United Nations Conference on Trade and Development

World Investment Report 1996

Investment, Trade and International Policy Arrangements

United Nations
New York and Geneva, 1996

Note

UNCTAD serves as the focal point within the United Nations Secretariat for all matters related to foreign direct investment and transnational corporations. In the past, the Programme on Transnational Corporations was carried out by the United Nations Centre on Transnational Corporations (1975-1992) and the Transnational Corporations and Management Division of the United Nations Department of Economic and Social Development (1992-1993). In 1993, the Programme was transferred to the United Nations Conference on Trade and Development. UNCTAD seeks to further the understanding of the nature of transnational corporations and their contribution to development and to create an enabling environment for international investment and enterprise development. UNCTAD's work is carried out through intergovernmental deliberations, technical assistance activities, seminars, workshops and conferences.

The term "country" as used in this study also refers, as appropriate, to territories or areas; the designations employed and the presentation of the material do not imply the expression of any opinion whatsoever on the part of the Secretariat of the United Nations concerning the legal status of any country, territory, city or area or of its authorities, or concerning the delimitation of its frontiers or boundaries. In addition, the designations of country groups are intended solely for statistical or analytical convenience and do not necessarily express a judgement about the stage of development reached by a particular country or area in the development process.

The following symbols have been used in the tables:

Two dots (..) indicate that data are not available or are not separately reported. Rows in tables have been omitted in those cases where no data are available for any of the elements in the row;

A dash (-) indicates that the item is equal to zero or its value is negligible;

A blank in a table indicates that the item is not applicable;

A slash (/) between dates representing years, e.g., 1994/95, indicates a financial year;

Use of a hyphen (-) between dates representing years, e.g., 1994-1995, signifies the full period involved, including the beginning and end years.

Reference to "dollars" ($) means United States dollars, unless otherwise indicated.

Annual rates of growth or change, unless otherwise stated, refer to annual compound rates.

Details and percentages in tables do not necessarily add to totals because of rounding.

The material contained in this study may be freely quoted with appropriate acknowledgement.

UNITED NATIONS PUBLICATION

Sales No. E.96.II.A.14

ISBN 92-1-104468-5

Preface

As part of the increasing globalization of economic activities, international production by transnational corporations is growing rapidly. The *World Investment Report 1996* provides an analysis of current global and regional trends in international production and looks into the particular theme of the interrelationships between investment and trade. It is a topic of particular interest at this time, given negotiations and discussions on international frameworks for investment in various fora -- a topic addressed in *WIR 96* in some detail.

More particularly, *WIR 96* deals with the following issues:

- The global and regional trends as regards foreign direct investment and, in particular, such investments in infrastructure.

- The linkages between trade and foreign direct investment, their role in development and their implications for national policies, particularly in the context of the changing global environment.

- The current international arrangements governing foreign direct investment, the policy options for developing these further and the issues that need to be considered in this respect, especially with a view towards safeguarding development objectives.

In discussing these issues, *WIR 96* is a contribution to a better understanding of the role of foreign direct investment in the world economy and the current discussion on the evolution of international arrangements for foreign direct investment.

Boutros Boutros-Ghali
Secretary-General of the United Nations

New York, August 1996

The *World Investment Report 1996* was prepared by a team led by Karl P. Sauvant and comprising Victoria Aranda, Richard Bolwijn, Persephone Economou, Masataka Fujita, Michael Gestrin, Padma Mallampally, Fiorina Mugione, Lilach Nachum, Ludger Odenthal, Jennifer Powell, Edmund Ruhumuliza, Jörg Weber and Zbigniew Zimny. Specific inputs were also received from Anna Joubin-Bret, Annalisa Caresana, Danielle Lecacheur, Mina Mashayekhi, Michael Mortimore and James Zhan. The work was carried out under the overall direction of Roger Lawrence.

Principal research assistance was carried out by Mohamed Chiraz Baly. A number of interns assisted at various stages during the preparation of *WIR 96*: Athina Alexiou, Mario Ardiri, Jelle Bartlema, Stefan Führer, Cynthia Hoekstra, Giuseppina Marinotti, Nguyen Phuong, Maria Popescu, Louis Toral and Katja Weigel. Production of *WIR 96* was carried out by Jenifer Tacardon, Medy Almario, Elizabeth Mahiga and Mary McGee. It was desktop-published by Teresita Sabico and graphics were done by Diego Oyarzun-Reyes and Martin Best. *WIR 96* was edited by Vince McCullough and copy-edited by Frederick Glover.

Experts from within and outside the United Nations system provided inputs for *WIR 96*. Major inputs were received from Arghyrios A. Fatouros, and also from Thomas L. Brewer, John Cantwell, John M. Kline and Robert E. Lipsey. Inputs were also received from Edward Dommen, Lucia Piscitello, Toshiko Matsuki, Terutomo Ozawa and Prasada Reddy. A number of experts were consulted and commented on various chapters. Comments, including during expert group meetings, were received from Philippe Brusick, Stephen Canner, Philippe Douvain, Harry Freeman, Murray Gibbs, Edward M. Graham, H. Peter Gray, Michael Hansen, Cory Highland, Jan Huner, Dwight Justice, Peter Koudal, Mark Koulen, James R. Markusen, Edouard Mathieu, Joel Messing, Lynn Mytelka, Deepak Nayyar, Herbert Oberhänsli, Adrian T. Otten, Antonio Parra, Stephen Pursey, Eric Ramstetter, Patrick Robinson, Pedro Roffe, Pierre Sauvé, M. Sornarajah, Anne-Christine Strandell, Kenneth Vandevelde, Louis Wells, Gerald T. West and Mira Wilkins. *WIR 96* benefited from overall comments and advice from John H. Dunning, Senior Economic Adviser.

Inputs were also provided by numerous officials in Central Banks, statistical offices, investment promotion agencies and other government offices concerned with foreign direct investment, as well as the International Bureau of Fiscal Documentation and executives of a number of companies. The advice of Obie Whichard was particularly important.

Financial contributions by the Governments of the Netherlands and Norway are gratefully acknowledged.

Contents

Part Two
Foreign direct investment and trade: interlinkages and policy implications

Page

Boxes

Figures

Page

Tables

Executive Summary

Investment, Trade and International Policy Arrangements

Foreign direct investment (FDI) has been growing rapidly in the recent past, faster, indeed, than international trade, which has long been the principal mechanism linking national economies. Moreover, as the global environment is changing and strategies of transnational corporations (TNCs) evolve, new configurations of TNC activities are emerging. This focuses renewed attention on what FDI means for trade, how FDI and trade are interlinked, and whether and how these interlinkages influence the economic growth and welfare of countries, particularly developing countries. These issues are of particular interest in the context of national policies for FDI and trade. But at a time when negotiations and discussions on international arrangements for investment are underway in various fora, they are also of interest at the international level. They are the special topic of this year's *World Investment Report*.

Part One outlines the latest trends in FDI and international production, explains some of the reasons behind these trends and looks at future prospects. Part Two examines the relationship between FDI and trade. And Part Three reviews current international arrangements regarding FDI; presents various policy approaches towards the further evolution of these arrangements; and identifies and analyses key issues.

Global and regional trends

World FDI flows reached a record high in 1995, ...

Investment inflows in 1995 increased by 40 per cent, to an unprecedented $315 billion. Developed countries were the key force behind the record FDI flows, investing $270 billion (an increase of 42 per cent over 1994) and receiving $203 billion (53 per cent higher). The spectacular growth of FDI among developed countries was accompanied by a hefty rise in flows into developing countries, which, at $100 billion, set another record in 1995; outward investment from developing countries also rose, reaching $47 billion. Investment flows to Central and Eastern Europe nearly doubled to $12 billion in 1995, after stagnating in 1994.

Investment flows are concentrated in a few countries. The ten largest host countries received two thirds of total inflows in 1995 and the smallest 100 recipient countries received only 1 per cent. Investment going to the top 10 host countries is also more important for their economies than it is for the bottom 100: the share of FDI stock in GDP for the smallest 100 recipients is below that of the top 10 recipients. In the case of outflows, the largest five home countries (the United States, Germany, the United Kingdom, Japan and France) accounted for about two thirds of all outflows in 1995.

Foreign direct investment is a major force shaping globalization. The outward FDI stock which the 39,000 parent firms invested in their 270,000 foreign affiliates reached $2.7 trillion in 1995. Moreover, FDI flows doubled between 1980 and 1994 relative to both global gross fixed capital formation and world GDP. And the value added of all foreign affiliates accounted for 6 per cent of world GDP in 1991, compared with 2 per cent in 1982.

...aided by a boom in mergers and acquisitions, increasingly used as a corporate strategy...

The latest surge in FDI flows reflects the fact that an increasing number of firms, including from developing countries, are becoming more active globally in response to competitive pressures, liberalization and the opening up of new areas for investment. These firms are once again using mergers and acquisitions (M&As) as a central corporate strategy for establishing production facilities abroad to protect, consolidate and advance their international competitiveness.

The value of all cross-border M&A transactions (including those involving portfolio investments) doubled between 1988 and 1995, to $229 billion. The value of majority-held M&A transactions (excluding those involving portfolio investment and minority-held FDI) increased by 84 per cent in 1988-1995, to $135 billion. In Western Europe -- the focus of M&A activity in 1995 -- majority cross-border sales of firms were $50 billion and purchases were $66 billion. Much of that was due to intra-European Union deals. But the highest levels of M&A transactions in 1995 -- $49 billion worth of sales and $38 billion worth of purchases -- were registered by the United States. Industries with high cross-border M&A activity include energy distribution, telecommunications, pharmaceuticals and financial services. There was also a notable increase in participation of small and medium-sized and services-related enterprises. Overall, the M&A boom that began in the late 1980s, but was dampened by the FDI recession of the early 1990s, helped FDI flows to rise to record heights in 1995.

...and is beginning to reflect the opening up of infrastructure to foreign participation.

New investment opportunities in infrastructure, partly because of liberalization and deregulation and partly because governments turn more and more to foreign firms for capital and technology, have aided FDI to reach record levels. Infrastructure, especially communications, attracted FDI flows of around $7 billion annually in the early 1990s. This is but a fraction of the total investment requirements in infrastructure, much of which remains unmet.

Investment outflows to infrastructure from the major home countries made up 3-5 per cent of their total outflows in 1995. In many countries, FDI flows account for less than 1 per cent of the gross fixed capital formation in infrastructure. For the United States, the largest outward investor, the share of infrastructure industries in its outward FDI flows between 1992 and 1994 averaged 4.9 per cent a year. United States TNCs have invested $14 billion in infrastructure as of 1994, 2.3 per cent of its total outward stock. This share is small when compared with the share of FDI in infrastructure in 1940; then, more than a third of the United States FDI stock in Latin America was in infrastructure. Subsequent waves of nationalizations and expropriations, however, led to dramatic declines, a trend that has only recently begun to reverse.

The revitalized interest of TNCs in infrastructure has been sparked by several factors. Recognizing that shortfalls in infrastructure services can hamper economic development, more governments are willing to privatize and relinquish control of state monopolies to attract foreign investment and technology and to realize efficiency gains. Between 1988 and 1995, infrastructure privatizations mobilized private capital of nearly $40 billion, more than half of which was foreign direct and portfolio investment. Furthermore, technological developments, notably in telecommunications, have turned infrastructure industries previously dominated by natural monopolies into competitive industries with potentially profitable investment opportunities. Capital raised from public sources in many countries is no longer sufficient to meet the financing requirements of infrastructure development. Privately sourced capital, often mobilized by TNCs, has therefore stepped in to help meet those requirements, including through new techniques of financing projects such as build-operate-transfer, build-own-operate, and build-own-transfer schemes.

Despite the still low levels of FDI flows in infrastructure, future prospects for increased TNC involvement are promising. Despite their high fixed costs, many infrastructure projects are attractive to foreign investors. Continuing FDI liberalization and infrastructure deregulation, coupled with the growth of investment guarantees, helps to lower the risks of nationalization. Potential for greater TNC involvement in infrastructure is especially conducive to attracting FDI, such as the establishment of science parks, export-processing zones and facilities for human resource development.

The world's largest TNCs are becoming more transnational...

The world's largest 100 TNCs (excluding banking and financial institutions), ranked by foreign assets, are all based in developed countries. They have roughly $1.4 trillion worth of assets abroad and account for around a third of the global FDI stock. That share has remained stable in the past five years. Royal Dutch Shell (United Kingdom/Netherlands) has topped the list of the top 100 TNCs every year since 1990. A composite index of transnationality that takes foreign assets, foreign sales and foreign employment together, presents a different ranking of the top 100 TNCs: Royal Dutch Shell falls to twenty-seventh, and Thomson Corporation (Canada) climbs to first place.

Salient features of the top 100 TNCs are:

- By country of origin, United States TNCs (with 32 in the top 100) are the largest group ranked by share of foreign assets in total assets in 1994.
- Japanese TNCs are the fastest growing group among the top 100, increasing in number from 11 in 1990 to 19 in 1994. Japanese TNCs in electronics were amongst the most important new entrants.
- European TNCs are prominent in capital- and research and development-intensive industries, such as chemicals and pharmaceuticals.
- By industry, TNCs in chemicals and pharmaceuticals score the highest rankings in transnationality index, followed by firms in food and electronics. Trading firms score lowest.

The future investment plans of the top 100 TNCs suggest a strong upward trend in FDI (as well as total investment), fueled partly by economic growth in major destinations, among which the developing countries are becoming more prominent. But intra-developed-country FDI will continue to feature prominently in future investments of the top 100. Transnational corporations based in North America view Europe as the most important future investment location, especially in high-technology and consumer-goods industries. Likewise, European TNCs see the United States as the most important location. Japanese TNCs, however, view Asia as the most promising. Transnational corporations from North America and Europe also have a positive view of Asia; this region is therefore expected to capture the largest growth of planned capital investments by the world's largest TNCs in the second half of the 1990s.

... and the largest developing-country TNCs are moving in the same direction.

The 50 largest TNCs based in developing countries, ranked by foreign assets, accounted for about 10 per cent of the combined outward FDI stock of firms in their countries of origin. These firms' ratio of foreign to total sales is high (30 per cent), but their ratio of foreign to total assets (9 per cent) is low. Their overall index of transnationality (21 per cent) is low, compared with that of the world's top 100 TNCs (42 per cent), reflecting their short history as important outward investors; but their plans for expansion suggest that they will become increasingly more transnational.

In 1994, Daewoo (Republic of Korea) ranked first among the 50 largest TNCs from developing countries on the basis of the ratio of foreign to total assets. Mexico's Cemex, the top TNC among developing country firms in 1993, ranked third. On the basis of the transnationality index, Creative Technology (Singapore), a producer of standard personal computer sound systems that holds more than 60 per cent of the global market share, was in first place in 1994. By country of origin, TNCs from China and the Republic of Korea, with eight entries each, were the largest groups among the top 50 developing country TNCs ranked by foreign-to-total asset share. By industry, TNCs in construction and electronics had the highest rankings.

Led by the United States, developed countries experienced rapid growth of FDI flows in 1995,...

Almost 90 per cent of the 1995 increases in FDI inflows (and outflows) were registered by developed countries. Because of this, the share of developed countries in world inflows increased from 59 per cent in 1994 to 65 per cent in 1995, while outflows rose from 83 to 85 per cent. The growth of developed country FDI was led by a few countries -- the United States, United Kingdom, France and Australia, in that order, in the case of inflows, and the United States, United Kingdom and Germany, in that order, in the case of outflows.

With large increases in inflows and outflows in 1995, the United States strengthened its position as the largest host and home country. With $60 billion, United States inflows were twice that of the United Kingdom, the second largest recipient among developed countries. Reflecting high levels of M&A-related investment by Western European TNCs, led by the United Kingdom and Germany, equity flows into the United States rose by 50 per cent. Reinvested earnings and intra-company loans (the other components of FDI) increased by 78 per cent and 36 per cent, respectively. Likewise, the $95 billion worth of United States outflows in 1995 reflected both record equity capital flows ($42 billion) and record reinvested earnings ($42 billion); 54 per cent of these outflows went to Western Europe.

The United Kingdom and Germany also registered record outflows in 1995, $38 billion and $36 billion, respectively. Large-scale investments in the markets for its main exports (the European Union and the United States) characterized FDI from the United Kingdom. German TNCs directed their attention to investment opportunities abroad, partly to escape cost increases and currency appreciations at home and partly because investments in the eastern part of the country have abated with the completion of the privatization programme.

Increases of 20 per cent in 1994 and 15 per cent in 1995 are strong signs that Japanese FDI outflows are recovering. Japanese TNCs are investing abroad faster than at home. However, 1995 FDI outflows were still less than half of the annual average in 1989-1991. Most Japanese FDI goes to East and South-East Asia and developed countries, and is aimed at establishing regional or global networks (efficiency-seeking FDI) or supplying local markets. Investment flows to Africa and Central and Eastern Europe have been small, accounting for only 0.1 per cent and 0.3 per cent of Japan's total outflows, respectively, in 1990-1994. To recover and increase their international competitiveness, Japanese affiliates are establishing "second generation" affiliates abroad. For example, 47 per cent of Japanese affiliates in Hong Kong, and 43 per cent of Japanese affiliates in Singapore, have already established their own foreign affiliates.

...while flows to developing countries advanced, and those to developing Asia boomed.

The current boom in FDI flows to developing countries, with inflows reaching $100 billion in 1995, is a reflection of sustained economic growth and continuing liberalization and privatization in these countries, as well as their increasing integration into the investment plans of TNCs. The share of developing countries in the combined outflows of the largest five developed-country outward investors rose from 18 per cent in 1990-1992 to 28 per cent in 1993-1994. Investment from developing countries to other developing countries is also increasing: in 1994, for example, more than half of the FDI flows from Asian developing countries were invested in the same region.

South, East and South-East Asia continued to be the largest host developing region, with an estimated $65 billion of inflows in 1995, accounting for two thirds of all developing-country FDI inflows. The size and dynamism of developing Asia have made it increasingly important for TNCs from all countries to service rapidly expanding markets, or to tap the tangible and intangible resources of that region for global production networks. European Union TNCs, in particular, after neglecting Asia in the past, are now changing course and investing more.

China has been the largest developing-country recipient since 1992. Although inflows are soaring in other countries as well, with 58 per cent of inflows to South, East and South-East Asia in 1995, China has been the principal drive behind Asia's current investment boom. Recent FDI policy changes in China may dampen these flows temporarily, however. China is moving towards national treatment, eliminating gradually some preferences for foreign investors, such as exemptions from import duties, that have distorted markets, encouraged "round-tripping", speculative investments and "phantom" foreign ventures. However, given China's outstanding growth performance and the continued opening of new areas to FDI, such as infrastructure, its attractiveness to foreign investors is unlikely to be affected seriously. Hence, Asia's investment boom will probably be sustained in the coming years.

Investment flows to Latin America and the Caribbean have risen, but continue to be "lumpy",...

Latin America and the Caribbean saw a 5 per cent increase of FDI inflows to $27 billion in 1995. Most, however, was concentrated in individual industries (automobiles in Mexico and Brazil, natural resources in Chile) or privatization-induced (in Argentina and Peru). Investment flows in Latin American countries are therefore susceptible to special circumstances in those industries or to privatization policies. Especially at the country level, investment flows are prone to wide year-to-year fluctuations which makes them "lumpy".

Argentina, Peru and Venezuela provide illustrations of lumpiness in FDI: when some large companies were privatized in the early 1990s, investment inflows soared. In the following years, however, they fell considerably, which was only partially offset by post-privatization investments. Investments in large mining projects or in industries such as automobile manufacturing may also cause "spikes" in FDI flows and lead to lumpiness. Lumpy FDI flows can not only change drastically the ranking of FDI recipients from one year to the next, but also the industrial composition of investment flows for a given country. For example, in Peru, communication and transport accounted for 42 per cent of its 1995 inward FDI stock, compared with 0.4 per cent in 1990; the "spike" in 1995 was the result of a large telecommunications privatization. With large-scale privatizations beginning to be implemented in Brazil and with the launching of large investment projects in automobiles, lumpy FDI will continue to shape the level and composition of flows to Latin American countries for some years.

...while Africa remains marginalized ...

The FDI stock in Africa doubled between 1985 and 1995. Inflows to Africa, however, have not been rising as rapidly as inflows to other regions. In 1995, they were almost the same as in 1994 - - $5 billion. The share of Africa in developing-country inflows therefore fell to 4.7 per cent in 1995 (from 5.8 per cent in 1994). But within Africa, there have been significant changes in the geographic pattern of FDI. In the 1980s, southern Africa accounted for more than 40 per cent of Africa's FDI stock, but its importance has diminished substantially since, and by 1993 it accounted for about a quarter of Africa's stock. In contrast, North African countries, which in 1980 accounted for a mere 12 per cent of total stock in Africa, have substantially improved their position, accounting for more than 30 per cent by 1993, due mainly to the rising levels of European investments. Investors from the developed countries have displayed uneven interest in Africa. Due to geographical proximity and post-colonial ties, Western European investors have always been more active compared with both United States and Japanese investors. Within Western Europe, France, Germany, Italy and the United Kingdom are the main investors in Africa.

Significant variations exist in the importance of FDI for African's recipient countries. For countries with large inflows, such as Nigeria, FDI is not as significant relative to the size of the domestic economy as it is for countries with small flows, such as Equatorial Guinea.

...and Central and Eastern Europe sees a surge in response to economic recovery.

Driven not only by waves of privatizations, but by economic recovery in some countries (Poland and the Czech Republic), FDI inflows to Central and Eastern Europe have soared to record levels. Having remained stagnant in 1994, inflows almost doubled in 1995, to reach an estimated $12 billion. The region accounted for 5 per cent of world inflows in 1995, compared with only 1 per cent in 1991. Hungary and the Czech Republic accounted for about two thirds of the increase in 1995, with inflows tripling to $3.5 billion and $2.5 billion, respectively. The 1995 FDI flows into the Russian Federation at an estimated $2 billion were double the 1994 level.

A significant share of the FDI received by Central and Eastern European economies -- 18 per cent in 1994 -- is from privatization of state enterprises. However, this share has declined considerably compared with 1989-1993 when, for the main recipient countries (excluding the Russian Federation), privatization-related inflows accounted for most FDI. The trend in FDI inflows and, in particular, non-privatization related FDI inflows, is correlated with the growth of domestic output: in most countries, FDI inflows picked up when GDP growth became positive. Thus, while many foreign investors rushed to establish a nominal presence in Central and Eastern Europe as countries began to liberalize their investment frameworks in the late 1980s and early 1990s, it was only when transition was well under way and negative growth rates of GDP began to reverse that TNCs began to invest significantly. The doubling of FDI into the region in 1995 reflects the recognition by TNCs that Central and Eastern European countries, particularly those in Central Europe, are well on the way to becoming market economies.

Foreign direct investment and trade: interlinkages and policy implications

The rapid growth of FDI and discussions about international arrangements related to such investment have drawn renewed attention to the relationship between trade and FDI. Does trade lead to FDI or FDI lead to trade? Does FDI substitute for trade or trade substitute for FDI? Do they complement each other? In other words, what does the growth of FDI mean for trade and -- most importantly -- what are the implications for growth and development?

Since FDI and trade are both handmaidens of growth and development, it is important to understand the interlinkages between the two.

Foreign direct investment and trade are of importance for economic performance, growth and development. They are, moreover, increasingly interrelated. These inter-linkages are important for several reasons:

- The role of trade as a positive factor in growth and development has long been recognized and reflected in trade policies. Foreign direct investment, as the principal method of delivering goods and services to foreign markets and the principal factor in the organization of international production, increasingly influences the size, direction and composition of world trade, as do FDI policies.

- The role of FDI as a positive factor in growth and development is being increasingly appreciated and is also increasingly reflected in FDI policies. Trade and trade policies can exert various influences on the size, direction and composition of FDI flows.

- Apart from the autonomous impacts of each on growth and development, interlinkages between trade and FDI must be taken into account if the developmental contribution of each is to be maximized, and if synergies between the two and broader growth and development objectives are to be maximized.

These considerations provide good reasons for looking more closely at the nature of the interlinkages between FDI and trade. Another reason is that national FDI and trade policies are generally formulated independently of each other, with the result that the two sets of policies may not always fully support one another in policy objectives and their efficient implementation. An improved understanding of the interlinkages can contribute to the formulation of national policies in the two areas that are mutually supportive. And, of course, it would also provide a background and basis for discussions at the international level as regards appropriate policy arrangements.

The relationship between trade and FDI in a given product is characterized by a sequential process of internationalization...

Historically, the relationship between FDI and trade for a given product has been characterized by a linear, step-by-step sequential process of internationalization, running from trade to FDI or from FDI to trade.

In manufacturing, market-seeking firms typically begin with domestic production and sales. They internationalize via exports, licensing and other contractual arrangements and by establishing foreign trading affiliates before they engage in FDI. As a result of this linear sequence, FDI in manufacturing is often viewed as an activity replacing trade. This perception has been strengthened, moreover, by the notion of a product cycle in which FDI takes place only when an innovating firm no longer finds exporting as profitable as producing abroad. This sequence of trade leading to FDI characterizes internationalization that is motivated by the search for markets, traditionally the dominant factor motivating TNCs. Manufacturing firms that seek low-cost inputs (especially labour), as part of their effort to improve efficiency and corporate performance may, however, begin their internationalization sequence with FDI, and this is trade creating.

The dominant characteristic of the relationship between trade and FDI in the natural resources sector is also linear. It begins either with imports, followed by FDI from the importing country in a process of vertical integration that may well lead to higher exports from the host country, or it begins with resource-seeking firms undertaking FDI and proceeding to export from host countries. The latter, common in non-renewable resources, accounts for most natural resource investments. In both cases, FDI is typically trade-creating, leading to exports or additional exports from the host country.

In the services sector, the dominant characteristic is that trade as an option to deliver many services abroad does not exist, and firms must move directly to foreign production if they want to satisfy international market demand. As a result, service firms do not enjoy the comfort of a gradual conquest of foreign markets through a linear sequential approach: the linear sequence is truncated. The need for local presence to deliver services is one reason underlying the shift of the world FDI stock towards services in the past 20 years. Establishing affiliates abroad has, in general, a smaller direct impact on home country exports of the service in question than establishing market-seeking manufacturing affiliates has on trade in a product.

The situation as regards FDI and trade in services is beginning to change under the impact of the growing transportability of services, and especially that of information-intensive services, or parts thereof, due to advances in telecommunications and information technologies. This may reduce the need for FDI to deliver these services to foreign markets. The technological advances that have increased tradability have also opened up possibilities for export-oriented FDI in some services or as regards particular services functions undertaken typically in-house by various firms (e.g., data processing, accounting).

....with associated trade and associated investment effects...

Apart from product-specific FDI and trade impacts of sequential trade-FDI interlinkages, there are also impacts from associated trade and associated FDI. The former include, for example, additions to exports of the home country due to intra-firm sales of services and intangible assets by parent firms to foreign affiliates, whether in manufacturing, natural resources or services. They also include additions to home country exports due to intra-firm sales of machinery and intermediate products by parent firms to their foreign affiliates. Similar exports from the parent firm occur in low cost input-seeking manufacturing FDI and in natural resource FDI. In addition, there could be further effects on trade due to exports by other firms in the same or other industries (or even sectors) of goods and services required by foreign affiliates.

Foreign affiliates in the services sector may also have an indirect impact on trade, as they may create demand for machinery and equipment necessary and/or for information-intensive support services provided either by headquarters personnel or services provided via communication lines. But again, this impact is not large. The exception is FDI in trading services, which plays a substantial role in facilitating the exports of goods from home or host countries, or both.

The internationalization sequence in a given product also gives rise to associated FDI. This begins when, for example, a firm exporting a manufactured product establishes marketing or other affiliates abroad; it continues when other firms (e.g., component suppliers, advertising firms, banks, insurance companies) follow suit once an investment in a particular product has been made. In natural resources, associated FDI can take place where certain services are required (e.g., shipping) or where foreign firms move into processing. Investment in a service may lead to the establishment of foreign affiliates in related services. More importantly, FDI in trading services can give rise to associated FDI in the production of manufactured and primary products by the same TNC or other TNCs.

...and implications for countries' trade.

The overall impact of market-seeking direct investment on the volume and composition of trade of a home or host country at the industry or aggregate level depends on the relative importance of these various direct and indirect effects. In general, FDI that follows trade can replace trade in a single product, but it is unlikely to do so -- and, in fact, is often complementary to trade -- at the sectoral and national levels. Some empirical studies suggest, indeed, that the trade-creating effect of FDI in manufacturing tends to outweigh the trade-replacing effect for the home country. Moreover, FDI seems to shift the composition of home country exports to host countries towards intermediate products and away from final products.

In natural resources, the impact of the FDI trade linkage was, and still is, trade creating. For one thing, host country exports of the resources involved expand. So do, generally, home country imports of the same resources and, also often, home country net exports due to increased exports of the resources after processing, or of manufactured goods based on these resources. The principal issues regarding this FDI-trade interlinkage relate to the retained value (or share of rents) accruing from the exploitation of, and trade in, host country resources and the role that these resources can (or should) play in development.   Many countries had severed the FDI-trade linkage through nationalizations, in the expectation that they could capture a larger share of the rents and promote domestic development more effectively.   More recently, a new relationship appears to have emerged in which many countries benefit from trade, technology and skill assets that TNCs possess, and firms benefit from stable supplies, without necessarily risking their capital.   Still, TNCs account for a fair share of the raw material trade of host countries.   In 1992, United States affiliates alone accounted for one tenth of all raw material exported from both developed and developing host countries.   This share is double that in the mid-1960s for all developed countries, and half that for developing countries.

Since the links between FDI and trade in services are limited, the effects of FDI on host developing countries are largely independent from, rather than intertwined with, those of trade.   As the tradability of some services increases, however, host countries, including developing countries, are able to participate more in the production and export of these services.   This might however, be accompanied by reduced technology transfer and skills development, as compared with the levels that TNCs traditionally have had to undertake for stand-alone service affiliates to function effectively.

Although the distinct characteristics of the FDI-trade relationship in the three sectors make it easier to understand the interlinkages between FDI and trade, the intersectoral nature of interlinkages in reality must be emphasized.   Many firms not only perform various activities but produce both good and services, so that classifying them sectorally is an oversimplification.   Moreover, associated trade and associated investment effects of internationalization through trade on FDI are often intersectoral. The crossing of sectoral boundaries, both in the framework of a single firm's activities and as regards indirect FDI and trade effects, makes it increasingly difficult to isolate separate trade and investment effects associated with the internationalization sequence of a particular product, firm or, indeed, industry or sector.

But what seems to be clear is that, first, trade eventually leads to FDI; and, second, on balance FDI leads to more trade.   The result, therefore, is an intensification of international economic interactions.

The world environment for trade and FDI is changing,...

The linear interrelationship between trade and investment continues to characterize a good part of FDI.   But something new is happening.   In the past 30 years or so, and particularly since the mid-1980s, the environment for FDI and trade has changed significantly.   The most important changes relate to the reduction of technological and policy-related barriers to the movement of goods, services, capital, professional and skilled workers, and firms.   More specifically, technological developments have greatly enhanced the ease with which goods, services, intangible assets and people can be transported, and tasks related to the organization and management of firms implemented over distances.   The liberalization of rules and regulations governing trade, investment and technology flows has meant that the new possibilities created by technology can actually be realized.   As a result, international production has grown substantially, as many firms have become TNCs.   For example, the number of parent firms headquartered in 15 major developed home countries nearly quadrupled between 1968/1969 and 1993, from 7,000 to 27,000.   Thus, there is a substantial presence of foreign affiliates in the world economy today.   While most are largely stand-alone affiliates, more are being drawn into closer interaction with each other.

...allowing firms greater choice of production locations and modalities of internationalization, making the internationalization sequence less important...

The principal effect of the new environment is that firms are freer to choose how to serve foreign markets: by producing at home and exporting, by producing in a foreign country for local sale, or by producing in a foreign country for export. They also have greater freedom to obtain foreign resources and inputs for production by importing them from foreign producers or by establishing production facilities that enable them to access resources where they are located, for producing raw, intermediate or final products for use elsewhere or sale in national, regional or global markets.

With competition driving firms to use the new possibilities to an increasing extent, more firms, especially in technologically sophisticated industries, immediately look at regional or world markets. Established TNCs in manufacturing and services in particular, can jump over the earlier steps directly to the FDI stage. Moreover, the internationalization sequence leading to FDI can begin anywhere within a TNC system -- innovation, the production of a new good and export can start in a foreign affiliate rather than the parent firm.

...and pushing TNCs to establish integrated international production systems,...

But the changes brought about by the new environment go further. As firms seize new regional and global opportunities, they combine ownership advantages with the locational advantages of host countries, and so strengthen their own competitive positions. With this purpose in view, firms -- particularly those that are already TNCs -- are increasingly organizing or reorganizing their cross-border production activities in an efficiency-oriented, integrated fashion, capitalizing on the tangible and intangible assets available throughout the corporate system. In the resulting international division of labour within firms, any part of the value-added chain can be located wherever it contributes most to a company's overall performance.

As a result, the simple, sequential relationship characteristic of TNCs in manufacturing gives way to a more complex relationship, in which intra-firm trade flows between parent firms and affiliates and among affiliates assume considerable and increasing importance. This is reflected, for example, in the increase in the share of intra-firm trade in total trade of United States TNC parent firms, as well as foreign affiliates, in 1983-1993. The high share of affiliate-to-affiliate trade in intra-firm trade by United States affiliates, and its growth, particularly in developing countries, is also striking. The share of exports to other foreign affiliates in intra-firm exports of foreign affiliates rose from 37 per cent in 1977 to 53 per cent in 1983 and to 60 per cent in 1993. A greater division of labour within TNCs, through either horizontal or vertical integration of activities dispersed among different locations, necessarily increases intra-firm investment and trade flows. Moreover, since the trade flows generated by integrated international production systems are related to the vertical or horizontal integration of production activities (or both), the structure of trade linked to such FDI involves relatively larger shares of intermediate products and services and intra-industry trade.

Nowhere can the difference that the new environment can make with respect to FDI-trade interlinkages be seen more clearly than in the European Union and in the contrasting experiences of Asia and Latin America. In the European Union, the share of exports relative to sales of United States affiliates to other (mostly European Union) destinations increased noticeably as a result of the restructuring of TNC activities to take advantage of European integration, from 14 per cent in 1957 to 31 per cent in 1993. In East and South-East Asia, export propensities of United States affiliates have been high since the 1960s, reflecting the integration of the former into the global division of labour by United States TNCs in electronics and other industries. In contrast, export propensities of United States affiliates in Latin America were traditionally much lower. However, when countries in this region began to liberalize their trade policies in the mid-1980s, export propensities rose faster than those in Asia.

... within which FDI and trade flows are determined simultaneously.

The decision to locate any part of the value-added chain wherever it is best for a firm -- be it transnational or national -- to convert global inputs into outputs for global markets means that FDI and trade flows are determined simultaneously. They are both immediate consequences of the same locational decision.

As a result, the issue is no longer whether trade leads to FDI or FDI to trade; whether FDI substitutes for trade or trade substitutes for FDI; or whether they complement each other. Rather, it is: how do firms access resources -- wherever they are located -- in the interest of organizing production as profitably as possible for the national, regional or global markets they wish to serve? In other words, the issue becomes: where do firms locate their value-added activities? In these circumstances, the decision where to locate is a decision where to invest and from where to trade. And it becomes a FDI decision, if a foreign location is chosen. It follows that, increasingly, what matters are the factors that make particular locations advantageous for particular activities, for both, domestic *and* foreign investors.

This creates new opportunities and challenges for countries.

Reduced obstacles to trade and FDI and the possibilities that they open up for TNCs to disperse production activities within integrated international production systems create new opportunities for countries. The challenge is to attract FDI and then to maximize the benefits associated with it in order to realize the opportunities arising from the new environment.

For example, integrating production within corporate systems along efficiency-oriented lines means that firms fragment activities more closely -- and narrowly -- in accordance with the static comparative advantages of different (domestic and foreign) locations. The division of labour that results provides potential opportunities for countries to participate in production and trade associated with TNCs, specializing in segments of goods and services production for which they have a comparative advantage. Moreover, as firms fine-tune their search for locational advantages, countries with a broad range of capabilities have the opportunity to attract specialized activities in various industries. Many firms in developing countries, particularly in Asia, but also in Latin America, are already part of regionally or globally integrated production systems of TNCs or are linked to them through subcontracting or other arrangements, exporting parts, components and/or selected products to affiliates and parent companies. There are, of course, always risks associated with participation in the international division of labour. Vulnerability may increase as specialization becomes more narrow, especially when it is susceptible to technological change and locational reorientation (e.g., data-processing).

Greater interconnectedness of FDI and trade also has potential implications for dynamic change and growth through technological upgrading and innovation in the countries attracting TNCs. As the international intra-firm division of labour within TNCs evolves, affiliates become focused on areas in which the local potential for innovation is greatest. Hence, there is a search for local sources of innovation in each affiliate, which can become part of a regional or global strategy of production and marketing. For developing countries, the extent to which the gains from participating in such integrated innovation within TNC systems are realized locally depends on the role assigned to local affiliates and on the extent to which this role is associated with networking with other firms (especially indigenous firms) in the same location, and hence becomes part of a wider system of technological and associated spillovers. Countries differ considerably in how they can act as centres of excellence for FDI in research-based products. A few developing countries have succeeded in becoming centres for the location of innovative activities of TNCs and become locked-into a dynamic process of technological upgrading. Others have not managed to attract FDI that carries technological spillovers and, therefore, have been locked-out. This is precisely where government policies become important in terms of creating the factors that make a particular location attractive for particular activities, or in exploring alternative (non-TNC related) avenues of dynamic upgrading.

There may also be benefits to countries due to the accelerated transformation of the industrial structures of host and home countries which is the allied consequence of the integration of FDI and trade. In general, countries -- developed and developing -- tend to benefit in efficiency from a restructuring in favour of industries in which the country is comparatively advantaged (and in which integrating TNCs expand their local operations), and in dynamic terms from a greater focus on activities in those industries in which the country's potential for innovation is greatest. For developing countries, the latter is particularly beneficial since foreign affiliates within those industries tend to develop greater capabilities as part of the regional or global strategies of their respective TNCs. Thus, these affiliates can make a greater contribution to local innovation through linkages and spillovers. However, the structural transformation that occurs because of opportunities created by integrated FDI and trade networks depends on local specificities. Many developing countries that have managed to attract FDI that is part of regionally or globally integrated production systems are involved in low-technology activities which have contributed to expanding and diversifying their economies, but which have limited consequences for technological upgrading. For a few, however, there has been more positive change.

From a wider perspective, the benefits of closer FDI-trade interlinkages -- whether for static efficiency, technological dynamism or industrial restructuring -- are by no means evenly distributed between countries, in part because of the uneven distribution of FDI. In the short and medium-term, poorer countries that generally attract little FDI may have few opportunities to capture such gains and may indeed be further marginalized unless there are strong national and international efforts for development. As more countries build up the human-resource and infrastructure capabilities that TNCs seek, the scope for these countries to share in the benefits can be expected to increase. The gains of greater participation in the international division of labour are also accompanied by costs to particular groups within economies, both developed and developing -- and more so when unemployment is high. Balancing the benefits against these costs poses a formidable challenge for policy makers.

Integrated FDI and trade requires coordinated policies.

The intertwining of FDI and trade presents new challenges for national policy makers. The need for coordinated policy approaches acquires greater importance with the emergence of integrated international production systems, as investment and trade flows are the life-blood of such systems. Transnational corporations internally integrate the trade and investment functions that most national governments still tend to view and address separately, sometimes creating a disjuncture between national policy instruments and integrated corporate transactions. National trade and FDI policies have typically evolved separately, frequently influenced by different goals, and administered by distinct, often loosely connected agencies. This historical and organizational separation is not suited to a world in which trade and FDI are closely interlinked. Inconsistent policies risk creating an environment in which trade and FDI policies may neutralize each other, or could even prove counterproductive. On the other hand, when formulated and implemented coherently, national trade and FDI policies become mutually reinforcing in support of national growth and development. Coordination can generate synergies that yield outcomes exceeding the expectations for separate policy choices. At the same time, policy coherence does not presuppose any particular overall policy approach (e.g., a liberal approach); it merely is a reflection of the fact that, since FDI and trade are inextricably intertwined, national policies on FDI and trade need to be coordinated.

Towards a multilateral framework for foreign direct investment?

The question of international arrangements governing FDI is now prominent on the international agenda...

Foreign direct investment and trade are inextricably intertwined, both at the microeconomic level of firms' strategies and operations and at the macroeconomic level of national economies. They contribute not only individually and directly to the development process, but also jointly and indirectly, through linkages with one another. Governments are increasingly establishing national policy frameworks to create a framework within which FDI and trade can flourish, knowing full well that, once an appropriate enabling framework is created, other factors determine FDI and trade flows.

The principal manner in which governments are pursuing this objective vis-à-vis FDI regimes is through liberalization. They reduce restrictive investment measures; strengthen standards of treatment; provide investment protection; and pay more attention to ensuring the proper functioning of the market. In 1995 alone, 106 of 112 regulatory changes in 64 countries that altered investment regimes were in the direction of greater liberalization or the promotion of FDI.

Despite these significant changes, the question has been raised whether current international arrangements have been overtaken by global economic reality and, therefore, a "catching up with the market" is necessary. The vigorous growth of bilateral and regional investment agreements, the inclusion of certain FDI-related issues in the Uruguay Round agreements and the beginning of negotiations on a Multilateral Agreement on Investment in the OECD suggest that many governments believe that this is, indeed, the case. Some governments -- but also TNCs, as well as labour organizations, consumer groups and other non-governmental organizations, all for their own reasons -- are driving the process, though, of course, there exists a diversity of views and approaches among these groups as to how international arrangements guiding FDI should be further developed.

...and is being pursued at the bilateral,...

At the bilateral level, key investment concepts, principles and standards have been developed through the conclusion of treaties for the protection and promotion of FDI (bilateral investment treaties or BITs). Their distinctive feature is their exclusive concern with investment. Introduced years ago, these treaties have remained virtually unchanged in their format, and the issues they address continue to be among the most important for investors. They contain mostly general standards of treatment after entry and establishment and specific protection standards on particular key issues. As far as development is concerned, BITs emphasize the importance of FDI for development and therefore seek to promote it; they generally recognize the effect of national laws and policies on FDI;

and they contain various exceptions or qualifications, e.g., exceptions for balance-of-payments considerations in relation to the principle of free transfer of funds.

The network of BITs is expanding constantly. Some two-thirds of the nearly 1,160 treaties existing in June 1996 were concluded in the 1990s (172 in 1995 alone), involving 158 countries. Originally concluded between developed and developing countries, recently more BITs are between developed countries and economies in transition, between developing countries, and between developing countries and economies in transition.

... regional...

At the regional level, the mix of investment issues covered is broader than that found at the bilateral level, and the operational approaches to deal with them are less uniform. This reflects, among other things, differences in interests and needs, levels of development, perspectives of future development and that investment issues are typically only one of the issues covered in a regional agreement. Most regional instruments are legally binding, although there are exceptions and the definition of investment varies considerably, depending on the purpose and context of an agreement.

Issues typically (though by no means uniformly) dealt with at the regional level include the liberalization of investment measures; standards of treatment; protection of investments and dispute settlement; and issues related to the conduct of foreign investors, e.g., illicit payments, restrictive business practices, disclosure of information, transfer pricing, environmental protection, and employment and labour relations. Where the questions of providing special treatment to certain partners on account of different levels of development arises, it is dealt with primarily through exceptions, derogations, safeguards and the phasing of commitments.

...and, in partial ways, the multilateral levels.

At the multilateral level, most agreements relate to sectoral or to specific issues, moving in on central FDI concerns from the outside. Particularly important among them are services, performance requirements, intellectual property rights, insurance, settlement of disputes and employment and labour relations. Attention is also being paid to restrictive business practices, competition policy, incentives and consumer protection.

It is at the multilateral level that concern for development is most apparent. This is particularly so in the case of the GATS, TRIPS and TRIMs agreements, as well as the (non-binding) Restrictive Business Practices Set, where special provisions are made that explicitly recognize the needs of developing countries.

Lessons can be learned from past efforts, including that the evolution of international arrangements for FDI has followed and interacted with developments at the national level and reflects the priorities and concerns of a particular period,...

In the 1980s, the earlier post-war approaches to investment, which often stressed restrictions, controls and conditions on entry and establishment of FDI, were reversed, mainly as a result of the debt crisis (which made FDI a more desirable alternative to bank lending) and of the changing perceptions of the role that FDI can play in growth and development. As a result, laws and policies in many developing countries began to change dramatically in the direction of liberalization, protection and promotion of FDI. Liberalization also expanded and deepened in developed countries. These changes are now being reflected in regional instruments, and in sectoral or issue-specific multilateral agreements.

Two lessons can be drawn from past pendular swings on FDI policies. One is that progress in the development of international investment rules is linked to the convergence of rules adopted by individual countries. The other is that an approach to FDI issues that takes into account the interests of all parties, and hence is to their common advantage, is more likely to gain widespread acceptance and, ultimately, to be more effective. In practice, this raises the question of how an appropriate balance of rights and obligations among affected actors can be found.

...that widespread recognition is emerging on the principal issues that need to be addressed in the FDI area,...

With the growing appreciation of the role of FDI in development and the convergence of national attitudes in favour of market-oriented policies, some issues have moved from the national to the international arena and have become standard substantive items in international discussions on FDI (even though the extent to which these are at present incorporated in specific international instruments varies considerably, as does the strength with which they are addressed). These include (but are not necessarily limited to) general standards of treatment of foreign investors; questions relating to entry and establishment and operational conditions; protection standards, including dispute settlement; issues relating to corporate behaviour; and other issues, such as the promotion of FDI.

In a rapidly globalizing world economy, the list of substantive issues entering international FDI discussions is becoming increasingly broader and may eventually include the entire range of questions concerning factor mobility. Issues that receive relatively little attention at this time may, therefore, acquire increased importance in the future.

...that, so far, progress has been made gradually, helped by increasingly greater transparency and monitoring,...

Regarding the functional characteristics of present arrangements, there are, with many variations, also some common features. Thus, restrictions are eliminated gradually (in the case of the OECD, for example, it took 25 years from the adoption of the Liberalisation Codes until the right of establishment was confirmed). Transparency is increased through the reporting of investment measures and relevant normative changes and monitoring, follow-up and dispute-settlement mechanisms of varying degrees of strength and binding force are set up. A key lesson from these functional approaches is that implementing and strengthening standards is a lengthy process. But it may well be that globalization pressures and changing corporate strategies will require faster normative responsiveness in the future.

...that the interrelations between investment and trade are seen increasingly in a common framework,...

The Uruguay Round of Multilateral Trade Negotiations was the first time that some investment issues were directly introduced as part of the disciplines of the multilateral trading system. This occurred most markedly in the negotiations of GATS which defines trade in services as including the provision of services through commercial presence. The TRIMs Agreement, in fact, focuses on one aspect of the policy interrelationship between trade and investment (performance requirements).

Possible future work on investment and competition may lead to even deeper policy integration. A major question is the extent to which this new trend should be accommodated through the development of concepts designed to capture the relationships between investment and trade.

...and, in particular, that development issues must be and can be addressed.

It was observed earlier that, for international agreements to be effective and stable, they need to take into account the interests of all parties, incorporate a balance of interests and allow for common advantage. This applies particularly to developing countries and, more generally, to agreements between countries at different levels of development. In particular, any agreement involving developed and developing countries must take into account the special importance of development policies and objectives. The development dimension can be addressed in international investment accords at all levels and in several ways.

Current international arrangements could either be allowed to evolve organically...

For analytical purposes, two basic approaches, two ideal types, regarding the further evolution of international arrangements for FDI can be distinguished.

One approach involves allowing current arrangements to evolve organically, while improving them actively by deepening and expanding them, as appropriate. The overarching rationale for this approach is that current arrangements are working well in providing an enabling framework that allows FDI to contribute to growth and development and are supporting high and growing volumes of FDI. Moreover, such arrangements allow for groups of countries to enter into agreements having the degree of "strength" that is suitable to their circumstances.

...or a comprehensive multilateral investment framework could be sought,...

Another approach involves the construction, through negotiation, of a comprehensive multilateral framework for FDI. The overarching rationale for this approach is that the globalization of business, increased volumes and the growing importance of FDI, intertwined of FDI and trade and the emergence of an integrated international production system require a similarly global policy framework. In brief, in this view a global economy requires a global policy approach to create a stable, predictable and transparent enabling framework for FDI.

...although, in reality, these two policy approaches are not mutually exclusive.

These two policy approaches have been presented for expositional purposes as stylized alternatives, to highlight differences, even at the risk of oversimplification. In reality, even the proponents of each option seldom make such a clear distinction. Those in favour of an approach that allows current arrangements to evolve organically include a diverse range of governments; their support for this approach, however, does not necessarily preclude support for an eventual multilateral framework. Conversely, governments seeking a comprehensive multilateral framework are actively strengthening bilateral, regional, interregional and specific multilateral agreements on FDI.

There appears, indeed, to be a consensus that greater international cooperation on FDI issues is desirable. This underlying consensus is reflected in both of the policy approaches. The differences among governments and others in their support for either of the above options -- or some combination of the two -- lie more in their opinions on how best to achieve greater cooperation. In this perspective, the two approaches can be seen as coexisting and, indeed, developing in a complementary manner.

The further development of international arrangements governing FDI needs to consider a number of issues,...

Since the further development of international FDI arrangements is being pursued at all levels, it is important to identify and analyse issues that need to be considered, especially with a view towards their implications for development. An examination of investment instruments provides a list of key issues that could reasonably be expected to be addressed:

- *Scope*. In any instrument on FDI, the forms and types of transactions and operations to which it applies need to be determined.

- *Investment measures* that affect entry and operations of foreign investors. Particularly relevant are issues relating to admission and establishment, ownership and control, operations, incentives and investment-related trade measures.

- Application, with respect to FDI, of certain *standards of treatment*. Particularly relevant are issues of national treatment, most-favoured-nation treatment, and fair and equitable treatment.

- Measures dealing with *broader concerns,* including the proper functioning of the market. Particularly relevant are issues relating to restrictive business practices, transfer pricing, transfer of technology, employment, the environment, and illicit payments.

- *Investment protection and the settlement of disputes*. Particularly relevant are issues relating to expropriations and property takings in general, abrogation (or unilateral amendment) of state contracts with investors, transfer of funds, and dispute settlement.

- *Procedural approaches*. There is also the issue of the legal character of a given instrument and the approach adopted regarding the mechanisms used to put it into effect.

Although extensive, this list of issues is by no means exhaustive. In addition, the relative importance of particular issues varies, of course, for different participants. While investment protection and liberalization, for instance, are especially important to TNCs, the implications for sustainable growth and development of all these issues are of particular significance for governments. Social policy questions, meanwhile, are special concerns of other groups, in particular trade unions and consumer groups.

...while always keeping at the forefront the development dimension.

Because the activities of TNCs have such pervasive consequences for the development prospects of all countries, and in particular those of developing countries and economies in transition, any international arrangement involving the latter groups of countries has to be particularly sensitive to development needs. Broadly speaking, the development objective needs to be:

- *safeguarded* by allowing countries in need of a transition period -- through exclusions, exemptions and temporary measures -- the time to adjust to more stringent standards of investment liberalization, it being recognized that many developing countries have already gone far on their own initiative;

- *advanced* by agreeing that developing countries can take appropriate measures to increase the benefits that they can reap from FDI, without infringing on the essential interests of foreign investors;

- *supported* by home country governments committing themselves to help developing countries attract FDI, in particular FDI that is most consonant with their development needs (e.g., because it embodies appropriate technology or is export-oriented). Governments of home countries can promote FDI flows to developing countries, e.g., through the provision of information and technical assistance; direct financial support and fiscal incentives; and investment insurance and tax-sparing provisions. While many home countries have already many measures in place in this respect, and some international instruments address this issue, not all do, and those that do, can be strengthened.

Experience has shown that development objectives can not only be accommodated but actually be promoted by international agreements. The further development of international arrangements for FDI needs to keep this objective at the centre of its attention.

The choice of forum will, of necessity, shape how the framework will evolve, with the main choices being either regional and interregional fora...

Investment issues are currently the subject of discussion or negotiation in a number of regional and interregional fora. One important recent initiative was the launching, in May 1995, of negotiations aimed at the conclusion of a Multilateral Agreement on Investment among the members of the OECD in time for the Organization's ministerial meeting in 1997. The main aim of these negotiations is to eliminate discrimination between foreign and domestic investors. The agreement is intended to provide a broad framework for international investment, with high standards for the liberalization of investment regimes and the protection of investment, and with effective dispute-settlement procedures. While this agreement is being negotiated among OECD members only, it is meant to become a free-standing international treaty open also to non-OECD members. Evidently, one of the main challenges will be to obtain the adherence of non-OECD members.

Other regional and interregional fora have already addressed investment issues, or are in the process of doing so, including APEC, ASEAN, SADC, NAFTA and MERCOSUR, as well as the initiatives pursued in the context of the Free Trade Area for the Americas and the European Energy Charter Treaty.

...or a multilateral forum.

Although multilateral rules on FDI could be established in an independent agreement, recent proposals aim at the negotiation of such rules in the framework of international organizations with global, or potentially global, membership. In particular, the WTO has been mentioned as an appropriate forum for such negotiations. An important consideration underlying this suggestion is that the intertwining of investment and trade requires a more integrated approach to international rule-making. This has already manifested itself in the work of the GATT and of the WTO. Thus, the WTO already deals with certain aspects of investment issues in the context of the agreements on trade in services, trade-related investment measures and trade-related aspects of intellectual property rights, and an agenda exists for the expansion and deepening of these rules. Negotiations on liberalization through the expansion of the GATS schedules of commitments are scheduled to take place before

1999, and the TRIMs Agreement provides for consideration of competition and investment issues by the same year.

Members of the WTO are discussing a proposal for a decision to be taken at the WTO's first Ministerial Conference in Singapore in December 1996 to create a body to conduct a work programme on trade and investment. If such a decision were taken, it is likely to provide for exploratory work rather than the immediate launching of actual negotiation of a set of investment rules.

Finally, the question of a possible future multilateral framework on investment was addressed at the 1996 UNCTAD IX Conference at which it was agreed that UNCTAD should identify and analyse implications for development of issues relevant to a possible multilateral framework on investment, beginning with an examination and review of existing agreements, taking into account the interests of developing countries and bearing in mind the work undertaken by other organizations. The areas of policy analysis and consensus-building, with a particular focus on the development dimension, are, indeed, areas in which UNCTAD can make a contribution.

Part One

Trends

Chapter I

Global Trends

A. Trends in foreign direct investment and international production

1. Overall trends

World economic growth and the response of transnational corporations (TNCs) to technological development, international competition and liberalization propelled global foreign-direct-investment (FDI) flows to unprecedented levels in 1995. Following the end of the FDI recession in 1993, investment *inflows* rose by 9 per cent in 1994 (to $226 billion) and by another 40 per cent (about $90 billion) in 1995 (table I.1 and annex table 1), to reach a record of $315 billion for inflows (table I.2). Investment *outflows* also hit new highs in 1995[1] -- $318 billion, or an increase of 38 per cent over 1994 (table I.1 and annex table 2).[2] In 1995, FDI growth was substantially higher than that of exports of goods and non-factor services (18 per cent), world output (2.4 per cent) and gross domestic capital formation (5.3 per cent).[3] Judging from Japanese and United States data for the first quarter of 1996, world FDI flows are expected to remain at a high level in 1996. As always, these figures do not capture the importance of various non-equity forms, including strategic alliances.

Developed countries were the key force behind the record 1995 flows. Inflows rose by 53 per cent in 1995, to $203 billion; outflows rose by 42 per cent in 1995, to $271 billion (table I.1). The United States was the star performer, with $60 billion of inflows and $96 billion of outflows. But the spectacular rise in FDI flows into developed countries did not detract from flows into developing countries. At $100 billion (an increase of 15 per cent over 1994), they, too, set a record in 1995, although their *share* in global inflows declined to 32 per cent, after having increased consecutively for the previous six years. While continuing to be small, FDI inflows to the group of 48 least developed countries increased as well, by 29 per cent in 1995, to $1.1 billion. With $47 billion in 1995

(15 per cent of outflows), developing countries scored another record in FDI outflows, accelerating their production-level integration into the world economy. After stagnation in 1994, FDI flows to Central and Eastern Europe nearly doubled, to $12 billion.

World FDI inflows have been highly concentrated over the past decade. The ten biggest recipients received 68 per cent of the total in 1995, compared to 70 per cent in 1985. The share of the smallest 100 recipients (including all least developed countries) has remained at a mere 1 per cent during the same period. In contrast, FDI outflows from the five largest outward investors -- the United States, Germany, the United Kingdom, Japan and France, in that order -- became more concentrated in 1995, accounting for two thirds of global outflows (figure I.1).

The surge in global FDI flows in 1995 partly reflects their cyclical nature. During 1991-1993, average real GDP growth in the Group of Seven countries, the principal sources of FDI, was 1.4 per cent. That growth rate picked up in 1994, to 2.9 per cent, and is estimated to have been 2.3 per cent in 1995 (World Bank, 1996, p. 5). Given that FDI flows respond to cyclical fluctuations in economic growth with a one or two year lag (UNCTAD-DTCI, 1993c), the 1995 surge is not surprising. However, the underlying upward trend in FDI flows over the past decade and the fact that each cyclical upswing in economic activity has led to progressively higher peaks in FDI flows suggest that other factors are also at work.

Table I.1. FDI inflows and outflows, 1983-1995

(Billions of dollars and percentage)

Year	Developed countries		Developing countries		Central and Eastern Europe		All countries	
	Inflows	Outflows	Inflows	Outflows	Inflows	Outflows	Inflows	Outflows
Value (billion dollars)								
1983-1987	58.7	72.6	18.3	4.2	0.02	0.01	77.1	76.8
1988-1992	139.1	193.3	36.8	15.2	1.36	0.04	177.3	208.5
1990	169.8	222.5	33.7	17.8	0.30	0.04	203.8	204.3
1991	114.0	201.9	41.3	8.9	2.45	0.04	157.8	210.8
1992	114.0	181.4	50.4	21.0	3.77	0.10	168.1	203.1
1993	129.3	192.4	73.1	33.0	5.59	0.20	207.9	225.5
1994	132.8	190.9	87.0	38.6	5.89	0.55	225.7	230.0
1995	203.2	270.5	99.7	47.0	12.08	0.30	314.9	317.8
Share in total (per cent)								
1983-1987	76	95	24	5	0.02	0.01	100	100
1988-1992	78	93	21	7	0.77	0.02	100	100
1993	62	85	35	15	2.70	0.09	100	100
1994	59	83	39	17	2.60	0.24	100	100
1995	65	85	32	15	3.80	0.09	100	100
Growth rate (per cent)								
1983-1987	37	35	9	24	-7	68	29	35
1988-1992	-4	3	15	16	298	46	1	4
1993	13	6	45	52	46	99	24	11
1994	3	-1	19	17	7	179	9	2
1995	53	42	15	22	106	-45	40	38

Source: UNCTAD, based on annex tables 1 and 2.

Figure I.1. FDI outflows from the five largest home countries, 1980-1995

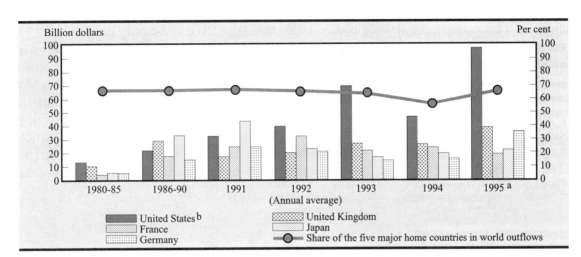

Source: UNCTAD, based on annex table 2.

a   Estimates.
b   Excludes FDI in the financial sector of the Netherlands Antilles, except for 1995.

Table I.2. Selected indicators of FDI and international production, 1986-1995

(Billions of dollars and percentage)

Item	Value at current prices, 1995[a] (Billion dollars)	Annual growth rate (Per cent) 1986-1990	Annual growth rate (Per cent) 1991-1994
FDI inflows	315	24.7	12.7
FDI outward stock	2 730	19.8	8.8
Sales of foreign affiliates	6 022 [b]	17.4	5.4[e]
Royalties and fees receipts	41 [d]	21.8	10.1
GDP at factor cost	24 948 [d]	10.8	4.3
Gross product of foreign affiliates	1 410 [e]	11.0[f]	11.4[g]
Gross fixed capital formation	5 681 [d]	10.6	4.0
Exports of goods and non-factor services	4 707 [b]	14.3	3.8[c]

Source: UNCTAD.

a   Estimates.
b   1993.
c   1991-1993.
d   1994.
e   1991.
f   1982-1989.
g   1989-1991.

Note: not included in this table are the value of worldwide sales by foreign affiliates associated with their parent firms through non-equity relationships and the sales of the parent firms themselves.

Most important among them is that, in response to technological and competitive pressures, companies from every developed country, as well as from an increasing number of developing economies, are becoming more active globally, either through FDI or non-equity investments. These companies seek to exploit new markets or take advantage of factors of production to build international production networks.   Mergers and acquisitions (M&As) are their favourite route to production abroad. In fact, a significant part of the increases in FDI in 1994 and 1995 is attributable to M&As (discussed separately in the next section). This is helped by the acceptance of privatizations with foreign-investor participation, especially in developing countries (table I.3), giving rise to new investment opportunities in industries previously closed to these investors, including in infrastructure. Important are also regional integration schemes (the single market programme in the European Union, NAFTA, MERCOSUR, APEC, ASEAN) that facilitate regionally integrated production networks for both insider and outsider firms.

Table I.3. FDI from privatizations in developing countries, 1989-1994[a]

(Millions of dollars and percentage)

Region	1989	1990	1991	1992	1993	1994	Cumulative 1989-1994
North Africa and Middle East							
FDI from privatization	1.0	-	3.2	19.2	302.0	121.9	447.3
Share of region's FDI inflows	0.1	-	0.2	0.9	8.0	3.3	2.9
Sub-Saharan Africa							
FDI from privatization	13.8	38.2	11.1	49.8	573.5	262.0	948.4
Share of region's FDI inflows	0.4	3.5	0.6	3.3	31.8	8.8	7.6
East Asia and the Pacific							
FDI from privatization	-	0.7	77.1	522.7	1 156.5	982.0[b]	2 739.0
Share of region's FDI inflows	-	0.01	0.4	1.9	2.5	1.9	1.5
South Asia							
FDI from privatization	0.1	10.6	4.2	41.8	16.2	14.1	87.0
Share of region's FDI inflows	0.02	2.3	0.9	6.7	1.9	1.1	2.1
Latin America and the Caribbean							
FDI from privatization	183.3	2 461.5	3 264.3	2 414.5	1 373.0	3 695.0	13 391.6
Share of region's FDI inflows	2.2	27.7	21.2	13.6	7.1	15.0	14.2
All developing regions							
FDI from privatization	198.2	2 511	3 359.9	3 048	3 421.2	5 075.0	17 613.3
Share of regions' FDI inflows	0.7	7.5	8.1	6.1	4.7	5.9	5.6
Memorandum:							
Central and Eastern Europe							
FDI from privatization	461.5[c]	488.9[c]	1 868.2	2 656.9	2 931.9	1 121.0	8 578[d]
Share of region's FDI inflows	..	..	76.3	71.0	52.5	19.0	48.5[d]

Sources: World Bank, privatization database and World Bank, 1996.

[a]   The World Bank's developing-country classification used in this table differs from that used elsewhere in this volume.

[b]   Excluding China, for which portfolio and direct investment cannot be distinguished for 1994.

[c]   FDI from privatization is larger than the recorded FDI inflows reported by the IMF in the balance-of-payments data.

[d]   1991-1994.

The recent boom in flows has also expanded the world's total FDI stock, valued at about $2.7 trillion in 1995 (table I.2 and annex tables 3 and 4). That stock belongs to some 39,000 parent firms and their 270,000 affiliates abroad (table I.4). About 90 per cent of parent firms in the world are based in developed countries, while two-fifths of foreign affiliates are located in developing countries (figure I.2). The global sales of foreign affiliates worldwide reached $6.0 trillion in 1993, continuing to exceed the value of goods and non-factor services delivered through exports ($4.7 trillion) -- of which about one quarter are intra-firm exports. In 1993, $1 of FDI stock produced $3 in goods and services abroad.

Figure I.2. Distribution of parent firms and foreign affiliates, by region, latest available year
(Percentage)

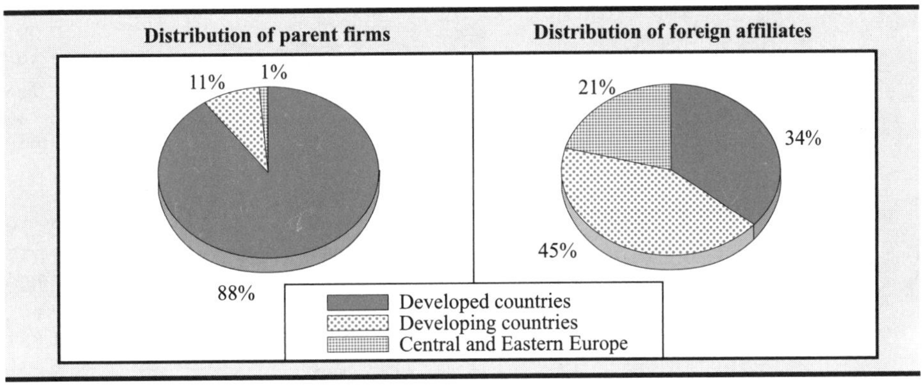

Source: UNCTAD, based on table I.4.

2. Cross-border mergers and acquisitions[4]

(a) Overall trends

Over the past ten years, the growth of the worldwide aggregate value of cross-border M&As has mirrored the growth of FDI flows (figure I.3). In the early 1990s, memories of previous unsuccessful cross-border M&As, coupled with the economic recession in many developed countries, led investors to adopt a more cautious approach to this type of investment. Along with FDI flows, such investments reached a cyclical trough in 1991. By 1995, the absolute value of cross-border M&A activities was once again large enough to affect the level, direction and composition of FDI flows, which rose to unprecedented heights.

Mergers and acquisitions are a popular mode of investment for firms wishing to protect, consolidate and advance their global competitive positions, by selling off divisions that fall outside the scope of their core competence and acquiring strategic assets that enhance their competitiveness.[5] For those firms, the "ownership" assets acquired from another firm, such as technical competence, established brand names, and existing supplier networks and distribution systems, can be put to immediate use towards better serving global customers, enhancing profits, expanding market share and increasing corporate competitiveness by employing international production networks more efficiently.

Table I.4. Number of parent firms and their foreign affiliates, by country, latest available year

(Number)

Area/economy	Year	Parent firms based in country	Foreign affiliates located in country[a]
Developed economies		34 199 [b]	90 786 [b]
Australia	1994	732	2 450
Austria	1993	838	2 210
Belgium and Luxembourg	1978	96	1 121
Canada	1995	1 565	4 708
Denmark	1992	800	1 289 [c]
Finland	1995	1 200	1 150
France	1993	2 216	7 097 [d]
Germany	1993	7 003 [e]	11 396 [f]
Greece	1991	..	798
Iceland	1995	50	40
Ireland	1994	39	1 040
Italy	1993	445 [g]	1 474 [g]
Japan	1995	3 967 [h]	3 290 [i]
Netherlands	1993	1 608 [j]	2 259 [j]
New Zealand	1995	263	2 277
Norway	1994	1 000	3 000
Portugal	1993	1 165	7 602
South Africa	1978	..	1 884
Spain	1995	236	6 232 [d]
Sweden	1995	3 520	5 550
Switzerland	1985	3 000	4 000
United Kingdom [k]	1992	1 443 [l]	3 376 [m]
United States	1993	3 013 [n]	16 543 [o]
Developing economies		4 148 [b]	119 765
Bolivia	1990	..	298
Brazil	1994	797	9 698
Chile	1995	..	2 028 [p]
China	1993	379 [q]	45 000
Colombia	1995	305	2 220
El Salvador	1990	..	225
Guatemala	1985	..	287
Hong Kong	1995	500 [c]	4317
India	1991	187	926 [r]
Indonesia	1995	313 [s]	3 472 [t]
Mexico	1993	..	8 420
Oman	1995	92 [t]	351 [t]
Pakistan	1993	57	758
Paraguay	1988	..	208
Peru	1990	..	905
Philippines	1995	..	14 802 [u]
Republic of Korea	1991	1 049	3 671
Saudi Arabia	1989	..	1 461
Singapore	1986	..	10 709
Sri Lanka [v]	1995	..	139
Taiwan Province of China	1990	..	5 733
Turkey	1995	357	136
Uruguay	1994	..	101
Former Yugoslavia	1991	112	3 900

/...

(Table I.4, cont'd)

Area/economy	Year	Parent firms based in country	Foreign affiliates located in country[a]
Central and Eastern Europe [w]		400	55 000
Albania	1994	..	118
Belarus	1994	..	393
Bulgaria	1994	26	918
Czech Republic	1995	..	20 337
CSFR	1994	26	..
Estonia	1994	..	1 856
Hungary	1994	66	15 205
Poland	1994	58	4 126
Romania	1994	20	..
Russian Federation	1994	..	7 793
Ukraine	1994	..	2 514
World		38 747	265 551

Source: UNCTAD.

[a] Represents the number of foreign affiliates in the country shown. The figures provided by the respective governments, however, may include the companies that are not normally considered as foreign affiliates according to the standard definition of affiliates (see the section on definitions and sources in the annex).

[b] Total does not include countries for which data are not available.

[c] 1991.

[d] 1992.

[e] Does not include holding companies abroad that are dependent on German-owned capital and which, in turn, hold participating interests of more than 20 per cent abroad (indirect German participating interests).

[f] Does not include the number of foreign-owned holding companies in Germany which, in turn, hold participating interests in Germany (indirect foreign participating interests).

[g] Not including the services sector.

[h] The number of parent firms not including finance, insurance and real estate as of March 1995 (3,695) plus the number of parent companies in finance, insurance and real estate industries as of December 1992 (272).

[i] The number of foreign affiliates not including finance, insurance and real estate as of March 1994 (3,006) plus the number of foreign affiliates in finance, insurance and real estate industries as of November 1995 (284).

[j] As of October 1993.

[k] Data on the number of parent firms based in the United Kingdom, and the number of foreign affiliates in the United Kingdom are based on the register of companies held for inquiries on the United Kingdom's FDI abroad and FDI into the United Kingdom conducted by the Central Statistical Office. On that basis, the numbers are probably understated because of lags in identifying investment in greenfield sites and because some companies with small presences in the United Kingdom and abroad have not yet been identified.

[l] Represents a total of 24 parent firms in banking and 1,443 non-bank parent firms in 1991.

[m] Represents 518 foreign affiliates in banking in 1992 and 3,376 non-bank foreign affiliates in 1991.

[n] Represents a total of 2,201 non-bank parent firms in 1993 and 89 parent firms in banking in 1989 with at least one foreign affiliate whose assets, sales or net income exceeded $3 million, and 723 non-bank and bank parent companies in 1989 whose affiliate(s) had assets, sales and net income under $3 million.

[o] Represents a total of 12,207 bank and non-bank affiliates in 1993 whose assets, sales or net income exceeded $1 million and 4,336 bank and non-bank affiliates in 1987 with assets, sales and net income under $1 million. Each affiliate represents a fully consolidated United States business enterprise, which may consist of a number of individual companies.

[p] Number of foreign companies registered under DL600.

[q] 1989.

[r] For 1988.

[s] For 1993.

[t] As of May 1995.

[u] This number covers all firms with foreign equity, i.e., equity ownership by non-resident corporations and/ or non-resident individuals, registered with the Securities and Exchange Commission from 1989 to 1995.

[v] Data for the number of investment projects.

[w] Data for parent firms and foreign affiliates are estimated.

Figure I.3. Worldwide cross-border M&As and FDI flows, 1987-1995

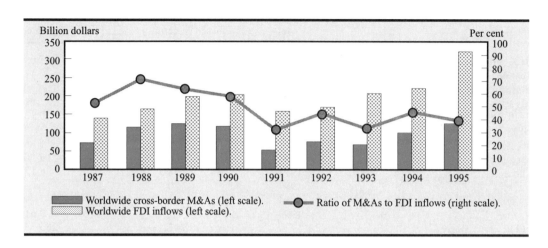

Source: KPMG, 1996 and UNCTAD, FDI database.

Note: only majority-held M&As.

The main cross-border M&A trends are:

- The total value of cross-border M&As (including both minority and majority cross-border M&As and related joint ventures) was $229 billion in 1995, twice the 1988 level. This was fuelled by a substantive number of cross-border M&As valued at over $1 billion (table I.5), accounting together for $71 billion. Majority cross-border M&As were valued at $135 billion in 1995. It is expected that their number and value will rise further in 1996 as firms seek to increase market share in slow growth industries.[6]

- Western Europe had the highest level of cross-border M&As of all regions. Most was intra-European Union. The United States, however, had the highest share of all countries (KPMG, 1996). Japanese cross-border M&As have increased three-fold in the past year, reflecting a shift from a traditional preference for greenfield investment.

- Most large-scale cross-border M&As have taken place in the energy distribution, telecommunications, pharmaceuticals and financial services industries.

- Cross-border M&As are no longer the sole province of large firms. Small and medium-sized firms appear to have played a significant role in the growth of cross-border M&As as well, particularly in the electronics, business services, personal services, healthcare, distribution, construction and engineering industries.

(b) Trends by region and major countries

In 1995, Western Europe was the focus of M&As, where foreign firms acquired companies worth $50 billion (annex table 7). Most acquisitions took place in the United Kingdom ($24 billion) and France ($10 billion). At the same time, Western European firms spent $66 billion for M&As abroad, $61 billion of which was due to European Union firms alone (annex table 8). Most of these cross-border purchases[7] were made by firms based in the United Kingdom ($18 billion), Germany ($15 billion) and France ($7 billion). Intra-European Union cross-border M&As, which comprised 42 per cent of all Western European purchases in 1995, increased from $20 billion in 1994 to $26 billion (23 per cent of all Western European FDI inflows) (KPMG, 1996). European firms made these purchases to adapt to the three-year old single European market, to create sufficient economies of scale in production and sourcing, and to reposition their networks on the European, rather than national level.[8]

In 1995, United States firms spent $38 billion in cross-border M&As, or 90 per cent of the equity component of FDI outflows from that country. Most were in the oil and gas industry. The largest were the Crown Cork & Seal purchase of Carnaudmetalbox (France) for $5.2 billion, the Central and Southwest purchase of Seeboard (United Kingdom) for $1.9 billion and the Southern purchase of South Western Electricity (United Kingdom) for $1.7 billion (table I.5). The value of United States firms acquired by foreign-based TNCs was $49 billion in 1995. The largest included the purchase by Hoechst (Germany) of Marion Merrell Dow ($7.1 billion), the purchase by Seagram (Canada) of MCA ($5.7 billion) and the Grand Metropolitan-Pillsbury (United Kingdom) purchase of PET ($2.6 billion) (table I.5).

In the past, Japanese TNCs have not engaged heavily in cross-border M&As, preferring instead greenfield investments (JETRO, 1996). Although purchases by Japanese TNCs increased more than three-fold in 1995, to $4.5 billion (from $1.1 billion in 1994), this was less than one-tenth of the amount spent by European firms and companies in the United States.

About one tenth of world-wide M&A sales takes place in developing countries (figure I.4). Before 1992, such transactions were almost entirely due to the privatization of firms in Argentina, the acquisition of domestic consumer-goods firms by foreign-based firms and the streamlining of core businesses by domestic conglomerates. Since 1992, Asian and Central and Eastern European firms have been the targets in the developing world, surpassing Latin America and the Caribbean. This

---

Box I.1. FDI and M&As: a comparison of the data

Changes in the levels of cross-border M&As are not always reflected in changes in FDI flows. This is because the foreign equity component of FDI flows contains only a part of the cross-border M&A transactions, namely, the foreign equity component of these transactions with a share of the total equity of at least 10 per cent. Mergers and acquisitions can take place through other types of transactions that are not included in FDI flows, such as minority investments (those that are classified as portfolio equity investments) and domestically raised capital (see accompanying figure). These ways of financing M&As have become more important in recent years. It is, therefore, possible to witness a large increase in M&As that is not fully reflected in FDI flows. By the same token, FDI flows contain elements, such as intra-company loans and reinvested earnings,[a] that are not part of M&As. Consequently, movements in FDI flows can take place independently of movements in M&As. In practice, however, there is a close relationship between movements in M&As and FDI flows.

FDI and cross-border M&As

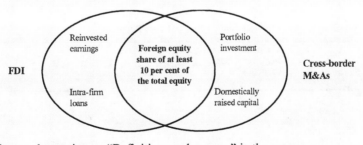

a For details, see the section on "Definitions and sources" in the annex.

Table I.5. Cross-border M&A deals with a value of above $1 billion, 1995

Acquiring company	Home country	Acquired company	Host country	Value (Billion dollars)	Industry
Hoechst AG	Germany	Marion Merrel Dow	United States	7.1	Pharmaceutical R&D and manufacturing
The Seagram Co. Ltd.	Canada	MCA Inc.	United States	5.7	Film production
Crown Cork & Seal Co.Inc.	United States	Carnaudmetalbox S.A.	France	5.2	Packaging products
Atlas (a joint venture of France Telecom/ Deutsche Telekom)	Belgium	Sprint	United States	4.2	Telecommunications
United Communication Industry PLC (via Total Access PLC)	Thailand	Intercity Paging Service PTE LTD	Sri Lanka	2.8	Telecommunications
Grand Metropolitan PLC (via Pillsbury)	United Kingdom	Pet Inc (United States)	United States	2.6	Pet foods
The Broken Hill Pty Co. Ltd.	Australia	Magma Copper Company	United States	2.4	Production and refining of copper
Zuerich Versicherungs- Gesellschaft (together with insurance partners)	Switzerland	Kemper Corp.	United States	2.0	Finance (fund management)
Interbrew S.A.	Belgium	John Labatt	Canada	2.0	Brewing
Wolters Kluwer NV	Netherlands	CCH Commerce Clearing House Inc.	United States	1.9	Business services (tax and business law information services)
Central and Southwest Corp.	United States	Seeboard PLC	United Kingdom	1.9	Electricity distribution
Softbank Corporation	Japan	Ziff-Davis Publishing Co.	United States	1.7	Publishing of computer magazines
Cadbury Schweppes PLC	United Kingdom	Dr. Pepper/ Seven-Up Co.	United States	1.7	Soft drinks
Southern Company	United States	South Western Electricity PLC	United Kingdom	1.7	Power station and distribution
Texas Utilities Co.	United States	Eastern Energy	Australia	1.6	Electricity distribution
Dresdener Bank AG	Germany	Kleinwort Benson Group PLC	United Kingdom	1.6	Investment bank
Pacificorp	United States	Powercor Ltd.	Australia	1.6	Electricity distribution
National Australia Bank Ltd.	Australia	Michigan National Corporation	United States	1.6	Banking
Veba AG	Germany	Cable & Wireless PLC	United Kingdom	1.5	Telecommunications
Telsource (consortium led by Koninklijke PTT Nederland NV and Swiss Telecom) (Netherlands)	Netherlands	SPT Telecom	Czech Republic	1.5	Telecommunications
Schweizerischer Bankverein (Swiss Bank Corp.)	Switzerland	SG Warburg's Investment Banking Business	United Kingdom	1.4	Investment banking

/...

reflects the growing availability and attractiveness of firms in Asia and privatization programmes in Central and Eastern Europe.

Transnational corporations based in developing countries have not engaged much in cross-border M&As ($8 billion in 1995) (figures I.5 and I.6). The precipitous jump in Asian cross-border purchases in 1992 was the result of a single transaction, the purchase of Midland Bank (United Kingdom) by Hongkong and Shanghai Banking Corporation (Hong Kong) for $7.2 billion (KPMG, 1996). Latin American and Caribbean cross-border purchases also increased in 1992 (figure I.6). Mexican purchases were valued at $3 billion and Martini & Rossi (Italy) was bought by the Caribbean-based Bacardi & Company for $1.5 billion. Since 1992, overall levels of purchases by developing country TNCs have declined.

(Table I.5, cont'd)

Acquiring company	Home country	Acquired company	Host country	Value (Billion dollars)	Industry
Utilcorp (consotium including AMP Investments and States Authorities Super-annuation Board)	United States	United Energy	Australia	1.4	Electricity distribution
Energy Corporation	United States	Citipower	Australia	1.3	Electricity distribution
BASF AG	Germany	Boots Pharmaceuticals	United Kingdom	1.3	Pharmaceuticals
Lyonnaise des Eaux Dumez S. A.	France	Northumbrian Water	United Kingdom	1.2	Water utility
International Property Corporation Ltd. (including P. Reichman, L. Tisch, Prince Al Waleed Bin Talal, E. Safra and M. Price)	Canada	Canary Wharf	United Kingdom	1.2	Real estate
Sodexho S. A.	France	Gardner Merchant	United Kingdom	1.2	Catering
International Paper Co.	United States	Carter Holt Harvey Ltd.	New Zealand	1.2	Paper and pulp
Daewoo Corp.	Republic of Korea	FSO Fabryka Samochodow Osobowych	Poland	1.1	Transport equipment
ING Internationale Nederlanden Group NV	Netherlands	Barings Investment Banking, Securities and Asset Management Divisions	United Kingdom	1.1	Banking
Colgate-Palmolive	United States	Kolynos	Brazil	1.0	Chemical and pharmaceuticals / oral-care products
SEE Corp.	United States	First Hydro	United Kingdom	1.0	Power generating stations
MCI Communications Corp.	United States	SHE Systemhouse	Canada	1.0	Information technology services
Tomkins PLC	United Kingdom	Gates Rubber	United States	1.0	Rubber and plastic products (for automobiles)
MCI Communications	United States	The News Corp.	Australia	1.0	Media company

Source: UNCTAD, based on data obtained from KPMG.

Figure I.4. Cross-border M&A sales in developed and developing countries, 1988-1995

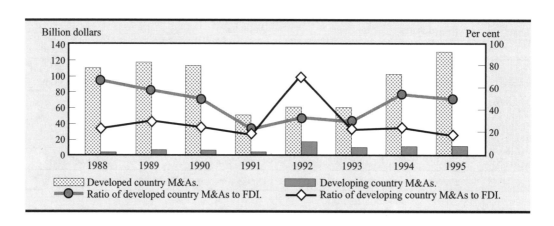

Figure I.5. Cross-border M&A purchases in developed and developing countries, 1988-1995

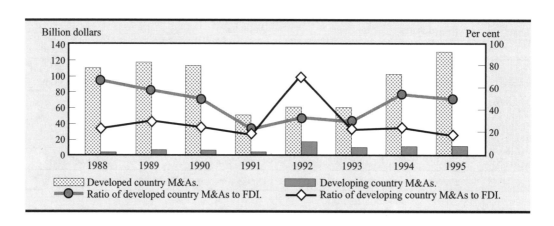

Figure I.6. Cross-border M&A purchases by enterprises in developing countries, 1988-1995

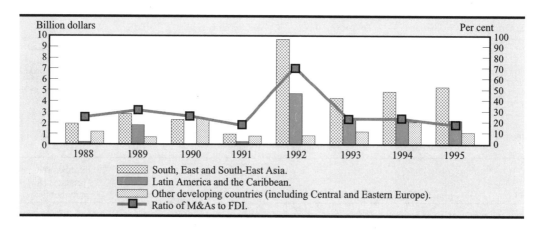

Sources: KPMG, 1996 and UNCTAD, FDI database.

Note: only majority-held M&As.

(c) Trends by industry

From a sectoral perspective, there are noteworthy trends in some industries:

- The value of service-related M&As increased by 146 per cent between 1993 and 1995 (figure I.7). Services firms have favoured M&As as a way of creating the necessary scale to allow them to serve customers abroad, as well as to take advantage of deregulation (Hamill, 1993).

- In 1994 and 1995, heightened competition in the pharmaceutical industry led to a wave of domestic and cross-border M&As. The reasons include the expiration of patents on many drugs discovered in the 1960s, declining profit margins and market shares, government-mandated cuts in healthcare costs, and a tendency towards vertical integration of pharmaceutical firms' distribution systems, services and general healthcare and healthcare delivery providers. Pharmaceutical companies have also been faced with the challenge of expanding product lines at competitive prices and coping with the high costs of research and development. Some of these M&As are expected to lead to more efficient production and lower costs. For example, the Hoechst/Marion Merrell Dow merger is expected to result in a 19 per cent reduction of the combined workforce.[9]

- The value of cross border M&As in banking and finance tripled in 1995, to $100 billion (annex table 9). The most significant included the Zuerich Versicherungs-Gesellschaft consortium (Switzerland) purchase of Kemper Corporation (United States) for $2 billion and the Dresdner Bank AG (Germany) purchase of Kleinwort Benson Group PLC (United Kingdom), for $1.6 billion; the insurance industry also had an unusually high level of cross-border M&As in 1994, valued at $9 billion (table I.5).

Figure I.7. Worldwide sectoral trends in cross-border M&As, 1988-1995

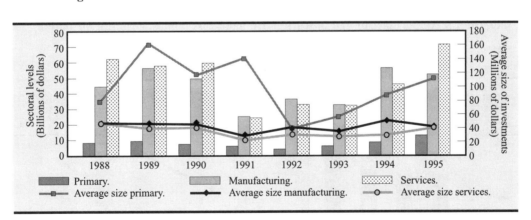

Sources: KPMG, 1996 and UNCTAD, FDI database.

Note: only majority-held M&As.

3. Foreign direct investment and international production

Between 1980 and 1994, the ratio of FDI stock to world GDP and the ratio of FDI flows to gross domestic investment doubled (figure I.8). The world gross product of foreign affiliates (a value-added measure of their output produced abroad) accounted for 6 per cent of world GDP in 1991 (the latest year for which data are available), compared with 2 per cent in 1982 (table I.6). For some countries, that share was considerably higher: for Indonesia and Malaysia, for example, the shares for 1991 were 16 per cent and 11 per cent, respectively.

Behind the increasing importance of FDI in host countries lies a strong push towards the transnationalization of firms. The ratio of FDI outflows to gross domestic capital formation and the ratio of FDI outward stock to GDP in developed countries almost doubled between 1985 and 1995, from 3 per cent to 6 per cent and from 7 per cent to 12 per cent, respectively.

Increasing transnationalization globally, however, masks divergent trends nationally. The United States, for example, experienced three phases in its transnationalization. First there was outward expansion from the 1950s to the late 1970s, then followed a reduction in transnational activities from the late 1970s to the mid- to late 1980s. Finally, in the late 1980s, there was a resumption of outward expansion. As a result, the ratio of gross product of foreign affiliates to United States GDP declined from 8.2 per cent in 1977 to 6 per cent in 1989 and then marginally increased to 6.2 per cent in 1991. For Japan, on the other hand, where transnationalization has proceeded along a linear path, the share of foreign sales of Japanese TNCs in their total sales in manufacturing increased constantly from 2.9 per cent in fiscal year 1980 to 6.4 per cent in fiscal 1990 and to 8.6 per cent in fiscal 1994 (MITI, 1996).

Increasing transnationalization has been reinforced by the emergence of new outward investors, many of which are from developing countries. For example, outward FDI from Taiwan Province of China increased rapidly, beginning in the mid-1980s. The share of outward FDI in the total capital stock of firms based in Taiwan Province of China averaged 1.8 per cent between 1983 and 1987, rising to 6.1 per cent between 1988 and 1992 (UNCTAD-DTCI, forthcoming a, table 23).

Figure I.8. Importance of FDI in world GDP and gross domestic capital formation, 1980, 1988, 1990 and 1993-1995

(Billions of dollars and percentage)

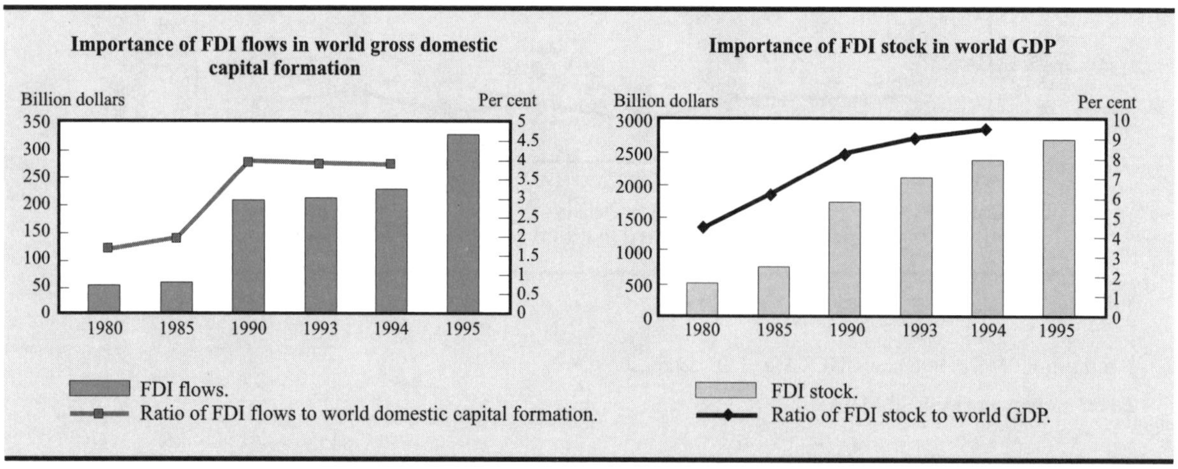

Source: UNCTAD, based on annex tables 1, 3, 5 and 6.

Foreign direct investment[10] has become not only the single largest item in net private capital flows to developing countries (54 per cent of the total in 1995),[11] but was also responsible for the continued upward trend in these flows in both 1994 and 1995. The halving of portfolio equity inflows from the 1993 peak of $46 billion to $22 billion in 1995 was more than offset by large and sustained increases in FDI inflows (figure I.9), although significant regional differences occurred.[12] In fact, FDI is often the only source of international private capital to most least developed countries that have not received the investment-grade ratings required for borrowing from abroad or tapping international capital markets.

The difference between FDI and portfolio investment trends is explained by the differences in the underlying factors and motivations between these two types of private capital flows, though both types of capital flows can be part of integrated corporate strategies. On the push side, the growth of institutional savings in industrial countries has given rise to a large pool of funds and, on the pull side, high returns in emerging stock markets make foreign investors more willing to face the accompanied higher risks. Bond financing -- the debt side of portfolio investment -- is determined by a country's

Table I.6. Sales and gross product of foreign affiliates, exports of goods and non-factor services and GDP, by region, 1982, 1990 and 1993

(Billions of dollars and percentage)

Region/country	Gross product of foreign affiliates [b]			Gross product of foreign affiliates as a ratio to home country GDP (Per cent)			Sales of foreign affiliates [a]			Sales of foreign affiliates as a ratio to exports of goods and non-factor services (Per cent)		
	1982	1990	1991	1982	1990	1991	1982	1990	1993	1982	1990	1993
Developed countries	410	1 102	1 120	5.2	6.7	6.5	1 770	4 272	4 525	121.2	136.3	131.5
Western Europe	180	609	631	5.9	8.8	8.8	785	2 360	2 564	89.3	117.6	121.7
European Union	164	572	592	5.7	8.7	8.7	718	2 216	2 416	87.6	118.1	122.3
Other Western Europe	15	37	39	9.6	10.6	11.0	68	145	148	111.7	109.9	112.7
North America	177	408	403	5.1	6.7	6.4	775	1 580	1 587	214.6	225.1	193.2
Other developed countries	48	86	86	3.5	2.5	2.2	210	332	374	95.3	78.3	72.8
Developing countries	143	274	288	5.7	6.6	6.5	626	1 062	1 457	113.7	111.6	133.5
Africa	23	33	33	6.8	8.6	9.4	99	129	143	119.5	126.4	157.7
Latin America and the Caribbean	58	97	103	7.5	8.9	8.9	255	377	500	226.9	236.9	293.6
Asia	61	141	150	4.6	5.4	5.1	265	547	802	77.9	82.4	99.1
West Asia	17	24	24	3.8	2.5	2.0	73	92.8	106	51.1	65.4	68.4
South, East and South-East Asia	44	117	126	5.0	7.4	7.5	192	454	695	97.4	87.0	106.8
Oceania	1.2	1.7	1.8	28.6	32.2	30.1	5	7	8	346.8	303.4	230.9
Central and Eastern Europe	0.1	1.5	2.9	0.0	0.7	1.3	.5	6	40	0.9	10.1	22.8
World	548	1 378	1 410	5.2	6.6	6.4	2 396	5 341	6 022	116.0	128.9	127.9

Source: UNCTAD estimates.

  [a] Worldwide sales are estimated by extrapolating the worldwide sales of foreign affiliates of TNCs from France, Germany, Japan and the United States on the basis of the shares of these countries in the worldwide inward FDI stock. Regional sales are estimated by applying the relevant shares of each region in the worldwide inward stock to the estimated worldwide sales.

  [b] Worldwide gross product is estimated by extrapolating the worldwide gross product of foreign affiliates of United States TNCs on the basis of the relative share of this country in the worldwide inward FDI stock. Regional gross products are estimated by applying the relevant shares of each region in worldwide inward stock to the estimated worldwide gross product.

(or firm's) ability to access international capital markets and the cost of borrowing from these markets vis-à-vis other sources of finance. Usually, the sound macroeconomic management of an economy is closely related with a good stock-market performance. Good macroeconomic management is also an important pull factor determining inward FDI. But

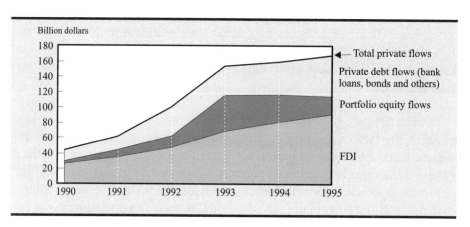

Figure I.9. Total private flows to developing countries, by type of flows, 1990-1995

Source: World Bank, 1996, p. 3.

Note: The World Bank's developing-country classification used in this table differs from that used elsewhere in this volume.

other pull factors such as the size of the market and the availability of resources not found elsewhere are also significant determinants of FDI. And on the push side, the forces driving FDI are different from those driving portfolio equity investment. It is not the size of institutional savings, but international competition that drives firms to invest abroad.

4. Foreign direct investment and infrastructure

(a) Trends

Transnational corporations are becoming increasingly involved in infrastructure development.[13] Investment flows from developed countries in the early 1990s into the main infrastructure industries (construction, communications and transport and storage) were around $7 billion annually (annex table 10). Throughout the 1990s, FDI inflows and inward stocks in infrastructure in selected major developed and developing recipient countries, as well as countries in Central and Eastern Europe, increased steadily, both in value and as a share of total investments (figure I.10 and annex table 11).

This reflects, of course, an increase in infrastructure FDI outflows (annex table 10). Such flows accounted for 8 per cent of total outflows in 1994 in the case of the United States (the largest outward investor), compared with 5 per cent only two years earlier. Likewise, the United States outward FDI stock in infrastructure rose steadily in the 1990s and, at $14 billion in 1994, accounted for 2.3 per cent of its global outward stock. For Japan, infrastructure FDI outflows accounted for nearly 7 per cent of total outflows between 1992 and 1994. But for most developed countries, infrastructure FDI outflows account, typically, for 3-5 per cent of total outflows (figure I.11 and annex table 10).

The growing importance of infrastructure is also reflected in the value of total assets in infrastructure owned by United States affiliates abroad. These were valued at $54 billion in 1992 or 3 per cent of the total assets of these affiliates, compared with $22 billion, or 1.6 per cent in 1989. The total assets of United States affiliates abroad rose by some 31 per cent between 1989 and 1992, while

Figure I.10. Inward FDI in infrastructure-related industries[a] as share of all industries in selected countries, various years[b]

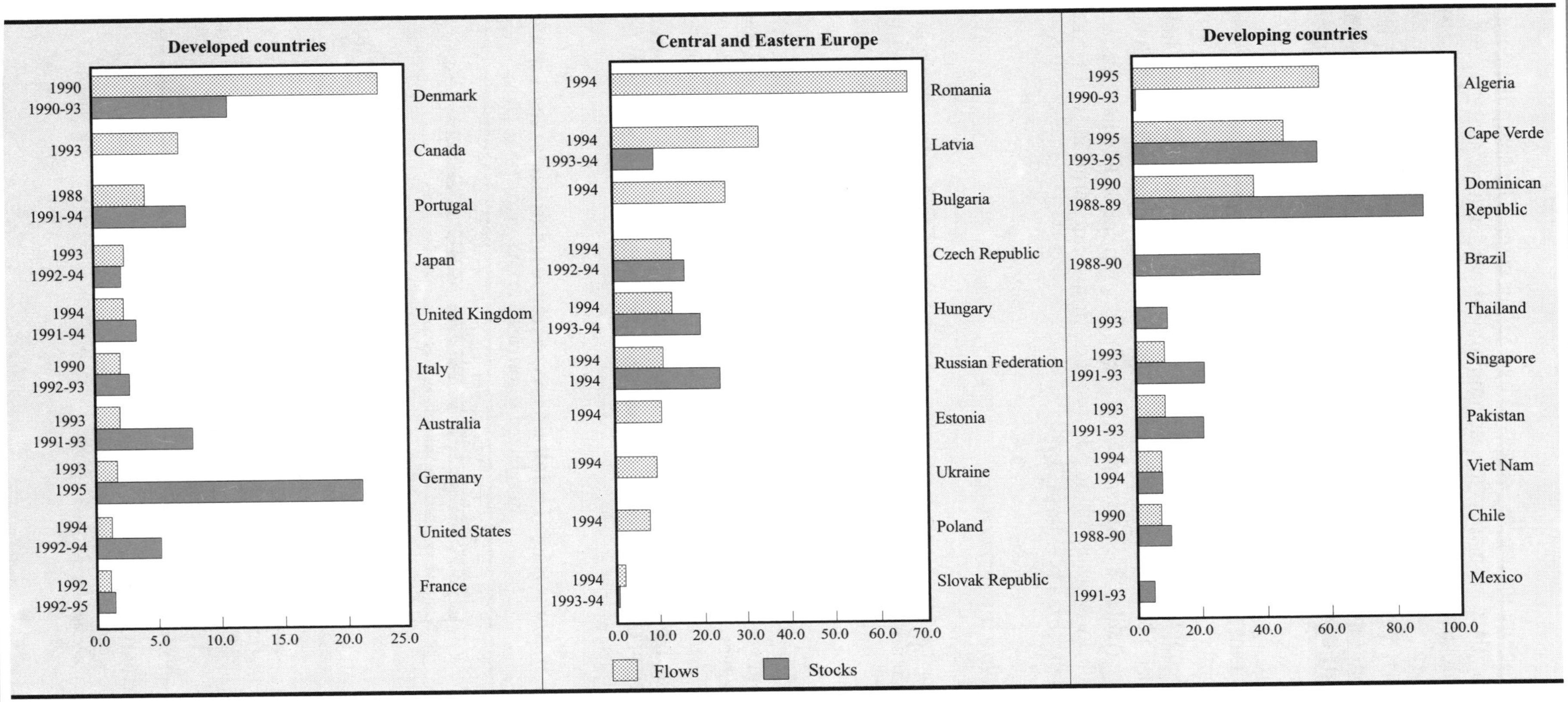

Source: UNCTAD estimates, based on annex table 10.

a   Includes construction, communications and transport storage.
b   Annual average for inflows of FDI.

assets in infrastructure industries increased by 153 per cent. The sharp increase in foreign affiliate assets has taken place primarily in telecommunications, whose share in the total assets in all infrastructure industries more than doubled between 1989 and 1992 (figure I.12).

Even so, FDI in infrastructure is still low compared to investments in other industries, with some notable exceptions (annex tables 10 and 11). Only in a few countries (e.g., Denmark, South Africa, Kenya and Nepal) does FDI account for a considerable share of total investment in infrastructure (table I.7).

However, a historical perspective on FDI in infrastructure points to significant potential for increased TNC involvement in this area. In 1940, United States foreign affiliates involved in infrastructure accounted for more than 22 per cent of the outward FDI stock held by United States firms, valued at $1.5 billion. In some regions, more than one third of United States investment went into infrastructure (table I.8). Subsequent waves of expropriation and nationalization led to a steady decline of FDI in infrastructure in the post-war era, in absolute terms as well as in relation to the total United States stock abroad (Kobrin, 1984).

(b) Financing infrastructure

The financial requirements for infrastructure are vast. Present growth rates in East Asia suggest that such investment requirements will be $1.4 trillion during the next decade; for China alone, the figure is over $700 billion. In Latin America, requirements are around $600-800 billion (World Bank, 1995b).

Because of the enormous resources needed to finance infrastructure projects, the risks involved and the severe budgetary constraints that many governments of developing countries face, external resources are expected to play a prominent role in overcoming these bottlenecks. Transnational corporations invest in infrastructure projects in the form of FDI (greenfield investments or acquisitions through privatizations), build-own-operate (BOO), build-operate-transfer (BOT), build-transfer-operate (BTO), or variants of these schemes (table I.9; and Sirtaine, 1994). Since FDI is

Figure I.11. Outward FDI in infrastructure-related industries[a] as share of all industries in selected countries, various years[b]

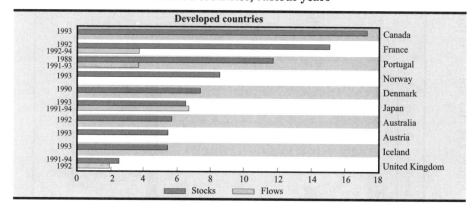

Source: UNCTAD estimates, based on annex table 10.
[a]   Includes construction, communications and transport storage.
[b]   Annual average for outflows of FDI.

**Figure I.12. The industry composition of total assets of United States abroad
in infrastructure, 1989 and 1992**

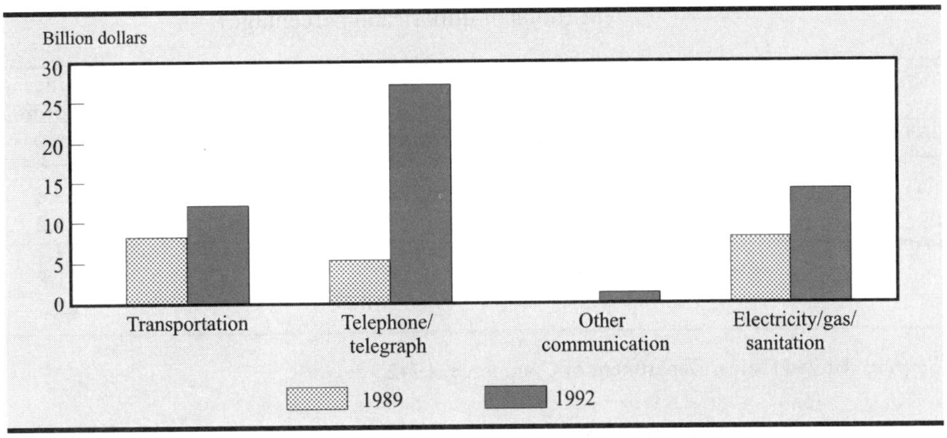

Billion dollars

Transportation | Telephone/telegraph | Other communication | Electricity/gas/sanitation

☐ 1989   ■ 1992

Source: United States, Department of Commerce, 1992 and 1994.
Note: non-bank affiliates of non-bank firms.

**Table I.7. Infrastructure FDI flows relative to total gross domestic capital formation
in selected countries, 1992**

(Millions of dollars and percentage)

Country	Total investment in infrastructure (Million dollars)	FDI flows into infrastructure[a] (Million dollars)	Ratio of FDI to total investment in infrastructure-related industries (Per cent)
Developed countries			
Denmark [b]	631	95.8	15.2
Finland	1 811	14.8	0.8
France	30 655	181.4	0.6
Greece	2 209	8.1	0.3
Italy [c]	38 715	24.6	0.6
Netherlands [c]	7 882	319.4	4.1
Norway [d]	3 636	4.2	0.1
South Africa	1 708	103.1	6.0
Sweden	6 103	6.8	0.1
United Kingdom [d]	17 312	527.7	3.0
United States	54 652	2 114.0	3.9
Developing countries			
Kenya	19	1.4	7.4
Korea, Republic of [b]	3 236	11.3	0.3
Nepal [c]	47	3.4	7.3
Pakistan	1 730	70.1	4.1
Venezuela [e]	881	4.6	0.5
Zimbabwe [f]	26	0.1	0.4

Source: UNCTAD estimates, based on annex table 11; and United Nations, 1995.

[a] Annual average flows in the early 1990s in most cases. For the specific period used for each country, see annex table 11.
[b] Includes only construction.
[c] 1990.
[d] 1991.
[e] 1989 includes transport and storage industries.
[f] 1985.

Table I.8. United States outward FDI stock in public utilities and transportation, by region, 1940

(Millions of dollars and percentage)

Region/country	FDI in public utilities and transportation	Total FDI stock	FDI in public utilities and transportation as a share of total FDI stock (Per cent)
Canada	407	2103	19.4
Europe	74	1420	5.2
Latin America	962	2771	34.7
Asia	50	422	11.8
Total	1 493	6 716	22.2

Source: United States, Department of Commerce, 1942.

defined as an investment involving control of a resident entity in one economy by an enterprise resident in another economy, the infrastructure facilities involved in schemes other than BTO can be regarded as foreign affiliates regardless of the method of financing the investment (figure I.13). Even BOT projects, where foreign investors own and control an infrastructure facility only for a specified period, can be considered as FDI because the time length -- typically 10 to 20 years -- is sufficiently long for the investment to qualify as FDI, despite the agreement to transfer eventually ownership and control of the facility back to the host country.

Governments in many developing countries, including those in Asia, have only recently begun to allow foreign investor involvement through BOT or related schemes to finance infrastructure projects. Two examples highlight this:

- In Viet Nam, the Government provided, in 1993 and 1994, the legal framework for BOT schemes. However, as of mid-1996, only one such project had been approved, a water-supply plant with a total investment of $30 million by two Malaysian companies, Emas Utilities and Sadec Malaysian Consortium.[14]

- In China, it was only in August 1995 that the Government promulgated a notice on screening and monitoring pilot BOT projects in infrastructure. In the same year,

Figure I.13. Ways of financing infrastructure projects

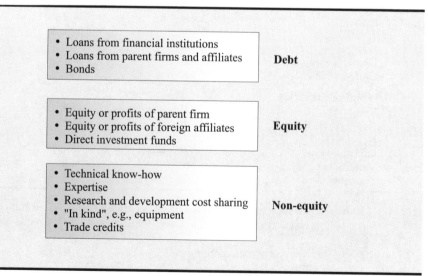

Source: UNCTAD.

Note: The financing of BOO, BOT or BTO projects falls under all of these financing methods.

the Guangxi Autonomous Region opened the Laibin Power Station to foreign investors for bidding. This marked the official recognition of the first trial BOT project. In reality, however, the BOT scheme had already been introduced during the early 1980s, including through such projects as Shajiao Power Plant B in Shenzhen by Hopewell (Holdings) from Hong Kong. Such (trial) BOT projects have been agreed for thermal power stations, hydro-power stations, highways, bridges and tunnels and city water works.

Table I.9. Forms of involvement by TNCs in infrastructure projects

Form	Description	Project examples
Privatization	A foreign investor acquires shares and/or assets of state-owned infrastructure through privatization.	Telecom (Argentina) was privatized in November 1990. A 60 per cent equity share was sold to a consortium (STET of Italy and French Telecom, both 17.5 per cent; J.P. Morgan of the United States, 10 per cent), with a selling price of $2.6 billion. An additional $1 billion investment took place in 1991-1992, and a further $3.4 billion investment is planned between 1993 and 1997. Entel (Chile) is gradually being privatized since 1986. Equity was sold to Telefónica of Spain (20 per cent equity), Chase Manhattan of the United States (11.7 per cent), Banco Santander of Spain (10 per cent). Annual investment between 1989 and 1992 was $40 million, and total investment between 1993 and 1998 is expected to be $300 million.
Build-operate-transfer	A foreign investor (or a consortium of private foreign and/or domestic companies) is selected, usually through a bidding process, to design, finance and build an infrastructure facility. The project company operates the facility for a pre-defined period of time during which the revenues received are supposed to cover the costs and provide an adequate return to the investor(s). At the end of that period, the ownership and the right to operate the facility are transferred to the government. Variants of this scheme include BLT (build-lease-transfer) and ROT (rehabilitate-operate-transfer).	A project to build three gas turbines in the Philippines. Project implementing company: Hopewell Energy (Philippines) Corp. Total project costs: $41 million. Minority investment in the project sponsoring company (Hopewell Project Management Co., Ltd.) by Japanese trading companies. Borrowing (bank loans and IFC loans): $30 million.
Build-own-operate	This arrangement is similar to BOT, except that the infrastructure facility is owned and operated by the project company indefinitely.	A project to establish two electric power stations in Indonesia. Project implementing company: P.T. Paiton Energy Co. (Indonesia). Total project costs: $1.8 billion. 20 per cent equity share in the project sponsoring company (Mission Energy B.V.) by Japanese trading companies. 30 year-term. Borrowing: $1.4 billion.
Build-transfer-operate	After an infrastructure facility is built and ownership is transferred to the government, the project company operates the facility and shares revenues with the government.	A project to install 1 million telephone lines in local area in Thailand. Project implementing company: Thai Telephone and Telecommunication. 20 per cent equity share by NTT of Japan and 3 per cent by Japanese trading companies. 30 year-term (25 years for operations). Revenue sharing: 56.9 per cent. Borrowing (bank loans and supplier credits): $1.0 billion.

Source: UNCTAD, based on Japan Institute for Overseas Investment, 1993.

Box I.2. Direct investment funds and infrastructure development

Direct investment funds have been created to invest in medium and long-term projects (5-10 years) in developing countries, mostly in infrastructure development, through equity (usually with a controlling stake of 10 per cent or more) or convertible debt. Foreign investors whose capital comprises direct investment funds are a diverse group that includes institutional and private investors, TNCs, other private companies, regional banks and multilateral organizations. Some TNCs or domestic private companies may already have considerable experience in the type of projects in which the fund plans to invest (e.g., power plants). Examples of direct investment funds are the AIG Asian Infrastructure Fund (which raised over $1 billion in 1994); Asian Infrastructure Fund (with $500 million capital); and Scudder Latin America Infrastructure Fund (with committed capital of $100 million) (see accompanying table).

What has triggered the emergence and proliferation of these funds are the enormous financial requirements of developing countries for infrastructure. By pooling resources through direct investment funds, foreign investors hope to lower the risk of investing in infrastructure projects in developing countries. The participation of regional or multilateral organizations with experience in financing private-sector development projects also helps to lower the risks involved.

Despite the enormous investment potential offered by infrastructure projects in developing countries, direct investment funds have not been investing heavily. The costs and risks involved in infrastructure development (including those from exchange-rate changes) have discouraged them from investing large amounts of capital unless a rate of return can be assured that can be high by usual international standards. Some host countries are themselves not always eager to have foreign equity participation. Others still need to clarify their regulatory and administrative procedures relating to foreign equity participation in infrastructure to alleviate any fears of expropriation. Overall, however, direct investment funds represent a potentially important source of foreign capital for the modernization of infrastructure in developing countries.

Selected direct investment funds for infrastructure projects

Fund	Core investors	Capital raised as of 1994
AIG Asian Infrastructure Fund	American International Group Government of Singapore Bechtel Enterprises	$ 1-1.2 billion
Alliance ScanEast Fund, L.P.	Equitable Life Assurance Society of American International Group International Finance Corporation European Bank for Reconstruction and Development	$ 22 million
Asea Brown Boveri Funding	Asea Brown Boveri	$ 500 million
The Asian Infrastructure Fund	Pergrine Investment Holdings Soros Fund Management Frank Russell Company International Finance Corporation Asian Development Bank	$ 0.5-1 billion
Central European Telec Investments, L.P.	Creditanstalt Bankverein International Finance Corporation	$ 42 million
Global Power Investments Company, L.P.	GE Capital Corporation Soros Fund Management International Finance Corporation	$ 0.5-2 billion
Scudder Latin America Trust for Independent Power	International Finance Corporation NRG Energy, Inc. CMS Energy, Inc. Corporacion Andida de Fomento	$ 100-300 million

Source: Anayiotos, 1994.

The principal sources of finance for TNC-controlled infrastructure projects are debt instruments (mostly loans from commercial banks and bilateral or multilateral financial institutions and, to a lesser extent, bonds). Around $27 billion in loans and bonds alone was raised for financing infrastructure projects in 1995.[15] Equity is also provided by TNCs (directly or indirectly through direct investment funds, see box I.2) and by other foreign investors, often together with equity funds from local private investors, multilateral and regional financial institutions or the host country's government. Assuming a ratio of equity to debt of 20 to 80, the value of equity in infrastructure-project financing in 1995 was around $5 billion, and the combined financial flows for infrastructure development in the form of both debt and equity was around $32 billion. However, only a part of equity financing is recorded as FDI for balance-of-payments purposes..

Privatization has been another important channel through which foreign investment (direct and portfolio equity) has entered infrastructure industries. In developing countries, the privatization revenues from infrastructure projects during 1988-1995 were $40 billion (table I.10), representing 37 per cent of all privatization revenues (World Bank, 1996, p. 122). Foreign investment accounted for about half of these revenues.

(c) Constraints and the potential for increased foreign direct investment in infrastructure

High fixed or sunk costs, long gestation periods, possible price ceilings and other regulations on the operation of an infrastructure facility imposed by host countries tend to dampen foreign investors' willingness to commit funds for infrastructure development. Political risk (expropriation or nationalization) is also present (box I.3). These constraints have induced foreign investors to minimize equity commitments to infrastructure projects, relying instead on debt (commercial loans and bonds).

There are also constraints that arise out of the very nature of some of the ways (e.g., BOT) in which infrastructure projects are financed through foreign capital. Given the perceived risk, investors require high rates of return (which, moreover, need to be backed up by legally binding assurances). This necessarily requires user fees comensurate with the rate of return, which, in many poorer developing

Table I.10. Infrastructure privatizations in developing countries, 1988-1995

(Millions of dollars and percentage)

Industry	Total revenues	Foreign investment	Foreign investment as a share of total revenues
Utilities	11 130	3 994	35.9
Power/gas/electricity	10 903	3 905	35.9
Water and sanitation	227	89	39.4
Telecommunications	21 293	14 253	66.9
Transport	7 518	2 178	29.0
Airlines	6 106	1 739	28.5
Railroads	453	99	21.8
Road transportation	431	64	14.8
Ports and shipping	528	276	52.3
Total	39 941	20 425	51.1

Source: World Bank, privatization database.

Note: Preliminary estimates.

countries, can be too high to be sustainable. In many other countries, the implied increases in user fees are substantial and may simply not be acceptable politically. As a result, negotiations of BOT and similar schemes -- in developing and developed countries -- are typically very complex and drawn out, and concentrated so far in a relatively limited number of countries.

Despite these constraints, there is considerable potential for TNC participation in infrastructure development, given the recognition that the size of the investment requirements is too big to be met from public sources alone. Through their affiliate networks, TNC systems are well suited to raise funds anywhere in the world and channel them to where they are needed, or use internally generated funds to meet the financial requirements of infrastructure development (UNCTAD-DTCI, 1995a, chapter III). By pooling financial resources, including through new instruments (box I.2), TNCs can share the cost and spread the risk associated with infrastructure development. Insurance against political risks is provided increasingly by bilateral or multilateral institutions (e.g., OPIC and MIGA -- box I.4), as well as export credit agencies. There is also considerable scope for TNC participation in infrastructure that is especially conducive to attracting FDI, such as science parks, export-processing zones and facilities for human resource development.

Governments are increasingly willing to open up infrastructure to both domestic and foreign private investors (table I.11). Countries in Latin America and the Caribbean, in particular, have taken

---

Box I.3. FDI in infrastructure: back into the future?

The history of FDI in infrastructure, particularly in developing regions, is characterized by large investments during the nineteenth and early twentieth centuries -- and by expropriations and nationalizations starting from the mid-1960s and reaching a peak in the early 1970s (UNCTAD-DTCI, 1993a, box I.1, p. 17). For example, American & Foreign Power (AFP), established in 1923 to hold General Electric's stock in energy and utilities overseas, invested heavily in energy/utilities infrastructure projects in 11 countries in Latin America and two in Asia before the Second World War. In the post-war period, despite the boom in the demand for energy, host-country governments imposed limits on energy-rates. AFP began to face declining revenues despite the growing demand for energy; as a result, it reduced such investments by half. Eventually, AFP faced nationalizations, expropriations, forced sales and forced reinvestments of the sales proceeds in most countries in which it was operating, and was almost forced out of the energy and utilities industries completely.

While the present environment in developing countries is favourable towards private foreign investment, a few incidents suggest that investments in infrastructure tend to be riskier than other investments. They highlight that, despite the overall positive attitudes towards foreign investors in most developing countries, governments often still prefer local to foreign ownership, especially in projects with a public good output. Moreover, the perception of the foreign investor as a contributor of capital and technology tends to diminish once an infrastructure project has been completed and the costs in terms of dividends and interest payments, as well as the frequent monopoly position of the foreign investor, become more apparent, decreasing the political cost of nationalization.

In projects in which a continuous foreign-investor presence is regarded as useful -- for example, because of technical problems or managerial complexities in running an infrastructure facility, or because the facility is part of a regional or global infrastructure complex -- foreign investors are less likely to be subjected to a forced exit. Debt obligations are also more likely to be met in the case of nationalization; hence foreign investors try to minimize their share of equity in a project. Raising capacity in the face of increased demand, even if ceilings on rate increases have been imposed by the government, can diffuse nationalize pressures. In the same context, unpopular rate increases should take place before the transfer of ownership of an infrastructure facility to the foreign investor. Involving local or other foreign partners to share the cost of financing and run an infrastructure facility, as well as sensitivity to environmental issues, can also be helpful. Finally, obtaining insurance against political risk from investment guarantee organizations (see box I.4), receiving government guarantees and agreeing on a reasonable dispute-settlement mechanism with the host-country government can all avert conflicts and forced exits.

Source: Wells and Gleason, 1995.

Table I.11. Measures for the liberalization of FDI in infrastructure, 1991-1995

Economy	Year	Measure
Africa		
Tunisia	1994	Grants financial incentives for infrastructure projects.
Asia		
China	1993	Opens construction of airports and aircrafts to FDI.
India	1994	Allows FDI in road projects on build-operate-transfer (BOT) basis; FDI in telephone services and television broadcasting companies is also permitted.
Indonesia	1994	Opens ports, shipping, airlines, railways, production, transmission and distribution of energy, mass media, water distribution and sanitation to FDI.
Pakistan	1994	Incentive package and guidelines for private sector participation in the power generation sector.
Philippines	1994	Authorizes the financing, construction, operation and maintenance of infrastructure projects by the private sector.
Taiwan Province of China	1994	Allows FDI in major transportation infrastructure projects.
Viet Nam	1993	Promulgates BOT regulations.
	1994	Streamlines the approval process for infrastructure projects, including BOT.
Central and Eastern Europe		
Albania	1995	Opens the power sector, water supply, transport, electric energy, telecommunication, waste material disposal and industrial zones and parks to FDI. Provides for the use of BOT schemes, management contracts and leasing.
Bulgaria	1995	Opens postal and telecommunication networks, roads, harbours, civil airports, water supply and irrigation, electric power supply and distribution to FDI and sets the framework for granting concessions.
Czech Republic	1994	Opens the energy sector to FDI.
Hungary	1994	Opens roads, railways, ports, public airports and telecommunications to FDI and sets the framework for granting concessions.
Ukraine	1993	Grants preferential treatment to investors in high priority sectors, such as infrastructure.
Latin America and the Caribbean		
Argentina	1992	Allows FDI in the privatization of the State gas company.
Bolivia	1994	Opens the privatization process to FDI including in infrastructure.
Brazil	1995	Authorizes public sector concessions to foreign and domestic investors in electric power generation and supply, telecommunications, sanitation, sewerage and water supply, transport, highway construction, ports and airports and natural gas distribution.

/...

big steps towards opening infrastructure to FDI during 1991-1995. Partly, this is the result of technological developments that have changed the parameters of providing certain infrastructure services and that have enabled competition to emerge in markets formerly considered as natural monopolies (e.g., telecommunications). Moreover, almost by necessity, certain infrastructure industries are now being viewed as global industries.

The realization of the FDI potential also rests on the growing awareness that shortfalls in the provision of infrastructure services have created severe bottlenecks for overall development in many

(Table I.11, cont'd)

Economy	Year	Measure
Colombia	1995	Opens television broadcasting to FDI.
Costa Rica	1993	Organizes the granting of concessions in public works and services and infrastructure.
Ecuador	1993	Organizes private sector participation in public services and infrastructure.
	1995	Regulates the participation of foreign investors in companies operating in radio and television.
Panama	1995	Organizes the granting of concessions in the electricity industry.
Mexico	1995	Opens land transportation of passengers and cargo to FDI.
Peru	1991	Organizes the granting of concessions in roads, public utility services, education and transport. Allows FDI in the electric power industry through concessions.
Venezuela	1994	Allows FDI in public works and services through concessions.
West Asia		
Turkey	1993	Authorizes and organizes the use of BOT financing and investments in major infrastructure projects.
	1995	Grants special incentives for infrastructure projects and BOT projects.
Republic of Yemen	1994	Opens the electricity, water and telecommunication projects to FDI.
Developed countries		
Australia	1992	Limits foreign investment to 20 per cent in commercial television and television broadcasting.
Japan	1991	Allows FDI up to 20 per cent in Nippon Telegraph and Telecom.
Portugal	1993	Opens the water production and distribution and basic sanitation services sector to FDI.

Source: UNCTAD, based on UNCTC, 1992a; UNCTAD-DTCI, 1993a, annex table 6; and various official gazettes and official publications on national legislation.

Note: table I.11 does *not* reflect existing policies of countries where the infrastructure sector had already been open to FDI prior to 1991, or where FDI is encouraged, but without specific legislative measures applicable to infrastructure. This table does not include privatization laws, even though a number of countries has included state-owned enterprises in infrastructure among those to be privatized, opening them up, in the process, to foreign investors. As of 1996, about 129 such privatization laws had been passed worldwide.

Box I.4. Infrastructure projects insured by MIGA

Institutions insuring (guaranteeing) FDI have registered a sharp increase in the demand for coverage of infrastructure investment in recent years. For instance, the share of "contracts of guarantee" for infrastructure projects in MIGA's portfolio rose from 4 per cent in 1994 to 12 per cent by March 1996, making this sector the fastest growing in its portfolio. Between 1991 and March 1996, MIGA issued some 30 contracts, with a coverage of $275 million for infrastructure projects which involve about $3.5 billion of FDI. This trend is likely to continue in the future, since about one third of the 1,000 preliminary applications for guarantees that MIGA had received by the end of May 1996 concern infrastructure projects (including 174 power projects and 68 projects in the telecommunications industry); about 42 per cent of these applications are from Asia and 37 per cent from Latin America and the Caribbean.

Source: MIGA.

---

developing countries. Governments are also aware that the availability and quality of infrastructure are factors determining a country's attractiveness to FDI (Wheeler and Mody, 1992; Mody and Wang, 1994). The quality of communication and transportation systems, in particular, have become more important in light of the complex strategies increasingly being pursued by TNCs (UNCTAD-DTCI, 1993a). The rationalization and dispersal of corporate functions on a regional or global level implies, among other things, that a sound telecommunications system is a prerequisite for attracting certain corporate functions, such as accounting, finance and research and development.

B. The largest transnational corporations

1. Trends and salient features of the top 100

In the same manner in which world FDI flows are dominated by a few countries, the world's 100 largest TNCs -- just 0.3 per cent of the TNC universe -- control most international production. The largest 100 (table I.12) (excluding banking and financial institutions), ranked by foreign assets, are all based in developed countries. Royal Dutch Shell[16] (United Kingdom/Netherlands) has topped the list for the past five years. These 100 TNCs have approximately $1.4 trillion worth of assets abroad and account for roughly a third of global FDI stock, a share unchanged over the past five years. The highlights of the trends in 1990-1994 are as follows:

- *Assets.* Both total and foreign assets grew by 6 per cent between 1990 and 1994.[17]

- *Sales.* Foreign sales grew by 5 per cent between 1990 and 1994. In 1993, the sales of the foreign affiliates of the top 100 TNCs accounted for a quarter of the estimated $6 trillion worldwide sales by foreign affiliates of all TNCs. In some industries, that share was even higher -- for example, foreign sales by the world's largest TNCs in electronics accounted for 80 per cent of estimated global sales in that industry.

- *Employment.* As of 1993, employment at home and abroad by the top 100 TNCs is estimated to be about 12 million, or 16 per cent of the estimated 73 million employed by all TNCs worldwide. About 5 million workers are employed by the foreign affiliates of the top 100 TNCs -- about one-sixth of all workers employed by all foreign affiliates. This share has not changed in the past five years, despite the corporate restructuring undertaken by firms. By contrast, labour productivity, calculated as sales per employee, appears to have risen significantly, by almost 30 per cent between 1990 and 1994.

Table I.12 . The top 100 TNCs ranked by foreign assets, 1994

(Billions of dollars and number of employees)

Ranking by: Foreign assets	Index[b]	Corporation	Country	Industry[a]	Foreign assets	Total assets	Foreign sales	Total sales	Foreign employment	Total employment	Index[b]
1	27	Royal Dutch Shell[c]	United Kingdom/ Netherlands	Petroleum	63.7	102.0	51.1	94.8	79000	106000	63.6
2	80	Ford	United States	Motor vehicles and parts	60.6	219.4	38.1	128.4	96726	337778	28.6
3	26	Exxon	United States	Petroleum	56.2	87.9	72.3	113.9	55000	86000	63.8
4	85	General Motors	United States	Motor vehicles and parts	..[d]	198.6	44.0	152.2	177730	692800	25.7
5	38	IBM	United States	Computers	43.9	81.1	39.9	64.1	115555	219839	56.4
6	30	Volkswagen	Germany	Motor vehicles and parts	..[d]	52.4	29.0	49.3	96545	242318	60.4
7	97	General Electric	United States	Electronics	33.9	251.5	11.9	59.3	36169	216000	16.7
8	82	Toyota	Japan	Motor vehicles and parts	.[d]	116.8	37.2	91.3	27567	172675	28.1
9	59	Daimler - Benz	Germany	Transport and communication	27.9	66.5	46.3	74.0	79297	330551	42.8
10	37	Elf Aquitaine	France	Petroleum	..d	48.9	26.2	38.9	43950	89500	56.7
11	32	Mobil	United States	Petroleum	26.2	41.5	44.1	66.8	27400	58500	58.7
12	74	Mitsubishi	Japan	Diversified	..[d]	109.3	67.0	175.8	11146	36000	31.0
13	8	Nestlé	Switzerland	Food	25.4	38.7	47.3	48.7	206125	212687	86.5
14	72	Nissan Motor	Japan	Motor vehicles and parts	..[d]	80.8	27.3	65.6	34464	143310	32.2
15	6	ABB Asea Brown Boveri Ltd[e]	Switzerland	Electrical equipment	24.8	29.1	25.6	29.7	194557	207557	88.4
16	68	Matsushita Electric	Japan	Electronics	..[d]	92.2	39.2	78.1	112314	265397	39.8
17	4	Roche Holdings	Switzerland	Pharmaceuticals	23.4	25.9	10.3	10.5	50869	61381	90.5
18	31	Alcatel Alsthom	France	Electronics	23.1	51.2	21.9	30.2	117000	197000	58.9
19	33	Sony	Japan	Electronics	..[d]	47.6	30.3	43.3	90000	156000	58.5
20	51	Fiat	Italy	Motor vehicles and parts	22.5	59.1	26.3	40.6	95930	251333	47.0
21	14	Bayer	Germany	Chemicals	22.4	27.4	21.9	26.8	78300	146700	72.5
22	83	Hitachi	Japan	Electronics	..[d]	92.5	19.8	56.8	80000	331852	27.7
23	10	Unilever[f]	United Kingdom/ Netherlands	Food	22.0	28.4	39.1	45.4	276000	307000	84.5
24	9	Philips Electronics	Netherlands	Electronics	..[d]	27.8	31.7	33.7	210000	253000	85.0
25	49	Siemens	Germany	Electronics	..[d]	50.6	30.1	52.1	158000	376000	47.3
26	55	Renault	France	Motor vehicles and parts	..[d]	41.2	16.7	32.5	39982	138279	43.7
27	18	British Petroleum	United Kingdom	Petroleum	19.5	28.8	30.8	50.7	48650	66550	67.2
28	67	Philip Morris	United States	Food	18.0	52.6	24.2	65.1	85000	165000	41.0
29	28	Hanson	United Kingdom	Building materials	18.0	34.0	10.3	17.7	58000	74000	63.3
30	78	Mitsui	Japan	Diversified	..d	82.5	64.5	171.5	23560	80000	29.5
31	62	Du Pont	United States	Chemicals	..d	36.9	18.6	39.3	35000	107000	42.0
32	79	Nissho Iwai	Japan	Trading	..d	55.5	34.3	118.4	2101	7245	29.0
33	20	B.A.T. Industries	United Kingdom	Tobacco	15.8	48.5	25.0	32.8	158205	173475	66.7
34	24	Hoechst	Germany	Chemicals	15.7	26.2	23.9	30.6	92333	165671	64.6
35	29	Rhône - Poulenc	France	Chemical	15.6	22.9	9.4	15.5	46430	81582	61.8
36	25	Ciba - Geigy	Switzerland	Chemicals	15.5	31.8	15.4	22.0	63095	83980	64.6
37	81	ENI	Italy	Petroleum	..[d]	54.3	10.9	31.1	19527	91544	28.1

/...

(Table I.12, cont'd)

Ranking by: Foreign assets	Index[b]	Corporation	Country	Industry [a]	Foreign assets	Total assets	Foreign sales	Total sales	Foreign employment	Total employment	Index [b]
38	87	Sumitomo	Japan	Trading	..[d]	59.0	48.5	167.7	..[g]	22000	24.2
39	21	Volvo	Sweden	Motor vehicles and parts	14.2	18.6	16.7	20.2	30664	75549	66.6
40	76	Chevron	United States	Petroleum	13.0	34.4	10.6	35.1	10636	45758	30.3
41	92	Toshiba	Japan	Electronics	..[d]	63.2	11.4	56.6	38000	190000	20.0
42	5	Sandoz	Switzerland	Pharmaceuticals	..[d]	14.9	11.3	11.6	51258	60304	88.8
43	89	Itochu Corporation	Japan	Trading	..[d]	62.5	36.1	162.3	2706	10140	22.7
44	54	Texaco	United States	Petroleum	11.7	25.5	16.6	32.5	10640	29713	44.2
45	41	BASF	Germany	Chemicals	11.3	25.7	19.6	27.0	40297	106266	51.5
46	48	VIAG AG	Germany	Diversified	11.2	23.3	8.6	17.8	41288	86018	48.0
47	95	Marubeni	Japan	Trading	..[d]	78.8	37.3	153.8	1915	10006	19.1
48	52	Dow Chemical	United States	Chemicals	10.4	26.5	8.6	16.7	24165	53700	45.3
49	70	Xerox	United States	Scientific and photo. equipment	10.2	38.6	7.9	16.8	32150	87600	36.7
50	3	RTZ	United Kingdom	Mining	..[d]	11.7	5.6	6.1	43112	44499	91.4
51	66	Honda	Japan	Motor vehicles and parts	..[d]	28.3	25.0	37.5	19668	92800	41.0
52	7	Electrolux	Sweden	Electronics	..[d]	11.3	12.9	14.0	94469	114103	87.3
53	91	ITT	United States	Diversified services	..[d]	100.8	7.8	23.8	23366	110000	21.2
54	23	Saint - Gobain	France	Building materials	..[d]	16.5	8.7	13.4	58364	80909	65.2
55	43	Procter & Gamble	United States	Soaps and cosmetics	9.6	25.5	16.1	30.3	57500	96500	50.0
56	100	AT&T	United States	Electronics	9.4	79.3	7.3	75.1	32820	304500	10.8
57	94	NEC Corporation	Japan	Electronics	9.3	47.7	11.6	43.3	17569	151069	19.3
58	11	Glaxo Wellcome[h]	United Kingdom	Pharmaceuticals	9.1	12.1	7.7	8.5	35523	47378	80.2
59	65	Hewlett - Packard	United States	Computers	9.0	19.6	9.5	25.0	39435	98400	41.4
60	1	The Thomson Corporation	Canada	Publishing and printing	9.0	9.4	5.9	6.4	43100	48600	92.3
61	13	Seagram	Canada	Beverages	9.0	11.7	6.5	6.8	..[g]	15805	78.6
62	19	News Corporation	Australia	Publishing and printing	9.0	19.4	7.3	8.4	..[g]	25844	66.8
63	86	Nippon Steel Corporations	Japan	Metal	..[d]	51.3	8.8	34.0	15000	50438	24.4
64	88	Amoco	United States	Petroleum	8.5	29.3	7.1	30.3	7541	43205	23.3
65	50	Robert Bosch	Germany	Motor vehicles and parts	..[d]	17.7	11.5	21.2	62343	153794	47.2
66	40	BMW AG	Germany	Motor vehicles and parts	8.2	17.1	17.9	25.9	50474	109362	54.4
67	16	Michelin	France	Rubber and plastics	8.0	13.1	9.9	12.2	..[g]	117776	72.0
68	71	Canon Inc.	Japan	Computers	8.0	23.9	14.1	21.0	35101	72280	33.5
69	64	Sharp Corporation	Japan	Electronics	..[d]	109.9	7.3	14.6	29000	42853	41.6
70	90	Veba	Germany	Trading	7.7	38.6	12.4	43.7	23894	126875	22.4
71	2	Solvay	Belgium	Chemicals	7.7	8.3	7.4	7.8	35695	39874	92.2
72	77	Pepsico	United States	Food	7.6	24.8	8.2	28.5	140170	471000	29.8
73	17	Total	France	Petroleum	..[d]	10.3	19.1	25.6	29340	51803	68.0
74	42	McDonald's	United States	Restaurants	..[d]	13.6	4.2	8.3	..[g]	183000	50.5
75	98	Chrysler	United States	Motor vehicles and parts	..[d]	49.5	6.6	52.2	24000	121000	15.4
76	63	Grand Metropolitan	United Kingdom	Food	..[d]	15.5	4.7	11.8	27006	64300	42.0
77	75	BHP	Australia	Metals	6.6	20.5	4.3	12.6	12000	48000	30.3
78	47	Johnson & Johnson	United States	Pharmaceuticals	6.6	15.7	7.9	15.7	42374	81537	48.1
79	45	Minnesota Mining	United States	Mining	6.4	13.1	6.2	12.1	32581	69843	48.9
80	22	Cable and Wireless	United Kingdom	Telecommunications	..[d]	11.1	4.8	7.1	31128	41348	65.9

/...

(Table I.12, cont'd)

Ranking by: Foreign assets	Index	Corporation	Country	Industry [a]	Foreign assets	Total assets	Foreign sales	Total sales	Foreign employment	Total employment	Index [b]
81	36	Digital Equipment	United States	Computers	6.0	10.6	8.3	13.5	43598	82800	57.2
82	69	Mannesmann	Germany	Industrial and farm equipment	..[d]	13.3	6.4	18.7	40487	124914	37.3
83	99	GTE	United States	Telecommunications	5.8	42.5	2.6	19.9	14793	111000	13.3
84	44	Carrefour	France	Trade	5.8	11.9	13.3	27.1	44200	90300	49.0
85	39	Thomson	France	Electronics	5.8	16.3	10.1	13.9	57148	98714	55.3
86	46	Sara Lee	United States	Food	5.8	11.7	5.8	15.5	84932	145874	48.3
87	15	Alcan Aluminum	Canada	Metal products	5.7	9.7	8.0	9.3	28000	39000	72.3
88	93	Atlantic Richfield	United States	Petroleum refining	5.6	24.6	2.6	15.0	4631	23200	20.0
89	56	Motorola Inc.	United States	Electronics	5.2	17.5	12.6	22.3	58900	132500	43.6
90	84	International Paper	United States	Paper	5.1	17.8	3.3	15.0	20500	70000	26.6
91	35	LVMH Moet-Hennessy	France	Beverages	..[d]	12.0	3.4	5.0	11737	18779	57.4
92	53	Alcoa	United States	Metals	..[d]	12.4	4.3	9.9	31400	61700	44.9
93	12	Akzo	Netherlands	Chemicals	4.9	6.9	11.2	12.0	51700	70400	79.3
94	34	Pechiney	France	Metals	4.9	9.9	8.3	12.8	33800	58234	57.5
95	73	RJR Nabisco	United States	Food and tobacco	4.9	31.4	4.9	15.4	33950	70600	31.9
96	58	Eastman Kodak	United States	Scientific and photo. equipment	..[d]	15.0	7.2	13.6	42000	96300	43.0
97	96	Kobe Steel, Ltd.	Japan	Metals	..[d]	28.3	2.5	14.8	5522	32485	17.0
98	61	United Technologies	United States	Aerospace	4.8	15.6	8.8	21.2	95600	171500	42.5
99	57	Norsk Hydro	Norway	Chemicals	4.7	13.8	4.5	9.8	16208	32416	43.5
100	60	Bridgestone	Japan	Rubber and plastics	..[d]	20.1	9.0	18.8	52000	89711	42.7

Source: UNCTAD.

[a]   Industry classification for companies follows that in the "Fortune Global 500" list in Fortune, 25 July 1994, and the "Fortune Global Service 500" list in Fortune, 22 August 1994. Fortune classifies companies according to the industry or service that represents the greatest volume of their sales. Industry groups are based on categories established by the United States Office of Management and Budget. Several companies are, however, highly diversified. These companies include Asea Brown Boveri, General Electric, Grand Metropolitan, Hanson, Sandoz, Total and Veba.

[b]   The index of transnationality is calculated as the average of foreign assets to total assets, foreign sales to total sales and foreign employment to total employment.

[c]   Foreign sales are outside Europe whereas foreign employment figures are outside the United Kingdom and the Netherlands.

[d]   Data on foreign assets are either suppressed to avoid disclosure or they are not available. In the case of non-availability, they are estimated on the basis of the ratio of foreign to total employment, foreign to total sales and similar ratios for the transnationality index.

[e]   The company's business includes electric power generation, transmission and distribution, and rail transportation. The company was formed by the merger of a Swedish and a Swiss firm. Data on foreign sales and assets are outside Switzerland.

[f]   Foreign sales, assets and employment figures are outside the United Kingdom and the Netherlands.

[g]   Data on foreign employment are suppressed to avoid disclosure.

[h]   Glaxo Wellcome was previously called Glaxo Holdings, but changed name after the acquisition of Wellcome, United Kingdom.   The data provided is for Glaxo alone up to 30 June 1994.

The highlights of the regional and country trends for the top 100 TNCs in 1990-1994 are as follows:

- By country of origin, United States TNCs, with 32 entries, constituted the largest group in the top 100 in 1994. These firms are involved in a wide range of industries, including oil and gas, chemicals and pharmaceuticals, metals, electric and electronics equipment, motor vehicles, food and beverages and diversified services. In the past five years, the international activities of United States TNCs in consumer goods have grown rapidly.

- Japanese TNCs constitute the fastest growing group among the top 100 TNCs, doubling in number from 11 in 1990 to 19 in 1994.[18] This suggests that individual Japanese firms have been investing heavily abroad, though the level of overall FDI outflows from Japan in the early 1990s was relatively low. The restructuring of many Japanese affiliates abroad, leading to a downsizing of existing operations and a decrease in the number of new establishments, did not discourage the expansion plans of TNCs seeking to preserve or increase their market shares (JETRO, 1994; Tejima, 1995). Japanese TNCs in electronics were amongst the most important new entrants, expanding through large acquisitions in the United States and new production facilities in East and South-East Asia. Japanese TNCs have the largest value of foreign sales in that industry, compared with top 100 TNCs from other countries.

- European TNCs in the list of the top 100 are prominent in research-and-development intensive industries, such as chemicals and pharmaceuticals where industry consolidation has triggered a wave of M&As. Transnational corporations in these industries have improved their position in the ranking, thanks to the fast growth of foreign assets through acquisitions. In addition, large-scale operations in foreign markets relative to size of home countries for some European TNCs lead to a high transnationality index. Transnational corporations based in the United Kingdom are the largest group among European countries, followed by Germany and France.

Foreign assets, foreign sales and foreign employment, taken in isolation, do not capture fully the extent to which TNCs have become international (see also UNCTAD-DTCI, 1995a, p. 24). Re-ranking the top 100 TNCs according to a composite index of transnationality[19] therefore presents a different picture. Royal Dutch Shell falls to twenty-seventh position, and Thomson Corporation (Canada) climbs up to first place. By industry, TNCs in chemicals and pharmaceuticals score the highest rankings, followed by firms in food and electronics. Trading firms rank lowest. But even this re-ranking does not take into account various non-equity forms (including strategic alliances) through which firms operate internationally.

2. Salient features of the top 50 transnational corporations from developing countries

The 50 biggest TNCs[20] based in developing countries (table I.13), ranked in terms of foreign assets, accounted for about 10 per cent of the combined outward FDI stock of their countries of origin. These firms' ratio of foreign to total sales is high (30 per cent), compared with the ratio of foreign to total assets (9 per cent). In 1994, more than half of the top 50 TNCs from developing countries were based in Asia; the rest were based in Latin America. In 1994, Daewoo (Republic of Korea) ranked first among the 50 largest TNCs from developing countries on the basis of the ratio of foreign to total assets. Cemex, the top TNC among developing country firms in 1993, fell to third place in 1994. Although the operations of Cemex outside Mexico continued to grow, changes in the Mexican exchange rate affected the value of its assets denominated in pesos,[21] and hence its ranking.

Table I. 13. The top 50 TNCs based in developing economies, ranked by foreign assets, 1994

(Millions of dollars and number of employees)

Ranking by: Foreign assets	Index[a]	Corporation	Economy	Industry	Foreign assets	Total assets	Foreign sales	Total sales	Foreign employment	Total employment	Index[a]
1	11	Daewoo	Korea, Republic of[b]	Electronics	..[c]	33000	16000	40000	100000	200000	33.0
2	10	Hutchison Whampoa Limited	Hong Kong	Diversified	..[c]	52192	12500	30168	15086	26855	34.4
3	8	Cemex S.A.	Mexico	Cement	2847	7893	744	2101	8073	20997	36.6
4	5	Jardine Matheson Holdings Limited[d]	Hong Kong	Construction	2539	6350	6463	9559	50000	220000	43.4
5	..	China State Construction Engineering Corp.	China	Construction	2189	..[e]	1010	..[e]	..[e]	..[e]	..
6	..	China Chemicals Imports & Exports	China	Trading	1915	..[e]	7914	..[e]	..[e]	..[e]	..
7	20	Samsung Co., Ltd.	Korea, Republic of[b]	Electronics	..[c]	38000	21440	67000	42235	195429	19.5
8	17	LG Group	Korea, Republic of[b]	Electronics	..[c]	25000	8600	43000	29061	59200	25.1
9	19	Grupo Televisa S.A. de C.V.	Mexico	Media	1371	3260	286	1288	..[f]	21600	22.2
10	34	Hyundai	Korea, Republic of[b]	Diversified	1293	9657	1610	13081	814	44835	9.2
11	15	Souza Cruz S.A.	Brazil	Tobacco	935	1246	316	3784	63	11387	28.0
12	23	Keppel Corporation Limited	Singapore	Diversified	817	9118	248	1377	2847	12113	16.8
13	25	San Miguel Corporation	Philippines	Food	806	2939	252	2599	2702	30965	15.3
14	14	Tatung Co. Ltd.	Taiwan Province of China	Electrical equipment	805	3983	1200	3621	9777	27769	29.5
15	7	Dong Ah Construction Industrial Co.	Korea, Republic of[b]	Construction	734	3431	1134	2547	6828	12630	40.0
16	41	Petroleo Brasileiro S/A - Petrobras	Brazil	Petroleum refining	715	30162	2316	26396	24	50295	3.7
17	..	China Metals and Minerals	China	Trading	710	..[e]	2270	..[e]	..[e]	..[e]	..
18	3	Acer	Taiwan Province of China	Electronics	665	2033	2079	3172	4164	9981	46.7
19	30	New World Development Co. Ltd.	Hong Kong	Diversified	624	6944	316	1721	2520	28000	12.1
20	2	Fraser & Neave Limited	Singapore	Diversified	590	2728	839	1491	6547	8365	52.1
21	39	Singapore Telecommunications LTD	Singapore	Telecommunications	577	4811	50	2490	411	11279	5.9
22	..	China Harbours Engineering	China	Construction	559	..[e]	409	..[e]	..[e]	..[e]	..
23	6	Sime Darby Berhad	Malaysia	Food	557	1189	1857	3159	7500	32000	43.0
24	21	Wing On International (Holdings) Ltd.	Hong Kong	Diversified	491	1499	62	393	188	2792	18.4
25	..	China Shougang Group	China	Metals	446	..[e]	980	..[e]	..[e]	..[e]	..
26	..	China Cereals, Oil, Foodstuff Import Export	China	Trading	440	..[e]	6200	..[e]	..[e]	..[e]	..
27	18	CMPC Empresas S.A	Chile	Paper	352	2612	380	891	1718	10465	24.2
28	42	Chinese Petroleum	Taiwan Province of China	Petroleum	349	14148	157	10748	19	21231	1.3
29	31	Formosa Plastic	Taiwan Province of China	Chemicals	327	1906	233	1491	60	3645	11.5

/...

(Table I.13, cont'd)

Ranking by: Foreign assets	Index[a]	Corporation	Economy	Industry	Foreign assets	Total assets	Foreign sales	Total sales	Foreign employment	Total employment	Index [a]
30	35	Empresas Ica Societad Contro- ladora SA	Mexico	Construction	321	3264	95	1386	2136	25267	8.4
31	26	Sadia Concordia S/A Industria e Comercio	Brazil	Food	313	1405	567	2784	57	32357	14.3
32	22	Desc SA de CV	Mexico	Diversified	313	1902	313	1633	3431	19288	17.8
33	..	China Foreign Trade Transportation Corp.	China	Transportation	300	..[e]	300	..[e]	..[e]	..[e]	..
34	16	Hong Kong and Shanghai Hotels Ltd.	Hong Kong	Hotel	292	2628	47	230	2756	5540	27.0
35	27	Grupo Industrial Bimbo S.A. de C.V.	Mexico	Food	..[c]	1221	252	1252	..[f]	42463	13.3
36	1	Creative Technology	Singapore	Electronics	224	445	638	658	883	2678	60.1
37	24	Amsteel Corpora- tion Berhad	Malaysia	Diversified	209	1459	80	1066	7800	28200	16.5
38	..	China Iron and Steel Industrial and Trading Group	China	Metals	188	..[e]	257	..[e]	..[e]	..[e]	..
39	36	Companhia Cervejaria Brahma	Brazil	Food	187	1755	80	1249	476	9606	7.3
40	33	Sam Yang Co., Ltd.	Korea, Republic of [b]	Diversified	170	1964	115	1487	864	5795	10.4
41	37	China Steel Corporation	Taiwan Province of China	Metal	170	5737	467	2492	6	9561	7.3
42	4	Hyosung Corporation	Korea, Republic of	Trading	117	553	2206	2812	470	1460	43.9
43	38	Evergreen Marine	Taiwan Province of China	Transport	117	1678	80	1152	91	1298	7.0
44	9	Grupo Sidek	Mexico	Tourism	114	2831	25	575	10438	10774	35.1
45	40	Tong Yang Cement Mfg Co., Ltd.	Korea, Republic of [b]	Cement	91	1733	39	736	116	2208	5.3
46	29	Charoen Pokphand	Thailand	Food	82	642	109	857	1077	8440	12.8
47	12	Malaysian Interna- tional Shipping Co., Ltd.	Malaysia	Transport	72	172	406	885	321	3004	32.8
48	28	Usiminas - Usinas Siderurgicas de Minas GE	Brazil	Steel	63	3949	564	2280	1375	10448	13.2
49	32	Vitro Societad Anonima	Mexico	Non-metallic	52	4338	800	2872	1000	36694	10.6
50	13	Aracruz Celulose S/A	Brazil	Paper	..[c]	2593	482	529	..[f]	3378	31.1

Source: UNCTAD.

[a] The index of transnationality is calculated as the average of foreign assets to total assets, foreign sales to total sales and foreign employment to total employment.

[b] The accounting standards of the Republic of Korea do not require the publication of consolidated financial statements including both domestic and foreign affiliates. The figures provided here are estimates of consolidated financial statements as provided by the companies in response to a survey by UNCTAD. Depending on the availability of the data on foreign components, the data for business group totals are used.

[c] Data on foreign assets are either suppressed to avoid disclosure or they are not available. In the case of non-availability, they are estimated on the basis of the ratio of foreign to total employment, foreign to total sales and similar ratios for the transnationality index.

[d] A subsidiary of Jardine Matheson Holdings of Bermuda.

[e] Data are not available.

[f] Data on foreign employment are suppressed to avoid disclosure or not available. In the case of non-availability of the data, they are estimated on the basis of other foreign component ratios for the transnationality index.

On the basis of the transnationality index, Creative Technology (Singapore), a producer of standard personal computer sound synthesis, holding more than 60 per cent of the global market share, was in first place in 1994.[22] Its overseas investments include both production plants and after-sales and support centres in the United States, Europe and South and South-East Asia.[23] Overall, however, the index of transnationality of the top 50 TNCs from developing countries is low (21 per cent, compared with 42 per cent for the world's top 100 TNCs).

Much developing country FDI is directed to other developing countries, usually within the same region. Intraregional investment now accounts for around 40 per cent of total FDI in East and South-East Asia. This pattern is reflected in the investments of the top 50 TNCs based in developing countries. Daewoo is the largest foreign investor in Viet Nam and Acer (Taiwan Province of China) is the largest investor in the Subic Bay, the Philippine's largest industrial zone.[24] In 1994, about 18 per cent of the Keppel Group's (Singapore) earnings came from projects in the Philippines and Viet Nam.[25] Ten of the top 50 TNCs are investing in infrastructure projects in developing countries, often in joint ventures with local partners, particularly in telecommunications. Transnational corporations based in Latin America have also begun to invest heavily abroad, mostly through privatizations in the same region. For example, USIMINAS (Brazil) has acquired, together with firms from Chile and Argentina, SOMISA (Argentina), a State-owned metal firm (CEPAL, 1995). Bimbo (Mexico) has invested in a new production plant in Chile and has concluded a joint venture agreement with a local company in Argentina.

Recent years have witnessed a strong expansion by TNCs based in the Republic of Korea, signalling a shift from an export to an outward investment-driven phase of the internationalization of its economy. The increased competitiveness of its firms reflects state-of-the-art production processes and products and specific advantages based almost completely on created assets (Dunning and Narula, 1996). What has motivated these TNCs to invest abroad is not only lower costs in the case of investment in other developing countries, but also the desire to access markets and technology. Large investments in developed countries to strengthen existing or acquire new competitive advantages have been undertaken by Samsung, Daewoo and LG, all ranked high in the list of the top 50. In some cases, these firms have invested through acquisitions. Samsung, for example, has recently acquired AST (United States) and Integrated Telecom Technology (United States), an ATM provider. LG Electronics has acquired a majority stake in Zenith (United States) and Hyundai has bought NCR Microelectronics, an affiliate of ATT (United States). Europe is the main target of investments by TNCs based in the Republic of Korea. Samsung has 11 production plants in Europe (United Kingdom, Germany, Spain and Hungary), employing 6,000 people.[26] Daewoo has consumer electronics plants in France and Austria and automobile plants in Central and Eastern Europe. LG Electronics produces refrigerators in Italy, video casette recorders in Germany and electronics home appliances in the United Kingdom, France and Spain. It also has plants in Romania, Russian Federation and Hungary and design centres in Germany, Russian Federation and Ireland.

3. Future investment plans

Based on a UNCTAD survey conducted in 1995,[27] future investment plans of the 100 largest TNCs suggest a strong upward trend in FDI (as well as domestic investment), fuelled by improved economic conditions and robust economic growth forecasts for several developing countries (figure I.14).[28] The present FDI pattern, whereby most investment originates in, and is directed to, developed countries will continue. Those TNCs based in North America view Europe as the most important investment location in the future, especially in high-technology and consumer-goods industries (figure I.15). Likewise, European TNCs view the United States as an important investment location and plan to improve their presence there. Japanese TNCs have a different orientation: for these firms, South, East and South-East Asia feature as the most promising investment locations in the future. This is not to say that TNCs from the other Triad members do not view positively developing countries, especially those in Asia. Indeed, many firms plan to invest heavily in that region, and in developing countries overall, over the next five years (figure I.15).

Planned capital investments by the world's largest TNCs in Asia are expected to experience the fastest growth in the second half of the 1990s, reflecting the region's large and rapidly growing markets for consumer products and services (Services of the European Commission and UNCTAD-DTCI, 1996). Oil-producing TNCs are also attracted by Asia's large oil and gas reserves. Chemical firms forecast a strong demand in that region. Akzo, BASF and Bayer (Germany) plan large production projects in China. Other corporations, such as Du Pont (United States) and Ciba-Geigy (Switzerland), that already have production facilities in China, are planning new plants.[29] Various infrastructure projects are in the pipeline in several countries in Asia, with telecommunications expected to attract the largest amount of FDI (Hatem, 1996).

Developing-country TNCs also plan to invest or expand existing capacity abroad. For example, in 1994, the overseas production of LG and Daewoo was only 3 per cent and 8 per cent, respectively, of their total production. Both firms plan to increase the ratio of foreign to total production to 45 and 60 per cent, respectively, by the year 2000 (Kim, 1996, p. 846). In 1996, LG Group announced and started the establishment of a large-scale electronics and semiconductor complex in Newport, SouthWales, United Kingdom, that will produce semiconductors, monitors and other TV and monitor components; the total investment of $2.6 billion will be fully completed in 2002 and the affiliate will employ 6,100 people.[30] The investment is the largest single investment in Europe of any non-European firm and is the largest overseas investment by a TNC from the Republic of Korea. The operations at the new LG plants in the United Kingdom will include research and development, product development, parts procurement, production, sales and services. Likewise, Taiwan Semiconductors (Taiwan Province of China) has entered into a joint venture with Altera (a United States microchip designer) and plans to expand production capacity by 30 per cent.[31] Although the expansion of Latin American TNCs is more limited than that of Asian TNCs, MERCOSUR is expected to boost the growth of intra regional FDI by TNCs based in that region (table I.14).

All of this points to increasing international activities by both developed and developing country TNCs and towards more complex forms of international production. They may well be accompanied by a further rapid expansion of FDI.

Figure I.14. Will FDI increase over the next five years?

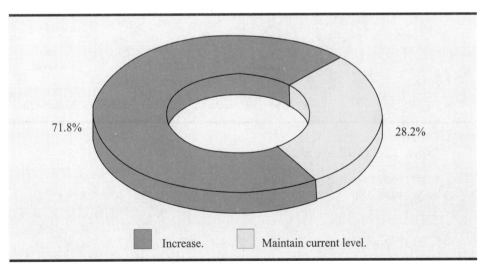

71.8% 28.2%

Increase. Maintain current level.

Source: UNCTAD, based on a 1995 survey of the top 100.

Figure I.15. Past [a] and future [b] patterns of TNC investments

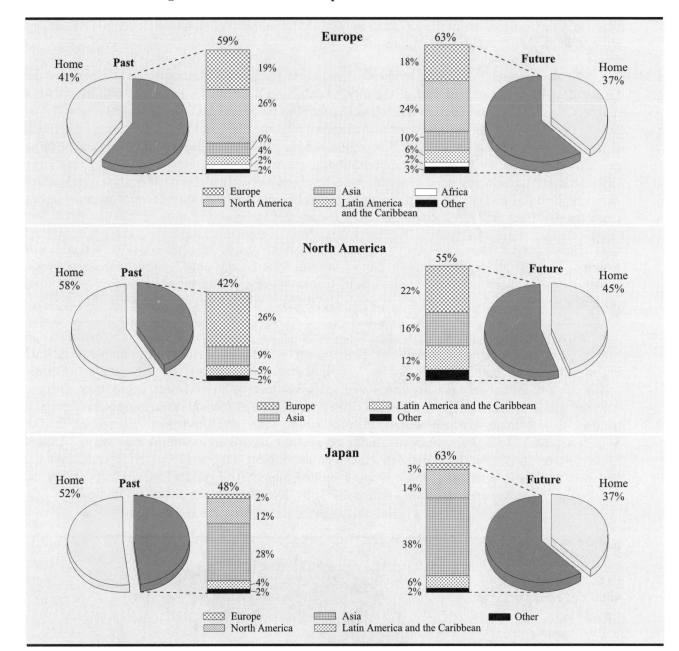

Source: UNCTAD, based on a 1995 survey of the top 100.

[a]   1990-1995
[b]   1996-2000

Table I.14. Future investment plans of selected TNCs based in developing economies

Corporation (home economy)	Host country	Investment projects
Acer (Taiwan Province of China)	Philippines	New production plants in electronics at Subic Bay to strengthen export capacity and take advantage of Subic Bay's transportation network.
Daewoo (Republic of Korea)	China, India and Viet Nam	Car factories to tap emerging local markets and reduce production costs.
	Mexico	Video plant worth $240 million in Baja, California, to gain market access to NAFTA.
	Poland, Romania and the Czech Republic	$3 billion investment in car plants to supply domestic and regional markets.
Hyundai (Republic of Korea)	India	Wholly owned car factory output for domestic and regional markets.
	United States	$1.3 billion investment in a semiconductor plant in Oregon to supply the local market and access technology.
	Brazil	Manufacturing car plant to increase production capacity in the host country.
	United Kingdom and Europe (specific location undecided)	$240 million investment in auto-dealerships in the United Kingdom and $1.5 billion investment in a consumer electronics plant in Europe to improve sales, avoid potential trade barriers and tap local engineering skills.
LG Electronics LG Semicon Co., Ltd. (Republic of Korea)	Newport, South Wales United Kingdom	$2.6 billion investment in a large-scale electronics and semiconductors complex.
Samsung (Republic of Korea)	United States	$1.5 billion investment in a semiconductor plant in Oregon to supply the local market and upgrade technology.
	Mexico	$581 million investment in the next four years in an industrial complex to gain market access to NAFTA and establish local supplier networks to reduce imports.
Singapore Telecom (Singapore)	China and Indonesia	Establish telephone networks; aims at becoming an important service provider in these countries.
YPF (Argentina) and Petrobas (Brasil)	Mexico and Argentina	50:50 joint company to exploit regional opportunities in upstream and downstream activities.
Vitro (Mexico)	United States	$126 million investment in expanding production capacity of its affiliate to serve the local market.

Source: UNCTAD, based on company reports.

Notes

[1] Global FDI inflows and outflows do not match because of differences in methodology and data collection among countries (see the section on "Definitions and sources" in the annex).

[2] The 1995 growth rates of FDI inflows and outflows expressed in SDRs were 32 per cent and 30 per cent, respectively.

[3] The 1995 data for exports of goods and non-factor services are World Trade Organization estimates; those for world output are United Nations estimates (United Nations, 1996). The 1995 data for gross domestic capital formation are estimates for the OECD member States only (OECD, 1995e).

[4] All data, discussion and figures in this section consider only cross-border M&As that result in the foreign investor holding more than 50 per cent of the acquired firm's voting shares, unless otherwise indicated. Data on minority investments (including portfolio investments and investments with equity of less than 50 per cent made with the intention of providing the investor with significant management influence) are not included on the assumption that portfolio investments account for the bulk of such investments.

[5] "When merger is the best way forward", *Corporate Finance*, January 1994, pp. 32-35.

[6] Gene G. Marcial, "The whisper stocks of 1996", *Business Week*, 25 December 1995, p. 89.

[7] Cross-border M&A sales and purchases describe the direction of these transactions; i.e., when a cross-border M&A takes place, it registers as both a sale in the country of the target firm, and as a purchase in the home country of the acquiring firm. Data addressing cross-border M&A activities on an industrial basis refer to sales figures.

[8] *Corporate Finance,* op. cit..

[9] "Hoechst toasts marriage to Marion, then announces plant closings, job cuts", *Medical Marketing and Media*, 31, 1, January 1996, p. 8.

[10] Data in this paragraph are from World Bank, 1996, table 1.1. Net private capital flows accounted for 72 per cent of aggregate net long-term resource flows to developing countries in 1995.

[11] The developing-country classification of the World Bank (and hence the FDI inflow figures in its publications) differs from the classification used by UNCTAD. Data for 1995 are World Bank estimates.

[12] The modest growth in FDI inflows to Latin America and the Caribbean did not offset the sizeable decline in portfolio equity flows to that region, where the bulk of the overall decline in portfolio flows took place (World Bank, 1996).

[13] Commonly defined, infrastructure, or social overhead capital, includes public utilities (e.g., power, telecommunications, sewage and sanitation), public works (e.g., roads, dams) and transportation (e.g., railroads, ports and airports) (World Bank, 1994, p. 2). By and large, these industries share a number of characteristics: their output is a public good (with a "free rider" problem arising frequently), and there are usually substantial fixed or sunk costs involved in their development, as well as significant economies of scale to be reaped. Other social services, such as education (schools), health (hospitals) and corrective facilities (prisons) share the same features and are therefore included in the definition of infrastructure.

[14] Information provided by the Ministry of Plan and Investment of Viet Nam.

[15] Richard Lapper, "Big increase in project finance", *Financial Times*, 1 March 1996.

[16] Traditionally, companies in the oil industry are prominent in the ranking of the top 100 TNCs because they hold most of their assets abroad in response to the geographical location of oil deposits and because the value of these assets is high reflecting the capital intensity of that industry.

[17] Since assets are expressed in nominal dollars, the growth of their value is affected by currency movements.

[18] A similar trend is also observed in the world's largest firms identified by *Fortune*. The number of Japanese firms included in the world's largest 500 firms increased from 111 to 149 between 1990 and 1994. In 1994, for the first time ever, a Japanese firm -- Mitsubishi -- led *Fortune*'s ranking of firms in terms of sales. Eight Japanese firms were included in the top 10 firms ranked in terms of sales, compared with only 1 in 1990. See, "The largest 500", *Fortune*, 7 August 1995.

[19] The composite index of transnationality is calculated as the average share of foreign assets in total assets, foreign sales in total sales and foreign employment in total employment.

[20] The inclusion of new information on TNCs based in China (Zhan, 1995) has added 8 Chinese TNCs to the list, changing significantly the ranking of the top 50 developing-country TNCs.

[21] Daniel Dombey, "Devaluation takes toll on Mexican industrial groups", *Financial Times*, 4 May 1995.

[22] Emily Thornton, "Sound off", *Far Eastern Economic Review*, 24 November 1994, p. 82.

[23] "200 Asia's leading companies", *Far Eastern Economic Review*, 28 December 1996, pp. 40-93.

[24] "Daewoo: Mr. Kim's one man empire", *The Economist*, 27 January 1996, pp. 60-61; "The Philippines", *Business Week*, 1 April 1996, pp. 37-41.

[25] Murray Hiebert, "It's a jungle out there", *Far Eastern Economic Review*, 25 April 1996, pp. 58-60.

[26] Marc Nexon, "Samsung: l'entreprise qui va nous dévorer", *L'Expansion*, 12 June 1996, pp. 42-49.

[27] UNCTAD undertook a survey of the top 100 TNCs based in developed countries to understand better their strategies and to analyze expected changes in their investment patterns over the next five years. In that survey, information on TNCs, such as total assets, sales, number of employees, number of affiliates, the geographical and industrial distribution of their activities abroad, and planned investments abroad, was collected. The rate of response of the survey was about 80 per cent. Developing country TNCs were not included in this survey.

[28] It is interesting to note that a survey of 260 TNC managers (not necessarily the largest TNCs) and opinion leaders of research institutions and investment promotion agencies showed a stronger interest in investing at home than abroad (Hatem, 1996, p.17). That survey was conducted in collaboration with Arthur Andersen and the Ministry of Economy of France, using the UNCTAD questionnaire. See Hatem, 1996, p. 8.

[29] Andrew Wood and Ian Young, "Foreign companies rush to invest", *Chemical Week,* August-September 1994, pp. 4-22.

[30] LG Group news release, 10 July 1996.

[31] "200 Asia's leading companies", *Far Eastern Economic Review*, 28 December 1996, pp. 40-93.

Chapter II

Regional Trends

A. Developed countries

Since the end of the foreign-direct-investment (FDI) recession in 1993, developed country inward and outward FDI flows have risen vigorously. Indeed, about two-thirds and 85 per cent of the 1995 increases in FDI inflows and outflows, respectively, have occurred in developed countries. The 1995 FDI stock in developed countries was about $1.9 trillion, and their outward stock was about $2.5 trillion, accounting for about 73 per cent and 92 per cent of the world's inward and outward stocks, respectively (annex tables 3 and 4).

The growth of developed country FDI was led by a few countries -- the United States, United Kingdom, France and Australia on the inflow side, and the United States, United Kingdom and Germany on the outflow side. This is mainly due to differences in economic growth or differences in the timing of the end of the recession as well as the size of mergers-and-acquisitions (M&As) for some developed countries (see chapter I).

1. United States and Western Europe

(a) Trends in foreign direct investment

United States FDI inflows increased by more than 21 per cent over the 1994 level, reaching $60 billion in 1995, more than the level of total inflows to all developing countries in 1992 and twice the size of inflows to the United Kingdom, the next most important recipient among developed countries (annex table 1). Increases in inflows in 1995 were recorded in equity capital flows and reinvested earnings. Reflecting a strong recovery of M&A activity by Western European TNCs, equity capital flows into the United States grew by 15 per cent, to $39.5 billion, or two-thirds of United States FDI inflows. In particular, large M&As were undertaken in pharmaceuticals and biotechnology. Reinvested earnings almost tripled from $4.5 billion in 1994 to $13.3 billion in 1995, reflecting good growth performance and prospects of the United States economy.

Germany was the largest investor in the United States in 1995 with $11 billion, followed by the United Kingdom with $10 billion. Japanese TNCs ranked fourth with almost $4 billion. After extensive restructuring by Japanese affiliates in the United States drew to an end in 1993 (reflected in negligible inflows of only $65 million in 1993), Japanese FDI picked up once again. The re-emergence of large Japanese FDI in the United States is expected to continue: for example, there was a large-scale acquisition of Ziff-Davis Publishing by Softbank Corporation for $1.8 billion in 1995; and Toyota and Nissan announced plans in 1994 to expand the size of plants in North America by 50 per cent and 18 per cent, respectively, by 1996-1997.

The United States invested heavily abroad in 1995, confirming its position as the largest source country in the world. United States outflows were almost $100 billion in 1995, $58 billion higher than those of the next biggest investor, the United Kingdom. The share of the United States in world outflows was about 30 per cent in 1995, twice as large as that in the latter half of the 1980s. While there was an overall decline in FDI outflows from other major home countries in the first half of the 1990s, United States outflows increased steadily (except in 1994 when they declined by 34 per cent) -- by 17 per cent in 1992, 77 per cent in 1993 and 109 per cent in 1995.[1] The outward stock of FDI in 1995 was about $710 billion, accounting for 26 per cent of world outward FDI stock.[2]

Record FDI outflows in 1995 reflected record equity capital outflows ($36 billion) and record reinvested earnings ($54 billion). Most United States FDI abroad -- about 60 per cent of FDI outflows in 1994-1995 -- is financed from reinvested earnings. Intra-company loans declined by 42 per cent ($4.7 billion) in 1995. The 1994 and 1995 levels of United States intra-company loans are low. In particular, United States finance affiliates in the United Kingdom have registered declining flows of intra-company loans in recent years. This can be explained by the desire of parent firms to retain funds to finance domestic investments given high growth rates and lucrative investment opportunities at home. Another explanation lies in the gap between United States interest rates and those found in other countries.[3] Higher interest rates in the United States mean that the cost of raising funds in domestic markets is greater, so parent firms raise funds abroad through finance affiliates and channel them back home as intra-company loans. As parent firms begin to pay back these loans, intra-company loans as a component of outflows can be expected to increase.

The United Kingdom is not only the most favoured location for United States FDI, but it is also attractive to firms from Western Europe and Japan,[4] especially through M&As. Examples of large scale investments in 1995 by Western European TNCs include acquisitions of Fisons by Rhône-Poulenc Rorer, a Swiss pharmaceutical company (£1.8 billion), Kleinwort Benson by Dresdner Bank (£1 billion), S.G. Warburg by the Swiss Bank Corporation (£860 million) and Barings by ING, a Dutch bank (£860 million). In fact, almost half of M&As in Western Europe in 1995 took place in the United Kingdom. Relatively low costs and corporate taxes in comparison with other European Union members have played a role in attracting FDI into the United Kingdom. Outflows from the United Kingdom in 1995 also reached a new record of $38 billion, going mostly into large-scale investments in the markets of its main export destinations. The European Union and the United States were the principal recipients.

Net disinvestments in manufacturing led to negative inflows (of $3 billion) to Germany in 1994. The high value of the mark, and relatively high corporate taxes and labour costs, all acted as disincentives to foreign investors. Although inflows to Germany rose sharply in 1995 (to $9 billion), they were mostly in real estate and holding companies and were made in anticipation of further appreciation of the mark. In contrast to inflows, outflows from Germany were a record $35 billion, almost equal to the second largest outward investor, the United Kingdom. With the privatization programme in the eastern part of the country largely completed by 1994, German firms are again directing their attention to opportunities abroad to escape cost increases and currency appreciations at home and improve their competitiveness. Germany's imbalance between outflows and inflows reached $26 billion in 1995, exceeding the Japanese imbalance in FDI by $5 billion and rekindling in some quarters a fear of job exports and "hollowing out".[5]

(b)   Has the Asian century arrived for the United States?

Since the late 1970s, United States trade with Asia and the Pacific (including Japan) has been higher than trade with Europe. In 1994, United States trade with developing Asia alone overtook trade with Europe (figure II.1).[6] Does this suggest that the gravity of international economic relations of the United States has shifted from the country's links across the North Atlantic towards its links across the Pacific? Has the Asian century arrived for the United States?

On the basis of trade data alone, this may appear so. But in today's world, trade is only one measure of economic integration, and no longer the most important one. Other modalities of delivering goods and services to foreign markets -- and, beyond that, organizing production -- also need to be taken into account.

Data on one of these modalities, FDI and sales associated with it, are available. If goods and services delivered to foreign markets through FDI are added to those delivered through trade, the picture looks entirely different (figure II.2): the volume of goods and services delivered in Europe by United States firms is nearly 50 per cent higher than that delivered on the other side of the Pacific, and it is five times that if developing Asia alone is considered.

The inclusion of FDI provides not only a more comprehensive and accurate picture of the integration of the various regions in exchanges of goods and services, it also draws attention to integration of production -- that is, the increased meshing of the production apparatus of different countries and regions through ownership linkages and division of labour. One measure of this is intra-firm trade, as such trade reflects precisely the international intra-firm division of labour.

Figure II.1. United States trade, by region, 1985-1994

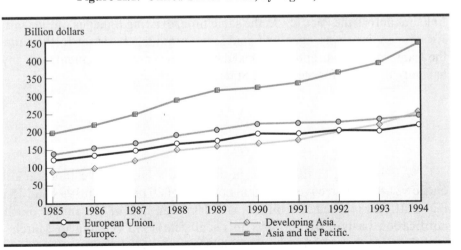

Source: IMF, 1995.

Indeed, the share of trade across the North Atlantic that is intra-firm (24 per cent) is substantially higher than the share of the United States intra-firm trade across the Pacific (15 per cent; 16 per cent for developing Asia alone) (United States, Department of Commerce, 1995).

The difference in the extent of production integration between the

Figure II.2. United States trade plus TNC affiliate sales abroad and foreign affiliate sales in the United Sates, by region, 1985-1993

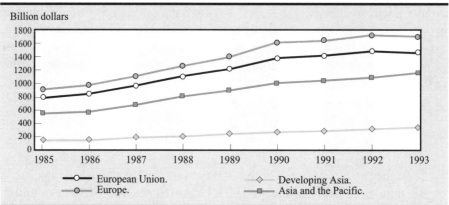

Source: IMF, 1995; and United States, Department of Commerce, various issues.

United States and Western Europe on the one hand and the United States and Asia and the Pacific on the other has three principle reasons: (1) the longer history of United States FDI in Western Europe and the response of United States TNCs to the efforts towards greater European integration (UNCTC, 1993); (2) the low United States inward foreign direct investment in Japan; and (3) the still relatively low FDI interpenetration between the United States and developing Asia.

Of course, this difference may slowly disappear. Trade data alone suggest this (figure II.1). Moreover, the rate of return on investments in Asia and the Pacific is higher than in Western Europe, 12.1 per cent compared to 9.4 per cent in 1994 (United States, Department of Commerce, 1995a). Partly as a result, the growth rate of United States FDI stock in Asia and the Pacific has been significantly higher than that in Europe during 1990-1994 (an annual average of 6.6 per cent compared to 4.3 per cent), a trend that is expected to continue in the second half of the 1990s.[7] Also, for developing Asia, the ratio of United States exports plus sales by foreign affiliates to that region's GDP has been increasing steadily, from 7.5 per cent in 1986 to 10.2 per cent in 1993, while for Western Europe that ratio has remained unchanged at about 12 per cent.

The regional integration efforts pursued in the framework of APEC are likely to strengthen linkages across the Pacific. At the same time, existing linkages of the United States across the North Atlantic are much stronger, and could well provide a basis for further integration -- for example, in the framework of a proposed Transatlantic Free Trade Agreement.[8] In any event, the Asian century has not yet begun for the United States.

2. Japan

(a)   Trends in foreign direct investment

After falling to fifth place in the world's largest investors' ranking in 1993, Japan's FDI outflows are again recovering, with increases of 20 per cent in 1994 and 15 per cent in 1995. In 1995, FDI outflows reached $21 billion, still less than half of the annual outflows of 1989-1991. On a notification basis, FDI outflows in fiscal year 1995 (ending in March 1996)[9] were higher than (notification) flows in fiscal year 1988, the start of the dramatic increase of Japanese FDI.[10]

What drives Japanese TNCs to invest abroad in the mid-1990s is a desire to recover or increase their international competitiveness, rather than to avoid trade frictions, a reason that was important during the investment boom in the latter half of the 1980s. Many Japanese firms consider overseas production as a necessity in the face of a more than 25 per cent increase in the exchange-rate value of the yen between 1993 and 1995. At the same time, economic recovery in the United States and dynamic growth in East and South-East Asia beckon.

Moreover, the transnationalization strategies of Japanese TNCs are becoming more multi-layered: increasingly, Japanese affiliates, particularly in Asia, are establishing affiliates abroad (JETRO, 1996). For example, 47 per cent of Japanese affiliates in Hong Kong, and 43 per cent in Singapore, had already established foreign affiliate networks in the region by 1993. Although not many Japanese affiliates in Thailand and Malaysia have invested in other Asian countries to date (only 4 per cent of the affiliates in both countries), 35 per cent of the affiliates in Thailand and 28 per cent in Malaysia are planning to do so within the next five years (JETRO, 1996, pp. 25-36).[11] By comparison, about one quarter of Japanese affiliates in the United States have established their own affiliates, and one third of these are located outside the United States (MITI, 1994, tables 2-1 and 2-43). By size of the capital base in fiscal 1992, 13 per cent of the capital of all Japanese foreign affiliates was owned indirectly by their ultimate parent firms. Such indirect FDI is not reflected in Japan's outward FDI statistics.

The recent increases in Japanese FDI have taken place in manufacturing and some services industries, unlike the late 1980s when most FDI went into financial services and real estate. Japanese FDI in such traditional industries as food, textiles and iron and non-ferrous metals, re-surfaced again in South, East and South-East Asia, this time by many small and medium-enterprises. Manufacturing FDI in that region exceeded that in North America in fiscal year 1994 for the first time, and continued to do so in fiscal 1995 ($5.1 billion in the former region and $4.8 billion in the latter on a notification basis).[12] By fiscal year 1994, chemicals became the second largest destination of FDI after electrical machinery, reflecting the global reorganization of that industry. Investment in transport equipment in developing countries (mainly in Latin America and South, East and South-East Asia) increased fourfold in 1994, reflecting a rising demand for automobiles.

Manufacturing TNCs, especially in electronic machinery and transport equipment, have been establishing global integrated production systems since the late 1980s to maximize efficiency. Indicative of this trend are that (MITI, 1995):

- One out of 20 Japanese affiliates in the world was a regional headquarters by 1993, signalling the emergence of multilayered networks.

- One fifth of foreign affiliates specializing in research and development were conducting research and development for their entire TNC systems by 1993, and that share is expected to increase to more than 40 per cent in the next five years.

- Intra-firm transactions among Japanese affiliates within the same TNC systems accounted for 48 per cent of the exports of these affiliates in Asia, 23 per cent in the European Union and 28 per cent in the United States in 1992.

Figures like these suggest that Japanese TNCs are leading in the establishment of regional or global networks. Efficiency-seeking FDI has become an increasingly important type of investment for Japanese TNCs. Foreign production is increasing, though its relative importance in total production in the manufacturing sector is still considerably lower than that of firms from Germany and the United States (figure II.3). Japanese FDI is expected to grow faster than domestic investment in the immediate future (Export-Import Bank of Japan, 1996), with most continuing to go to East and South-East Asia and the United States. Africa and Central and Eastern Europe have not attracted much Japanese investment so far, and only 3 per cent of Japanese TNCs plan to increase their investments in these regions in the near future.

Figure II.3.   Share of foreign production in total production of all manufacturing firms in Japan, Germany and United States, 1986-1994

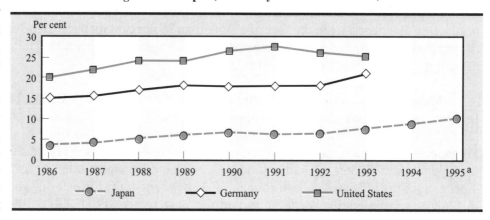

Source: MITI, 1996, figure I.4.
a   Estimates.

(b)   Why is Japanese foreign direct investment in Africa and Central and Eastern Europe so small?

Africa and Central and Eastern Europe (CEE) each accounted for only 0.2 per cent of Japan's FDI stock worldwide as of March 1996, and for 0.1 per cent and 0.3 per cent, respectively, of Japan's total FDI outflows during 1990-1994 (table II.1).[13] This share is well below that of other major home countries, such as France, the United Kingdom and the United States in the case of Africa, and Germany, the United States and France, in the case of CEE. Austria and Italy are also major home countries in the latter region. The pattern of Japanese exports to Africa and CEE parallels the outward FDI pattern.

Regardless of the nationality of TNCs, market-seeking FDI in Africa and CEE is low, either because of small populations or low purchasing power, or both. Furthermore, cost-productivity configurations, another "pull" factor for FDI, are more attractive in other regions, as is the general economic performance. Finally, Africa and CEE compete, of course, with other host regions for FDI, especially Latin America and Asia; in particular, Asia is the most prefered location for Japanese investors in developing countries.[14] Still, a number of specific factors explain the exceptionally small FDI from Japan in Africa and CEE:

- *A small Japanese support-services network.* Japanese trading companies (*sogo shosha*), which have played a vital role in initiating and organizing Japanese FDI abroad (Kojima and Ozawa, 1984), are far less represented in Africa and CEE than in the rest of the world. Japanese trading companies (including non-*sogo shoshas*) have approximately 5,500 foreign affiliates worldwide; only 85 of them are located in Africa and about 60 in CEE (Toyo Keizai, 1996). Although *sogo shoshas* have been operating in Africa since the 1960s, they have not yet established strong networks and the knowledge and experience needed to support FDI in Africa (UNCTAD/ECA, 1995). The small presence of Japanese banking affiliates is also a limiting factor. Of 1,150 Japanese foreign banking (including insurance) affiliates, only 12 are located in Africa and only 2 (both in Hungary) in CEE. In countries where the domestic financial sector is underdeveloped, the provision of banking services by Japanese affiliates is particularly important, especially since Japanese TNCs tend to use their own banking affiliates.[15] The assistance for undertaking FDI abroad provided by the Government of Japan is also skewed in favour of other developing regions. The Japan External Trade Organization (JETRO) has a world-wide network of 79 offices to assist Japanese firms, but only eight of these offices are in Africa and five in CEE, compared with 16 in South, East and South-East Asia.[16]

- *Weak linkage between official development assistance and FDI.* Japanese official development assistance and FDI are closely linked in some developing countries because a part of Japan's aid is tied to the purchase of Japanese products, or is associated with investment-facilitating activities, such as infrastructure development. Renewed commitments by the Government of Japan to support Africa's development have translated into increased aid recently, but this has not yet begun to stimulate Japanese FDI in Africa. In 1993, Africa received more than 10 per cent of Japan's bilateral official development assistance, making it the largest recipient region after Asia; however, about four fifths of this assistance is spent on humanitarian purposes or basic human needs, while in Asia a substantial part of bilateral official development assistance (58 per cent of the total in 1993) is in loan aid for the purpose of improving the region's economic and social infrastructure (Japan, Ministry of Foreign Affairs, 1995). Japan's assistance to CEE countries is channelled through multilateral organizations, such as the EBRD, and has not led to higher Japanese FDI.

- *Moderate trade relations.* Weak trade relations between Japan and Africa and CEE have certainly not facilitated FDI, neither as a sequential nor as a complementary activity. In 1990-1994, Africa accounted for only 1.2 per cent of Japanese exports, CEE for 0.7 per cent (table II.1).

Table II.1. The relative importance of Japanese FDI outflows and exports to Africa[a] and CEE, 1990-1994

(Percentage)

Home country	The region's share in total FDI outflows (1990-1994 annual average)		The region's share in total exports (1990-1994 annual average)	
	Africa	CEE	Africa	CEE
Japan	0.1[b]	0.3	1.2[b]	1.1
Memorandum:				
European Union	0.3[c]	2.1[c]	2.7	5.2
Austria	0.2[c]	29.2[c]	1.1	12.3
France	0.5[c]	0.9[c]	5.9	3.2
Germany	2.2[c]	4.4[c]	1.9	8.2
Italy	0.3[c]	2.5[c]	2.8	6.8
Sweden	-	0.5	1.0	3.4
United Kingdom	2.9[c]	0.5[c]	2.8	2.8
United States	0.3	1.0	1.4	1.9

Source: UNCTAD, based on data provided by Fuji Research Institute Corporation; OECD, 1995d and IMF, 1995.

a   Excluding Liberia for all countries in this table.
b   If Liberia were included, the respective figures for Japan are 1.2 and 1.6 per cent.
c   1990-1993.

- *Availability of similar resources in other regions.* Japanese labour-intensive investments typically take place in neighbouring Asian countries, not only because of low labour costs and relatively skilled labour, but also because of a familiarity with Asia's business culture. For natural resource-seeking FDI, Asia, Canada and Oceania have been the main host regions. Although both CEE or Africa have abundant cheap labour, Asia's geographical proximity to Japan means lower transportation costs for goods exported back to Japan. This is an important consideration, given that 15 per cent of sales of all Japanese affiliates abroad were made to Japan in fiscal 1993 (MITI, 1995, table 2-13-13).

- *Psychological distance.* Although geographical distances have been significantly reduced due to technological developments in communications and transportation, Japan's psychological distance to Africa and CEE, especially when compared with Asia, is greater. In some geographically distant countries in Latin America, a large influx of Japanese immigrants has made psychological distances smaller.

Despite these factors, there are ways of changing Japanese investors' negative impressions of these two regions as FDI locations. Unfamiliarity with these markets is an important drawback for Japanese investors. Japanese affiliates in Western Europe may play a role as catalyst by educating parent firms or even by investing directly in these regions. This is already happening: examples are Fujitsu's investment in Poland via ICL, a Japanese affiliate in the United Kingdom; Kyocera's investment in the Czech Republic through its affiliate, AVX in the United Kingdom; and Alps Electric's in the Czech Republic through its affiliate in Ireland.[17] The possible enlargement of the European Union to include some countries in CEE may strengthen this trend. Meanwhile, the creation of a free trade area between North African countries and the European Union may increase the attractiveness of the former countries as an export platform to Europe. Japanese electronic manufacturers that use the United Kingdom as a production base for serving the European market may find it advantageous to move at least part of their value-added activities to North Africa. In other words, Japanese TNCs may establish Europe-wide regional core networks, with some operations being transferred to CEE or North Africa, or both.

A possible source of future FDI are Japanese small and medium-sized enterprises (which account for some 15 per cent of Japan's outward FDI stock and for about half of Japan's equity investment cases (UNCTAD-DTCI, 1993b). Traditionally, these firms have preferred to locate in Asia; but rising costs there are making that less attractive. In fact, the number of affiliates of Japanese small and medium-sized enterprises that withdrew from Asia exceeded that of newly established affiliates in 1994.[18] In this respect, CEE may become more attractive to them, a possibility further encouraged by the governments of this region which try to attract FDI from small and medium-sized enterprises by giving them special preferences.

B. Developing countries

The current boom in investment flows to developing countries, $100 billion in 1995, is a reflection of sustained economic growth and continuing liberalization and privatization in these countries, as well as the increasing integration of the developing countries into the investment plans of TNCs. With some 40 per cent of the total, China was the single largest recipient of FDI flows among developing countries in 1995. Even so, inflows into developing countries other than China rose by some 16 per cent between 1993 and 1994, and by another 10 per cent between 1994 and 1995.

Record FDI flows into developing countries in the 1990s have taken place during a time of almost stagnant outflows (1992-1993) as well as during periods of rapidly growing outflows (1994-1995) from the developed world. Two developments underlie this trend: the growing importance of developing countries as sources of FDI (especially for other developing countries) and the increase in the value and share of total outflows from the developed countries going to developing economies:

- Outflows from the developing countries rose from $39 billion in 1994 to $47 billion in 1995, with an increasing share going to other developing countries. Intraregional FDI accounted for 37 per cent of inward FDI stock of nine Asian economies[19] in 1993, compared to one quarter in 1980 (UNCTAD-DTCI, 1995a, table II.3). For the ASEAN countries, one quarter of FDI flows came from newly industrializing economies in 1990-1992, a share that rose to nearly 40 per cent in 1993-1994 (JETRO, 1995 and 1996). More generally, more than half of the FDI flows from developing countries (57 per cent) were invested within the same region in 1994 (JETRO, 1996, table I-15).

- The share of developing countries in the combined outflows of the world's five largest outward investors rose from 18 per cent in 1990-1992 to 28 per cent in 1993-1994. In other words, developed-country TNCs are investing more than they used to in developing countries, both in absolute terms and as a share of their total outward investments.

The concentration of FDI in the largest 10 developing-country recipients has increased, from 69 per cent of annual average FDI flows into developing countries in 1990-1992 to 76 per cent in 1993-1995 (figure II.4). However, that increase was on account of China alone: the largest 10 recipients other than China accounted for 58 per cent of the annual average FDI inflows to developing countries (other than China) in 1990-1992, compared with 41 per cent in 1993-1995 (figure II.4).

Figure II.4. The concentration of FDI inflows in the developing world, 1985-1995

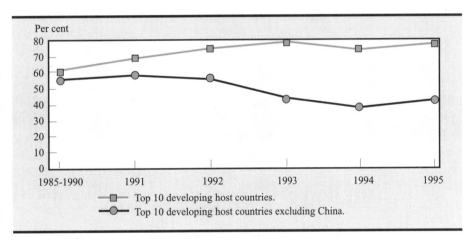

Source: UNCTAD estimates, based on annex table 1.

1. Asia

(a) Trends

South, East and South-East Asia and the Pacific have strengthened their role as the largest developing-country FDI recipient region, with an estimated $65 billion of inflows in 1995 (an increase of 21 per cent over 1994), accounting for 65 per cent of total developing-country FDI inflows. East and South-East Asia alone received an estimated $62 billion in 1995, while South Asia saw a doubling of inflows, to an estimated $2.7 billion in that year, mainly as a result of a tripling of inflows into India.   Inflows of FDI to four ASEAN member States (Indonesia, Malaysia, Philippines and Thailand) increased from $8.6 billion in 1994 to $14 billion in 1995.   West Asia's FDI inflows were about $2.5 billion in both 1994 and 1995, having declined from their 1993 peak of $3 billion.

With 58 per cent of the region's inflows, China has been the principal driver behind the current investment boom in that region and to the developing world as a whole.   However, although the absolute size of FDI inflows has been considerably smaller in other countries in the region, investment flows in these countries have also soared, especially when compared with the size of their economies.

The size and dynamism of developing Asia have made it increasingly important for TNCs to be established there, to service rapidly expanding markets or to tap the tangible and intangible resources of that region for their global production networks.   European Union TNCs, in particular, after having neglected Asia in the past decade or so, seem to be changing course and investing more, often in large scale projects (table II.2).   In that, they are supported by a range of programmes of the European Commission (box II.1), and may be further encouraged to do so in the future by the Asia-Europe Investment Promotion Action Plan to be launched as a result of the Asia-Europe summit in March 1996 (box II.2).   Thus, given appropriate policies, FDI flows to Asia should continue to grow. This will be even more so when India begins to realize its FDI potential and the Central Asian countries recover.

In addition, the region's infrastructure-financing requirements for the next decade will play a role in sustaining FDI flows to Asia.   Countries are dismantling barriers to FDI in this sector, giving rise to new and large investment opportunities for TNCs.   And privatization, still lagging well behind other regions, is showing signs of taking off, particularly in telecommunications.

Finally, Asian developing economies themselves are increasingly becoming outward investors, reflected in the liberalization of their outward FDI regimes and, in some cases, the provision of incentives for such investments (UNCTAD-DTCI, 1995a).   In 1995, the region accounted, with $43 billion, for 90 per cent of all developing-country outflows; Hong Kong is the single largest outward investor among the developing countries. Asian economies played an important role in the recovery of FDI outflows from the FDI-recession of 1991-1992, accounting for about two-thirds of increases in outflows during 1993-1994.   Most outward FDI goes to other countries of the region to take

Table II.2. Examples of large-scale European Union investments in Asia announced in 1995

Firm name	Home country	Host country	Investment amount (Million dollars)	Industry
BASF	Germany	China	4 000	Petrochemicals
Fiat	Italy	China/India	2 000	Transport equipment
GEC Alsthom	France	Republic of Korea	2 100	Transport equipment (High speed train)
Siemens	Germany	Indonesia	1 700	Utilities/power
Mercedes-Benz	Germany	China	1 000	Transport equipment
National Power	United Kingdom	Pakistan	756	Utilities/power
Siemens Power Ventures	Germany	Pakistan	507	Utilities/power

Source: UNCTAD, based on various sources.

advantage of cost differentials and liberal trade regimes that allow export-oriented FDI to flourish, facilitated by ethnic and cultural links. Malaysian and Thai TNCs, for example, directed more than 60 per cent of their FDI outflows to Asia in 1995; some four-fifths of Hong Kong's outward FDI went to China in 1995; a good part of Singapore's outward FDI is distributed to other Asian countries (especially ASEAN countries and China); and about 60 per cent of China's outward FDI has remained within the Asian region (UNCTAD-DTCI, forthcoming b).[20] But Asian TNCs are also increasingly targeting other parts of the world, including developed countries. As part of the Asia-Europe dialogue, in fact, special efforts are being made to increase Asian FDI in the European Union (UNCTAD-DTCI, forthcoming b).

(b) China: is the heat beginning to cool down?

China's FDI inflows rose by 147 per cent between 1992 and 1993, but only by 23 per cent in 1994 and 11 per cent in 1995. Inflows increased from $28 billion in 1993 to $38 billion in 1995, almost equivalent to the average annual inflows of all developed countries in the first half of the 1980s. This raises the question of whether China's FDI growth is sustainable. This has implications for the level

---

Box II.1. Promoting European FDI in Asia

As part of an overall approach to strengthen its economic links with Asia, the European Union has designed a number of support programmes to facilitate FDI by European firms in Asia. The most important ones are:

- *The Asia-Invest Programme.* This programme comprises a wide range of instruments to promote business contacts between Asian and European companies. It includes a "Business Priming Fund", which gives assistance to European companies for market research and monitoring activities and the organization of courses for executives aimed at the improvement of language skills and cultural knowledge. The programme also features the "Asia Enterprise and Asia Partenariat", which provides part-financing for business meetings that facilitate contacts and match-making between potential European and Asian investors. The "Asia Investment Facility", the third important component of the Asia-Invest Programme, comprises activities designed to identify, evaluate and promote specific investment opportunities. These activities include, for instance, identifying investment opportunities for European companies in Asia and their subsequent dissemination through workshops and publications. This set of instruments is complemented by several additional measures to improve the access of European companies to information on Asian markets, such as the establishment of European Business Information Centres in several Asian cities.

- *The European Community Investment Partners.* This scheme comprises four different financing facilities that assist in the formation of joint ventures between European and Asian partners. Support is available at every stage, from part-financing of activities to identify possible partners and support for feasibility studies, through equity participation in new ventures and assistance in developing human resources once a joint venture has been established. A new facility offers grants for the preparation of privatizations or build-operate-transfer and build-own-operate infrastructure schemes, as well as grants and interest-free loans to companies for certain training activities.

- *Financing facilities of the European Investment Bank.* Since 1993, the European Investment Bank has been mandated to engage in investment projects in 14 Asian economies[a] that fulfil certain criteria. So far, the Bank has approved ECU 340 million for joint ventures between Asian and European firms; for projects inducing a high technology transfer between Asia and Europe; for projects fostering closer relations between the two regions; and for projects that lead to environmental improvements or foster regional integration.

Source: Services of the European Commission and UNCTAD-DTCI, 1996.

[a]   Bangladesh, Brunei Darussalam, China, India, Indonesia, Macau, Malaysia, Mongolia, Pakistan, Philippines, Singapore, Thailand, Sri Lanka and Viet Nam.

of FDI flows to Asia and to the developing world as a whole. It is particularly relevant in light of China's recent FDI-policy changes and developments in its relations with two of the largest source economies, Hong Kong and Taiwan Province of China.

On the policy front, China is moving towards national treatment -- an effort to level the playing field for domestic and foreign firms and facilitate its entry into the World Trade Organization. Policy measures since 1994 are meant to eliminate preferences for foreign investors that have distorted markets and have led to a bias against domestic firms. Among them are the unification of the tax system and the elimination of the exemption of import duties granted to foreign affiliates:

- In the tax reform undertaken in 1994, the turn-over tax regime and the individual income- tax regime were unified. As a result, both domestic and foreign firms are now governed by a unified set of rules on value-added, consumption, business operations and individual income taxation. A notable exception, however, is the corporate income tax regime, under which foreign investors still enjoy preferential treatment.

- Since April 1996, foreign affiliates face the same duties and import-related taxes as domestic firms on all imported equipment, materials and all other items (including when these imports are made by newly approved FDI projects as part of their investments). Although overall tariff rates had already been lowered considerably at the beginning of 1996 (from 35.9 per cent to 23 per cent), the abolition of the preferential import duties awarded to foreign investors is important, given that nearly 70 per cent of China's FDI is "in kind" -- that is, imported capital equipment (Zhan, 1993 and UNCTAD-DTCI, 1995a, pp. 59-60).

Box II.2. The Bangkok summit and follow-up

At the beginning of March 1996, the first Asia-Europe summit was held in Bangkok, Thailand. Participants were the heads of State and Governments from ten Asian nations and the fifteen member countries of the European Union (with the head of the Government of Italy acting also as President of the Council of the European Union), and the President of the European Commission. During that meeting, a wide range of issues were discussed, focusing especially on establishing a political dialogue and reinforcing economic relations and cooperation between Asia and Europe.

Both sides stressed that there is large, yet unexplored, potential for economic cooperation in trade, capital flows and the exchange of expertise and technology. In particular, the need to raise European FDI in Asia was stressed, as was the wish to encourage Asian FDI in Europe. To strengthen the economic ties between Asia and Europe, it was agreed to liberalize trade and investment frameworks further. Some follow-up meetings on these issues before the next summit in the United Kingdom in 1998 have been scheduled, among them:

- A government and private-sector working group meeting in early July 1996 to deal with the objectives, scope and context of an investment promotion action plan.

- An informal senior officials' meeting in Brussels in July 1996 on measures to promote economic cooperation between Asia and Europe, especially regarding trade and investment issues.

- In 1997, the economic ministers will meet in Japan to discuss various economic issues.

- The inaugural meeting of the Asia-Europe Business Forum will be held in France in October 1996. At this meeting, business representatives and senior officials will discuss ways to foster cooperation between the private sectors of Asia and Europe. A second forum will be held in Thailand. A business conference held in 1997 will complement the activities of the business fora.

- Several studies concerning the economic synergies between Asia and Europe have been planned as a basis to develop policy measures in the future.

Source: "Chairman's statement of the Asia-Europe Meeting", Bangkok, 2 March 1996.

- Provinces and cities are now strictly forbidden to grant tax incentives to foreign investors over and above those stipulated by the central Government.

China has also become more selective in screening FDI projects to ensure compliance with economic development objectives. This is reflected in the Government's newly adopted guidelines for FDI that are in line with the national development plan and the country's industrial policies.[21] In addition, the country is targeting large TNC investments. This is reflected in the incentives aimed at attracting large TNCs in capital- or technology-intensive projects.[22]

The Government has introduced measures to prevent speculative investment, for example in real estate, and has forced some "phantom" foreign affiliates to terminate operations.[23] Also, it has strengthened monitoring by promulgating "Administrative procedures for appraising foreign invested property" in early 1994. The appraisals aim at preventing some foreign investors from seeking extra gains or incentives by over-valuing or over-quoting their investments, or using inferior capital equipment.

These policy changes could have a significant impact on FDI flows. The movement towards national treatment discourages "round-tripping" (that is, capital outflows that are repatriated back to China disguised as FDI, taking advantage of tax and regulatory incentives to foreign investors) and "phantom" foreign ventures (Zhan, 1995). Tighter screening and monitoring of FDI projects may significantly reduce the overvaluation of FDI that takes place through the mis-invoicing of imports of equipment (UNCTAD-DTCI, 1995a, pp. 59-60). Furthermore, recent policy measures will reduce short-term speculative investments. Finally, tight monetary policies -- likely to be pursued by the Government in the near future[24] to curb inflation and cool the overheated economy -- will have a bearing on FDI: since FDI projects usually have to be coupled with domestic capital (an entry requirement for FDI in some industries), more expensive domestic capital discourages domestic investments and hence diminishes the ability of foreign investors to find joint-venture partners.

Moreover, outward FDI from Hong Kong, Macau and Taiwan Province of China, the top FDI sources for China, is losing momentum as the transfer of labour-intensive production to China slows down. Partly due to the fact that most labour-intensive production has already moved out from these economies and partly due to increases in labour and land costs in the coastal regions, export-processing production has become less attractive in China than in several other Asian countries. The share of these three economies in China's cumulative FDI inflows has, indeed, declined from 72 per cent in 1993 to 63 per cent in 1995. Furthermore, the return of Hong Kong to China in 1997 may have implications for FDI flows, depending on the smoothness of the transition and China's capability of maintaining Hong Kong as a competitive international business centre (box II.3).

As a result of these developments, FDI inflows to China may well be approaching a temporary peak. Inflows in 1996 may be affected by a rush to have FDI projects approved and contracts signed

---

Box II.3. Hong Kong after 1997: implications for FDI in China

According to the scenario of "one country, two systems", Hong Kong after 1997 will remain "a separate customs territory" with full membership in WTO. Within one sovereign State, there will be two separate and independent economic, financial and social systems. All trade and investment flows from Hong Kong to China will be treated as "foreign". Investments from Hong Kong into China -- whether by Hong Kong TNCs or by affiliates of foreign-based TNCs in Hong Kong -- will continue to enjoy the same status as before,[a] including as far as data reporting is concerned.

   [a]   Wang Liaoping, Deputy Director-General, Foreign Investment Administration, MOFTEC, speech at the seminar on China's FDI, Hong Kong, 11 June 1996.

---

before the new policies abolishing preferential treatment for foreign investors come into effect.[25] Indicative may be the development of contractual FDI which, in 1994-1995, was considerably lower than in 1993. Between 1993 and 1995, the number of projects approved -- a useful indicator for predicting actual flows in the forthcoming years -- fell from over 83,200 to less than 37,200 (figure II.5); the 1994-1995 increase in actual flows was the outcome of the 1992-1993 boom in FDI approvals.

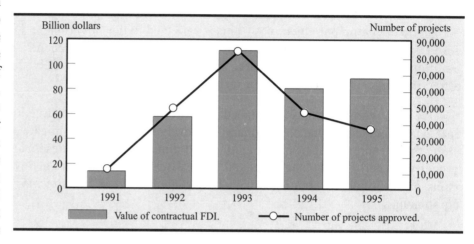

Figure II.5. Number and contractual value of approved FDI projects, 1991-1995

Source: Zhan, 1993; and data provided by MOFTEC.

China's attractiveness to foreign investors, however, remains bright. China's growth performance is outstanding. With an average annual GDP growth of 12 per cent in 1991-1995 and anticipated growth of 8 to 9 per cent in 1996, China is one of the fastest growing economies in the world, and this trend is expected to continue. The liberalization of FDI policies is still under way. Some industries that had been off limits to foreign investors (such as air transport, general aviation, retail trade, foreign trade, banking, insurance, accounting, auditing, legal service, the mining and smelting of precious metals, and the prospecting, extraction and processing of diamonds and other precious non-metal minerals) are being opened gradually. There is a significant potential for FDI participation in infrastructure, and several build-operate-transfer schemes have already been concluded. Foreign investors are now allowed to acquire state-owned firms. Furthermore, investments from other major source countries, such as Japan and the Republic of Korea, are increasing. The European Union is also pursuing new initiatives to increase its presence in the Chinese market. Finally, to the extent that the Chinese currency becomes convertible, profit repatriation will be easier, making it more attractive to invest in China. As a result, the already great importance of FDI for China's economy (table II.3) is likely to grow.

Table II.3. The importance of FDI in China, 1991-1995

Item	1991	1992	1993	1994	1995
Actual FDI flows (billion dollars)	4.4	11.2	27.5	33.8	37.5
Average amount per project (million dollars)	0.9	1.2	1.3	1.8	2.5
FDI as a ratio to gross domestic investment (per cent)	4.5	8	13.6	18.3	..
Volume of exports by foreign affiliates (billion dollars)	12.1	17.4	25.2	34.7	..
Share of exports by foreign affiliates in total exports (per cent)	17	20.4	27.5	28.7	31.3
Share of industrial output by foreign affiliates in total industrial output (per cent)	5	6	9	11	13
Number of employees in FDI projects (million)	4.8	6	10	14	16
Tax contribution as share of total (per cent)	..	4.1	..	..	10

Source: Zhan, 1993; and data provided by MOFTEC.

Thus, while FDI inflows to China may fall below $30 billion in the next few reason to believe that this would be mainly a temporary adjustment rather than a resp in general economic factors. China will remain one of the top FDI destinations in the world.

2. Latin America and the Caribbean

(a)   Trends

Latin America and the Caribbean saw an increase of 5 per cent in FDI inflows between 1994 and 1995, to an estimated $27 billion. Mexico remained the largest recipient in the region, with nearly $7 billion in inflows in 1995. Brazil, Argentina and Chile followed closely with an estimated $4.9 billion, $3.9 billion and $3.0 billion, respectively. Outflows from the region amounted to an estimated $3.8 billion in 1995. Brazil (with $1.4 billion) and Chile (with nearly $0.6 billion) were the largest investors from Latin America.

Together, inflows to Argentina, Brazil, Chile and Mexico accounted for an estimated two-thirds of all FDI flows to Latin America and the Caribbean in 1995. Most was industry-specific (automobiles in Mexico and Brazil, natural resources in Chile) or privatization-induced (e.g., in Argentina and Peru). This raises the issue of the extent to which FDI in Latin America and the Caribbean is "lumpy", in the sense that it is fuelled by special conditions in a few industries or is tied to privatization policies both of which may be short-lived.

(b)   "Lumpiness" of foreign direct investment

Investment flows to some countries in Latin America and the Caribbean have shown wide year-to-year fluctuations. Flows to Peru, for example, increased from $371 million in 1993 to $2.3 billion in 1994, most of which was in response to the privatization of the Peruvian Telephone Company. The estimated FDI inflow due to this single privatization was $1.4 billion (World Bank, 1996). Likewise, flows to Argentina fell from $6.3 billion in 1993, a record level attributable mostly to FDI from the privatization of telecommunication, airlines and petroleum state-owned enterprises, to $1.2 billion in 1994. And flows to Venezuela rose from $451 million in 1990 to $1.9 billion in 1991, after a large influx of FDI from the privatization of the telephone and airline companies, before falling to $629 million in the following year. Such "spikes" in the FDI trend for Latin America and the Caribbean lead to "lumpy" FDI flows, not only for the countries concerned, but also for the region as a whole.

Lumpy FDI flows are the outcome of substantial investments by TNCs in projects with unusually large investment requirements. In Latin America and the Caribbean, most of these projects are found in infrastructure, mining and petrochemical industries and are triggered by the privatization of state-owned firms. Projects with large capital requirements, however, are also found in manufacturing, especially in automobiles, an industry in which TNCs (such as Volkswagen, Fiat, General Motors and Ford) have been engaging in large greenfield investments in recent years.

Lumpy FDI flows can also change dramatically the industrial composition of FDI flows from one year to the next. Hence, sudden shifts in the shares of particular industries in total FDI flows from year to year may well reflect lumpy FDI flows received by these industries in a given year. For example, communication and transport accounted for 42 per cent of Peru's inward stock by 1995, compared with 0.4 per cent in 1990 (IDB and IRELA, 1996).

The lumpiness of flows to Latin America and the Caribbean implies that caution should be exercised when comparing investment flows across years, industries or recipient countries. Averaging values of FDI flows over several years can smooth some of the lumpiness. Certainly at the world level, the lumpiness of FDI flows in a few countries is unlikely to make a big difference in the aggregate value of these flows. For individual countries, however, lumpy FDI flows may lead to record FDI levels in one year followed by a quick reversal in the next, as in Peru.

Future flows in Latin America and the Caribbean will continue to be characterized by lumpy investments. Brazil, currently embarking on a large privatization programme with FDI involvement, may well experience a surge in FDI. Given that Brazil is one of the top FDI recipients in the region and that privatization programmes in other countries are still in progress, lumpy FDI inflows are likely to continue to shape the level of flows to the region as a whole over the next few years.

3. Africa

At $5 billion, FDI inflows to Africa in 1995 were almost the same as those in 1994 (table II.4). Investment flows to Africa are highly concentrated. An oil-producing country, Nigeria, accounted for 61 per cent of the average annual inflows to sub-Saharan Africa during 1993-1995. The concentration of FDI flows appears to be less for North Africa where Egypt, the largest recipient, accounted for an estimated 48 per cent of the sub-region's inflows over the same period.

This section looks at changes in the pattern of FDI in Africa since the 1980s, based on data and information collected for the forthcoming *World Investment Directory,* volume V, *Africa* (UNCTAD-DTCI, 1996a):

- In terms of recipient countries, FDI in Africa has become less concentrated over time. In the 1980s, southern Africa accounted for nearly two thirds of Africa's inward stock. That share fell to less than a quarter by 1995 (table II.4), mostly on account of disinvestments in South Africa during the apartheid era and the increased interest of European investors in North Africa. The latter has been encouraged by association agreements between the European Union and some North African countries (Martin, 1996), the latest of which was a trade and investment agreement between the European Union and Tunisia in 1996.

Table II.4. FDI stocks and inflows to Africa, by sub-region, 1980-1995

(Millions of dollars and percentage)

Region/ Sub-region	Flows						Stocks							
	1980-1984		1985-1990		1991-1995		1980		1985		1990		1995	
	Value	Share	Value	Share	Value	Share	Value	Share	Value	Share	Value	Share	Value	Share
North Africa[a]	415	30.1	1 278	46.4	1 584	41.7	4 429	11.9	8 988	23.7	16 109	30.7	20 557	30.3
Southern Africa[b]	255	18.5	5	..	71	1.9	23 831	63.8	16 423	43.4	16 367	31.2	16 524	24.4
Rest of Africa	711	51.4	1 485	53.6	2 138	56.4	9 074	24.3	12 481	32.9	20 029	38.1	30 714	45.3
Total Africa	1 381	100	2 768	100	3 793	100	37 334	100	37 892	100	52 505	100	67 795	100

Source: UNCTAD estimates based on UNCTAD-DTCI, 1996a.

a Algeria, Egypt, Libyan Arab Jamahiriya, Morocco and Tunisia.

b Botswana, Lesotho, Mozambique, Namibia, South Africa and Zimbabwe.

- The fact that FDI in Africa has become less concentrated geographically is also reflected in the changes in the pattern of royalties and fees payments to foreign firms by African countries (table II.5), most of which typically take place on an intra-firm basis. In 1980, southern Africa accounted for 93 per cent of the region's royalties and fees payments to foreign firms (and South Africa accounted for 94 per cent of that share). By 1993, southern Africa's share had dropped to 86 per cent, again mostly on account of the decline in these payments by South Africa. Interestingly, payments by North African countries remained constant between 1980 and 1993, which suggests that firms (including foreign affiliates) in this sub-region have not had extensive technology agreements despite increases in FDI.

- Although small, royalty and fee receipts by African countries -- about a fourth of the value of payments in 1993 (table II.5) -- underscore that Africa (especially, but not only, South Africa), too, is home to TNCs. A sample of these firms (table II.6) shows that they operate from a variety of countries in a diversified range of industries.

- In terms of source countries, FDI in Africa has become less concentrated as well (UNCTAD-DTCI, 1996a). Western Europe remains, however, the largest investor; more than half of the largest foreign affiliates operating in Africa are from there (table II.7). Among the Western European investors, France, Germany, Italy and the United Kingdom have been the traditional dominant sources of FDI for Africa, but Belgium is now beginning to emerge as an important

Table II.5.   Royalties and fees paid to, and received from, foreign countries, selected African countries, 1980-1993

(Millions of dollars)

Sub-region and country	Payments to foreign countries				Receipts from foreign countries			
	1980	1985	1990	1993	1980	1985	1990	1993
North Africa	9.4	2.5	9.6	9.1	..	..	..	..
Algeria	-	1.3	2.3	..	..	..	..	..
Morocco	9.4	1.2	7.3	9.1	..	..	..	..
Southern Africa	212.2	130.3	168.2	173.7	17.0	11.3	54.1	50.1
Botswana	..	..	7.8	2.1	..	..	..	..
Lesotho	..	..	1.0	1.1	..	..	..	..
South Africa	202.2	122.0	130.0	124.0	17.0	11.2	54.0	50.0
Swaziland	1.0	0.6	9.3	12.2	..	0.1	0.1	0.1
Zimbabwe	9.0	7.7	20.1	34.3	..	..	..	..
Rest of Africa	5.4	3.6	26.7	16.3	1.0	2.5	9.9	1.7
Benin	..	0.2	..	..	..	..	..	..
Burkina Faso	1.0	0.1	..	..	..	..	..	..
Burundi	..	0.1	0.1	0.1	..	..	..	..
Cameroon	..	0.8	-	0.2	..	1.6	0.3	1.7
Ghana	4.0	0.2	0.2	0.7	..	..	..	..
Kenya	..	2.0	6.0	7.2	..	..	..	..
Madagascar	..	..	..	6.0	..	..	..	..
Senegal	0.4	0.2	..	..	1.0	0.9	1.6	..
Seychelles	..	..	1.4	2.1	..	..	..	..
United Republic of Tanzania	..	..	19.0	..	..	..	8.0	..
Total	227.0	136.4	204.5	199.1	18.0	13.8	64.0	51.8

Source: UNCTAD-DTCI, 1996a.

investor. The United States, the second largest investor in Africa, also saw a decline in its share of Africa's inward stock, from 32 per cent in 1985 to 25 per cent in 1993.

African countries vary widely in terms of the importance of FDI for their economies (figure II.6). Two indicators of the significance of FDI -- the ratio of FDI flows to gross domestic capital formation and the ratio of FDI stock to GDP -- yield similar results in terms of their country rankings (figure II.6). The largest host African countries normalized by the size of economies include some of the major FDI recipients in Africa, such as Egypt and Morocco, as well as some of the smallest recipients, such as Equatorial Guinea, Namibia, the Gambia and Sierra Leone. However, the small size of domestic investment makes the amount of FDI received by the latter group of countries very significant to their economies. Likewise, the group of the 10 host countries that rank the lowest according to this share includes countries that receive fairly large amounts of FDI (e.g., Nigeria and

Table II.6. African TNCs, by industry, 1993

(Millions of dollars)

Company	Home country	Industry	Sales
All industries (except finance and insurance)			
Anglo American Industrial Corp. Ltd.	South Africa	Diversified	21 180.3
Barlow Rand Ltd.	South Africa	Diversified	11 573.9
O K Bazaars Ltd.	South Africa	Distributive trade	1 619.0
Consol Ltd.	South Africa	Paper	809.9
Basil Read Pty. Ltd.	South Africa	Construction	113.2
Bearing Man Ltd.	South Africa	Distributive trade	61.8
Berzach Brothers (Holdings) Ltd.	South Africa	Construction	42.5
Berger Trading Holdings Ltd.	South Africa	Distributive trade	15.0
Conserverie Chérifiennes	Morocco	Food	13.7
Benguela Concessions Ltd.	South Africa	Mining	6.3
Société Agricole Tolaise Arabe-Libyenne (SAFAL)	Libyan Arab Jamahiriya	Agriculture	1.0
Zambia Consolidated Copper Mines Ltd. (ZCCM)	Zambia	Mining	0.9
Cairo General Contracting Co.	Egypt	Construction	..
Consumers Cooperative Society	Egypt	Distributive trade	..
Omnium Nord African	Morocco	Diversified	..
Finance and insurance			**Assets**
Banque Algerienne de Developpement	Algeria	Finance	15 375.0
Nedcor Bank Ltd.	South Africa	Finance	13 702.5
Banque Misr	Egypt	Finance	11 800.0
Banque du Caire (SAE)	Egypt	Finance	5 319.8
Commercial Bank of Ethiopia	Ethiopia	Finance	2 196.4
Union Bank of Nigeria	Nigeria	Finance	1 450.3
Ghana Commercial Bank	Ghana	Finance	919.0
Libyan Arab Foreign Bank	Libyan Arab Jamahiriya	Finance	634.0
Zambia National Commercial Bank Ltd.	Zambia	Finance	209.8
Chinguity Bank	Libyan Arab Jamahiriya	Finance	151.0
Ecobank Ghana Ltd.	Togo	Finance	86.0
Ecobank-Bénin S. A.	Togo	Finance	49.0
Société Inter-Africaine de Banque (SIAB)	Libyan Arab Jamahiriya	Finance	30.0
Banque Commerciale du Niger (BCN)	Libyan Arab Jamahiriya	Finance	18.0
Banque Commerciale du Sahel S. A.(BCS-SA)	Libyan Arab Jamahiriya	Finance	11.0

Source: UNCTAD-DTCI, 1996a.

Tunisia). Another indicator also shows that the importance of FDI varies from country to country: foreign affiliate employment ranges from 0.1 per cent in Algeria to about 28 per cent in Mauritius (table II.8).

Finally, it should be noted that African countries are making considerable efforts to establish an appropriate FDI framework. As part of these efforts, African countries had concluded (by June 1996) 258 bilateral investment treaties for the promotion and protection of FDI, and 155 treaties for the avoidance of double taxation (table II.9). North Africa's intensity of bilateral investment treaties for the promotion and protection of FDI, at 15.9 treaties per country, is the highest among all developing regions (figure II.7). Reflecting the low intensity of bilateral investment treaties for sub-Saharan Africa, however, Africa's overall intensity of bilateral investment treaties, at 4.6 treaties per country, lags behind that of other developing regions.

Table II.7. The largest foreign affiliates in Africa,[a] by home country of parent firm, 1993

(Millions of dollars and percentage)

Home area/country	Number All industries excluding finance and insurance[b]	Number Finance and insurance	All industries excluding finance and insurance:[b] sales	Finance and insurance: assets	All industries excluding finance and insurance:[b] sales	Finance and insurance: assets
Developed countries	349	154	57 883	122 479	97.8	91.8
Western Europe	254	129	14 189	94 654	24.0	71.0
European Union	242	125	13 971	94 315	23.6	70.7
France	121	68	11 674	22 626	19.7	17.0
Germany	11	2	93	16	0.2	0.0
Italy	9	3	356	3 006	0.6	2.3
United Kingdom	66	40	1 765	42 464	3.0	31.8
Other Western Europe	12	4	218	339	0.4	0.3
Norway	1	..	..	..	..	..
Switzerland	11	4	218	339	0.4	0.3
North America	48	12	1 325	5 652	2.2	4.2
Other developed countries	25	1	3 869	53	65.4	0.0
Japan	4	..	435	..	0.7	..
South Africa	20	1	38 254	53	64.6	-
Mixed ownership	22	12	3 676	22 120	6.2	16.6
Developing countries	25	48	162	7 869	0.3	5.9
Africa	3	17	1	1 138	-	0.9
Latin America and the Caribbean	2	2	16	224	-	0.2
South, East and South-East Asia	7	7	26	534	-	0.4
West Asia	11	16	106	3 632	0.2	2.7
Mixed ownership	2	6	14	2 341	-	1.8
Central and Eastern Europe	1	..	..	..	..	..
Not specified	44	17	1 128	3 000	1.9	2.3
Total	419	219	59 174	133 348	100.0	100.0

Source: UNCTAD-DTCI, 1996a.

[a] Based on the ten largest affiliates (or fewer where the largest ten affiliates are not available) in all countries in Africa in both "all industries" (except finance and insurance) and the finance and insurance sector.
[b] Primary sector, secondary sector and tertiary sector except for finance and insurance affiliates.

Table II.8. Employment in foreign affiliates in selected African countries
(Number and percentage)

Country	Year	Employment in foreign affiliates	Share in total national labour force [a]
Algeria	1995	10 779 [b]	0.1
Egypt	1995	375 160	3.4
Kenya	1995	27 565	2.5
Malawi	1991	26 680	5.5
Mauritius	1994	50 000 [c]	27.7

Sources: UNCTAD-DTCI, 1996a; and United Nations, 1995.
[a]   Data for national employment are from 1990-1992.
[b]   Estimates.
[c]   Only in export-processing zone.

Figure II.6. Significance of inward FDI to host African countries[a]

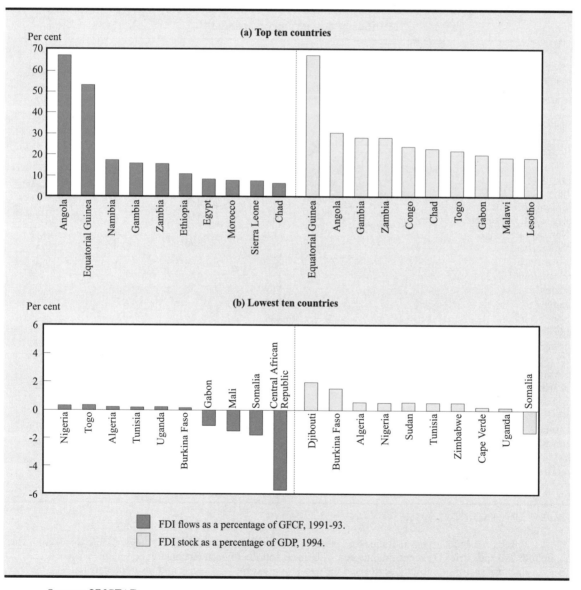

Source: UNCTAD.
[a]   Excludes Liberia.

Figure II.7. The intensity of BITs, by region, June 1996

(Number)

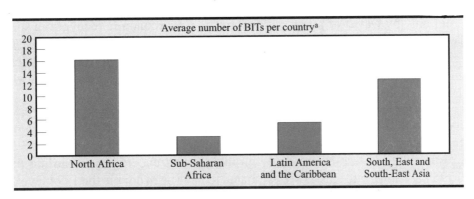

Source: UNCTAD, database.

a   Number of bilateral investment treaties concluded by countries in each region divided by the total number of countries in that region.

Table II.9. Bilateral treaties for the promotion and protection of FDI and the avoidance of double taxation, 1996

(Number of treaties)

Region/country	North Africa[a]		Southern Africa[b]		Rest of Africa		All Africa	
	BIT [c]	DT [d]	BIT[c]	DT[d]	BIT[c]	DT[d]	BIT[c]	DT[d]
Developed countries	44	41	13	9	119	65	176	115
Western Europe	41	34	10	6	115	56	166	96
European Union	34	28	8	5	88	46	130	79
France	4	4	-	-	11	14	15	18
Germany	4	3	1	1	31	4	36	8
United Kingdom	3	3	1	2	14	10	18	15
Japan	1	1	-	-	-	1	1	2
United States	2	3	1	-	4	1	7	4
Developing countries	42	14	3	-	13	20	59	34
Asia	18	6	2	-	3	6	23	12
South, East and South-East Asia	7	3	2	-	3	6	12	9
West Asia	11	3	-	-	-	-	11	3
Africa	18	8	-	-	10	14	28	22
Latin America and the Caribbean	3	-	1	-	1	-	5	-
Central and Eastern Europe	16	5	-	1	7	-	23	6
Total	102	60	16	10	140	85	258	155

Source: UNCTAD-DTCI, 1996a.

a   Algeria, Egypt, Libyan Arab Jamahiriya, Morocco and Tunisia.
b   Botswana, Lesotho, Mozambique, Namibia, South Africa and Zimbabwe.
c   Bilateral investment treaties, as of June 1996.
d   Double taxation treaties, as of March 1996.

C. Central and Eastern Europe

1. Trends

Driven not only by waves of privatizations, but also by economic recovery in some countries (e.g., Poland and the Czech Republic), FDI inflows to Central and Eastern Europe (CEE) have soared to record levels. Having remained stagnant in 1994, FDI inflows to CEE nearly doubled in 1995, to reach an estimated $12 billion (table II.10). The region now accounts for 5 per cent of world inflows, compared with only 1 per cent in 1991.

Hungary and the Czech Republic account for the largest share of the *increase* of FDI in the region; driven to a large extent by privatizations, inflows to both tripled in 1995, to $3.5 billion and $2.5 billion, respectively. Despite economic turbulence and uncertainty regarding private-sector reforms, the 1995 FDI flows into Russia are estimated to have been double the 1994 level. Investment flows into Romania continued to show a steady growth, rising to an estimated $550 million in 1995, while inflows to Poland were just under $2 billion.

Table II.10. FDI inflows into Central and Eastern Europe and their importance in the host economies, 1991-1995

(Millions of dollars and percentage)

Country	Inflows					Stock		Stock distribution 1995 (Per cent)	FDI inflows per capita 1995 (Dollars)	FDI inflows as percentage of GFCF, 1994	FDI stock as percentage of GDP, 1994
	1991	1992	1993	1994	1995	1994	1995				
Albania	..	20	58	53	70	130	200	0.6	20.3	-	7.2
Armenia	..	..	..	8	10	8	18	0.1	2.8	-	0.2
Azerbaijan	..	..	..	-	110	-	110	0.3	14.6	-	..
Belarus	..	7	10	15	20	32	52	0.2	2.0	-	0.2
Bulgaria	56	42	55	106	135	263	398	1.2	15.4	4.9	2.6
Croatia	..	..	..	..	..	..	..	..	..	..	..
Czech Republic	..	..	654	878	2 500	2 508	5 008	14.9	242.8	9.1	7.0
Estonia	..	82	162	214	188	458	646	1.9	122.9	-	10.0
Georgia	..	..	..	..	..	..	..	..	..	..	..
Hungary	1 462	1 479	2 349	1 144	3 500	6 434	9 934	29.6	346.0	13.9	15.6
Kazakhstan	..	100	150	185	284	435	719	2.1	16.6	-	2.4
Kyrgyzstan	..	..	..	10	15	10	25	0.1	3.2	-	0.4
Latvia	..	29	45	215	250	289	539	1.6	97.8	-	5.0
Lithuania	..	10	12	31	50	53	103	0.3	13.5	-	1.0
Moldova	..	17	14	23	32	54	86	0.3	7.2	-	1.5
Poland	291	678	1 715	1 875	2 510	4 879	7 389	22.0	65.4	13.5	5.1
Romania	40	77	94	340	373	551	924	2.8	16.3	9.8	1.9
Russian Federation	..	700	700	1 000	2 000	2 400	4 400	13.1	13.6	0.2	0.9
Slovakia	..	..	199	203	250	890	1 140	3.4	46.7	-	7.2
Slovenia	..	111	113	84	130	308	438	1.3	66.8	-	2.4
Tajikistan	..	..	..	10	15	10	25	0.1	2.5	-	0.5
Ukraine	..	200	200	159	200	559	759	2.3	3.9	-	0.7
Uzbekistan	..	40	45	50	115	135	250	0.7	5.0	-	0.6
Yugoslavia	118	64	25	..	..	400	400	1.2	..	..	..
Total	1 966	3 657	6 600	6 603	12 757	20 808	33 565	100	31.5	-	3
Memorandum:											
Argentina	2 439	4 179	6 305	1 200	3 900	22 900	26 800	..	112.8	9.6	8.1
United Kingdom	16 208	14 934	14 475	10 085	29 910	214 200	24 410	..	513.5	6.6	20.9

Source: UNCTAD estimates, based on annex tables 1, 3 and 5; and EBRD, 1995.

The European Union continues to account for most FDI flows into CEE. It also accounts for some three-quarters of the FDI stock in Hungary and Bulgaria, two-thirds of the FDI stock in the Czech Republic, Poland, Slovakia and Slovenia, and a little over 50 per cent of the stock in the Baltic Republics. Even in some more distant countries of the CIS, the European Union accounts for most inward FDI stock.[26] The dominant position of the European Union is only challenged in the Russian Federation, where Switzerland and the United States together account for 51 per cent of its inward FDI stock. In contrast to the United States, which is usually the second largest investor in CEE (accounting for 15 per cent of its inward FDI stock), Japan accounts for a minuscule 1 per cent of that region's inward stock (see section A).

Japanese companies are also falling behind investors from the newly industrializing countries of East and South-East Asia pursuing export-oriented investment strategies aimed at supplying the European Union market. In particular, companies from the Republic of Korea have recently increased their presence in CEE, particularly in Poland and Romania (TNCs based in the Republic of Korea now rank first in Romania).[27]

The FDI pattern in CEE reflects the pattern of its international trade. The European Union is the most important trading partner for all CEE countries, reflecting intra-firm trade flows between European Union parent firms and their CEE affiliates and the importance of the region as a production base for exports to the European Union. The United States and Japan rank a distant second and third in the region's trade balance. Both trade and FDI patterns reaffirm CEE's (and, in particular, the Visegràd countries) clustering around the European Union, the single most important Triad member for that region. The regional core strategies of some TNCs, especially in the automobile industry, include plans for rationalizing production Europe-wide.

This trend is likely to continue given push factors, such as corporate restructuring in the European Union (especially in Germany) and increased competition at home and in export markets from traditional and new competitors (especially from the newly industrializing economies in Asia). At the same time, the relatively cheap and skilled labour force, geographical proximity and cultural affinity, market-access considerations, and the economic recovery and regained political stability continue to be important pull factors for future investment flows into the region. In particular for the European Union's small and medium-sized TNCs, the geographical proximity will continue to make it an attractive location compared with low-cost countries in other regions (Hansen, 1996).

2. Foreign direct investment and economic growth: the link in Central and Eastern Europe

A significant share of the FDI received by CEE economies -- 18 per cent in 1994 -- is from the privatization of public enterprises. However, this share has declined considerably compared with 1989-1993 when, for the main recipient countries (excluding Russia), privatization-related inflows accounted for most FDI. These investments are "lumpy" and their timing reflects privatizations in host countries. As such, privatization-related FDI flows cannot be said to lead or lag domestic economic growth. It appears, however, that trends in FDI inflows, in particular, non-privatization related FDI inflows, coincide with the growth of domestic output, particularly in the Visegràd countries and the Baltic States: in all countries for which data are available, FDI inflows picked up once GDP growth became positive (figure II.8).

While many foreign investors rushed to establish a nominal presence in CEE when countries began to liberalize investment frameworks in the late 1980s and early 1990s, it was only when the transition process was well under way and negative GDP growth rates began to reverse that TNCs began to invest significantly in that region. Transnational corporations discriminated among CEE economies, investing first in those countries whose economic performance had improved and where policy reversals regarding role of the private sector seemed unlikely. Hence, in determining whether FDI leads or lags economic growth, individual economies, or groups of economies, have to be examined separately.

- Among the Visegràd countries, Poland was the first to make the turnaround in economic growth after the initial transition shock, and the first to receive significant FDI inflows. Inflows have grown steadily, seemingly stabilizing at a level below those of the Czech Republic and Hungary. Inflows into the Czech Republic and Hungary are, however, much more volatile because much is related to privatization. For example, over 70 per cent of the 1993 jump in inflows into Hungary was linked to privatization; the 1995 jump was also the result of large utility and telecommunication sell-offs.[28] Likewise, some 60 per cent of the Czech Republic's inflows in 1995 are related to the privatization of the telecommunications company, SPT Telecom,[29] and a major oil refinery.[30] Non-privatization related FDI flows to Poland are thus significantly higher than in Hungary and the Czech Republic, reflecting the better growth performance of the former (figure II.9). At the same time, non-privatization inflows to the Czech Republic have been growing at a much steadier pace than in Hungary, mirroring the higher GDP growth rates in 1995 (and the even higher forecast for 1996) in the former (figures II.10 and II.11).

  The Visegràd region, which has the highest growth rates and the strongest aspirations to integrate with Western Europe, accounted for over 65 per cent of inflows to the region in 1995, and is expected to continue to attract most of that region's FDI (EIU, 1996). Inflows to Hungary and the Czech Republic are expected to stabilize at a level below that of Poland after the last wave of privatizations. Only in Slovakia has the good economic performance not been coupled with significant increases in FDI inflows. This is not only linked to unclear FDI policy signals, but also reflects a significantly smaller domestic market (low GDP and GDP per capita).

- In the Baltic States, Latvia's steep economic decline in the early part of its transition caused investors to hold back initially. After positive growth rates were registered in 1994, however, Latvia overtook Estonia as the largest FDI recipient in that sub-region, even though much of its 1994 jump in inflows consisted of a sell-off in the telecommunications sector (EIU, 1996). Estonia's improved economic performance, on the other hand, has not yet led to large FDI gains. Likewise, Lithuania's slow start in receiving FDI, despite having registered positive GDP growth rates in 1994, reflects the small size of the domestic market; its GDP per capita is only about half the size of its neighbours.

- In Russia, FDI appears to be leading output growth. Russia's 1995 jump in inflows was partly in response to the increased stabilization of the economy, despite a projected 1995 negative growth rate of 3 per cent after four years of double-digit negative growth. It also reflects the fact that TNCs were eager to invest in Russia to establish "first-mover" advantages in anticipation of more favourable future prospects

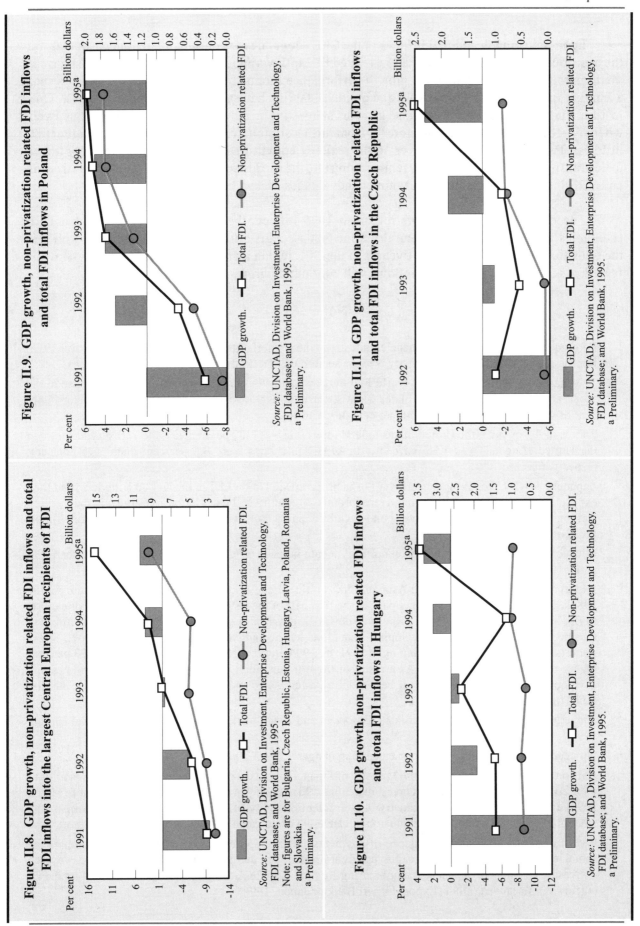

Figure II.8. GDP growth, non-privatization related FDI inflows and total FDI inflows into the largest Central European recipients of FDI

GDP growth. — Total FDI. — Non-privatization related FDI.

Source: UNCTAD, Division on Investment, Enterprise Development and Technology, FDI database; and World Bank, 1995.
Note: figures are for Bulgaria, Czech Republic, Estonia, Hungary, Latvia, Poland, Romania and Slovakia.
a Preliminary.

Figure II.9. GDP growth, non-privatization related FDI inflows and total FDI inflows in Poland

GDP growth. — Total FDI. — Non-privatization related FDI.

Source: UNCTAD, Division on Investment, Enterprise Development and Technology, FDI database; and World Bank, 1995.
a Preliminary.

Figure II.10. GDP growth, non-privatization related FDI inflows and total FDI inflows in Hungary

GDP growth. — Total FDI. — Non-privatization related FDI.

Source: UNCTAD, Division on Investment, Enterprise Development and Technology, FDI database; and World Bank, 1995.
a Preliminary.

Figure II.11. GDP growth, non-privatization related FDI inflows and total FDI inflows in the Czech Republic

GDP growth. — Total FDI. — Non-privatization related FDI.

Source: UNCTAD, Division on Investment, Enterprise Development and Technology, FDI database; and World Bank, 1995.
a Preliminary.

Economic growth and FDI inflows in the CEE economies are closely related: in particular, for the countries examined non-privatization-related FDI inflows appear to have taken off in response to the turnaround in these economies' growth performance (not disregarding the fact that factors such as market size, regulatory frameworks and political stability have all played a significant role). This, in turn, further strengthens economic growth, suggesting a movement towards a virtuous cycle whereby economic growth leads to more FDI that further stimultates growth which leads to higher FDI inflows. Two caveats apply, however, in the region's growth-FDI relationship, both closely linked to the transitional character of CEE's reintegration into the world economy: FDI related to privatization and FDI linked to establishing "first-mover" advantages escape this interrelationship.

The doubling of FDI into the region in 1995 reflects the recognition by TNCs that CEE economies, particularly those in Central Europe that are registering high growth rates, are well into the transition process. As the attractiveness of the CEE region increases with further progress in this regard, it is likely that investment inflows will continue to grow.

Notes

[1] Foreign direct investment in the financial industry in the Netherlands Antilles is excluded except for 1995. For the reason to exclude this industry, see the section on "Definitions and sources" in the annex.

[2] The shares of the United States in world FDI outflows and stocks are, however, lower than those in the 1960s and 1970s when the United States was also the dominant investor, accounting for more than 45 per cent of world outflows and about 40 per cent of world stock.

[3] For example, in 1993, the United States federal funds rate was 3.02 per cent and the Treasury-Bill rate in the United Kingdom was 5.25 per cent. In 1995, these rates were 6.0 per cent and 5.46 per cent, respectively.

[4] Japanese TNCs have invested nearly half of their European Union FDI in the United Kingdom, and they expect that the country will be the tenth most promising country in the world for investment in the medium and long-term, according to a survey conducted by Japan's Export-Import Bank in 1995 (Export-Import Bank of Japan, 1996).

[5] Michael Lindemann, "German 'job exporting' debate is renewed", *Financial Times*, 2 November 1995, p. 4.

[6] Exports from the United States to Asia and the Pacific, already higher than those to Europe during the 1980s, grew at a considerably higher pace in the first half of the 1990s and exceeded the value of exports to Europe by 38 per cent in 1993. Exports to developing Asia alone are now only slightly below those to Europe. On the import side, developing Asia alone has accounted for a higher share of United States imports than Western Europe beginning in 1991; by 1994, imports from developing Asia were 23 per cent higher than those from Europe. As a result of these trends, total trade between the United States and developing Asia exceeded total trade between the United States and Western Europe in 1994 for the first time (figure II.1).

[7] See, e.g., a survey among United States, European and Asian managers and business experts in Hatem, 1996.

[8] "In need of fastening, the Atlantic friendship in danger", *The Economist,* 27 May 1995, p.13.

[9] Data on outward FDI reported by the Ministry of Finance are based on notifications by companies prior to their investments. Companies that invest more than 100 million yen abroad (30 million yen prior to March 1994) are required to notify the Ministry of their intention to invest. These data tend to overestimate the amount of actual FDI because of inclusion of cancelled or deferred FDI (Ramstetter, forthcoming).

[10] Investment outflows (based on balance-of-payments data and approvals) significantly underestimate the actual level of investments because reinvested earnings are not included. According to a 1995 survey, the reinvested earnings of Japanese manufacturing foreign affiliates accounted for 35 per cent of total FDI outflows in fiscal year 1994 (Export-Import Bank of Japan, 1996).

11 Based on a JETRO survey conducted in May 1995.

12 Sectoral data are only available on a notification basis.

13 As virtually all Japanese investments in Liberia are motivated by the country's status of a tax haven, FDI there has been excluded from Africa's total. Japan accounted for more than four fifths of inward FDI stock of Liberia in 1993 (UNCTAD-DTCI, 1996a). With Liberia, Africa accounts for 1.5 per cent of Japan's outward FDI stock.

14 Looking at the medium (the next three years) and the long term (10 years ahead), eight out of the 10 most preferred countries for Japanese TNCs are in Asia (the remaining two being in developed countries) (Export-Import Bank of Japan, 1996). One reason is that the operations of Japanese affiliates in that region are very profitable: in fiscal year 1994, the ratio of current income to sales of Japanese affiliates in that region was 4.1 per cent, compared, for example, with 1.9 per cent in the United States and 1.2 per cent in Europe (MITI, 1996).

15 For example, one fifth of funds raised by Japanese affiliates in host countries were through affiliates of Japanese banks in the same countries in 1992 (MITI, 1994, table 2-21-12).

16 Information provided by JETRO.

17 Information provided by Fuji Research Institute Corporation.

18 *Nihon Keizai Shimbun*, 9 May 1996, based on a survey by MITI. There were 92 affiliates of small and medium-sized TNCs that withdrew in 1994, while 86 affiliates were established by them.

19 China, Indonesia, Hong Kong, Malaysia, Philippines, Republic of Korea, Singapore, Taiwan Province of China and Thailand.

20 It must be noted that a good part of Hong Kong's (perhaps some 30 per cent) and Singapore's (perhaps 50 per cent) FDI is undertaken by foreign affiliates established there; see Low, Ramstetter, Yeung, forthcoming.

21 Guiding Catalogue of Industries for Foreign Investment, promulgated on 27 June 1995.

22 These include measures allowing foreign firms to sell on the domestic market products that China would otherwise need to import; measures helping foreign firms to obtain foreign exchange; measures allowing large TNCs to set up investment and/or holding companies in China; and measures opening new investment areas to TNCs.

23 By early 1994, over 7,500 ventures had been deprived of their status as foreign affiliates (*China Economic News,* 18, 16 May 1994).

24   Dai Xanglong, Governor, People's Bank of China, *International Business*, 6 May 1996.

25 A grace period has been granted to those projects which had already been approved before 1 April 1996, but for which actual investments have not yet taken place.

26 Data are available for Belarus, where the European Union accounts for 38 per cent of FDI; Moldova (68 per cent); and Ukraine (43 per cent).

27 See, for example, "Daewoo takes over Romanian shipyard", *Financial Times*, 28 May 1996, p. 5.

28 Information provided by Privatization International, London.

29 "Czech telecom stake sold for record $1.5bn", *Financial Times*, 29 June 1995, p. 13.

30 Newsletter of the Embassy of the Czech Republic, Washington, D.C., United States, volume IV, No. 2, February 1996.

Part Two

Foreign direct investment and trade: interlinkages and policy implications

Introduction

The rapid growth of foreign direct investment (FDI) and the discussions about international policy arrangements related to such investment have drawn renewed attention to the relationship between FDI and trade. Does trade lead to FDI or FDI lead to trade? Does FDI substitute for trade or trade substitute for FDI? Do they complement each other? In sum, what does the growth of FDI mean for trade -- and, most importantly, what are the implications for the economies involved?

This Part explores linkages between FDI and trade, as they have evolved and are evolving, and in the context of the changing global environment for international transactions and the changing nature of FDI. It then identifies briefly implications with respect to trade and FDI policies for growth and development.

The inter-linkages between FDI and trade are important for several reasons:

- The role of trade as a handmaiden of growth and development has long been recognized and reflected in trade policies. Foreign direct investment, as the principal mode of delivering goods and services to foreign markets, and the principal factor in the organization of international production, increasingly influences the size, direction and composition of world trade, as do FDI policies.

- The role of FDI as a handmaiden of growth and development is being increasingly appreciated and is now largely reflected in FDI policies. Trade and trade policies can exert various influences on the size, direction and composition of FDI flows.

- Apart from the autonomous impacts of trade and FDI on growth and development, there are interlinkages between the two which, if ignored, may reduce the developmental contribution of each, and, if seized, can create synergies with broader growth and development implications. Yet these are still relatively unknown and not well understood. One of the principal reasons for this lack of knowledge and understanding is that the theoretical explanations of these two distinct yet interlinked activities have largely gone their separate ways, and attempts to integrate the theories of trade and FDI are, despite considerable progress in recent years, still at a stage of infancy (see annex to Part Two).

- Finally, understanding the interrelationship between FDI and trade can help in the formulation of policies for FDI and trade in that they support one another in terms of policy objectives and their efficient implementation. An improved understanding of the interlinkages would also provide a background and basis for discussions at the international level as regards appropriate policy arrangements.

Trade-FDI linkages can be analyzed in different ways: by type of FDI, by strategy of transnational corporation (TNC), by sector of economic activity, by group of countries and their levels of development, or by the evolution of thinking and theorizing about the subject. The discussion in this Part takes a mixed approach. It consists of two chapters:

- Chapter III reviews the interrelationships between FDI and trade as they have evolved, focusing on the dominant characteristics of the relationship in the manufacturing, natural resources and services sectors. This relationship, reflecting the methods of internationalization of firms and the modes of delivery of products to foreign markets, has generally involved a linear, step-by-step progression, running from trade to FDI, and consisting predominantly of bilateral linkages between home and host countries. The inclusion of the two other sectors complicates the sequence (and the relationship): it can run from FDI to trade in some natural resources industries, or it can become truncated, as in many service industries. In each case, the review begins with a discussion of the sequence, focussing especially on the step that leads to FDI; then reviews the impact of trade once this step has been taken; points to associated trade and associated FDI effects; and, finally, discusses the development implications of the relationship.

- Chapter IV reviews briefly the changes in the international environment that have brought about the emergence of new types and patterns of FDI, alongside the still dominant ones discussed in chapter III, and focuses on the FDI-trade relationship under conditions of efficiency-seeking integrated international production. Since about the late 1960s, and especially since the mid-1980s, the relationship between FDI and trade has begun to change, as a result of changes in the nature and composition of FDI under the influence of new and changing strategies of TNCs, spurred in turn by technological progress related to transport, communications and information transmission; liberalized policies with respect to international trade, FDI and technology flows; and the existence of a multitude of affiliates already established by TNCs. Although historically important types of FDI continue to exist, and even characterize the majority of cases of products and firms entering international production, FDI is becoming increasingly associated with integrated international production within the transnational corporate systems of firms pursuing complex integration strategies, under which firms disperse their activities regionally or globally across production sites from which to serve regional or international markets. The result is a more complex interrelationship between FDI and trade, reflecting the greater choice for firms engendered by the liberalizing environment for international transactions. The discussion then turns to implications of a closer FDI-trade relationship for countries, both developed and developing. The chapter concludes by touching upon policy implications at the national level of the changing FDI-trade relationship, in particular the question of the need for coherence between national FDI and trade policies, in light of the intertwinedness of FDI and trade.

Given the importance of both FDI and trade for development, understanding the interaction between the two is particularly important for policy makers at the national and international levels. Although the discussion does not lead to specific policy prescriptions, it seeks to provide some of the analytical underpinnings for them.

Chapter III

Foreign direct investment and trade: the traditional sequential relationship

The sequence and pattern of international transactions at the country level are determined mainly by cross-border activities of firms. The dominant characteristics of the sequential internationalization process can be distinguished according to the sector of a firm's activities. These characteristics largely determine the relationship between trade and foreign direct investment (FDI) for any product, once the sequence of internationalization is complete. At the same time, the indirect effects of this internationalization influence the relationship between FDI and trade that emerges at the industry, sectoral or intersectoral levels.

A. The manufacturing sector

1. The sequence

Historically, manufacturing firms have traded with foreign enterprises and buyers before undertaking FDI. For a number of reasons, most firms still begin their internationalization sequence today in this way.[1]

- Trade is easier and less risky than FDI. Trade can be short-term, one-off transactions in which claims can be settled quickly. Foreign direct investment is long term and involves the direct commitment of assets by a parent firm in an environment that requires more knowledge, experience, managerial and organizational capacity than exports.

- Exports can be in any amounts, while foreign production requires a minimum size to be economically efficient. Exports are often a test of the existence of a market for a manufacturing affiliate.

- Before modern communication, it was difficult for a parent firm to supervise and control foreign affiliates on a day-to-day basis.

When possible, trade has therefore usually occurred before FDI. For a firm producing a specific product, the internationalization sequence has typically followed this pattern:

- Domestic production and sales are traditionally the principal objectives. Foreign markets enter the purview of most entrepreneurs later.

- When foreign markets become interesting, exports begin usually with arm's-length sales, initially through domestic or foreign agents. In the past, FDI did not enter into the reckoning.

- Intermediaries are replaced by export departments at headquarters, leading, perhaps, to some FDI, e.g., in storage facilities or foreign trading affiliates.

- Exports are often followed by licensing of foreign producers to manufacture a product with proprietary technology.

- Once experience with these and other, mostly non-equity, forms of production abroad has been gained, firms gradually begin to build up production capacities, beginning with assembly operations or other partial production (sometimes in joint ventures with local partners), before turning towards production in majority or wholly-owned foreign affiliates, often as stand-alone clones of their parent companies.

- While a firm may simultaneously export to many countries, investment in production facilities usually begins in one country, typically not too distant from the home country in "psychological" distance -- that is, the distance measured in "factors preventing or disturbing the flows of information between firms and market" (Johanson and Wiedersheim, 1993), such as differences in language, culture, political systems, level of education and level of development.

- If successful, the experience with the first foreign producing affiliate can lead to affiliates in other countries, on the basis of separate, local market-oriented, multi-domestic strategies, relying on stand-alone affiliates (UNCTAD-DTCI, 1993a).

- Eventually, foreign affiliates may begin to export.

There is plenty of evidence that this linear, step-by-step sequence of servicing foreign markets captures accurately the development of foreign activities by many manufacturing companies (box III.1). While, certainly, not every firm goes through all these steps (e.g., licensing agreements do not always precede producing affiliates), the precedence of exporting over FDI as a way of entering foreign markets has been the dominant characteristic of internationalization (Wilkins, 1974; Nicholas, 1982; Johanson and Vahnle, 1993).

Given that the threshold of cost and risk for foreign production has traditionally been seen as higher than for domestic production, a firm needs special competitive advantages to move from exports to FDI to overcome the natural disadvantage of being an outsider. In case of firms falling under the product-cycle paradigm, this ownership specific advantage is new product. But it may also be the possession of trade marks or brand names, superior technology, managerial competence or the ability to supply high-quality, differentiated goods. When firms have such advantages, "the impetus to engage in foreign production was entirely based on the perceived net economic benefits of such production vis-à-vis exports from a home based factory" (Dunning, 1993, p.106). Four factors have been of special importance in influencing the shift from exports to FDI (Dunning, 1993, pp. 106-109):

Box III.1. Linear sequence in manufacturing: Singer & Company

Singer was one of the first United States-based companies that internationalized its operations. In August 1850, I. M. Singer invented a sewing machine and established I. M. Singer & Company in New York in 1851 to manufacture and sell the machines in the United States. To protect this innovative product, Singer had applied for and obtained domestic and some foreign patents by 1851. Until 1855, the company concentrated on fine tuning its operations in the domestic market.

The first step towards internationalizing took place in 1855, when Singer & Co. sold its French patent for the single thread machine to a French merchant for a combination of lumpsum payment and royalties. This proved to be a bad experience for Singer as the French merchant was reluctant to pay royalties and handled competitors' products, leading to disputes and discouraging Singer from selling foreign patents to independent business persons. By 1856, Singer stopped granting territorial rights to independents in the domestic market due to bad experiences and began establishing its own sales outlets. Independent agents were not providing user instructions to buyers and failed to offer servicing. They were also reluctant to risk their capital by providing instalment payments as well as carrying large inventories.

Learning from its domestic problems, Singer used franchised agents as a mode of entry abroad; they sold and advertised the company's product in a given region. By 1858, Singer had independent businesspersons as foreign agents in Rio de Janeiro and elsewhere. Between September 1860 and May 1861, the company exported 127 machines to agents in Canada, Cuba, Curacao, Germany, Mexico, Peru, Puerto Rico, Uruguay and Venezuela. Due to its domestic experience, Singer sped up the linear sequence, sometimes simultaneously using both franchised agents and its own sales outlets.

Singer also started extending its policy of establishing sales outlets to foreign markets. By 1861, it had salaried representatives in Glasgow and London. They established additional branches in England, to each of which the machines were sold on commission. By 1862, Singer was facing competition in England from imitators. Foreign sales of Singer machines increased steadily as the company was able to sell machines abroad at prices lower than in the United States because of the undervaluation of the dollar. In 1863, Singer opened a sales office in Hamburg, Germany, and later in Sweden. By 1866, the European demand for Singer machines surpassed supplies and competitors were taking advantage of Singer's inability to supply the machines. After the civil war, the United States currency appreciated; at the same time, wages in the United States began to rise, increasing manufacturing costs and affecting firms' international competitiveness. As a result, some United States firms started establishing factories abroad.

In 1868, Singer established a small assembly factory in Glasgow, with parts imported from the United States. The venture proved to be successful and, by 1869, Singer decided to import tools from the United States to manufacture all parts in Glasgow. By 1874, partly due to the recession at home, Singer was selling more than half of its output abroad. Then, Singer started replacing locally-financed independent agents with salaried-plus-commission agents. By 1879, its London regional headquarters had 26 offices in the United Kingdom and one each in Paris, Madrid, Brussels, Milan, Basel, Capetown, Bombay and Auckland.

By the 1880s, the company had a strong foreign sales organization, with the London regional headquarters taking the responsibility for sales in Australia, Asia, Africa, the southern part of South America, the United Kingdom and a large part of the European continent. The Hamburg office was in charge of northern and middle Europe, while the New York office looked after sales in the Caribbean, Mexico, the northern part of South America and Canada. By 1881, the capacity in Singer's three factories in Glasgow was insufficient to meet demand. Therefore, in 1882, Singer established a modern plant in Kilbowie near Glasgow with the latest United States machine tools and with a capacity equivalent to that of its largest factory in the United States. In 1883, Singer set up manufacturing plants in Canada and Australia. Through experience, Singer learned that it could manufacture more cost effectively in Scotland than in the United States for sales in Europe and other markets.

Source: Wilkins, 1970.

- Government policies, especially tariffs or other barriers on imported goods, have been a powerful encouragement, prompting exporting firms to begin production in a host country, sometimes, when trade barriers were high, on a sub-optional scale. In this case, the linear sequence leading to FDI was speeded up by import restrictions.

- Competition of firms in oligopolistic industries frequently prompts rivals to follow competitors abroad in establishing themselves in important foreign markets, again speeding up internationalization.

- Foreign production could be undertaken because of the need to reduce transportation and production costs.

- Proximity to customers and markets is important. Presence in the market permits firms to cater better to the special needs of customers in host countries through the adaptation of products or production to local tastes.

These factors alone, however, are not sufficient for foreign production through FDI. They need to be combined with the desire of firms to internalize the markets for ownership-specific advantages.

The linear sequence continues to characterize the internationalization sequence for most firms in the manufacturing sector, especially for new entrants. This is true for large and small firms, be they from developed or developing countries or economies in transition. A recent survey of 807 British companies found that "a majority of companies, and in particular manufacturing companies, tend to build up their overseas activity in a series of stages, typically starting with exports, then establishing a small office presence, building up to a sales, marketing and distribution operation and finally, in some markets, establishing an investment in production facilities" (United Kingdom, Department of Trade and Industry, 1996, p. 3). Even large, experienced TNCs with extensive international networks of integrated affiliates still use this step-by-step approach to enter some new markets, especially small ones (for which FDI is not justified) and difficult ones (such as Japan; Ozawa, 1992, pp. 39-41). Where, however, markets for identical or similar products exist that are served by local companies, TNCs may chose to enter directly with FDI, including through mergers and acquisitions.

As a result of this sequence, FDI has often been viewed as replacing trade. This perception found its expression in the dominant paradigm of the 1960s and 1970s, the product-cycle paradigm, explaining the sequence from domestic production of a new product to its export and then foreign production by United States firms -- after World War Two the world's most important source of FDI (Vernon, 1966).[2] The paradigm was originally developed to explain the two largest FDI flows at that time: United States FDI to Europe (and especially to the then European Economic Community) and to developing countries (mainly Latin America). It dealt with individual products and stages in the life of these products. The starting point was that the comparative advantage of the United States (and the ownership-specific advantages of its firms) was in innovation, and that exports therefore were heavily weighted with new products still in development. It was therefore necessary for production to take place near the home base of the innovating firm. Once production became routine, the United States was no longer a suitable place for production which would move overseas. At first the innovating firm would move production to foreign affiliates, so that it could continue to earn rents on its firm-specific assets, i.e., its superior knowledge of how to produce and market the product. However, that superiority would eventually be lost as local and other foreign firms learned the techniques of production and the innovator's firm-specific assets in the product disappeared.

Thus this sequence, though dealing with a single product, is relevant also indirectly to the producer of this product, the firm. It describes the path of the firm in becoming a TNC -- the firm invents a new product, begins as a local producer, turns into an exporter and eventually becomes a foreign investor. The path ends with production diffused to many firms as the product matures into a standard product. From a single product perspective, there is a shift from export to foreign production; from a (single-product) firm perspective, the establishment of a plant abroad replaces exports as the mode of servicing the foreign market of such a product, giving rise to market-seeking FDI.

The literature is full of single-product examples of substitution between FDI and exports, in many cases induced by trade restrictions rather than developments in the market. One of the first books dealing with the linear sequence used by United States firms investing in Europe observed, for example: " ... by imposing a 33 1/3 per cent tariff on tires the Government had extended an invitation to Mr. Firestone to manufacture tires in England rather than pay $1,000 a day in import duties ..."; in the case of Kodak, " ... its German and French factories, and its English camera division, date from the levying of high duties by those countries" (Southard, 1931, p.177).[3]

More recent examples of the substitution of FDI for trade can be found in Latin America. Witness the Argentine motor industry. Under the pressure of restrictions on imports, foreign automobile firms set up production in the country: "Between December 1958 and November 1961, Argentine authorities approved automotive investment plans submitted by foreign firms to the tune of US $97 million. This resulted, by 1961, in the establishment of 22 automotive firms, wholly or partly foreign-owned, in a country with an estimated market potential for motor vehicles in the half-decade ahead of at most 200 to 300 thousand units per annum" (Felix, 1964, pp. 393-394); United States exports of automobiles grew rapidly from 1958, to a peak in 1962 of over $73 million and then fell sharply to $23 million in 1967 and $12 million in 1973 (Felix, 1964).[4] Local production of foreign affiliates substituted for imports (or, from the viewpoint of the home countries, exports). However, the line of causality did not run from higher FDI to lower trade; it ran from import restrictions to smaller imports by the host country (or exports from the home country), to higher FDI.

It is important to note that the discussion above relates to market-seeking FDI, which has traditionally accounted for the dominant share of manufacturing investments. Although low-cost labour-seeking investment also forms a part of manufacturing FDI, it is discussed in chapter IV, since it is only one variant of efficiency-seeking FDI that aims at exploiting the economies of locational dispersion and integrated production, with a view towards serving regional and global markets.

2. Impact of foreign direct investment on trade

So, foreign production can substitute for trade in a *single* product. But the impact on trade of establishing a foreign affiliate does not stop there. While replacing exports, an affiliate usually generates demand for other products, such as capital goods or intermediate goods and services. These may be provided by other parts of the parent company, its suppliers or independent companies at home, or firms in third countries. This may lead to new trade for home and host countries -- associated trade; if it pulls domestic suppliers of goods and services abroad, it can also lead to new investment -- associated investment. Only when the configuration of these indirect effects is known can their full impact on trade and FDI be assessed. It may happen -- and, in fact, it does frequently -- that the shift from exports to FDI turns out to be both trade-replacing and trade-supporting and, on balance, often trade creating. In addition, FDI can also change the composition of trade.

The FDI-trade relationship is further complicated by the fact that, over time and as TNCs mature, strategies change, as do trade relations. Exporters from a home country can become importers into it from foreign affiliates; importers into a host country can also become exporters from it.

Most systematic evidence relates to developed countries. It suggests that the trade-creating effect of FDI in manufacturing for the home country tends to outweigh the trade-replacing effect. The largest number of such studies relate to United States TNCs, and they use a variety of data sets:

- With respect to the relationship between United States exports and United States FDI across manufacturing industries, one study found a positive correlation between an expansion of United States exports and the expansion of outward FDI, with the strength of this association declining as the level of FDI rose (Bergsten et al., 1978). The conclusion was that, in the early stages of FDI, foreign affiliates are on average highly dependent upon exports from the parent company of intermediate products and complementary final products; but as local operations expand, dependency upon supplies from the parent firm is reduced.

- Another study found that the level of production by United States affiliates in a host country had a favourable impact on United States exports in an industry to that country (Lipsey and Weiss, 1981). Foreign production by United States affiliates was, however, negatively related to the exports of countries other than the United States to the same market, underlining the importance of FDI to compete for market shares.

- An investigation based on a cross-section of United States TNCs for 1970 found that there was a positive and generally significant correlation between outward FDI (measured in terms of foreign affiliate production) and the value of manufacturing exports by parent firms in each of five regions, and in all but three of 14 industries covered (Lipsey and Weiss, 1984). In other words, the increase in exports to a host country, associated with increased foreign affiliate production in that country, was not offset for the parent company by reductions in exports to other countries. The positive effect on parent company exports of intermediate products was stronger than the positive impact on parent-company exports of finished products.

- Studies of Swedish TNCs have also shown a positive relationship between foreign affiliate production and parent firm exports (Swedenborg, 1979 and 1985).

- A study of foreign affiliate production and exports in 1982 of the world's largest industrial firms also found a positive correlation between the two (Pearce, 1990). It showed that, moreover, FDI was more closely related to intra-firm exports than to inter-firm exports.

- And looking at manufacturing exports of United States and Sweden, and changes over time for Sweden, another study found that the relationship with foreign affiliate production was neutral or complementary. It also concluded that the complementarity between FDI and home country exports was more clearly visible for Swedish than for United States exports, and that there was no weaking of the relationship as the size of FDI increased (Blomström et al., 1988).

Some of these studies demonstrate that, although the level of home-country exports to a host country tends to increase, the composition of these exports shifts, particularly towards exports of components and other intermediate products, and, in relative terms, away from exports of final or finished products (Lipsey and Weiss, 1984; Pearce, 1990).

From the numerous studies of the effect of inward FDI in manufacturing on manufacturing trade of host developed countries, the balance of evidence suggests that both imports and exports are increased, but with some exceptions and qualifications. One of the main reasons is that FDI tends to be concentrated in the most trade-intensive industries, and often especially in those in which the host country has a comparative advantage (or in which that comparative advantage can be developed).[5]

B. The natural resources sector

The relationship between trade and FDI in the natural resources sector is determined by the fact that extraction and production are location-bound and that an important part of the demand for the resources is international. In some natural resource industries, the dominant characteristic of the relationship has also been a linear, step-by-step sequence similar to that in manufacturing, except that trade usually consisted of imports (i.e., was home country-demand led). However, in other resource-based industries, FDI preceded trade. These two categories can be roughly associated with the distinction between renewable (agriculture and forestry) and non-renewable (mining and petroleum) resources, respectively.

Initially, the demand for many raw materials came primarily from developed countries. The most important factors determining where production would start and whether it required FDI (then leading to trade or supporting already existing trade) were: production *pre-conditions* in the location of deposits of non-renewable resources or the climatic conditions required to cultivate renewable resources; and the availability of production *capabilities* (including capital, technology and skills). The principal variants of the resulting FDI-trade relationship are:

- If a (host) country has both, production pre-conditions and capabilities, as was the case with some renewable resources (such as tea, cotton or coffee), arm's-length exports to countries short of the resources involved would take place. In principle, the same applies to non-renewable resources, e.g., oil and copper. Foreign direct investment could occur at a later stage, either as a result of the backward vertical integration of firms from home countries, or the forward vertical integration of producers in the natural resource rich countries (box III.2) -- in both cases supporting or expanding existing trade.

- If production pre-conditions exist, but capabilities do not, as with many non-renewable resources, then FDI by foreign firms is necessary to begin production and exports. In this case, FDI clearly leads to trade -- exports from host countries and imports into home countries (or elsewhere).

1. The sequence

Non-renewable resources are characterized by the importance of geology, the capital-intensive and high-risk nature of their exploitation, and the fact that most metals are fairly homogenous products sold in world markets. Historically, the first step was the search for oil and mineral deposits.

This explains flows of FDI to explore and then extract resources, leading to a trade linkage between host and home countries (or other countries). The process generally started from FDI, because of the advantage of home country firms in resource discovery and exploitation. The highly capital-intensive nature of the activities involved (requiring large-scale investment) and oligopolistic competition (requiring TNCs to secure direct control over supplies) contributed to, and sustained, FDI.

Box III.2 Standard Oil: changing trade roles of a natural resources sector TNC

Standard Oil did not start out as a typical TNC in the non-renewable resources. Distinct from its European counterparts, it did not have to go abroad to get access to oil because it originated in a country well endowed with it. In addition, it did not start out as a natural resources company: during its first few decades, its principal business was the processing and distribution of oil rather than its extraction. In the second half of the nineteenth century, when the company was established by John D. Rockefeller, oil extraction in the United States was a competitive business with many small producers and low profit margins. Buying oil cheap and investing in refineries, pipelines and other transportation facilities in the United States, Standard Oil soon became almost a monopolist in the domestic market for the distribution of oil and oil-based products.

While building up the domestic market, the company also began its internationalization process in a sequence typical for a manufacturing rather than for a natural resources TNC. Its first step into foreign markets was exporting oil to Europe, mainly through independent export merchants or representatives of foreign importers. Already in the 1860s, much of the oil production of the United States was sold abroad, mainly to Europe. From the 1880s onwards, benefitting from its experience with the domestic market, Standard Oil began selling its oil products abroad through its trading affiliates. Then, these affiliates entered the processing stage, that is, they began to refine oil, in particular in countries where restrictive trade policies hampered the import of refined oil products from the United States (e.g., Mexico, Cuba and Canada).

Standard Oil took the first step into foreign oil extraction in 1898, when one of its member firms, Jersey Standard Oil, acquired Canadian Imperial Oil. The principal purpose was not so much access to oil (Imperial's oil production was not substantial), as gaining control over Imperial's refining and marketing facilities in Canada.

Standard Oil, or rather its successor companies, began to look towards a more intensive expansion in foreign markets only after the United States Supreme Court decided to dissolve the Standard Oil trust in 1911. It soon learned that, contrary to Standard Oil's prior experience in its home market, it had to control the extraction of oil, not only its processing and distribution, to be successful in an oligopolistic international market. Since that time, Standard Oil companies started investing on a large scale in foreign production of oil, exploring new sources and purchasing foreign oil-producing properties. Before World War One, Jersey Standard Oil acquired stakes in oil extraction in Peru, Romania and the Dutch East Indies. At the same time, New York Standard Oil purchased producing properties in Palestine, Syria and Asia Minor and entered into exploration agreements in China and Venezuela. The selection of these places reflected basically the location of the main known oil reserves at that time.

When, after World War One, fears of oil shortages arose in the United States, its leading oil companies intensified their search for foreign oil to supply, inter alia, the domestic market. In the 1920s and 1930s, Standard Oil like other United States oil companies expanded its exploration and production, *inter alia*, to Russia and several countries in Latin America and in the Middle East. Part of the production was sent back home, and part was sold in third markets. When the United States introduced tariffs on imported oil products in the 1930s, some Standard Oil companies stopped importing into the home country and dealt in oil exclusively in third markets, thus becoming truly international traders.

After World War Two, all major United States oil TNCs expanded FDI activities, with a view towards supplying the rapidly growing markets of Europe and Japan. Access to oil reserves was crucial, because it reduced risks and provided flexibility of supply. With time, investment in marketing surpassed that in production once again; but, in contrast to the period between 1860 and 1940, Standard Oil companies, like other United States-based oil TNCs, used these investments to sell oil of their foreign affiliates all over the world, rather than exporting oil products from the home country.

Sources: Lipsey, 1996; Wilkins, 1970 and 1974.

While the exports of a host country often go to the home country of the parent firms, they can also be destined for third countries, which, sometimes, had been served by exports from the home country, before these were displaced by exports from the host country. This applies, for example, to the United States in the case of copper, lead, petroleum, bauxite, gold and zinc. In particular, the United States oil industry was already selling about two-thirds of its output to foreign markets when it started to undertake overseas investment in oil exploration and extraction (Jones, 1996).

In the second group -- mostly renewable resources industries -- the process normally begins with the demand for resource-related manufactured goods in developed countries being served by independent indigenous companies. Renewable resource products are imported by firms of the home country (as a rule, a developed country), normally in the first instance through arm's length contracts, i.e., by trade between independent companies. Then, for various reasons -- ranging from the minimization of transaction costs (such as the need to ensure the security of supplies, and thus reduce the costs of accommodating potential opportunism on the part of an independent supplier) to the exploitation of economies of scale, and depending on the resource involved -- home-country firms undertake FDI in a backward vertical integration process to internalize markets for raw materials and thus assume control of foreign activities. While in commodities such as sugar, tea, bananas and rubber, foreign-owned plantations became important, in the case of other agricultural raw materials (such as cotton and tobacco) production often remained in the hands of local commercial interests or peasant farmers. In these latter commodities, long-term non-equity contracts with local producers are in some cases arranged directly by home-country processing companies. In other cases, trading TNCs become involved in establishing such contracts, sometimes eventually leading to FDI by these firms in the plantations or other farming operations. For some plantations, imports become almost completely intra-firm through FDI, and so large vertically and horizontally integrated TNCs are created. In the 1950s and 1960s, for example, a high proportion of world trade in bananas was controlled by two United States TNCs, United Fruit and Standard Fruit, both vertically and horizontally integrated (box III.3).

Box III.3. Backward integration in renewable resources

Problems of quality control arising from information asymmetry encouraged the sequential transition from imports to FDI through vertical integration in tropical fruit products, such as bananas. Bananas are highly perishable. Moreover, production is at a distance from the major consumer markets. The shift from arms-length trade to FDI (and therefore intra-firm trade) was undertaken to ensure adequate supplies, and as an important means of quality control. Consistent quality was better assured by vertical integration. Banana production offered few economies of integration, and in fact numerous small producers co-existed with major companies. It was the coordination of production and marketing in which the economies of integration and internalization were found.

Large integrated TNCs also developed in tea and sugar-cane but, in these cases, trading TNCs also played a role in the transition to non-equity contracts and FDI. In the nineteenth century, numerous British tea-plantation companies had flourished in South Asia (an early example of trade giving rise to FDI in purely resource-based TNCs rather than in vertically integrated processing firms), but later they came under the control of large British managing agencies or trading TNCs. In some other British packaging and marketing companies, imports led to FDI again through backward vertical integration into tea production. Most FDI in sugar plantations also took the form of vertical integration -- for instance, United States sugar refineries invested in Cuban sugar factories. However, British sugar plantations in Guyana were bought by Booker McConnell, a trading TNC that also owned a shipping company which transported most of Guyana's sugar to the United Kingdom. In renewable resources especially, trading TNCs had a prominent role in shaping and reinforcing the FDI/trade relationship.

Source: Casson et al., 1982.

Occasionally, this sequence is also followed in resource extraction (mining), especially when trading TNCs from the home country are involved in initiating the supply of raw material imports on behalf of home-country manufacturers. For example, the iron ore industry developed as one in which two-fifths of trade took place under long-term, non-equity contracts between major producers and consumers, while another two-fifths of raw material imports were sold under short-term contracts (Vernon and Levy, 1982). This is also illustrated by metal trading (in particular, German) firms, which served the raw material import needs of home-country metal-processing firms through long term non-equity contracts, and later succeeded in the international vertical integration of mining, smelting, refining, sale and manufacture of the most important non-ferrous metals -- such that non-equity contracts led to FDI, and trading TNCs became extractive and processing companies.

2. Impact of foreign direct investment on trade

The dominant relationship between FDI and trade in natural resources is a linear and sequential one, in which either FDI leads to imports by home countries or imports by home countries lead to FDI (as a result of which those imports become intra-firm trade). In both cases, FDI does not replace trade -- it augments trade. Foreign affiliates play an important role in the primary sector exports of host countries. For instance, in 1992, United States foreign affiliates alone accounted for 11 per cent of primary commodity exports from both developed and developing countries (table III.1); in 1966-1992, their share increased from 7 to 11 per cent in developed host countries and more than halved in developing countries.[6]

Table III.1. Exports by United States majority-owned foreign affiliates in the primary sector from host countries, 1966-1992

(Billions of dollars and percentage)

Countries and items	1966	1977	1982	1985	1989	1992
All host countries						
Host countries' exports of raw materials[a]	77.7	431.8	731.6	648.8	735.5	824.7
Exports by primary sector affiliates[b] as percentage of countries' exports of raw materials	13.8	24.5	13.8	12.4	7.3	10.8
Developing host countries						
Host countries' exports of raw materials[a]	30.9	231.6	361.9	283.9	275.6	336.4
Exports by primary sector affiliates[b] as percentage of countries' exports of raw materials	25.2	35.1	16.3	14.8	8.3[c]	11.2[c]
Developed host countries						
Host countries exports of raw materials[a]	37.9	161.1	285.2	279.8	371.4	447.6
Exports by primary sector affiliates[b] as percentage of countries' exports of raw materials	6.6	10.4	14.6	13.7	7.8[c]	10.5[c]

Sources: United States, Department of Commerce, *US Direct Investment Abroad* (various issues); and UNCTAD, *Handbook of International Trade and Development Statistics* (various issues).

[a]   Including SITC groups 0 through 4.
[b]   Including exports by affiliates in petroleum and "other industries" (agriculture, mining, construction, transportation, communications and retail trade). In 1966, primary sector includes only petroleum and mining.
[c]   Data for Africa, Middle East and New Zealand included in these figures are estimates.

Given the nature of the investments, primary sector foreign affiliates of United States firms are also more export-oriented than manufacturing affiliates, if data for United States firms are indicative. In developing countries in 1966, only 8 per cent of the total sales of manufacturing affiliates were export sales; that ratio was almost 60 per cent for petroleum and close to 90 per cent for mining affiliates (United States, Department of Commerce, 1976). At that time, United States foreign manufacturing affiliates existed to serve their host-country markets; therefore, the majority of host country exports of affiliates from developing countries, almost three quarters in 1966, originated in primary sector affiliates (Lipsey, 1988). Later, this role, relative to both exports of all affiliates and host country exports, declined. It fell also in absolute terms, when exports by foreign affiliates in the primary sector plunged from $81 billion in 1977 to $38 billion in 1992, reflecting the changing relationship between developing host countries and natural resource TNCs. As newly independent developing countries sought to obtain a higher share of the returns from the extraction and exports of their natural resources by foreign affiliates, governments pursued indigenization policies, or nationalized natural resource affiliates to break the link between FDI and trade, though the timing and extent varied.

Since then, the FDI-trade relationship has been gradually redefined. While state companies could sell such products as copper, for which a competitive world market existed, for products like bauxite, in which no open market existed, they often formed joint ventures with TNCs. These provided foreign mineral companies with the benefits more commonly associated with vertical integration (including assured sources of raw materials), without the risks associated with ownership of capital-intensive assets. Joint ventures also provided host countries with the inputs they needed for the successful extraction and/or processing of raw materials, and with an assured market. Non-equity arrangements, too, have grown in importance. At the same time, FDI in natural resources has increased in absolute terms, at least as far as major home and host countries are concerned, and even though the share of natural resources in total FDI stocks in developing countries has not changed much (table III.2). Thus, governments of developing countries and TNCs have established new relationships based more frequently on various non-equity arrangements, contracts and joint ventures.

Table III.2. The primary sector in FDI stock for the largest developed home countries and the largest developed and developing host countries, 1970-1990

(Billions of dollars and percentage)

Countries and sector	1970	1975	1980	1985	1990
Outward stock in primary sector					
Developed countries[a]	29	58	88	115	160
share in total outward stock	22.7	25.3	18.5	18.5	11.2
Inward stock in the primary sector					
Developed countries[a]	12	17	18	39	94
share in total inward stock	16.2	12.1	6.7	9.2	9.1
Developing countries[b]	..	7	17	31	46
share in total inward stock	..	20.6	22.7	24	21.9

Source: UNCTAD, FDI database.

[a]   Australia, Canada, France, Germany, Italy, Japan, Netherlands, United Kingdom and the United States; together these countries accounted for almost 90 per cent of outward and 72 per cent of inward FDI stocks in 1990.

[b]   Argentina, Brazil, Chile, China, Colombia, Hong Kong, Indonesia, Malaysia, Mexico, Nigeria, Philippines, Republic of Korea, Singapore, Taiwan Province of China, Thailand and Venezuela; together these countries accounted for 68 per cent of total inward FDI in developing countries.

Investment in natural resources also leads to associated trade and associated investment. For host countries, FDI can lead to the export of resource-based products, especially where foreign parent firms move into processing and refining and the manufacture and distribution of final products (although most of these activities, typically, were located outside the original host country).[7] For home countries, it can also lead to exports of manufactures. These can be created directly (e.g., as exports of agriculture or mining equipment to host countries), or indirectly (e.g., as exports of manufactured consumer goods to the host country by other firms). But evidence suggests that this effect is not as strong as the positive impact of FDI on home country exports in manufacturing: for the world's largest firms, the positive effect of foreign production on parent company exports has been strongest in research-and-development-intensive manufacturing industries, and weakest in resources-based sectors (Pearce, 1990).

It is, however, important to distinguish between natural resources investments in developed and developing countries. The FDI-trade relationship follows the same path, but in developed countries it tends to overlap more with manufacturing and services, since companies may simultaneously undertake other investments. An example is the investment in the United States by Shell and British Petroleum: extraction was the first important phase, but was combined with associated FDI, e.g., the development of manufacturing (petrochemical plants) and services (filling stations). As a result of the establishment of downstream manufacturing and services facilities in the host country, the relationship between FDI and trade was characterized, from the beginning, by the export of higher value-added products (petrochemicals), and FDI had a more favourable impact on the trade of the host country. Host developing country governments have also sought to integrate natural resource facilities into domestic development, ideally by turning them into growth centres for resource-based industrialization. The objective for some has been to convert foreign-owned ventures, which produced raw materials for export, into national industries exporting and selling domestically processed or manufactured goods. Host developing countries, therefore, have become particularly interested in TNCs willing and able to participate in downstream, higher value-added activities.

C. The services sector

1. The truncated sequence

The provision of many services requires interaction between producers and consumers: since they are non-storable, they have to be produced when and where they are consumed. As a result, they cannot be transported and therefore traded crossborder. Their delivery abroad requires the movement of either producers or consumers, or through affiliates, that is, FDI. In addition, there are services that are so market sensitive that they need to rely on foreign affiliates, even though, in principle, they could be traded (boxes III.4 and 5). Thus, the dominant characteristic of the services sector is that trade as an option to deliver services abroad exists only to a very limited extent, and that firms therefore need to move directly to foreign production (although this may change owing to the increasing tradability of services). When doing so, they frequently use non-equity arrangements and minority joint ventures, although these can also be intermediary steps towards FDI. Naturally, the reasons for choosing non-equity or low- equity forms vary greatly from industry to industry (box III.6).

In any event, as service firms do not enjoy the comfort of a gradual conquest of foreign markets through a linear approach, the linear sequence is truncated. This is one of the reasons for the shift of the world FDI stock towards services in the past 20 years: as services have grown in importance to become the largest sector in the world economy, FDI in services has also expanded, and now accounts for half of the world's FDI stock and 60-65 per cent of FDI flows.

Many service companies take their first steps towards internationalization to support the international activities of their (goods producing) home country customers. Trading companies -- wholesale and marketing companies -- were among the first to establish themselves abroad to support export and/or import activities of home-based manufacturing or primary sector clients. Many banks establish their first offices abroad to serve their home-country clients travelling or living abroad, or their home-country corporate customers exporting or producing abroad. Some needs of both groups of customers can be served through correspondent relationships with foreign banks, but when business grows, the need to establish an office, subsidiary or branch becomes more urgent, given the

---

Box III.4. The truncated sequence of a transportable service: the case of advertising

Unlike trade in many services, trade in advertising has always been technically possible. Ever since there were post services, an ad could be produced in one location and mailed to another destination. With the increasing sophistication of communication and computer techniques, these possibilities have become more apparent. In addition, the output of advertising can be stored and does not have to be consumed simultaneously with production. Yet, the overwhelming portion of international transactions in advertising has always taken place through FDI (Weinstein, 1974).

Foreign delivery of advertising services by United States agencies

(Exports from the United States as per cent of total foreign delivery [a])

1986	1990	1993
3.9	2.5	5.9

Source: United States, Department of Commerce, *Survey of Current Business* (various issues).

[a] Exports plus sales of foreign affiliates in host countries.

There are several reasons for this:

- Successful advertisements have to use good psychology to get potential buyers interested in the products. New York copywriters, no matter how gifted, may have difficulty in striking the right note for an advertising campaign directed to consumers in, say, Latin America. The need to respond to national characteristics of consumers' mentality, determined by factors such as language and culture, requires, in most cases, a presence in the market.

- Much production has to take place abroad because the interaction between the "consumers" of ads and suppliers is difficult to maintain when they are based elsewhere.

- The cost of moving production to another country and setting up a foreign affiliate is relatively cheap because advertising production is less capital-intensive than other services or manufacturing (Terpstra and Yu, 1988). This puts aside an important consideration that could prevent FDI in favour of the trade option.

- Restrictions on foreign-made advertisements in the form of high taxes on ads produced abroad, the prohibition of ads in foreign languages or using foreign actors, and requirements that commercials be filmed locally have in the past been additional factors forcing agencies to set up affiliates in host countries (UNCTC, 1979).

As a result, although advertising services could be traded, their delivery to foreign markets, as well as the sequence of steps in the internationalization of advertising agencies, have always been truncated, because exporting has never been a practical option. Nothing illustrates this better than the growth of one of the oldest advertising agencies, J. Walter Thompson (box III.5).

Source: UNCTAD.

risk of losing business. A similar motive -- "follow thy customer" -- drives advertising and accounting companies abroad (box III.5). In all these cases, exports are not a viable alternative because of the non-transportability of the services involved, or because their nature requires a presence in the market. Once abroad, these service TNCs are also able to capture the business of domestic companies by offering services better or cheaper than those provided by local companies, or both, and/or unique services unavailable in the local markets of host countries (Sauvant and Zimny, 1987, p. 40).

Services TNCs can also go abroad without following customers, to seek new markets, exploiting ownership-specific advantages. Moreover, when competitors in oligopolistic service industries expand abroad, there may be a need to follow them to protect their positions in the oligopoly; such considerations are important in industries like banking, advertising, airlines, insurance and hotels. Another motive can be to produce services which have to be located where the resources are; examples include hotel services or airport facilities.

Box III.5. J. Walter Thompson's internationalization

J. Walter Thompson (JWT) was established in 1878, when a New York businessperson purchased an advertising company and renamed it after himself. During the 1890s, JWT began to expand in the United States, establishing branches in Boston, Chicago and Cincinnati (Henderson, 1960). Its expansion was based on pioneering advertising methods and products.[a]

The agency was the first United States advertising agency to go abroad. The first foreign affiliate was established in the United Kingdom in 1899; it was a small sales office looking for and servicing European advertisers who wished to run campaigns in the United States (West, 1987). Later on, it was turned into a full "production" agency, creating advertising campaigns and selecting and booking media space. The London affiliate followed closely the procedures and production processes developed in the United States. It applied the experience and technical knowledge of the parent company and offered the same standards of services. Those were new in the United Kingdom and were attractive for local clients. The United Kingdom experience, where FDI was, in fact, preceded by an "exporting" office, was possible because, although the affiliate was selling advertising products to foreign clients, it continued to address in these products its known domestic consumers. Besides, the psychological distance between the United States and the United Kingdom was small. The affiliate rapidly became the largest advertising agency in the United Kingdom, servicing both United Kingdom clients and United States TNCs investing in the United Kingdom.

When it came to servicing domestic clients abroad, JWT had to follow them abroad and establish foreign affiliates. Thus, when General Motors Export Corporation chose JWT as its advertising agency in 1927, JWT agreed to open an affiliate in every country in which General Motors had an assembly plant operation or distributor. The reward was that General Motors placed all domestic and international advertising contracts exclusively with JWT (West, 1987). As a result, the international expansion of JWT in the 1920s and 1930s paralleled closely General Motors' international expansion. Within a few years, JWT opened up 10 offices in Europe and another 10 offices in Egypt, South Africa, India, Australia, Canada, New Zealand and South America (Merron, 1991).

The international expansion of JWT has continued since (Buck, 1987). It broadened its clientele to include some of the largest United States manufacturing TNCs, such as Kodak, Kellog and Ford. Much of this expansion took place through mergers and acquisitions of existing local advertising agencies.

In 1987, JWT was acquired by the United Kingdom communications group WPP. The selling price for the agency, which once changed hands for $500, was $566 million. However, it continues to operate independently, and its ties with WPP are mainly financial.

Source: UNCTAD.

[a]   "J. Walter Thompson company", *Fortune*, November 1947, pp. 216-230.

Box III.6. Non-equity arrangements in services

There are four groups of service companies and reasons for the use of non-equity forms:

• Hotels, restaurants, fast-food and car-rental companies. Their preferred way to produce abroad is a management contract or franchising. In most cases, the agreement is sufficient because it protects the contractor's assets related to technology, operating methods or information flows and with respect to the performance of the contractee. On the other hand, non-equity forms do not involve (by definition) equity stakes, which can be both substantial and, in some parts of the world, risky, as in the case of hotels.

• Business and professional services such as accounting, consulting and legal services whose main assets are human capital, reputation, connections and brand names. They do not require expensive fixed assets that could be the basis for capital equity; but their key competitive advantages can be codified and easily transferred and controlled through non-equity arrangements, such as partnerships.

• Business services such as engineering, architectural and technical services, and some advertising requiring adaptation to local tastes, accounting and legal services (especially those whose provision is based on local standards and procedures). Partnerships or minority joint ventures with local partners provide access to local specialized knowledge and facilitate individual customization of products. In such industries as engineering and construction, joint ventures with local firms can help TNCs win contracts from governments of host countries and could, in the past, reduce the risk of nationalization.

• The risk of providing some services in such industries as investment banking and property and casualty insurance is so high that firms prefer that this risk be shared by a consortia.

Sources: Dunning, 1989, p. 53; and UNCTC, 1989, p. 98.

---

2. Impact of foreign direct investment on trade

Little is known about the trade impact of service TNCs. The data that exist for United States TNCs show that parent companies are considerable exporters of services, accounting for a third of total United States service exports and about one quarter of all exports of manufacturing parents in 1989 (table III.3). As a group, they showed a surprisingly high export propensity (6 per cent), even when compared with manufacturing parent firms (11 per cent). How these exports are affected by services FDI is difficult to say. To a large extent, it depends on whether the service is tradable or not.[8] If it is not, there is little or no direct impact. For tradable services (e.g., insurance, re-insurance, consultancy, legal services), exports can be a step in a sequence leading to foreign production which may reduce exports of the service. Foreign direct investment can also have an indirect impact on home-country exports. It may create demand for machinery and equipment necessary for the functioning of the foreign affiliate and/or for information-intensive support services provided either by headquarters personnel travelling to affiliates or via communication lines. This impact is, however, much smaller than that of FDI in manufacturing. For example, the value of manufacturing affiliates' imports from the United States was 14 per cent of total sales of manufacturing affiliates in 1988; for services' affiliates (excluding trading affiliates dealing mainly in goods), the figure was only one per cent (Zimny, 1993, p. 4).

In developing economies, the most obvious indirect impact of foreign service affiliates on trade is that of trading affiliates which help to export goods produced in a host economy. This is especially important in countries that enjoy a comparative advantage in some manufacturing products but have not yet acquired an advantage in marketing those products (UNCTC, 1989, p. 120). Other indirect impacts of FDI in services result from such producer services as financial, transportation, telecommunications, insurance or advertising services, which are inputs into the production of traded goods (and other services). If such services are provided by foreign affiliates because they are not available from local firms or are more efficient than those available from local firms, FDI makes a positive indirect contribution to exports from a host country; these services are then exported indirectly. It is not possible to assess how large the contribution is, but there is evidence that the linkages between exports from host countries and the production of services by foreign affiliates are strong.

Perhaps a proxy indicator of the importance of indirect exports of services can be the high concentration of local sales of foreign service affiliates of United States TNCs in countries with the largest exports of goods by foreign affiliates. In Asia, 86 per cent of local sales of services by foreign affiliates was in six countries, which in turn accounted for over 90 per cent of United States affiliates' exports from the region in 1988. In Latin America, three countries, responsible for 72 per cent of merchandise exports by foreign affiliates, generated 70 per cent of sales of services by foreign affiliates in the region. Among all developing countries, 11 countries accounted for 74 per cent of goods exported and 64 per cent of local sales of services by United States foreign affiliates (Zimny, 1993, p. 34). Finally, there is evidence (UNCTAD, 1994b) that another important group of customers of foreign service affiliates in host developing countries are large domestic companies. These are often large exporters. Services provided by foreign affiliates can therefore be embodied not only in goods exported by other foreign affiliates but also in goods exported by domestic companies.[9]

Thus, the truncated sequence in services means that the interaction between FDI and trade remains limited. But, as noted above, indirect effects on trade in goods can be important. Moreover, as a result of limited tradability, firms that wish to sell their services in foreign markets need to establish affiliates abroad which are miniature versions of parent firms. This means that the factor proportions used at home need to be replicated in host countries, which often includes inputs of skilled human capital. If such capital does not exist in host developing countries, it has to be created by TNCs through training or imported. If new skills spread within the host economy through the turnover of

Table III.3. Exports of services by TNCs from the United States, 1989

(Billions of dollars and per cent)

Item	Exports (Billions of dollars)	Services-export propensity[a] (Per cent)
United States cross-border exports of services	118.2	
Exports of services by TNCs:	48.8	
Petroleum TNCs	1.1	6.0
Manufacturing TNCs	6.1	6.0
Services TNCs	41.7	6.1
Financial services excluding banking	25.8	9.0
Business, rental and hotel services	5.4	5.6
Trading services	0.1	..
Construction	0.1	..
Transportation, communication and public utilities	10.2	3.5
Memorandum:		
Manufacturing TNCs, total exports of goods and services and export propensity	169.7	10.9

Source: United States, Department of Commerce, 1991.

a   Exports as a proportion of total sales.

skilled staff or indirect channels, including demonstration effects and competitive pressures, the pool of human capital of the host economy increases. The recognition of the role that services FDI can play in spreading skills and enhancing the competitiveness of manufactures is broadening the range of issues influencing country policies towards services FDI.

D. The importance of intersectoral linkages

The relationship between FDI and trade has been examined separately for manufacturing, natural resources and services. At the same time, it is evident that there are numerous intersectoral extensions -- that is, FDI and trade in all three sectors are often inextricably intertwined. The following, in particular, needs to be re-emphasized:

- Classifying firms by sector is often a simplification because many perform a spectrum of activities. Natural resources firms in, for example, the petroleum industry, are often integrated from the extraction and transport of resources, through the manufacturing of products to their marketing and distribution. Similarly, many manufacturing firms produce services -- in fact, many are, in the balance of their value added, actually service firms; for example, IBM is a service company, although it appears annually in the list of the United States largest industrial firms. Services firms are perhaps the easiest to classify because, typically, they concentrate on the production of services only, although there are exceptions, such as telecommunication firms producing both services and hardware. To the extent that firms engage in international activities, therefore, what they do can affect FDI or trade, or both, in more sectors than one. The most obvious example is FDI in such services as trading, transportation and financial services by manufacturing TNCs.

- Although the analysis above has focused on the internationalization of individual products through trade and, eventually, FDI, it has also drawn immediate attention to the importance of associated trade and associated investment by the same firm, as well as in the same industry, other industries and, indeed, other sectors.

This crossing of sectoral boundaries, both in a single firm's activities and as regards indirect FDI and trade effects, makes it increasingly difficult to isolate specific trade and investment effects associated with the internationalization sequence of a particular firm and product.

* * *

The interlinkages between FDI and trade are complex. They reflect the differing sequential processes of internationalization of individual products in the different economic sectors. They also need to take into account the intersectoral and indirect effects of trade and FDI in any particular product. In natural resources, trade often leads to FDI, and FDI is necessarily trade-supporting and/ or trade-creating. In manufacturing, in which market-seeking FDI could either replace or complement trade in a particular product, empirical studies suggest that, on balance, FDI and trade at the industry and country levels are positively related to each other. In tradable services, the situation is similar to that in manufacturing. In non-tradable services, the only thing that matters is trade associated with FDI which is, by definition, positively related to FDI.

Thus, what seems to be clear is that, first, trade eventually often leads to FDI; and second, that, on balance, FDI leads to more trade. The result is, therefore, an intensification of international economic transactions. The emergence of integrated international production systems multiplies the intersectoral intertwinedness of investment and trade and makes it increasingly likely that the two support one another, although it also makes it difficult, though not entirely impossible, to project the pattern of the FDI-trade relationship.

Notes

[1] There are, of course, cases in which trade did not precede FDI, such as some British investment in, e.g., breweries in the post-colonial United States and South Africa. Recent examples include FDI by developing country firms in developed countries to acquire technology or foreign manufacturing factories through takeovers.

[2] In fact, the origins of the idea that FDI and home-country exports are substitutes can be traced even further back, to a time when FDI was considered as basically a flow of capital. As such, it could be a substitute for trade as a way of bringing about factor-price equalization (Mundell, 1957).

[3] The author named the phenomenon of production in a foreign country "the new export technique", describing it in the following way: "Not new in the sense of being post-war [World War I], but new in that, although utilized by an increasing number of companies in the past fifty years, it has been adopted by a surprisingly large number within the past decade" (Southard, 1931, pp. 131-132).

[4] This example of the replacement of imports by local production is not usually cited as a successful case of the inducement of FDI and the development of local production. The reason is that local production was characterized by inefficiently small scale and high costs, the bill for which had to be paid by local consumers.

[5] Examples are the United Kingdom (Dunning, 1958, 1985; Steuer, 1973), Portugal (Simoes, 1985), Belgium (van den Bulcke, 1985), Germany (Juhl, 1985), and Sweden (Swedenborg, 1985). However, United States-owned manufacturing affiliates in Australia were concentrated more in import-competing than in export-oriented local industries, perhaps because Australia protected its industries so strongly (Brash, 1966). In the United States, on the other hand, inward FDI was found to be essentially unrelated to the pattern of United States commodity trade (Pugel, 1985). In addition, in such countries as Canada (Safarian, 1966, 1969), Japan (Ozawa, 1985) and France (Michalet and Chevalier, 1985), there is no tendency for foreign affiliates to export more than indigenous firms in the equivalent industries, in contrast to evidence of just such an effect in countries like the Netherlands (Stubenisky, 1970), Belgium (van den Bulcke, 1985), the United Kingdom (Dunning, 1976) and Portugal (Simoes, 1985).

[6] Much of the early FDI in developing countries was, in fact, in natural resources. Developing countries supplied the resources, and TNCs supplied capital, technical expertise and market access. There were only limited markets in developing host countries for raw materials, and few could bear the costs of extraction; the output from these investments was valuable primarily as exports. The historical predominance of natural resources FDI is reflected in the data for the United States. In 1929, investment in primary production was 75 per cent higher than that in manufacturing, although that ratio is inflated by the inclusion of all petroleum operations. However, even a more accurate measure shows FDI in primary production larger than in manufacturing as late as 1957. It was not until 1966 that the data show larger investment in manufacturing. By the mid-1980s, the stock of manufacturing investment was more than twice that in primary products, and close to three times as large if investment in distribution, mainly of manufactured products, is included with manufacturing (United States, Department of Commerce, various years).

[7] This is indicated by the fact that, for example, developing countries accounted in 1982 for 34 per cent of world production of iron ore, but for only 16 per cent of steel production; for 42 per cent of the production of copper ore, but 31 per cent of blister and 21 per cent of refined copper; and for 53 per cent of the production of bauxite, but only 19 per cent of alumina and just 10 per cent of aluminium (Yachir, 1988).

[8] "Exports" and "tradability" focus here on cross-border transactions between residents and non-residents. This is a narrower definition of trade in services than that used in the General Agreement on Trade in Services which includes the following four categories of the international supply of services (GATT, 1994, p. 328):

(a)   from the territory of one country into the territory of any other country;

(b)   in the territory of one country to the service consumer of any other country;

(c)   by a service supplier of one country, through commercial presence in the territory of any other country;

(d)   by a service supplier of one country, through presence of natural persons of a country in the territory of any other country.

9   A study on embodied services trade in Australia found that, on average, 20 per cent of the value of Australian exports consisted of value added by service industries, a remarkable share given that Australia exports mainly natural resources. Projections are that trade in goods will increasingly involve trade in embodied services. Estimates of the total exports of services embodied in goods for Canada (based on the assumption that exports of goods contain the same proportion of services as all goods) suggest such exports are larger than direct exports of services and more dynamic than merchandise exports (Grubel, 1988, p. 72). In case of developing countries, an old study of linkages in Puerto Rico in 1963 found that producer service industries exported directly about 20 per cent of their output. Another 20 per cent were exported indirectly which altogether made these industries a major exporter among 26 industries which were studied (Weisskoff and Wolff, 1977). No studies have been undertaken on the services provided in host developing countries by TNCs and exported indirectly.

Chapter IV

Foreign direct investment and trade relationships in a liberalizing and globalizing world economy

The preceding chapter described the dominant characteristics of the relationship between FDI and trade for the majority of products, firms and industries as they prevail today. But new relationships are emerging, with implications for countries and development. This is due to the changed environment within which firms operate and to which they have to adapt strategies and structures to remain competitive.

A. The new environment for foreign direct investment and trade

In the past thirty years or so, and particularly since the mid-1980s, the environment for international transactions has changed considerably, altering the form and purpose of foreign direct investment (FDI) and the activities of transnational corporations (TNCs), with consequences, in turn, for interlinkages between FDI and trade. The most important changes in the international environment relate to the reduction of technological and policy-related barriers to the movement of goods, services, factors of production and firms and to the fact that international production is now part of the world economy.

- *Improvements in technology.* Progress in information and communication technologies has not only made it possible for firms to process and communicate vastly more information at reduced costs, but to manage, day-to-day, far-flung and widely dispersed production and service networks (UNCTAD-DTCI, 1993a, chapter V). Moreover, advances in combining information and telecommunication technologies have increased the transportability of many information-based services, enabling them to be traded across distances without necessarily being embodied in people or goods. At the same time, advances in transportation have further facilitated the movement of goods and people.

- *Liberalization of policies*. Recent years have witnessed an acceleration in the liberalization of policies governing trade and investment flows, as well as flows of technology and finance capital. Trade liberalization, which began in the post-war years with the General Agreement on Tariffs and Trade, reached a new high with the conclusion of the Uruguay Round, when the average tariff on industrial goods in developed countries had fallen below 4 per cent (GATT, 1994) and many countries had taken steps towards opening services industries to foreign participation. The liberalization of FDI regimes has also proceeded rapidly since the early 1980s, typically with unilateral liberalization of national FDI policies, the conclusion of bilateral investment treaties and the creation of regional, sectoral or multilateral agreements that cover aspects of FDI (chapter V).

- *Rise of international production*. International production is now an integral and important part of the world economy. Numerous TNCs have emerged and established foreign affiliates. For 15 major developed countries, the number of TNCs headquartered in them nearly quadrupled between 1968/1969 and 1993, from 7,000 to 27,000 (table IV.1). Worldwide, there are now almost 40,000 TNCs, with some 270,000 foreign affiliates (not counting non-equity linkages). The number of affiliates per TNC has been rising -- from around four at the beginning of the 1990s to almost seven in the middle of this decade (see chapter I; and UNCTC, 1992a). Most TNCs emerged as a result of sequential, step-by-step processes and most foreign affiliates established in the process were more or less stand-alone.

The liberalization of trade and FDI regimes, along with technological improvements has:

Table IV.1. Number of parent TNCs, by country, 1968/1969 and 1993

Country	1968/1969	1993
United States	2 468	3 013
United Kingdom	1 692	1 443 [a]
Germany	954	7 003
France	538	2 216
Switzerland	447	3 000 [b]
Netherlands	268	1 608
Sweden	255	3 520 [c]
Belgium and Luxembourg	253	96 [d]
Denmark	128	800 [a]
Italy	120	445
Norway	94	1 000
Austria	39	838
Spain	15	744 [a]
Portugal	5	1 165
Total of above	7 276	26 891
World	..	38 747

Source: UNCTAD.

[a] For 1992.
[b] For 1985.
[c] For 1995.
[d] For 1978.

- Improved access to foreign markets, so that firms can choose more freely the modality -- FDI, trade, licensing, subcontracting, franchising -- they prefer to serve these markets and organize production.

- Improved access to foreign factors of production so that firms can obtain more easily and widely what they need for production, including such non-mobile resources as unskilled, cheap labour and competitive price-quality combinations of skilled labour and human resources for research and development.

- Permitted firms to capitalize on the tangible and intangible assets available throughout their corporate systems to maximize the overall efficiency of their systems.

- Created larger markets, giving firms greater opportunities to expand, but also leading to increased regional and global competitive pressures on firms, forcing them to look continuously for ways to stay competitive.

- Changed the relative importance of different factors that determine the location of FDI. Most importantly, tariff and non-tariff barriers have been lowered considerably and, so, one of the most important traditional FDI determinants, the size of national markets, has decreased in importance. At the same time, cost differences between locations, the quality of infrastructure, the ease of doing business and the availability of skills have become more important.

The potential dynamic of this situation lies in the interaction of these factors, each fuelling the other: enabled by liberalization and made possible by progress in technology, competition among firms drives more firms to exploit the new environment in the most optimal manner to maintain or increase competitiveness. Opportunities that arise when the operating framework becomes global need to be seized -- lest one risks losing to the competition. For many firms, this means that the traditional objectives of FDI -- to seek national markets for manufactured goods or services or to seek a regular flow of location-specific resources at the right price -- becomes easier, or FDI is no longer needed as much as before to reach national markets that were protected by trade barriers. At the same time, FDI that facilitates or generates trade benefits from the removal of FDI restrictions.

In some industries, however, firms, regardless of size or the country in which they are located, no longer have a choice whether or not to partake in the regionalization or globalization of their activities to stay competitive. But they have more choices than before as regards which modality to use for this purpose, and they need to consider them consciously. Increasingly, such choices are not only to obtain or expand access to markets and resources, but to combine markets and resources through production and trade, with a view towards creating new sources of competitiveness and strengthening existing ones. In these efforts, TNCs have inherent advantages over others, arising out of their corporate systems (each comprising a parent company and its affiliates) that they have already in place. Their portfolio of locational assets becomes increasingly important (UNCTAD-DTCI, 1995a, Part Two). Firms that do not have such a portfolio may need to acquire it. Firms that have already a dispersed collection of stand-alone foreign (and domestic) affiliates have an opportunity to turn these, in the framework of complex integration strategies, into integrated international production systems that transform global inputs into outputs for global markets. Competitive pressures push them to do so to reap economies of geographical diversification and integration of production. "Efficiency-seeking" FDI -- FDI that seeks to optimize gains from integrating geographically dispersed manufacturing and service activities within their corporate systems -- is the hallmark of those TNC strategies that are responding directly to the new environment. The specialization associated with efficiency-seeking FDI may be based on particular products, processes or functions.

The new environment and its implications are relevant not only for large firms from developed countries, but also for firms from developing countries and for small and medium-sized enterprises. Some pressures are not new, and have manifested themselves earlier in simple integration strategies which involved limited specialization and integration between parent firms and individual foreign affiliates (UNCTAD-DTCI, 1993a). What is new is the more complex form that efficiency-oriented strategies are taking, the extent to which value-added activities are fragmented and dispersed and the growing scale on which this is happening. This makes it all the more important to look at the relationship between trade and FDI under conditions of integrated international production.

B. Foreign direct investment and trade: the relationship in the new environment

1. The decreasing relevance of the sequence

Even in today's rapidly changing economic environment, establishing operations in a foreign country requires that some disadvantages are overcome. Thus, the need for ownership advantages to offset these disadvantages still holds good, especially knowledge-based assets that are unique to a firm. Similarly, greater risk is attached -- or perceived by many firms -- to operating in a foreign environment which gives exports an advantage. For these reasons, most firms still need to develop ownership-specific advantages, generally through home-based innovation and production, before producing abroad. Thus, the sequential process still holds good for most firms and products.

For more and more firms and established TNCs, however, the sequence may change in several ways:

- The process can be speeded up either through a faster progression from one step to the next, or through leapfrogging directly to FDI. There is some evidence that this is happening. For example, a study of 228 outward direct investments from Australia (65 per cent of which originated in 1970-1979) showed that, in 39 per cent of the cases, there was no pre-existing host country presence (Welch and Luostarinen, 1993, p. 163). Support for the idea of leapfrogging is also provided by an empirical study of Swedish firms which moved into the Japanese market directly through FDI (Hedlund and Kverneland, 1983). Leapfrogging over steps in the traditional process is more likely to occur in high-technology firms: a survey of 807 British companies found that "low technology manufacturing companies in general followed the process of exports before investment more frequently than high-technology companies" (United Kingdom, Department of Trade and Industry, 1996, p. 19). Mergers and acquisitions make leapfrogging easier.

- The sequence can begin anywhere within a TNC system, i.e., no longer only in the home country. Innovation and production can be undertaken by a foreign affiliate and the sequence starts from there. A variation is that foreign affiliates get product mandates, i.e., the responsibility for a product, product group or activity, including research and development, marketing and sales, for the corporate system as a whole. For example:[1] at BASF (Germany), cancer and immune-system research is carried out in the company's affiliate located in the United States, and the results are disseminated to pharmaceutical companies around the world directly or through affiliates located in different countries; at Rhône Poulenc (France), the production and distribution of vaccines is controlled by a Canadian affiliate (box IV.1); and at Nestlé, the company's confectionery business is operated by its United Kingdom affiliate.

Thus, to the extent that TNCs convert their collection of foreign affiliates into more integrated international production systems, the sequence of internationalization can be compressed, or certain stages skipped, and it can begin anywhere in the corporate system.

Box IV.1. Product innovation and internationalization by affiliates: the case of Rhône Poulenc

In 1989, the Institut Merieux, an affiliate of Rhône Poulenc (France), was merged with Connaught Bio Sciences (Canada). This was an attempt by Rhône Poulenc to obtain better access to the United States vaccine market; it also resulted in the centralization of research and development of vaccines in the Canadian affiliate. With more than $700 million in sales in 1994, the affiliate is the world's largest manufacturer of human vaccines. All research is carried out by the Canadian affiliate for global customers. Once a new product is developed, it is introduced to all major markets simultaneously for therapeutic testing.

Source: Rhône Poulenc, *Annual Reports*, 1994 and 1995.

---

2. Integrated international production and the relationship between foreign direct investment and trade

(a) Complex integration strategies and corporate systems of production and trade

In complex integration strategies, any value-added activity can be located, at least in principle, in any part of a TNC system, and integrated with other activities performed elsewhere to produce goods for national, regional or global markets. The decision of where to locate an activity is based on its expected contribution to the overall performance of the corporate system as a whole. A firm's organizational structure becomes correspondingly complex, involving multi-directional linkages and flows within the firm and with unrelated firms.[2] The first signs of this strategy were that not only foreign affiliates in natural resources but also in manufacturing and services began to export, first to their parent firms and then to other foreign affiliates -- the beginnings of an international division of labour within corporate systems. Before the more recent broad-based liberalization of international transactions, regional integration efforts were particularly conducive to the creation of integrated international production systems (boxes IV.2 and IV.3).

The pursuit of integrated strategies by TNCs may involve either vertical or horizontal integration, depending upon product characteristics and marketing portfolios and the type of FDI that they are undertaking. Vertical integration involves the geographic dispersion of interrelated activities that are located at different points along the value-added chain of a particular product among affiliates and even unaffiliated firms (e.g., through outsourcing). The integration takes place where it is most efficient to deliver the final product to national, regional or global markets. Vertical integration is driven mainly by country-specific differences in resource availability or resource cost (generally resulting in simple integration), by differences in cost-productivity combinations, transport costs, and by plant- and firm-level economies of scale. It is particularly relevant to the integration of TNCs' value-added activities in developing countries with those in developed countries. Horizontal integration involves the geographic dispersion of production of a differentiated product among the units of a corporate system, and is driven mainly by market specifications and, again, economies of scale, especially at the firm level. It is more likely to occur with respect to the operations of TNCs

---

Box IV.2. Integrated international production in the automobile industry: Toyota's network for auto parts in South-East Asia

Exports of motor vehicles from Japan amounted to nearly four million vehicles in 1995. About 32 per cent were by the Toyota Motor Company, which exported almost 38 per cent of domestic production. In addition, Toyota's overseas production increased from 152,000 vehicles in 1985 to 1,253,300 in 1995 -- more than a third of its total automobile production. In 1995, the number of vehicles produced overseas by Toyota exceeded, for the first time, its exports from Japan. At the end of 1995, Toyota had some 143,000 employees, more than 70,000 outside Japan.

Toyota has established integrated manufacturing systems in all three of its main markets -- North America, Europe and Asia. At the end of 1995, Toyota had 35 overseas manufacturing affiliates in 25 countries, more than a third of which were in Asia. Plants in China, Indonesia, Malaysia, Philippines, Taiwan Province of China and Thailand produced 370,962 vehicles, nearly a third of the company's overseas production in 1995.

Although Toyota's vehicle production in the region, as elsewhere, partly results from Asian countries' restrictions on imports of automobiles, the company has responded to the regional industrial cooperation policies of the ASEAN countries by establishing (in consultation with individual governments) a network of affiliates for parts supply to local and regional markets (including Japan). Toyota's intra-firm trade of parts and components in the region is coordinated by the Toyota Motor Management Company in Singapore (see accompanying figure). Toyota exports diesel engines from Thailand, transmissions from the Philippines, steering gears from Malaysia and engines from Indonesia. In 1995, intra-firm exports among these affiliates accounted for about 20 per cent of exports of parts and components of the company's manufacturing affiliates worldwide. Exports of these affiliates geared to other destinations outside the ASEAN market accounted for another 5 per cent.

Toyota also plans to undertake specialized production of various models in its Asian affiliates, both for local sales and exports within and/or outside the region. These include Toyota's all purpose-vehicle (the Kijang) in Indonesia and a compact car in Thailand for possible exports in Asia but also to destinations in South America and the Middle East.

Transaction amount of parts and components in 1995: $100 million

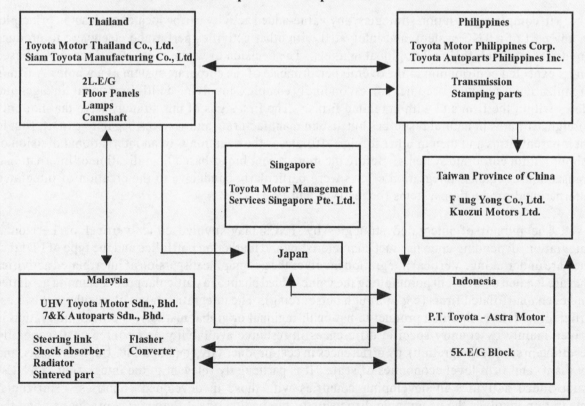

Source: UNCTAD, based on Toyota, 1994 and 1996, "The automobile industry: Toyota and Japan"; Toyota, 1994 and 1995 annual reports; WTO, 1995, pp. 109-114; and OECD, 1992 and 1994.

Box. IV. 3. Honda's European Union network of operations in motorcycles

Honda Motor of Japan has 100 affiliates in marketing, production and research and development outside Japan. It is the world's largest producer of motorcycles, although the majority of its sales now is from cars. Honda has established production facilities for motorcycles in Asia, Europe and North America.

Honda's activities in Europe began with the direct exporting of made-in-Japan models of motorcycles, quickly followed (in 1961) by FDI in Germany for marketing support and after-sales service. This was almost immediately followed by the establishment (in 1962) of Honda Benelux N.V. (Belgium), Honda's first overseas production affiliate to assemble and market a limited variety of models suitable for local tastes and for exporting to nearby markets in the rest of Europe. The company's quick -- indeed almost simultaneous -- move from exports alone to FDI was aimed at establishing strong bonds with its customers, a key consideration for competitiveness in the automotive industry. In Honda's case, a further consideration was that overseas motorcycle production represented a learning process for the overseas production of cars in order to enter automobile production for which the domestic market in Japan was already dominated by earlier entrants, Nissan and Toyota. In other words, motorcycle production abroad was also -- and quite considerably -- useful as a way of gaining information and experience for car production abroad.

The success of its first affiliate in production (and marketing) was critical for building much needed confidence in the company in its ability to manage industrial relations successfully, as well as assemble motorcycles cost-effectively, using local labour in a Western environment. The experience proved invaluable for Honda's subsequent ventures abroad, especially for a motorcycle assembly plant (in 1977) and, later, a car assembly plant, in Ohio, United States.

Honda's European operations in motorcycles are closely integrated and, moreover, have supply links with Japan, the United States and Brazil (see accompanying figure):

- After Honda Benelux N.V., other key assembly affiliates were set up: Honda Italia Industriale (Italy), wholly-owned, in 1977, and Montessa Honda (Spain), majority owned (88 per cent), in 1987. All started as final assemblers of different models, differentiated mainly by size, engine power, engineering features and style in response to the different demand conditions in each local market. They were designed to ship out models to each other, making each location an integral part of joint production and marketing. Such an arrangement results in economies of scale in production and in joint distribution and marketing, since any given model is produced only at one location, but a full line of models is offered in all locations.[a]

- A line of models from these European affiliates, as well as from other production sites (United States, Brazil and Japan), is also shipped and marketed to all other European markets, including the United Kingdom, as well as the United States and Japan. Some models are exported to developing countries. At the same time, Honda of America (United States) exports large motorcycles (CC 1500) to Europe, and Moto Honda da Amazonia Ltda (Brazil) exports medium-size motorcycles (CC 125).

- Initially, engines and key parts were supplied from Japan. But in 1985, Honda acquired a 25 per cent stake in Peugeot Motorcycles (France) and started producing small engines for scooters or mopeds that were supplied to both Honda Italia Industriale and Montessa Honda. Likewise, Honda Italia Industriale began to manufacture medium-size engines for its models, as well as for Montessa Honda. The engines for large-size models were still supplied from Japan. Montessa Honda currently produces no engines, but makes frames and other parts and components locally.

In 1995, Honda Benelux stopped producing motorcycles and shifted to production of car parts. In 1996, Honda's Italian operation is expected nearly to double output of motorcycles to 80,000 units, emerging as Honda's production base for the European Union. About 60 per cent of output is shipped to other markets. Its Spanish plant presently produces 45,000 units, about 70 per cent of which is exported.

Simultaneously, Honda's affiliates in Germany have become regional headquarters, coordinating production and marketing throughout the European Union. Research and development, engineering and designing for all European motorcycle models are also being carried out at Honda R&D Europe (Germany). Honda's German operations have thus emerged as the nerve centre for all its affiliates in the European Union.

To conclude, Honda has been, step by step, rationalizing its European network of operations in motorcycles. To begin with, it skipped the conventional sequence of internationalization that begins with export, by starting almost at the outset of its entry into Europe with FDI, followed by further FDI in several locations. It then took advantage of the increasingly liberalized framework for trade and investment within the European Union to integrate its European Union operations, both horizontally, through affiliate specialization in particular models of motorcycles, as well as vertically, through specialization of affiliates in the region in the production of intermediate products.

/...

(Box IV.3, cont'd)

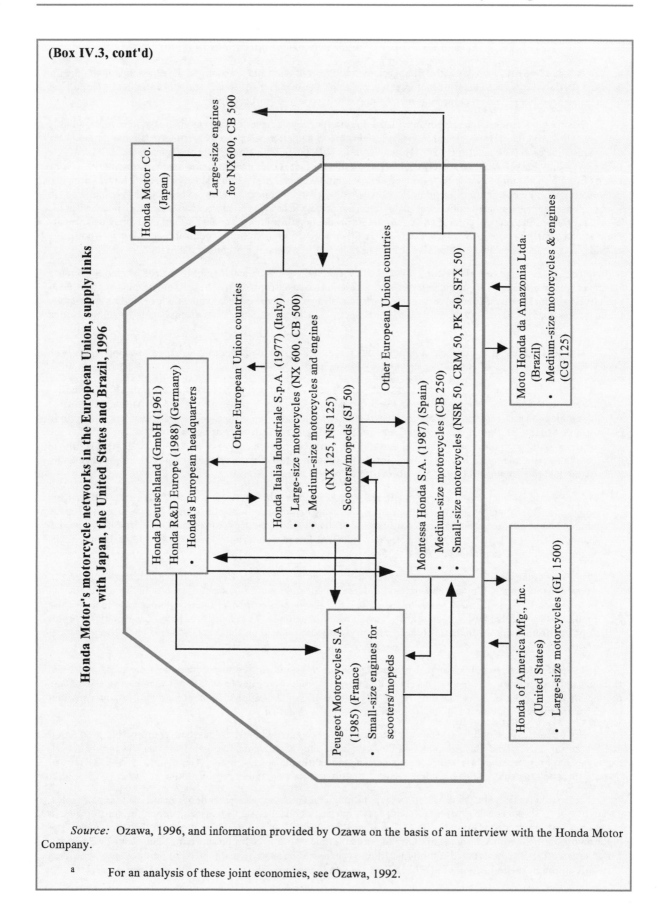

Honda Motor's motorcycle networks in the European Union, supply links with Japan, the United States and Brazil, 1996

Source: Ozawa, 1996, and information provided by Ozawa on the basis of an interview with the Honda Motor Company.

a   For an analysis of these joint economies, see Ozawa, 1992.

in advanced industrialized countries. In both cases, the result of such strategies is to create, for each TNC, a network of intra-firm and (in the case of certain kinds of vertical integration), inter-firm relationships within which resources, information, goods and services flow.

(b) Intra-firm trade

Intra-firm trade across national boundaries is an essential feature of all international production through FDI and has reached considerable proportions relative to countries' trade: the share of intra-firm exports by parent firms based in the country and affiliates of foreign firms located in the country in total exports of the country ranges from 38 per cent in the case of Sweden to 24 per cent in the case of Japan. The corresponding share of intra-firm imports in total country imports ranges form 14 per cent in Japan to 43 per cent in the United States.[3] The geographical extension of a firm through FDI involves -- even in stand-alone affiliates -- flows of intermediate goods and services from one or more members of a corporate system to others. However, the volume of intra-firm flows tends to increase, and the direction and nature of intra-firm flows and their geographic spread to change with the complexity of corporate integration. Indeed, such flows are an indicator of the degree of integration of production and geographical dispersion within TNCs. Many flows are not measured and reported, especially as far as the provision of services within transnational corporate systems is concerned. To the extent that they are reported -- especially the intra-firm flow of goods -- they are one of the most important indicators of the manner and extent in which FDI and trade are intertwined in a globalizing economic environment.

Within the traditional structures of manufacturing TNCs pursuing multidomestic strategies and generating FDI-trade linkages, intra-firm sales tend to be limited, comprising mainly flows of equipment and services from parent firms to each of their affiliates. In simple integration strategies, the direction of intra-firm trade is affected by the positioning of foreign affiliates in the value chain of a TNC's international production system. If foreign affiliates are located downstream, intra-firm trade consists mainly of parent firms' exports to affiliates; if they are upstream suppliers, they generate intra-firm imports for parent companies. With the growing importance of efficiency-seeking FDI by firms pursuing complex regional or global strategies, a multiplicity of linkages develops, and intra-firm trade becomes more important for TNCs, due to increased specialization and geographic dispersion of activities. Intra-firm sales are, moreover, no longer confined mainly to flows between parent firms and affiliates in one or both directions; *inter-affiliate* flows (exports of affiliates to one another) within TNC systems assume greater importance. In fact, the patterns of the latter are more important indicators of complex corporate integration strategies as they signal the emergence of true international corporate systems.

Data on trade by United States parent firms and their affiliates abroad illustrate the high and growing importance of intra-firm trade for TNCs. During 1983-1993, the share of intra-firm exports in total exports of United States parent firms rose from 34 per cent to 44 per cent; and the share of intra-firm imports in total imports rose from 38 per cent to almost one half. At the same time, the shares of intra-firm exports in total exports, and of intra-firm imports from parent firms in total imports from the United States, of United States foreign affiliates rose from 55 per cent to 64 per cent and from 83 per cent to 86 per cent, respectively (table IV.2). In manufacturing alone, the figures are considerably higher (and, for some industries, reach three quarters of the total), and are also increasing. For foreign affiliates, the share of intra-firm trade in their total trade reached in 1993 80-90 per cent in some manufacturing industries (table IV.2). Data for TNCs based in Japan (MITI, 1996) and Sweden,[4] as well as for parent firms and affiliates operating in France,[5] confirm the importance of intra-firm trade in several manufacturing industries, especially those characterized by high research-and-development intensities and firm-level economies of scale.[6]

When it comes to patterns of intra-firm trade, data show, indeed, that the intra-firm division of labour within United States TNC systems (parent firms and foreign affiliates) has become more complex: affiliate-to-affiliate exports within the same corporate systems have increased in importance as a share of total intra-firm trade from 30 per cent in 1977 to 44 per cent in 1993 (table IV.3). Trade with other foreign affiliates was particularly striking for developed country affiliates (where it accounted for almost half of total intra-firm exports in 1993), reflecting greater integration within the parts of TNC systems located in those countries (and especially those in Europe). However, it was also noticeable for developing-country affiliates, although with geographical variations (table IV.3).

If exports from parent firms to foreign affiliates are excluded and only intra-firm exports by foreign affiliates are considered, the shift towards increased trade among foreign affiliates within United States TNC systems is even more impressive: worldwide, the share of exports by these affiliates to other foreign affiliates in total intra-firm exports of such affiliates rose from 37 per cent in 1977 to 60 per cent in 1993 (table IV.3). In 1983-1993, it rose faster for developing country affiliates -- particularly those located in Asia -- than for developed country-based affiliates.

(c) The increasing tradability of services

The new environment can also be expected to bring about fundamental changes in the way in which international production is organized in the services sector. So far, foreign affiliates in this sector have largely been stand-alone clones of their parent corporations. Although, if United States data can be generalized, export propensities of foreign service affiliates are relatively high (table IV.4), the low share of intra-firm trade suggests that the intra-firm division of labour in this sector is still quite underdeveloped.[7]

Table IV.2. Shares of intra-firm trade in the international trade of United States parent companies and their foreign affiliates, by industry, 1983 and 1993

(Percentage)

	Parent firms				Foreign affiliates[a]			
	Share of intra-firm exports in total exports		Share of intra-firm imports in total imports		Share of intra-firm exports in total exports[b]		Share of intra-firm imports in total imports[c]	
Sector and industry	1983	1993	1983	1993	1983	1993	1983	1993
Petroleum	13.8	32.1	21.8	30.5	47.8	47.3	54.8	75.8
Mining	8.6	..	..	..	19.4	15.5	43.7	79.2
Manufacturing	43.0	48.5	60.6	63.4	70.3	74.2	83.4	82.5
General machinery	61.5	74.9	74.9	75.8	76.1	84.3	92.7	87.0
Electronics	32.6	39.2	54.1	45.2	73.1	76.6	89.2	93.2
Transport equipment	49.3	45.9	84.5	77.0	89.3	87.9	81.3	76.1
Wholesale trade	9.2	13.8	6.2	10.3	37.5	57.0	88.6	93.4
All industries	33.8	44.4	37.9	48.6	55.2	64.0	82.8	85.5

Source: UNCTAD, based on United States, Department of Commerce, 1986a and 1995a.

a   Data relate to non-bank majority-owned foreign affiliates of non-bank United States parent firms.

b   Shares of foreign affiliates' exports to the respective parent companies and to other affiliates of those companies in total exports of the affiliates.

c   Shares of foreign affiliates' imports from the respective parent companies in total imports from the United States. (Data on foreign affiliates' imports from other affiliates, and on their imports from other countries are not available.)

This, however, can be expected to change, given the growing transportability of some services. In particular, rapid technological developments in telecommunications and computers in the 1980s have made some services, especially information-intensive ones, more tradable by providing "the means for overcoming the inherent obstacle to trade in many services -- the intangibility, non-storability, and hence non-transportability of these services" (Sauvant, 1990, p. 116). The affected service industries include financial services, consulting and engineering, professional services, international reservation services in the air transportation and hotel industries, research and development, education and data services and information-intensive operations in other industries (UNCTAD, 1993; UNCTAD-DTCI, 1994b; and UNCTAD, 1995b). One implication of the increased tradability of information-intensive services is that this may reduce the need for FDI to deliver those services to foreign markets: trade options are created for firms that, in the past, could not serve foreign markets or had to serve them through foreign affiliates or the temporary movement of labour. In other words, tradability overcomes truncated internationalization of firms and of the delivery of service products abroad, making affected service products more like manufacturing products in their options to enter foreign markets.

Beyond that, information technologies are beginning to change the way in which service TNCs (as well as service-producing departments of other TNCs) can carry out their operations: they can increasingly split production processes into parts and allocate some operations to foreign affiliates in

Table IV.3: Value and relative importance of exports of United States foreign affiliates to other foreign affiliates of United States TNCs, by region and country, 1977, 1983 and 1993[a]

(Billions of dollars and percentage)

	1977			1983			1993		
	Value	Share in total intra-firm exports[b]	Share in total intra-firm exports of foreign affiliates	Value	Share in total intra-firm exports[b]	Share in total intra-firm exports of foreign affiliates	Value	Share in total intra-firm exports[b]	Share in total intra-firm exports of foreign affiliates
Developed economies	35.0	46	67	58.7	46	65	140.5	49	67
Canada	0.9	4	8	1.1	3	5	1.7	2	4
Europe	33.3	68	85	55.8	70	85	132.4	71	86
Japan	0.5	30	56	0.9	28	52	4.3	27	53
Developing economies	12.6[c]	15[c]	16[c]	14.3	26	31	27.3	29	40
Latin America	4.9	29	34	9.3	36	43	8.6	21	33
Mexico	0.1	12	33	0.2	7	18	0.8	4	8
Other Latin America	4.8	30	34	9.2	40	44	7.9	36	47
Developing Asia	2.2	23	27	3.0	16	20	16.6	35	46
Hong Kong	1.0	36	41	0.8	25	34	2.2	23	35
Singapore	0.3	23	30	0.5	10	13	8.8	43	50
Republic of Korea	..	..	..	0.1	10	17	0.3	16	32
Malaysia	0.2	28	40	0.8	30	46	1.8	37	46
Taiwan Province of China	..	..	..	0.2	12	16	1.2	34	52
All economies	49.8	30	37	73.0	40	53	167.8	44	60

Source: UNCTAD, based on United States, Department of Commerce, 1981, 1986a, and 1995a.

[a]   Data relate to exports by non-bank majority-owned affiliates of United States parent firms.
[b]   Total intra-firm exports include parent-to-affiliates, affiliates-to-parent and affiliates-to-affiliates exports.
[c]   Data for Africa, Middle East and Israel included in these figures are estimates.

accordance with factor costs or other considerations. The result is that foreign affiliates no longer need to be free-standing and miniature versions of parent firms. Rather, they can fulfil specialized tasks in the framework of a global intra-firm division of labour, and trade the results via international communication networks. One consequence is to extend the integrated international production systems of all TNCs into the international production of services.

An example of this development is the export of data services from developing countries. Such exports arise from decisions by firms to transfer labour-intensive service parts of their production processes to foreign affiliates in countries that can produce these services cheaper. For TNCs from the United States, such outsourcing was initiated years ago, but expanded greatly in the 1980s. While initially only simple services requiring low- or semi-skilled labour were involved (e.g., mailing lists), more recently highly skilled operations such as the development of computer systems and software, programming, engineering, design and system analysis are outsourced (box IV.4).

Table IV.4. Export and import propensities of United States majority-owned foreign affiliates in services, 1982, 1989 and 1993

(Percentage)

Industry of affiliate	Export propensity[a]			Import propensity[b]		Net export propensity[c]	
	1982	1989	1993	1982	1989	1982	1989
Services	36.0	26.7	26.8[d]	5.3	7.3	30.7	19.4
Construction	9.5	..	15.2	1.2	..	8.3	..
Transportation		27.1	26.6[e]		0.1	..	27.0
Communications and public utilities	9.2	..	..	1.3	..	7.9	..
Petroleum services	40.4	29.8	30.6	8.2	2.0	-2.6	27.8
Wholesale trade	41.7	29.4	30.1	12.4	12.9	29.3	16.5
Retail trade	2.2	1.6	3.1	2.8	3.3	-0.6	-1.7
Finance, excluding banks	37.8	25.5	26.9	0.0	0.0	37.7	25.5
Finance	53.9	24.8	33.2	0.0	..	53.9	..
Insurance	26.3	25.5	20.2	0.0	..	26.3	..
Business and other services[f]	19.8	25.1	19.3	1.5	1.5	18.3	23.6
Management consulting and public relation services	69.2	47.6	30.1	..	..	..	..
Computer and data-processing services	15.4	17.4	18.6	..	..	..	..
Engineering and architectural services	27.8	27.8	19.3	..	..	..	..
Goods	33.5	34.2	38.7	8.7	11.0	24.8	23.2
Primary[g]	63.5	78.9	41.5	2.1	5.3	61.4	73.6
Petroleum and coal	16.6	20.4	30.1	0.6	0.9	16.0	19.5
Manufacturing	33.9	36.5	40.3	12.8	13.2	21.1	23.3
All industries	34.6	31.3	34.0	7.2	9.5	27.4	21.8
Memorandum:							
Services net of trading, including petroleum trading	..	24.7	23.3[d]	..	0.9	..	23.9

Source: UNCTAD, based on United States, Department of Commerce, various years.

[a]   Exports of goods and services as percentage of total sales (local plus exports).
[b]   Based on total imports (goods and services) from the United States only.
[c]   Equals export minus import propensity.
[d]   Excluding transport and communications.
[e]   Based on exports to United States only.
[f]   Including over 25 service industries, from hotels to health and legal services to certification and testing services.
[g]   Agriculture and mining.

Box IV.4. The growth of the global office

Offshore back offices are similar for most firms. Materials, usually documents or magnetic media, are sent by air from the United States, Canada or Europe to processing facilities offshore. Processing usually takes the form of data entry, statistical analysis or information processing that involves decision making by trained employees. After processing, the results are returned to originating data-processing locations by courier, air freight, dedicated line, satellite or telephone modem. The turnaround time for offshore offices varies from several days to weeks, depending on the urgency and complexity of the work. The scale of offshore back offices is substantial. For example:

- New York Life insurance clients mail their health insurance claim forms to an address at Kennedy Airport in New York. The claims are sent overnight to Shannon Airport in Ireland, and then by courier to the firm's processing centre in Castleisland, about 60 miles from Shannon. The processing affiliate is linked via transatlantic telecommunication lines to the parent company. After processing, the claims are returned by dedicated line to the insurance firm's data-processing centre in New Jersey, and checks or responses are printed out and mailed to the clients. The motivation to move a part of the production process of insurance payments to Ireland was twofold: lower labour costs and difficulties in finding enough skilled personnel to process insurance claims at home. In addition to savings on labour costs, the company makes more use of its computers which are operated from Ireland in off-hours.

- American Airlines assembles accounting material and ticket coupons in Dallas, Texas, for transport on its scheduled flights to Barbados for processing by its offshore subsidiary, AMR Information Services/Caribbean Data Services. In Barbados, details of 800,000 American Airlines tickets are entered daily on a computer screen, and the data are returned by satellite to its data centre in the United States.

- Data entry for the white pages telephone directory for Montreal was handled on a contract basis in Asia, using labour intensive double entry, with two workers entering data and then checking for errors by electronic comparison of files.

While these are only examples, all indications are that a greater division of labour in the international production of services is emerging.

Source: Wilson, 1992, pp. 6-8, and "The growth of the global office," *New York Times*, 18 October 1988.

---

3. Evidence from selected regions

The new environment for international transactions and its impact on the interrelationship between FDI and trade can best be observed in regions within which the frameworks for trade and FDI have been considerably liberalized; which have a substantial complement of foreign affiliates in their economies; and in which the countries are all in a similar position to use progress in communication and transportation technologies.

The European Union is such a region, and the response of TNCs to European integration, and the changes in their patterns of FDI and trade are, therefore, instructive. So are the experiences of developing countries in Asia and Latin America: both regions had a sizeable complement of foreign affiliates and had comparable access to communication and transportation technologies, but differed in the degree of liberalization implemented until recently.

(a) Europe

Perhaps the best example of the movement from a simple to complex FDI-trade relationship -- in fact, a laboratory in this respect -- is European economic integration. Before 1 January 1958, when the European Common Market was formed, Europe was divided into segmented markets, each protected by substantial tariff and non-tariff barriers. For this reason, as well as the shortage of United States dollars at that time (which limited imports), foreign firms, including firms from the United

States, had little choice but to engage in FDI in each of these segmented markets if they wished to sell to European consumers.

As first tariff, and later non-tariff barriers were lowered within Europe, United States firms found that a large, dynamic market was emerging and that they could organize their new investments -- and restructure existing ones -- in the European Community in such a way as to take advantage of economies of scale and specialization within the framework of a regional strategy of production and marketing. This led to a big increase in United States FDI in Europe, increased plant specialization in Europe by multiproduct United States TNCs, and increased intra-European exports, which were often also intra-firm exports. This can be indirectly observed in the changing distribution of affiliate sales to local (national) markets in Europe, to the United States, and to third markets (including markets of other European Community member countries). Thus, while, in 1957, 85 per cent of affiliates' sales were directed to customers in local national markets, 1 per cent went to the United States and 14 per cent to other markets, mainly in Europe (Dunning 1996), the share to other markets increased over time, to reach 31 per cent in 1993 (table IV.5). In 1966 and 1977, half of the exports to these other (mainly European) markets were to other affiliates, a share that increased to 59 per cent in 1993 (table IV.5). This process of rationalization of production by United States TNCs has particularly influenced manufacturing affiliates: they have steadily become less oriented towards local markets and more towards markets of other countries (table IV.5). Thus, progress in the liberalization of international transactions within Europe allowed United States TNCs to integrate better their European production which was then reflected in increased intra-European Union and increased intra-firm trade (see also UNCTC, 1993).

At the same time, the growth of FDI and its reorganization within Europe has not detracted from the growth of United States parent firm exports to affiliates in Europe since the early 1980s (table IV.6). With a few exceptions -- noticeably in industries producing goods that are less dependent on product or process innovation (e.g., food, drink and tobacco) and in certain services -- the pattern also holds good at the industry level.

Table IV.5. The distribution of sales by affiliates of United States TNCs located in Europe between the local market, United States and other foreign markets, 1966-1993

(Billions of dollars and percentage)

	1966	1977	1982	1986	1989	1993
Total sales	41	220	364	397	573	716
Manufacturing affiliates only	22	104	145	191	292	356
Share of sales to the local market (per cent of total sales)	76	66	63	63	66	64
Manufacturing affiliates only	74	62	59	58	59	57
Share of sales to the United States (per cent of total sales)	2	4	5	4	5	4
Manufacturing affiliates only	2	2	2	4	6	4
Share of sales to other foreign countries (per cent of total sales)	22	30	33	33	29	31
Manufacturing affiliates only	24	35	39	39	35	38
Share of sales to other affiliates (per cent of sales to other foreign countries)	49	50	44	54	57	59

Sources: UNCTAD, based on United States, Department of Commerce, various years.

(b) Developing countries in Asia and Latin America

The impact of a liberal trade and investment environment on the trade-FDI relationship in developing countries can be seen in the export propensities of foreign affiliates in Asia and Latin America since they reflect the strategies of TNCs to exploit the comparative advantages of host countries with a view towards serving regional or international markets.

Much of United States FDI in manufacturing in developing countries immediately after World War II was undertaken by market-seeking TNCs relying on stand-alone affiliates, established in response to trade barriers. Overwhelmingly, they were meant to serve host-country markets: in 1957, only 16 per cent of their sales were exports (Lipsey, 1988). Small as exports were for United States manufacturing affiliates, there was a sharp contrast between affiliates in developing countries and those in developed countries. The latter group exported 16 per cent of their output in 1957, while the former exported only 5 per cent. There were also contrasts among developing countries: United States affiliates in Asia exported over 20 per cent of production, about the same as those in Europe, while affiliates in Latin America exported only 4 per cent (Lipsey and Kravis, 1982).

Over the next 20 years, the export orientation of manufacturing affiliates increased substantially in almost every region and industry (table IV.7). Affiliates in developed countries exported about a third of output in 1977, almost twice that in 1957. The figure for affiliates in developing countries

Table IV.6. Changes in sales of United States affiliates in Europe, exports of United States parent firms to affiliates in Europe, and intra-European exports of United States affiliates, 1982-1993

(Percentage)

Industry	Ratio of 1993 value to 1982 value		
	Sales of affiliates	United States-Europe exports by parent firms to affiliates	Intra-Europe exports by affiliates[a]
Manufacturing	246.0	226.7	244.2
Food, drink and tobacco	285.6	85.9	349.5
Chemicals and allied products	250.1	206.0	245.2
Primary and fabricated metals	153.1	154.5	184.9
Machinery (except electrical)	334.1	288.9	245.7
Electrical and electronic equipment	182.1	254.6	200.2
Transport equipment	253.4	474.1	254.9
Other manufactured products	267.2	191.6	218.6
Wholesale trade	196.1	200.5	146.0
Finance[b] and insurance	591.6	..	1,214.7
Business services	308.2	1,543.8	343.1[c]
All industries	196.3	216.7	189.4

Sources: Adapted from Dunning, 1996, table 9; based United States, Department of Commerce, 1985 and 1995a.

[a] Figures for intra-European Union exports of United States affiliates are exports by such affiliates to third countries. Although data on exports to Europe are not given separately, it is estimated on the basis of other data available that overall these account for 80 to 90 per cent of all exports of affiliates other than those to the United States.

[b] Excluding banking.

[c] All services.

was 18 per cent, more than three times that in 1957. Exports increased more rapidly relative to total sales in Latin American than in European affiliates, and still faster in Asian affiliates. By 1977, Asian affiliates were exporting well over half of their output, led by those in Hong Kong, Singapore, Republic of Korea and Taiwan Province of China, which, as a group, exported 80 per cent of production. In these countries, exporting had become the chief focus of United States manufacturing affiliates.

Since 1977, the trend has been towards further increases in export propensities, but with regional variations (table IV.7). Affiliates in developed countries continued to become more export-oriented, albeit at a slower pace than before. The major changes were in the developing countries that had lagged in exports earlier. They began to catch up. United States affiliates in Latin America increased export propensities rapidly after 1982, with an almost 40 per cent rise in Brazil and a much greater increase in Mexico between 1982 and 1986. In Asia, some countries that were not part of the earlier export boom began to move towards higher exports, with United States affiliates in the Philippines and Thailand approaching the export ratios of the four newly industrializing economies and Malaysia (table IV.7). In contrast, affiliates in the four newly industrializing economies in Asia all shifted their focus to local markets in various degrees, ranging from a small shift in Singapore (the smallest of the four), to a large decline in export propensity (from 68 per cent to 28 per cent) in the Republic of Korea (the largest market). The decline in export propensities did not reflect a decline or even a slower growth in the exports of affiliates in these countries or, for that matter, a substantial decrease in their share in host country exports (table IV.8). They were still growing faster than those of affiliates in developed countries. However, aside from affiliates in Singapore, they were no longer

Table IV.7. Export propensities of United States majority-owned foreign affiliates in manufacturing, 1966-1993 [a]

(Percentage)

	1966	1977	1982	1986	1989	1993
All economies [b]	18.6	30.8	33.9	38.4	37.8	40.3
Developed economies	20.4	33.1	36.6	39.3	38.0 [c]	40.6 [c]
Developing economies	8.4	18.1	22.0	32.5	36.7 [c]	38.7 [c]
Latin America and the Caribbean	6.2	9.7	11.9	20.0	22.0	22.2
Brazil	3.0	8.9	12.4	16.9	16.4	17.0
Mexico [c]	3.2	10.4	10.8	34.5	33.7	32.1
Developing Asia	23.1	57.0	60.6 [c]	67.5 [c]	64.4	64.4 [c]
India	6.9	3.6	..	4.1	..	..
Malaysia	..	76.2	81.5	≥83.7	74.7	84.9
Philippines	19.9	25.7	26.5	39.4	33.7	37.3
Thailand	..	≤38.0	..	58.5	73.3	61.2
Newly industrializing economies	..	81.2	76.0 [c]	76.2 [c]	67.9	67.0
Hong Kong	..	80.5	77.4	71.8	68.6	55.0
Republic of Korea	..	68.4	..	58.0	38.5	27.9
Singapore	..	93.2	91.8	89.7	87.2	85.9
Taiwan Province of China	..	71.4	59.4	63.7	46.4	38.8

Source: UNCTAD, based on United States, Department of Commerce, various years.

[a]   Exports (total sales minus local sales or sales to the United States plus sales to other countries) as per cent of total sales.

[b]   Developed and developing economies.

[c]   Exports by manufacturing affiliates in Africa and Republic of Korea in 1982, Africa and Middle East in 1986 and Israel and New Zealand in 1989 and 1993, included in these figures, are estimates.

the leaders in export growth. In these years, affiliates in Malaysia and Thailand, starting from relatively small exports, and affiliates in Mexico joined those in Singapore at the top of the export-growth standings (United States, Department of Commerce, various years).

Export propensities of United States affiliates in Asia were particularly high in selected industries, notably electronics (table IV.9), in which United States TNCs established affiliates in Asia as part of their integrated networks of production and trade. Initially, these were intended to take advantage of low labour costs in selected countries and, subsequently, other conditions that made it profitable to locate operations in more countries in the region. As a result of the export-intensive activities of United States TNCs (as well as Japanese firms), some Asian economies have been integrated into the international division of labour in the electronics industry, and some have been shifting specialization in production for international markets. Moreover, these affiliate activities are beginning to give rise to networks of indigenous suppliers linked indirectly (through affiliates) or directly (through contractual arrangements) to foreign markets as exporters of electronic products (UNCTAD-DTCI, 1995a, chapter IV).

Differences in host-country policies partly explain differences in export propensities among foreign affiliates. In the 1960s and the 1970s, Latin American host countries, in the light of balance-of-payments constraints and domestic industrialization objectives, sheltered their markets through high trade barriers. Foreign direct investment in the manufacturing sector was of the market-seeking kind, and TNCs relied on stand-alone affiliates. Under these circumstances, the linear sequence from trade to FDI was forced as high trade barriers stunted the growth of manufacturing exports, while tariff protection plus the lack of domestic competition permitted TNCs to run sub-optimal -- but profitable -- operations without any great risk. By contrast, in more liberal trade regimes, like those of Hong Kong and Singapore, and, to some extent, other Asian economies, manufacturing FDI became rapidly

Table IV.8. United States majority owned foreign affiliates' shares in host-economy exports of manufactures, 1966-1993

(Percentage)

	1966	1977	1982	1986	1989	1993
All economies	6.5	8.2	8.0	8.3	8.4	8.6
Developed economies	6.9	8.5	8.1	8.6	8.7 [a]	9.0 [a]
Developing economies	3.5	6.0	6.9	6.7	6.6 [a]	7.1 [a]
Latin America and the Caribbean	6.1	9.0	12.8	12.9	15.2	14.1
Brazil	3.3	11.4	14.1	15.1	14.2	13.1
Mexico	9.4	20.3	29.0	23.6	35.9	20.9
Developing Asia	3.7	6.2	6.4 [a]	5.6 [a]	5.3	6.0 [a]
India	1.6	0.3	..	0.3	..	..
Malaysia		9.3	≥18.5	18.5	10.6	11.2
Philippines	17.9	17.7	18.8	18.2	12.5	16.7
Thailand	..	≤4.7	..	5.7	9.4	5.7
Taiwan Province of China	..	6.2	4.1	3.4	3.5	2.7
Newly industrializing economies	..	7.0	5.5 [a]	5.0	6.3	8.0
Hong Kong	..	8.1	6.6	4.6	8.8	9.9
Republic of Korea	..	1.4	..	1.0	1.0	0.9
Singapore	..	18.7	14.5	18.1	18.7	23.7

Source: UNCTAD, based on United States, Department of Commerce, various years; and UNCTAD, *Handbook of Trade and Development Statistics*, various years.

a   Exports by manufacturing affiliates in Africa and Republic of Korea in 1982, Africa and Middle East in 1986 and Israel and New Zealand in 1989 and 1993, included in these figures, are estimates.

**Table IV.9. Sales and exports by United States affiliates[a] in Asia in
the electronics industry: selected data, 1977, 1983 and 1993**

(Millions of dollars and percentage)

	1977	1983	1993
Total sales	2 306	5 099	14 073
Total exports	2 282	4 595	10 765
Exports to the United States	1 674	3 442	6 465[b]
Exports to parent firms	1 633	3 362	6 740[b]
Exports to third countries	608[b]	1 153	4 300
Imports			
Imports from the United States	700[b]	2 111[b]	2 817
Imports from parent firms	672	2 041	2 666
Country exports	5 652	13 655	99 358
Export/sales ratio	99	90	76
Ratio of exports to third countries to total exports	27	25	40
Ratio of affiliate exports to country exports	40	34	11
Import/foreign sales ratio	30	41	20

Source: UNCTAD, based on United States Department of Commerce, various years.

[a]   Data relate to majority-owned non-bank affiliates of United States transnational corporations.

[b]   Data for Thailand in 1977, India and Indonesia in 1983 and Australia in 1993, included in these figures, are estimates.

export-oriented. As Latin American countries liberalized, affiliate export propensities increased there as well, benefiting from access to the corporate systems of parent companies (box IV.5). This was particularly the case in Mexico after 1982, as affiliates switched from local to export markets in the face of the debt crisis (UNCTC, 1992b).[8]

Undoubtedly, factors other than policy-related ones are also at work. In particular, plants in countries with small markets tend to export more than those in large countries to achieve a minimum efficient scale. But if that were the only explanation, it would be hard to explain why foreign firms -- having a choice of where to locate -- would choose to produce in small countries. There must be substantial advantages to offset the smallness of their markets, and these advantages must be in line with the changing strategies of TNCs, in the direction of exploiting local production advantages for regional and global markets.

C. Some implications for countries

Reduced obstacles to FDI and trade and the possibilities that they open up for TNCs to disperse production activities within integrated international production systems carry potential benefits and costs for countries. The nature of these benefits and costs, and how they compare with those that have traditionally been associated with trade and FDI, are not yet clear. This section explores tentatively some possible implications, especially for developing countries, of the relationship between FDI and trade in the new environment.

Static effects. Integrating production within corporate systems along efficiency-oriented lines means that firms fragment activities more closely -- and narrowly -- in accordance with the static comparative advantages of different locations. The division of labour that results provides potential opportunities for countries to participate in production and trade associated with TNCs, specializing in segments of goods and services production for which they have a comparative advantage. Moreover, as firms fine-tune their search for locational advantages, countries with a broad range of capabilities have the opportunity to attract specialized activities, not only as regards individual products and their components but also as regards functional activities of TNCs, such as finance, accounting and data processing. Thus, while a stand-alone affiliate may have produced an entire range of final products for its local host country market, an affiliate in an integrated system -- or an independent firm associated with a TNC system -- can concentrate on the production of intermediary or final goods for which the local productive capabilities of a host country are particularly well suited, and which it increasingly produces for exports to regional markets or the world market, as part of the global strategy of the TNC. Many firms in developing countries, particularly in Asia, but also in Latin America, are already part of regionally or globally integrated production systems of TNCs or are linked to them through subcontracting or other arrangements, selling or exporting parts, components and/or selected goods or services to affiliates and parent companies. Many of these countries initially become involved in the global production structures of TNCs through simpler forms of integration geared towards labour-intensive operations of parent firms. Subsequently, some of them have moved, through FDI or through non-equity arrangements, to more important, higher-technology activities. An example is the electronics industry.

Box IV.5. Corporate systems and host-country trade

In pursuing export-oriented strategies, host countries can benefit from the presence of foreign affiliates. Exporting involves costs regarding market research and the acquisition of other information and, importantly, it requires access to markets. Most TNCs have already paid these costs, and corporate systems provide privileged and advantageous access to world markets to foreign affiliates and other firms linked to them (UNCTAD-DTCI, 1995a).

The trading networks of TNCs can, indeed, account for some features of countries' trade behaviour. For example, at the time of the Latin American debt crisis, affiliates of United States TNCs in Latin America -- and, especially in such heavily indebted countries as Brazil, Chile and Mexico that had been exporting before the crisis -- were able to switch sales from host-country markets to export markets more quickly and thoroughly than local firms. Affiliates in Colombia and Venezuela, which had done little exporting before the crisis, were much less able to do so. Initially, much of the shift involved almost cutting off local sales rather than increasing exports, but after four or five years, the affiliates were increasing both local and export sales. Export propensities of firms other than United States affiliates also rose, but not as rapidly as those for United States affiliates. It seems reasonable to assume that the affiliates were able to switch from domestic to export markets more quickly than local firms because parent firms already had connections to outside markets. Another possibility is that affiliates did not wish to sell in local markets in exchange for depreciating currencies, while local firms, buying as well as selling in these currencies, were more willing to do so. Local firms, more dependent on local markets than TNCs, may also have been more reluctant to antagonize local customers (Blomström and Lipsey, 1993; UNCTC, 1992b).

Further evidence of the importance of TNC networks for the exporting of affiliates can be found in South-East Asia. There, affiliates of United States TNCs in the four newly industrializing economies, and in Indonesia, Malaysia and Thailand tended to export to markets in which there are other affiliates of the same parent firms -- sibling affiliates. Specifically, given the size of a market, as measured by population or real GDP, and given its total imports of the products of an affiliate's industry, the larger the affiliate's parent-firm's exports to its affiliates in that market, the higher the exports to that market by the parent firm's affiliates in these seven countries. In contrast, parent firms' exports to non-affiliates in a market were associated with lower exports by the affiliates from these seven countries to that market (Lipsey, 1995). However, the positive effect of parent firms exports to affiliates in a market on Asian affiliates' exports to that market was much larger than the negative effect of the parent firms' exports to non-affiliates. Thus, parent firms' exports to the world market are positively associated with Asian affiliate exports. Sibling affiliate production in a market seems to compete with Asian affiliate exports, but that effect is hardly ever statistically significant (Lipsey, 1995). The same positive influence of parent-firm exports to a market on affiliate exports to that market can be seen even more strongly in some individual industries: it is large and significant in electronic components and accessories, and smaller and only marginally significant in office and computing machinery (Lipsey, 1995).

Source: UNCTAD.

There are, of course, always risks associated with such participation in the international division of labour, and these risks may be greater when the participation is tied to transnational corporate systems whose options are worldwide and which are constantly under pressures to improve their competitiveness. Moreover, vulnerability may increase as specialization becomes more narrow, especially where it is susceptible to technological change and easy locational re-orientation (e.g., in the case of activities based on the cost of labour alone).

Dynamic effects. Greater interconnectedness of FDI and trade also has potential implications for dynamic change and growth through technological upgrading and innovation in the countries attracting TNCs. As the international intra-firm division of labour within TNCs evolves, affiliates become not only more closely aligned with the static comparative advantages of various locations, but increasingly focused on those areas in which the local potential for innovation is greatest. Since, in today's competitive world, TNCs cannot rely on profits that arise from protected market positions that may have been enjoyed by stand-alone affiliates, the importance of earnings created through innovation and productivity gains (resulting, e.g., from advantageous combinations of high skills with lower costs in host countries) increases. Hence, there is a search for local sources of innovation and higher productivity in each affiliate, which can become part of a regional or global strategy of production and marketing. Geographically dispersed innovations and productivity gains can be combined through a global strategy and, where they are relevant to more than their immediate local applications, they can be spread throughout the corporate system as an input into further improvements.

For developing countries, the extent to which the gains from this dispersion and integration of innovation within TNC systems are realized locally depends on the particular role assigned to local affiliates by their parent firms and the extent to which this role is associated with networking with other firms (especially indigenous firms) in the same location, and hence becomes part of a wider system of technological and associated spillovers. The prospects for technological upgrading through assembly-type activities, for instance, are limited. Such activities tend to be more geographically mobile and less connected to the local economy in which they are located. In fact, if, as a result of a shift by a TNC to an integrated system of FDI and trade, a former stand-alone affiliate that had been active in all functions in the vertical chain (from research to distribution) is confined to the assembly of imported research-based components, which it then exports for further (perhaps more sophisticated) processing and marketing in the form of final products, the affiliate may have less scope for innovation than before. Its lack of research or technological initiative will mean that, in this case, the affiliate makes no contribution to transforming the local pattern of comparative advantage; it may actually help to "lock-out" the country from developments within the industry. In contrast, technologically dynamic research-related FDI is attracted principally to countries having some locational assets of interest to TNCs. Such countries can become part of a local inter-firm network or locational agglomeration of activity and evolve into centres of excellence. The competitive advantages of TNCs interact positively with the location advantages of host countries, so that both the innovativeness of the companies and local economic growth or development are increased. Far from being subject to possible shifts to other countries, the level of such FDI in a host country is likely to rise steadily and can become increasingly focused on innovative tasks. As a result, the comparative advantage of the host country in the relevant industry can be progressively enhanced and is more firmly grounded in a coherent local system, being less dependent upon the locational decisions of any particular TNC. Affiliates in these centres of excellence are likely to become increasingly specialized in the production and export of research-related products, and hence in more innovative and higher value-added activities. The host country can thus become "locked-in" to a path of technological upgrading and continuous economic development.

So far, only a few developing countries have succeeded in becoming centres for the location of innovative activities of TNCs, leading to exports based on their newly developed comparative advantage. Perhaps most notable is Singapore in research and development in biotechnology. Others have managed to attract FDI that carries technological spillovers. But again others have not managed to attract such FDI. This is precisely where government policies become important in terms of creating the factors that make a particular location attractive for particular activities, or in exploring alternative (non-TNC related) avenues of dynamic upgrading.

Industrial restructuring. Countries can also benefit from the accelerated transformation of the industrial structures of host and home countries which can be the allied consequence of the integration of FDI and trade. In general, countries -- developed and developing -- tend to benefit in efficiency from a restructuring in favour of industries (or activities within industries) in which the country is comparatively advantaged (and in which integrated TNCs establish or expand local operations), and in dynamic terms from a greater focus on activities in those industries in which the country's ratio of skills to cost is internationally competitive and/or its potential for innovation is greatest. For developing countries, the latter is particularly beneficial since foreign affiliates within those industries tend to develop greater capabilities as part of the regional or global strategies of their respective TNCs. Thus, these affiliates can make a greater contribution to local innovation through linkages and spillovers.

Structural transformation depends on local specificities. Many developing countries that have managed to attract FDI that is part of regionally or globally integrated production systems are involved in low-technology activities that have contributed to expanding and diversifying their economies, but which have limited consequences for technological upgrading. In a few others, integrated production helped to upgrade industries, leading to more dynamic restructuring, in line with the specific capabilities that the economies have been able to foster (UNCTAD-DTCI, 1995a, ch. V). For example, in the Republic of Korea this took the form of an upgrading within manufacturing, although the linkage was mainly between the investment and trade of domestically-owned firms operating under technology licences (non-equity contracts) from Japanese TNCs (Koo, 1985). In Singapore, a smaller economy with less scope for moving into heavier capital-intensive industries, but in which integrated FDI and trade has long been sought in industries with the greatest potential for local innovation and export, TNC activity in recent times has shifted towards smaller research-intensive industries and thereby contributed importantly to the dynamic restructuring of the economy (Lall, 1994). Upgrading in manufacturing was more limited in Hong Kong; the structural shift was more towards the territory becoming an international or regional service and financial centre, in which integrated FDI and trade concentrated more on those services in which tradability has recently increased most, notably in investment banking (Chen, 1983).

Home countries may also benefit from a faster restructuring of industrial profiles as the outward FDI of domestically-owned TNCs becomes more closely entwined in trading networks. Outward FDI increases in locally declining industries as they are subject to greater import competition, and resources are thereby released for the expansion of rapidly growing industries (UNCTAD-DTCI, 1995a; Ozawa, 1992). The linkage between FDI and exports in the more dynamic industries also facilitates faster expansion of, and encourages a greater focus on, the most promising avenues for local innovation, while drawing on the complementary innovative inputs provided by specialized affiliates in other parts of the TNC system.

* * *

To conclude, the new environment and the shift towards integrated international production that it allows carry the potential for new opportunities for countries. But the potential to benefit from closer FDI-trade interlinkages -- whether for static efficiency, technological dynamism or industrial restructuring -- is by no means evenly distributed between countries, in part because of the uneven distribution of FDI.   The majority of developing countries, especially low-income and least-developed economies that attract limited FDI even of the traditional market-seeking and resource-seeking type, has so far had few opportunities to participate in the production-cum-trade structures of TNCs and the finer and wider division of labour that their activities engender.   They may thus risk further marginalization due to this increased specialization within TNC systems, unless greater national and international efforts for their development are made. At the same time, the experience of the more successful developing countries suggests that, as more countries build up the human resource and infrastructure capabilities that TNCs seek, the scope for these countries to share in the benefits can be expected to increase.   Indeed, the expanded scope for specialization within the production structures of TNCs pursuing complex integration strategies could well increase those opportunities.   The gains of greater participation in the international division of labour are also accompanied by costs to particular groups within economies, both developed and developing -- and more so when unemployment is high. Balancing the benefits against these costs poses a formidable challenge for policy makers.

D. National policy implications

The greater intertwining of FDI and trade presents new challenges for national policy makers. Transnational corporations internally integrate the trade and investment functions that most national governments still tend to view and address separately, sometimes creating a disjuncture between national policy instruments and the transactions they are seeking to influence. National trade and FDI policies have typically evolved separately, frequently influenced by different immediate goals and measurements, and administered by distinctive, loosely connected agencies.   This institutional separation is not suited to a world in which trade and FDI are closely interlinked (Dunning, 1992) because it can lead to inconsistent policies that can create an environment in which trade and FDI policies neutralize each other, or even prove counterproductive; policy incoherence can mean missed opportunities whose results may not be immediately realized (box IV.6).

On the other hand, when formulated and implemented in a coordinated fashion, national trade and FDI policies can become mutually reinforcing in support of national growth and development objectives.   Coordinated approaches can generate synergies that yield outcomes exceeding the expectations for separate policy choices. At the same time, it should be noted that policy coordination does not presuppose any particular overall policy approach (e.g., a liberal approach); it merely is a reflection of the fact that, since FDI and trade are inextricably intertwined, national policies on FDI and trade need to be coordinated. This section does not intend to discuss this matter in full; rather it seeks to provide some examples and outline part of the problem.

* * *

For most countries, FDI policies developed largely as an adjunct to trade policies and were expected primarily to serve national trade-policy goals. Developed home countries, which usually viewed FDI by domestic firms as a natural corollary to strong international trade, were often slow to recognize interactive implications of trade and FDI policies. These effects frequently appeared first on national policy agendas when a debate arose about the complementary versus substitution nature of FDI and trade in the context of "export of jobs".

For example, the United States treated FDI as a corollary to its trade policy which has traditionally been at the centre of its foreign economic policy. This approach was founded on the belief that FDI followed trade in accordance with the product-life cycle (see chapter III) and the activities of innovative and highly competitive domestic firms. National attention focussed on the

---

Box IV.6. Policy coordination in the automotive industry

Record bilateral trade deficits in the 1980s led the United States to seek voluntary export restraints on Japanese automobiles. This spurred significant FDI in the United States by Japanese automobile manufacturers as well as their suppliers. Whether United States trade and FDI policies are judged coordinated in this case depends partly on what objectives were being pursued. For some, FDI-based growth in Japanese transplant operations was likely not an anticipated or desired outcome. For them, a liberal United States policy towards inward FDI undermined the effectiveness of a protective trade policy. However, if the policy objective was to improve the bilateral trade balance, a different and more complex calculation is necessary. Interactive trade and FDI effects must be estimated, over a specified period of time, by measuring factors such as the substitution of domestic (United States or transplant) output for imported automobiles, the impact of transplant operations on United States market share, the input of imported components to transplant production, the price vs. quantity changes in imported cars, etc.. There is little evidence that such considerations were carefully evaluated during the policy-making process to determine whether trade and FDI policy would be mutually reinforcing, neutral or counterproductive in their interactive effects.

The complexity of FDI-trade relationships was also reflected in the 1988 United States Omnibus Trade Act which defined Japanese transplant operations in the United States as part of the Japanese automobile market in order to increase the sale of United States auto parts to all Japanese-owned firms (Kline, 1991). However, if cars produced by transplant operations were exported to Europe, United States policy supported the view that such products should be considered as United States and not Japanese automobiles (and therefore not included under European restraints on Japanese automobile imports).

For Canada, the need for coordination between trade and FDI policies in the automotive industry has been clearer. Lacking a large internal market, Canada's prospects to expand automotive production depended on a liberal trade and FDI relationship, principally with the United States. The initial United States-Canada Automobile Pact administered trade flows through quotas in the automotive industry between the two countries. However, lacking strong national automobile companies, Canada's ability to benefit from this agreement depended on correspondingly liberal FDI policies that would facilitate the establishment and/or expansion of automotive TNCs. The trade and investment policies were essentially handled separately, but required coherence in implementation and results. In other industries, the application of Canadian trade and investment policies was notably more restrictive.

Mexico's experience in the automotive industry adds a contrasting yet related case of trade and FDI policy coordination. Counting on the drawing power of a large internal market, Mexico initially combined import restrictions with FDI-regulated domestic production requirements. Although these coordinated policies attracted market-seeking TNCs, the import-substitution strategy yielded uncompetitive operations which were largely isolated from an increasingly integrated international automobile industry. Beginning in the mid-1980s, however, Mexico progressively liberalized trade and FDI policies, paving the way for the country becoming a major producer and exporter of automotive products (UNCTAD-DTCI, 1995a). Coherent changes to both national trade and FDI policies were essential to this result.

Subsequently, Mexico was incorporated into an expanded continental automotive arrangement through negotiation of the North American Free Trade Agreement (NAFTA) that explicitly addresses coordination of trade and FDI policies, including through explicit rules-of-origin for the automotive industry (which, in a sense, moves elements of import substitution to the regional level). These rules represent a key component of the countries' common framework for interactive trade and FDI policies that will influence TNC behaviour in the expanded and integrating North American market.

Source: UNCTAD.

FDI-trade relationship in the mid-1960s, shaped by debates over whether FDI was a complement to, or a substitute for, United States exports. The central policy objectives and associated measurements in this debate were clearly trade-based; outward FDI was judged largely according to its apparent impact on domestic jobs and its associated impact on the balance of trade. Other policy implications of the FDI-trade relationship surfaced when expanded overseas production by United States TNCs reduced the effectiveness of United States export restrictions imposed for national security reasons. Attempts to extend these "trade" controls extraterritorially have led to intergovernmental conflict and have not always been successful.

Early experiences in Europe offer a regional example of a lack of coordination between trade and FDI policies. The Common Market's lowering of internal trade barriers facilitated trade flows between member countries. But, in doing so, it undermined national FDI policies in countries such as France, which administered FDI restrictions to limit domestic market competition, particularly from large United States TNCs. For example, when General Motors encountered resistance against its plans to establish an assembly plant in Strasbourg, it negotiated an agreement with the Government of Belgium and established a plant in Antwerp, from which it exported vehicles to France duty free (Bergsten et al., 1978). Because there was no common European FDI policy, TNCs could invest in Common Market countries that had more liberal inward FDI policies and still gain access to the French market through liberalized trade channels.

Among developing countries, the broadly interactive effects of trade and FDI policies was perhaps better recognized. At first, FDI was regarded as an instrument to improve a country's trade position rather than valued for its (productive) worth. Hence, in pursuing national development objectives, usually domestic industrialization, many developing countries' inward FDI policies favoured those projects that promoted import-substitution.[9] These countries purposely linked trade and inward FDI policies, for instance by using tariff protection to create an artificial location advantage as an inducement to attract domestic market-serving (and thereby import-substituting) production capacities.

Although consistent in terms of mutually-supportive trade and FDI policies, this import-substitution approach proved unsatisfactory for most countries, especially as international economic conditions evolved towards an integrated global economy. Some countries, particularly in Asia, shifted to an export-oriented strategy that required a more complex consistency between trade and FDI policies. To the extent that this approach relied on TNCs, it sought to attract a different type of FDI, one motivated more by efficiency-seeking rather than domestic market-seeking objectives. National trade and FDI policy coordination thus demanded that liberalized inward FDI rules in targeted industries be matched with trade-policy measures, including lowered import barriers for needed inputs, a realistic foreign exchange regimes and easy export licensing and trade financing. Policies that aim at increasing exports would not only seek to attract foreign affiliates that produce goods and services for export, but FDI that upgrades a country's capabilities in telecommunications, transportation, utilities, financing and other producer services. They would also consider, e.g., permissive regulations governing the movement of managerial personnel and liberal import policies for needed inputs, including capital equipment and essential raw materials and components.

National policies that include the use of export-processing zones illustrate a specialized application of a consistent trade-and-FDI-policy package. There are hundreds of such zones. They require coordinated trade and FDI policies to promote value-added processing, domestic employment and increased exports. Specific trade-policy mechanisms, such as tariff-drawback schemes, are central to their operations. However, although the focus is trade-oriented, the zones' success is largely dependent on corresponding FDI policies that will attract foreign as well as domestic enterprises. Restrictive FDI policies regarding entry, local inputs, technology transfer, or management-training mandates would discourage TNCs from locating facilities in these zones. For most developing countries, export-processing zones that depended only on domestic firms would not be considered as successful.

Some issues also arise regarding outward FDI policy, for example in vertically integrated industries in which FDI in overseas natural resources extraction is desirable to provide inputs for national fabrication processes, be they for the domestic market or for exports. Japan's early industrial strategy selectively promoted FDI in resource extraction, matching it with liberal import regulations for raw materials, protective policies against competitive FDI or manufactured goods imports, and export-promotion programmes to assist final product sales.

More recent FDI-promotion strategies in some newly industrializing Asian economies demonstrate a similar consistency between trade and FDI programmes. Governmental promotion of outward FDI is targeted at opportunities where FDI can secure essential natural resources or technologies, or provide local market-distribution facilities to pull through home country exports (UNCTAD-DTCI, 1995a). In cases such as Singapore, both inward and outward FDI policies are linked to trade relationships. For instance, foreign investors in labour-intensive industries whose exports become less competitive are sometimes encouraged to participate in ventures that shift certain operations to more cost-effective neighbouring locations, as a way to keep Singapore tied into the higher value-added activities of a TNC's global corporate system (UNCTAD-DTCI, 1995a).

* * *

The need for policy coordination between national trade and FDI policies acquires greater importance with the emergence of integrated international production systems, as investment and trade flows are their life-blood. Deceptively simple in concept, national policy coordination can prove complex and difficult in practice. Traditional trade and FDI policies usually serve multiple national goals that may overlap or conflict. National policy "tool kits" contain a wide array of programmatic instruments and mechanisms, often administered by separate government agencies, whose interactive effects are sometimes hard to foresee. Unfortunately, there is no standard policy package that assures policy consistency for all countries. Effective coordination among policy choices and implementation programmes depends on many variables, including a country's stage of development, the quality of national factor endowments, the relevance of outward FDI policies, and the coordination and competence of administrative agencies. When several sets of interrelated policies have different initial objectives and varying implementation mechanisms, the matrix of potentially interactive effects becomes complex, complicating the pursuit of coherent and reinforcing actions. Policy simplicity, therefore, coupled with direct and measurable programme implementation, can help clarify resultant effects and the possible need for policy adjustments.

Coordination becomes even more complex if the effects of other closely related policies are considered, for example, with respect to technology or competition. Trade, FDI, technology and competition are probably the four most interactive domains of national policy that affect TNC operations. Industrial policy approaches, sometimes tied to strategic trade-theory concepts, can involve an even wider array of domestic and international policies. For most national economies, however, the closely interrelated effects of FDI and trade policies constitute the essential core where the task of assuring policy coordination must begin.

E. Conclusion

The ability and freedom of firms to exercise choice with respect to the location of their production and, hence, the investment and trade they undertake, has increased significantly in recent years. Partly as a result, FDI and trade have become more closely interconnected in the framework of efficiency-oriented, integrated international production strategies pursued by TNCs. For countries and regions in which such production is located, this means that FDI and trade support one another to a greater extent than before. Because of the extension of specialization within TNC systems, the scope for functional and product specialization among countries is increased, and there are more opportunities for trade in accordance with comparative advantage. At the same time, these new interrelationships increase the scope for altering and upgrading the comparative advantage of countries, particularly of developing countries, because production capacity can increasingly be located wherever the necessary capabilities are found. These opportunities are, however, open particularly to countries in which parts of the interconnected FDI-trade networks of TNCs are located. Thus, the immediate relevance of the new, closer linkages between FDI and trade for development depends partly on the extent to which developing countries actually participate in the integrated organizational structures of TNCs.

From a national policy perspective, the emergence of these more complex interlinkages between FDI and trade, alongside the traditional, simpler relationships, draws attention to the importance of national policy coordination between FDI and trade policies. The strong trend in the recent past towards the liberalization of trade and FDI reflects a recognition that there are inefficiencies that arise from trade-restriction induced FDI and FDI-restriction induced trade. It is difficult, however, to influence one without influencing the other. With the shift of the environment to one in which firms' choices regarding trade and FDI are greatly broadened, and in which the decision in favour of one can have immediate implications for the other, it becomes even more important that liberalized policies for FDI and trade mesh as closely with one another as possible.

* * *

Does trade lead to FDI or FDI lead to trade? Does FDI substitute for trade or trade substitute for FDI? Do they complement each other? What does the growth of FDI mean for trade -- and, most importantly, what are the implications for the economies involved?

As the discussion in this chapter suggests, these questions increasingly need to be reformulated, as the issue becomes more and more: how do firms access resources -- wherever they are located in the world -- in the interest of organizing their production as efficiently as possible for the national, regional and global markets they wish to serve? In other words, the issue becomes: where do firms locate their value-added activities and why? In these circumstances, the decision where to locate is a decision where to invest and from where to trade. And it becomes a FDI decision, if a foreign location is chosen. Hence, once a locational decision has been made, investment and trade flows are determined simultaneously. It follows from there that, increasingly, what matters are the factors that make particular locations attractive for particular activities for domestic *and* foreign investors.

Notes

1 Based on information obtained from companies' annual reports.

2 For a discussion of complex integration strategies and structures as well as other strategies and strtuctures adopted by TNCs, see UNCTAD-DTCI, 1993a, Part Two.

3 The data are as follows:

Intra-firm trade and its share in total trade, various countries and years[a]

(Billions of dollars and percentage)

Country	Intra-firm exports		Intra-firm imports	
	Value	Share in country exports	Value	Share in country imports
France [b]				
1993	56	34	28	18
Japan [c]				
1983	33	22	17	15
1993	92	25	33	14
Sweden [b]				
1986	11	38	1 [d]	3
1994	22	38	4 [d]	9
United States				
1983	71 [e]	35	99 [e]	37
1993	169	36	259	43

Source: UNCTAD, based on France, Ministère de l'Industrie, Direction générale des stratégies industrielles, unpublished data ; Sweden, Industrial Institute for Economic and Social Research and NUTEK unpublished data ; Japan, Ministry of International Trade and Industry (MITI), 1986 and 1996; United States, Department of Commerce, various issues.

[a] Intra-firm exports and imports include exports and imports, respectively, by parent firms of TNCs originating in the country and by affiliates of foreign firms that are located in the same country.

[b] Data cover only manufacturing.

[c] Data cover primary and manufacturing sectos and "other services", including business services, hotels, motion pictures, utilites and other miscellaneous services.

[d] Data on imports by affiliates of foreign firms located in Sweden are not available.

[e] In 1983, intra-firm exports and imports do not include trade by foreign affiliates in the United States with other foreign affiliates located abroad.

4 Based on data from the Industrial Institute for Economic and Social Research, Stockholm.

5 Based on data from France, Ministry of Industry, Directorate-General of Industrial Strategies.

6 Data for Japanese TNCs, available only for parent firms as a whole, indicated somewhat lower shares of intra-firm trade in total trade by TNCs: 32 per cent of exports and 29 per cent of parent firm imports in 1992. In the case of Japanese TNCs, too, there was a modest increase in the share of intra-firm trade in total trade between the early 1980s and the early 1990s (UNCTAD-DTCI, 1995a, p. 195).

7 For example, TNCs in business and other services exported less than 2 per cent of their output to, and imported 0.2 per cent of it from, their foreign affiliates in 1989. The comparable figures for manufacturing firms were 5.1 per cent and 4.1 per cent, respectively. Exceptions among service industries, with much higher percentages, include financial and trading services and data services (Zimny, 1993, pp. 8-10).

8 Although information on import propensities of United States foreign affiliates is limited because of lack of data on total imports of these affiliates, data on affiliate imports from the United States suggest that affiliates in developing countries have a higher ratio of imports to exports than those in developed countries,

although the ratios for developing country affiliates have been declining somewhat. In the past, when foreign affiliates in Latin American countries had lower propensity to export, they had a higher ratio of imports to exports. More recently the ratios in the two regions have converged (United States Department of Commerce, various years).

[9]   Until recently, outward FDI policy was considered largely irrelevant in these countries because conditions of capital shortage seemed to relegate them to a host-country status only; see UNCTAD-DTCI, 1995a.

Annex

Integrating the theories of FDI and trade

Traditionally, conceptual models of FDI and international trade have been developed separately. Foreign-direct-investment theory tries to explain why individual firms (or groups of firms) invest in particular countries, and uses the notions of ownership, internalization and location advantages as determinants of investment choices (Hymer, 1976; Casson, 1982; Dunning, 1992). Trade theory, developed much earlier, has put emphasis on why countries trade with each other in a general equilibrium framework and has developed the principle of comparative advantage as the determinant of trade patterns: countries sell what they produce relatively cheaply and buy what they produce relatively expensively. During the past 20 years or so, the "new trade theory"[a] has contributed to broadening the comprehension of trade patterns and in particular of the growth of intra-industry trade by incorporating industrial organization concepts of product differentiation, increasing returns to scale and imperfect competition in the traditional comparative advantage framework. But even these important developments in international trade theory continued to assume that firms produce goods and services in one location, excluding the possibility of incorporating FDI into their reasoning. On the other hand, FDI (and TNC) theory is quite successful in explaining the variety of trade flows that can be directly or indirectly created and/or diverted by different kinds of TNCs. However, the nature of the analysis, based on the behaviour of individual firms does not allow for generalizations, as regards patterns at the aggregate industry or country levels.

In spite of the limitations of theory, the growth of TNCs, their ability to replace and complement trade with sales by foreign affiliates (now higher in value than world exports), the internalization of one-third of world trade within TNC systems and the direct involvement of TNCs in arm's-length trade in another third have made the interlinkages between FDI and trade increasingly important. A clearer understanding of the FDI-trade relationship can only be provided within a unified theory of FDI and trade.

Contributions towards developing such a theory have been made since the early 1980s, by international trade theorists who have started to relax the restrictive hypothesis that firms are national and allowed for the possibility for them to own and employ factors of production located in different countries. The models developed within this new strand of economic literature have focused mainly on either vertical or horizontal FDI, where the first consists of the geographical separation of different stages of the value-added chain and the second consists of the duplication of the entire production process, except for headquarters activities, in several countries.[b]

In these integrated models, the activities of firms are divided into two categories. The first consists of "headquarters" activities, which involve engineering, managerial and financial services, as well as services of reputation, trademarks and so forth, which can be transferred at no cost even to distant production facilities. This set of activities is often simply indicated as research and development. The second consists of the actual production process, which can be further divided into upstream (intermediate goods) production and downstream (final goods) production. All these activities are assumed to have increasing returns to scale. Firms can geographically separate production facilities from headquarters because of the absence of transport costs of headquarters services, but they concentrate these in one location in order to reap associated scale economies. In the two-country equilibrium framework -- typical of trade analysis-- that these models adopt, there is no place for a distinction between foreign regional and national markets, or for complex internationally integrated strategies. In case of firms engaging in these activities in two countries, firms perform headquarters activities in the home country and either transfer plant production to the host country (vertical FDI), or undertake plant production both at home and in the host country (horizontal FDI).[c]

Firms now compete not only through price and quantity but also through production configuration, that is, they choose to be national or transnational in order to maximize their profits, taking into consideration competitors' behaviour. The central issue that these models have to solve is how individual firms' choices determine the aggregate combination of national and transnational corporations, which is usually referred to as the sector regime. This is the international production part of the analysis. Once the international distribution of activities is found, the international trade pattern is usually easier to derive.

Integrating vertical FDI into trade theory

One variant of the integrated theory introduces vertical FDI, explained in terms of factor-proportion asymmetries between countries, into international trade theory (Helpman, 1984; Helpman-Krugman, 1985). This theory represents an extension of the "new trade theory", which has introduced differentiated goods and increasing returns to scale in standard comparative advantage two-country, two-goods and two-factor models. Headquarters services in the differentiated sector, the finished differentiated goods and the homogeneous goods are assumed to be, respectively, the most capital intensive, of intermediate capital intensity, and the most labour intensive. Final goods transport costs and impediments to trade are not considered. Increasing returns to scale and zero transport costs make it optimal for firms to concentrate individual activities. The choice firms face as to where to locate headquarters activities and plant production is determined by factor prices.

If countries are completely identical in terms of factor-proportions, there is no FDI and no inter-industry trade, but there is intra-industry trade of varieties of the differentiated good as predicted by the new trade theory. When there are small differences in relative factor endowments there is a partial specialization of the relatively capital-abundant country in the differentiated capital-intensive goods and of the relatively labour-abundant country in the homogeneous goods. There is both inter-industry and intra-industry trade, the capital-abundant country becoming a net exporter of varieties of the differentiated goods and an importer of the homogeneous goods. This partial specialization brings about factor price equalization and new trade theory predictions still hold true. When factor-endowment differentials increase (above the factor price equalization-via-trade-set), new trade theory predicts a complete specialization of at least one country in the sector in which it holds its comparative advantage. But if differentiated sector firms are free to invest abroad, they will exploit factor price differentials by relocating headquarters activities in the capital-abundant country and plant production in the other. If differences are not too high, the capital-rich country is still a net exporter of the differentiated goods. But when countries' asymmetries increase above a certain limit, the capital-abundant country specializes in the capital-intensive production of research-and-development services and becomes a net importer of all varieties of the differentiated goods, as well as the homogeneous goods.

This variant of the theory integrating FDI and trade thus demonstrates that the possibility for firms to invest abroad reverses trade patterns when countries are very different in terms of relative factor endowments. In this case the capital-abundant country exports headquarters services in exchange for finished varieties of the differentiated good and for the homogeneous good, instead of simply exporting the differentiated good. Foreign direct investment generates complementary trade flows of finished goods from foreign affiliates to parent companies (intra-firm) or to the home country (arm's-length) and intra-firm transfers of intangible headquarters services from parent companies to foreign affiliates. If production is divided into upstream and downstream production, the FDI-trade relationship can be developed further with the emergence of intra-firm parent-to-affiliate exports of intermediate inputs. Factor-proportions models require large differences in countries' relative factor endowments for FDI to take place and a principal implication is that TNCs are more important between countries the greater the difference between them. They apply best to vertical investments from developed countries to developing countries.

Integrating horizontal FDI into trade theory

The explanation of horizontal FDI that is important in the case of investments between developed countries has been the object of another strand of international trade models which allow for firms to invest abroad (Markusen, 1984; Brainard, 1992; Horstmann-Markusen, 1992; Markusen-Venables, 1995). These models are essentially based on the tension between plant-level scale economies, on the one hand, and firm-level scale economies and transport costs, on the other. (Some of these models assume identical factor proportions between countries and identical factor intensities of headquarters activities and production activities.) In general, vertical FDI is excluded from the analysis by assumption.

Under these assumptions, one motivation to invest abroad is represented by multi-plant economies of scale generated by high fixed costs of research and development and other headquarters activities (Markusen, 1984). Research and development and headquarters activities are thus the international-trade-cum-FDI-models equivalent of the concept of "knowledge capital", developed by the business literature on TNCs. A second motivation for FDI is to overcome transport costs, geographical and cultural distance costs and all kinds of impediments to trade, including tariffs and non-tariff barriers to trade. Both motivations are counterbalanced by concentration advantages, that is, increasing returns to scale at the plant level. The higher the value of multi-plant economies of scale and transport costs relative to plant-level scale economies, the more likely is the presence of TNCs (Brainard, 1992).

These models based on the trade-off between proximity and concentration postulate a substitution relationship between trade and FDI at the firm level, and also at the country level. Firms either export, or produce and sell locally abroad: in the latter case there is a transfer of intangible headquarters services which does not increase merchandise trade. At the country level, assuming identical factor endowments, firms are either all national or all TNCs, and the co-existence of both types of firms is possible only in the exceptional case of perfect balance between proximity and concentration advantages. In other words, when countries are identical there is either intra-industry FDI or intra-industry trade of goods. The theory is successful in explaining the rise of FDI among developed countries but not in its prediction that this should replace trade flows.

A further development of the theory to allow for the separation of upstream and downstream production predicts exports of intermediate goods from parent companies to their foreign affiliates when firms decide to invest in downstream affiliates. This version thus introduces an element of complementarity between horizontal FDI and international trade (Brainard, 1992). A second elaboration of the theory introduces asymmetries between countries in terms of market size, factor endowments and technological efficiency (Markusen-Venables, 1995). Countries' asymmetries affect the choice between being national or multi-plant transnational and make it relatively convenient to be national and located in the advantaged country. It is, in this case, possible for national and transnational firms, and therefore trade and FDI, to exist simultaneously. Moreover, as the disadvantaged country develops in terms of local market size, factor endowments and technological efficiency, more and more firms open foreign affiliates in it. Thus TNCs' presence and FDI increase as countries become more similar, contrary to the predictions of models integrating vertical FDI and trade.

Conclusions

It can be argued that, because they are constrained by a simple two-country general equilibrium framework, the international production and trade models described above cannot significantly represent real TNCs' behaviour and empirical trade-FDI relationships. Indeed, there are relevant empirical phenomena which these models do not take into account: for instance, the role of governments in reshaping countries' comparative advantages and in influencing trade patterns, the importance of macroeconomic factors such as structural unemployment or growth, and market imperfections such as information asymmetry and limitations on knowledge computational capabilities of decision makers (Dunning, 1995). Continued empirical testing will throw light on the principal limitations of the theoretical FDI and trade-integrated models reviewed here, while more intense co-operation between international microeconomics, macroeconomics and business disciplines will point to the direction for future improvements. A major issue for future research is the extension of static models to include dynamic considerations, in order to represent the role of TNCs in transferring capital and technology and contributing to host and home countries' economic development. In an evolutionary perspective, however, the contribution of these recent models, particularly in the light of the fact that until the 1980s trade models were based on the hypothesis that only national firms exist, is considerable.

Source: UNCTAD.

[a]   See, for example, Krugman, 1986.

[b]   Recent research has already demonstrated the possibility to include vertical and horizontal integration motives for TNCs in a unified model (Markusen, Venables, Konan and Zhang, 1996).

[c]   The models described here focus on international production through FDI and do not consider the choice between FDI proper and non-equity arrangements. There are other international trade models that focus on the internalization decision (i.e., the choice between FDI and production abroad through contractual arrangements) and consider transaction and organizational costs as main determinants of this choice (Ethier, 1986; Horstmann-Markusen, 1987). There are also other models that emphasize oligopolistic market structures and strategic FDI motivated by the pre-emption of foreign competitors (see Motta, 1993, for a review of strategic investment models).

Part Three

Towards a multilateral agreement on foreign direct investment?

Introduction

As the analysis of the previous chapters indicates, foreign direct investment (FDI) and trade are inextricably intertwined both at the microeconomic level of firms' strategies and operations and at the macroeconomic level of national economies. Investment and trade not only contribute individually and directly to development, they also contribute jointly and indirectly through linkages with one another. Governments have therefore increasingly established national policy frameworks to create a framework within which FDI and trade can flourish and contribute to growth and development. Beyond that, they are beginning to pay more attention, at the national level, to the need for policy coordination between investment and trade policies.

The question arises whether a framework for FDI is also needed at the international level and, if so, to what extent it needs to be in tune with the existing multilateral trade framework. Although this issue has been addressed in various international fora over the past half century, it is now receiving broad attention, including as a potential issue for future work by the World Trade Organization.

Foreign direct investment is becoming increasingly important in the world economy, including in many developing countries. It has become more important than trade in terms of delivering goods and services to foreign markets and, in addition, it has become an important mechanism for organizing production internationally. All governments now recognise the role of FDI in development and are actively competing for it. At the same time, the question has been raised whether the present international arrangements governing FDI have been overtaken by global economic reality and, therefore, whether a "catching up with the market" is necessary (Robertson, 1996). The vigorous growth of bilateral and regional investment agreements, the inclusion of some FDI-related issues in the Uruguay Round agreements and the beginning of negotiations on a Multilateral Agreement on Investment in the OECD suggest that many governments believe that this is, indeed, the case. Governments, as well as especially transnational corporations (TNCs), but also labour organizations, consumer groups and other non-governmental organizations, all for their own reasons, are driving the process -- though there is a diversity of views and approaches among these groups as to how current international arrangements guiding FDI should be further developed.

The issue is therefore now prominent on the international policy agenda. Part Three identifies and analyzes issues that are relevant for the further development of international arrangements for FDI, and especially their implications for development. More specifically, it lays out the extent to which FDI issues have so far been covered at the bilateral, regional and multilateral levels and draws a number of lessons from past experiences; presents policy approaches towards the further evolution of international arrangements; reviews key issues that, judging from existing international investment instruments, one could reasonably expect to be addressed in the further development of international arrangements on FDI; and reviews relevant fora. The discussion is exploratory and is meant to contribute to informal dialogue about the issues.

Chapter V

International arrangements for foreign direct investment

It is now widely recognized among policy-makers that the potential benefits of foreign direct investment (FDI) for economic development and growth can far exceed the potential costs. Foreign direct investment is perceived as a key vehicle to obtain foreign technology, managerial skills and other vital resources; to integrate into international marketing, distribution and production networks; and to improve the international competitiveness of firms and the economic performance of countries (UNCTC 1992c; UNCTAD-DTCI, 1995a). Governments strive to create a favourable climate to attract FDI by establishing an enabling framework, knowing, however, that other factors (such as growth and macroeconomic stability) carry the principal weight in investors' location decisions. Governments have done so through the liberalization (UNCTAD-DTCI, 1994a, ch. VII) of FDI regimes by reducing restrictive measures on entry and operations. Many have also adopted or agreed to general standards of treatment and provided specific guarantees in key areas such as the transfer of funds, expropriation and dispute settlement. Increasingly, moreover, governments are paying attention to ensuring the proper functioning of markets, for instance, through the adoption of competition rules, and consumer and financial reporting standards. These trends, which are part of a broader liberalization process, are, in turn, an extension of the general tendency to pursue market-oriented policies as a means to achieve greater economic efficiency. For most developed countries, this represents a continuation, deepening and expansion of their historically liberal approach to FDI. For many developing countries and transition economies, however, the liberalization of FDI policies means a dramatic change from the more interventionist development models of past decades (UNCTAD-DTCI, 1996c, Introduction) (table V.1 and figure V.1).

To influence the location decisions of foreign investors in an increasingly open and highly competitive global environment, governments have also sought to attract FDI with promotional measures. Among these, incentives programmes are offered to encourage FDI into certain industries,

Table V.1. Regulatory changes, 1991-1995

(Number)

Item	1991	1992	1993	1994	1995
Number of countries that introduced changes in their investment regimes	35	43	57	49	64
Number of changes	82	79	102	110	112
Of which:					
In the direction of liberalization or promotion[a]	80	79	101	108	106
In the direction of control	2	-	1	2	6

Source: UNCTAD, based on various sources.

[a]   Including measures aimed at strengthening market supervision, as well as incentives.

activities or locations, often in exchange for performance requirements. Some programmes are directed specifically at foreign investors, others are addressed to local as well as foreign investment (e.g., regional development incentives), while, for particular investments considered of special importance to the country, incentives are often negotiated on an *ad hoc* basis. Though aimed at facilitating FDI, incentives can be market-distortive in ways similar to incentives to trade. In this respect, FDI incentives do not contribute to a more liberal FDI regime (UNCTAD-DTCI, 1996b).

These trends at the national level have created a greater degree of policy convergence among developed and developing countries. However, while the trend towards liberalization and facilitation of FDI in national regimes is pervasive, it is by no means uniform: considerable differences exist in national policy regimes that reflect a diversity of national priorities, concerns and objectives (UNCTAD-DTCI, 1994a, ch. VII). Independent of any differences, there is the overarching recognition of the obligation of foreign investors to comply with the national laws and regulations of the countries in which they operate.

Figure V.1. Types of changes in laws and regulations, 1995

(Percentage)

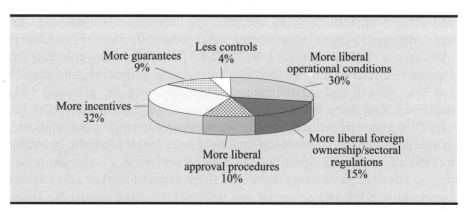

Source: UNCTAD.

A. Present international arrangements

Over the past half-century, it is striking how the number of instruments dealing with FDI has increased and how their coverage has become broader. At the same time, there have been sharp swings in attitudes of countries towards FDI, from protection, to restrictions and control, to facilitation and liberalization (Sauvant and Aranda, 1993; Sornarajah, 1994; Muchlinski, 1995), although there have often been considerable discrepancies between pronouncements of governments, including at the multilateral level, and the practices they follow.

The origins of international arrangements governing FDI can be traced back to the rules of customary international law developed between the eighteenth and twentieth centuries. Their twin foundations were the principles of State sovereignty and exclusive territorial jurisdiction on the one hand, and the legal doctrine of State responsibility for injuries to aliens and their property on the other. The international law of foreign investment has altered between emphasis on each of these foundations. At the end of the nineteenth century, prevailing perceptions of the doctrine of State responsibility were challenged by the Latin American States, which developed their own international law approach to the treatment of foreign investors, generally known as the Calvo Doctrine. Its main tenets were: (a) that, under international law, States are required to accord to aliens the same treatment as afforded to their own nationals under national law; both discrimination against aliens and the grant to them of privileges not available to nationals are thus condemned; (b) claims by aliens against the host State (particularly those based on contracts) must be decided solely by the domestic courts of that State; and (c) diplomatic protection by the State of the investor's nationality can be exercised only in cases of direct breach of international law and under restrictive conditions.

Efforts to create conventional multilateral rules for FDI started as early as the 1940s in the framework of the Havana Charter. (Unless otherwise indicated, all instruments referred to in this chapter are contained in UNCTAD-DTCI (1996c), *International Investment Instruments: A Compendium*, which also contains a summary examination and review of the instruments.) But it soon became obvious that the positions of countries on FDI at that time were too far apart to allow consensus. Even within the OECD, a proposal for a comprehensive agreement to protect FDI in the 1960s did not come to fruition,[1] and only a few multilateral initiatives dealing with specific aspects of FDI protection materialized.[2]

At the regional level, certain groupings began to introduce and implement common liberalization rules for FDI, mainly within the OECD and in the context of regional efforts to promote free trade and economic integration, particularly with the creation of the European Economic Community in 1958. (Economic integration -- especially efforts that are far advanced -- are a special case since investment rules are typically part of a wider set of rules and, therefore, allow trade-offs that may not be possible elsewhere.) To protect investment between developed and developing countries (mainly against the risk of expropriation[3]), bilateral investment treaties began to be concluded during that time.

In the 1970s, and in the context of concerns over the impact of transnational corporations (TNCs), developing countries imposed widespread controls, restrictions and conditions on FDI entry and operations.[4] This trend was also reflected in some regional instruments of the time (e.g., Decision 24 of the Andean Pact), while, at the multilateral level, efforts concentrated -- mainly at the insistence of developing countries, but also of trade unions and consumers -- on the formulation of standards of behaviour for TNCs. Lengthy negotiations on a Code of Conduct on Transnational Corporations and a Code on the Transfer of Technology eventually did not lead to agreed instruments.[5] But other multilateral instruments dealing with specific issues were concluded, such as the Tripartite Declaration of Principles Concerning Multinational Enterprises and Social Policy. Already in the 1980s, some efforts within the United Nations that focused on developing standards to ensure the proper functioning of markets, notably the Set of Multilaterally Agreed Equitable Principles and Rules for the Control of Restrictive Business Practices and the Guidelines for Consumer Protection, were successfully concluded.

Although many international instruments relevant to FDI exist, many have only a limited effect, and only the most dynamic of them (i.e., those that have continued to evolve and adapt or that address current concerns) are active components of the present international arrangements for FDI. In recent years, the development of international rules on FDI has proceeded mostly at bilateral and regional levels. Multilateral negotiations and agreements are also expanding; but, so far, those successfully concluded relate to sectoral or to specific issues only (table V.2) (UNCTAD-DTCI, 1996c; Brewer and Young, 1996a).

This chapter looks at bilateral, regional and multilateral agreements on FDI in terms of the various levels at which they presently function and their main elements (table V.3 and annex table 13). Investment standards elaborated by private institutions -- notably business organizations, trade unions, professional associations, consumers and other interested groups -- have, to some extent, also influenced the construction of international FDI rules[6] (table V.2), but they are not surveyed here.

1. Bilateral level

At the bilateral level, key investment concepts, principles and standards have been developed through the conclusion of treaties for the protection and promotion of FDI (bilateral investment treaties -- BITs).[7] Their distinctive feature is their exclusive concern with investment. Introduced four decades ago, these treaties have remained virtually unchanged in their format, and the issues they address continue to be among the most important for FDI (table V.3). They usually begin with declarations on the importance and beneficial role of FDI for development. Typically, BITs contain broad, open-ended definitions of foreign investment, inclusive of non-equity forms, different types of investment assets and most aspects of the life of an investment; many extend to portfolio investment. Investors covered are companies and individual nationals of one of the contracting parties, although the application of BITs is often restricted to investors who have real links with one of the two States involved. While they encourage governments to facilitate and welcome FDI, they avoid, in general, a direct regulation of the right of establishment, referring this matter to national laws (thus implicitly recognizing the right of governments to regulate entry of FDI);[8] an exception to this general approach is found in BITs signed by the United States which extend the national and most-favoured-nation (MFN) treatment standard to the entry and establishment of foreign investors (Vandevelde, 1992, 1993).[9] Most BITs also do not explicitly address ownership and control issues. On the other hand, some operational restrictions are covered. In particular, some BITs prescribe the admission of senior foreign personnel involved in an investment.[10] However, only a few BITs (those signed by the United States, as well as some Canadian and French BITs) prohibit performance requirements. Most BITs prescribe -- separately or in combination -- national treatment, MFN and fair and equitable treatment, and treatment according to international law. Of these standards, MFN is prescribed more often than national treatment, although an exception is usually provided for membership in regional integration agreements. National treatment itself is typically stated in broad and general terms, but, often, is qualified by a number of exceptions. In addition, BITs prescribe specific standards of investment protection on, notably, the transfer of funds, expropriation and nationalization and the settlement of disputes both between the treaty partners and between investors and the host State. By providing protection, BITs seek to promote FDI; yet they seldom provide for pro-active promotion measures by home countries. They also do not deal with broader issues related to the proper functioning of markets.

On the other hand, the similarity in both structure and substantive coverage of BITs should not conceal that differences in the strength of provisions exist to accommodate specific country concerns (table V.4).

Table V.2. Main international instruments[a] dealing with FDI, 1948-1996

Year[b]	Title	Setting	Level	Form	Status
1948	Havana Charter for an International Trade Organization	International Conference on Trade and Employment	Multilateral	Binding	Not ratified
1948	Draft Statutes of the Arbitral Tribunal for Foreign Investment and of the Foreign Investments Court	International Law Association	Non-overnmental	Non-binding	Not adopted
1949	International Code of Fair Treatment for Foreign Investments	International Chamber of Commerce	Non-governmental	Non-binding	Adopted
1957	Treaty Establishing the European Economic Community	European Economic Community	Regional	Binding	Adopted
1957	Agreement on Arab Economic Unity	Agreement on Arab Economic Unity	Regional	Binding	Adopted
1958	Convention on the Recognition and Enforcement of Foreign Arbitral Awards	United Nations	Multilateral	Binding	Adopted
1961	Code of Liberalisation of Capital Movements	OECD	Regional	Binding	Adopted
1961	Code of Liberalisation of Current Invisible Operations	OECD	Regional	Binding	Adopted
1962	United Nations General Assembly Resolution 1803 (XVII): Permanent Sovereignty over Natural Resources	United Nations	Multilateral	Non-binding	Adopted
1963	Model Tax Convention on Income and on Capital	OECD	Regional	Non-binding	Adopted
1965	Common Convention on Investments in the States of the Customs and Economic Union of Central Africa	Customs and Economic Union of Central Africa	Regional	Binding	Adopted
1965	Convention on the Settlement of Investment Disputes between States and Nationals of other States	World Bank	Multilateral	Binding	Adopted
1967	Revised Recommendation of the Council Concerning Co-operation Between Member Countries on Anticompetitive Practices Affecting International Trade	OECD	Regional	Non-binding	Adopted
1967	Draft Convention on the Protection of Foreign Property	OECD	Regional	Non-Binding	Not open for signature
1969	Agreement on Andean Subregional Integration	Andean Common Market	Regional	Binding	Adopted

/...

(Table V.2, cont'd)

Year[b]	Title	Setting	Level	Form	Status
1970	Agreement on Investment and Free Movement of Arab Capital among Arab Countries	Arab Economic Unity	Regional	Binding	Adopted
1970	Decision No. 24 of the Commission of the Cartagena Agreement: Common Regulations Governing Foreign Capital Movement, Trade Marks, Patents, Licences and Royalties	Andean Subregional Integration Group	Regional	Binding	Superseded
1971	Convention Establishing the Inter-Arab Investment Guarantee Corporation	Inter-Arab Investment Guarantee Corporation	Regional	Binding	Adopted
1972	Joint Convention on the Freedom of Movement of Persons and the Right of Establishment in the Central African Customs and Economic Union	Central African Customs and Economic Union	Regional	Binding	Adopted
1972	Guidelines for International Investment	International Chamber of Commerce	Non-overnmental	Non-binding	Adopted
1973	Agreement on the Harmonisation of Fiscal Incentives to Industry	Caribbean Common Market	Regional	Binding	Adopted
1973	Treaty Establishing the Caribbean Community	Caribbean Community	Regional	Binding	Adopted
1974	United Nations General Assembly Resolution 3201 (S-VI): Declaration on the Establishment of a New International Economic Order and United Nations General Assembly Resolution 3202 (S-VI): Programme of Action on the Establishment of a New International Economic Order	United Nations	Multilateral	Non-binding	Adopted
1974	United Nations General Assembly Resolution 3281 (XXIX): Charter of Economic Rights and Duties of States	United Nations	Multilateral	Non-binding	Adopted
1975	The Multinational Companies Code in the UDEAC (Customs and Economic Union of Central Africa)	Customs and Economic Union of Central Africa	Regional	Binding	Adopted
1975	Charter of Trade Union Demands for the Legislative Control of Multinational Companies	International Confederation of Free Trade Unions	Non-governmental	Non-binding	Adopted
1975	International Chamber of Commerce Rules of Conciliation and Arbitration	International Chamber of Commerce	Non-governmental	Non-binding	Adopted
1976	Declaration on International Investment and Multinational Enterprises	OECD	Regional	Binding/non-binding[c]	Adopted

/...

(Table V.2, cont'd)

Year[b]	Title	Setting	Level	Form	Status
1976	Arbitration Rules of the United Nations Commission on International Trade Law	United Nations	Multilateral	(Model)	Adopted
1977	ILO Tripartite Declaration of Principles Concerning Multinational Enterprises and Social Policy	International Labour Office	Multilateral	Non-binding	Adopted
1977	International Chamber of Commerce Recommendations to Combat Extortion and Bribery in Business Transactions	International Chamber of Commerce	Non-governmental	Non-binding	Adopted
1979	Draft International Agreement on Illicit Payments	United Nations	Multilateral	Binding	Not adopted
1979	United Nations Model Double Taxation Convention between Developed and Developing Countries	United Nations	Multilateral	(Model)	Adopted
1980	The Set of Multilaterally Agreed Equitable Principles and Rules for the Control of Restrictive Business Practices	United Nations	Mutltilateral	Non-binding	Adopted
1980	Guidelines Governing the Protection of Privacy and Transborder Flows of Personal Data	OECD	Regional	Non-binding	Adopted
1980	Unified Agreement for the Investment of Arab Capital in the Arab States	League of Arab States	Regional	Binding	Adopted
1980	Treaty Establishing the Latin American Integration Association (LAIA)	LAIA	Regional	Binding	Adopted
1981	International Code of Marketing of Breast-milk Substitutes	World Health Organization	Multilateral	Non-binding	Adopted
1981	Convention for the Protection of Individuals with Regard to Automatic Processing of Personal Data	Council of Europe	Regional	Binding	Adopted
1981	Agreement on Promotion, Protection and Guarantee of Investments among Member States of the Organisation of the Islamic Conference	Islamic Conference	Regional	Binding	Adopted
1981	Treaty for the Establishment of the Preferential Trade Area for Eastern and Southern African States	Preferential Trade Area for Eastern and Southern African States	Regional	Binding	No longer in effect
1982	Community Investment Code of the Economic Community of the Great Lakes Countries (CEPGL)	CEPGL	Regional	Binding	Adopted
1983	Draft United Nations Code of Conduct on Transnational Corporations	United Nations	Multilateral	Non-binding	Not adopted
1983	Treaty for the Establishment of the Economic Community of Central African States	Economic Community of Central and African States	Regional	Binding	Adopted

/...

(Table V.2, cont'd)

Year[b]	Title	Setting	Level	Form	Status
1985	Draft International Code of Conduct on the Transfer of Technology	United Nations	Multilateral	Non-binding	Not adopted
1985	United Nations General Assembly Resolution 39/248: Guidelines for Consumer Protection	United Nations	Multilateral	Non-binding	Adopted
1985	Convention Establishing the Multilateral Investment Guarantee Agency	World Bank	Multilateral	Binding	Adopted
1985	Declaration on Transborder Data Flows	OECD	Regional	Non-binding	Adopted
1987	Agreement for the Establishment of a Regime for CARICOM Enterprises	Caribbean Common Market	Regional	Binding	Adopted
1987	Revised Basic Agreement on ASEAN Industrial Joint Ventures	ASEAN	Regional	Binding	Adopted
1987	An Agreement Among the Governments of Brunei Darussalam, the Republic of Indonesia, Malaysia, the Republic of the Philippines, the Republic of Singapore and the Kingdom of Thailand for the Promotion and Protection of Investments	Agreement among the ASEAN countries	Regional	Binding	Adopted
1989	Fourth ACP-EEC Convention of Lomé	ACP-EU	Regional	Binding	Adopted
1990	Criteria for Sustainable Development Management: Towards Environmentally Sustainable Development	United Nations	Multilateral	Non-binding	Adopted
1990	Charter on a Regime of Multinational Industrial Enterprises (MIEs) in the Preferential Trade Area for Eastern and Southern African States	Preferential Trade Area for Eastern and Southern African States	Regional	Binding	Adopted
1991	Decision 291 of the Commission of the Cartagena Agreement: Common Code for the Treatment of Foreign Capital and on Trademarks, Patents, Licenses and Royalties	Andean Subregional Integration Group	Regional	Binding	Adopted
1991	Decision 292 of the Commission of the Cartagena Agreement. Uniform Code on Andean Multinational Enterprises	Andean Subregional Integration Group	Regional	Binding	Adopted
1991	The Business Charter for Sustainable Development: Principles for Environmental Management	International Chamber of Commerce	Non-overnmental	Non-binding	Adopted
1992	Guidelines on the Treatment of Foreign Direct Investment	World Bank	Multilateral	Non-binding	Adopted
1992	Articles of Agreement of the Islamic Corporation for the Insurance of Investment and Export Credit	Islamic Conference	Regional	Binding	Adopted
1992	North American Free Trade Agreement	Canada, Mexico and the United States	Regional	Binding	Adopted

/...

(Table V.2, cont'd)

Year[b]	Title	Setting	Level	Form	Status
1992	The CERES Principles	CERES	Non-governmental	Non-binding	Adopted
1993	Permanent Court of Arbitration Optional Rules for Arbitrating Disputes between Two Parties of which only One is a State	Permanent Court of Arbitration	Multilateral	Binding	Adopted
1993	Treaty Establishing the Common Market for Eastern and Southern Africa	Common Market for Eastern and Southern Africa	Regional	Binding	Adopted
1994	Marrakesh Agreement Establishing the World Trade Organization. Annex 1A: Multilateral Agreements on Trade in Goods. Agreement on Trade-Related Investment Measures	World Trade Organization	Multilateral	Binding	Adopted
1994	Marrakesh Agreement Establishing the World Trade Organization. Annex 1B: General Agreement on Trade in Services and Ministerial Decisions Relating to the General Agreement on Trade in Services	World Trade Organization	Multilateral	Binding	Adopted
1994	Marrakesh Agreement Establishing the World Trade Organization. Annex 1C: Agreement on Trade-Related Aspects of Intellectual Property Rights	World Trade Organization	Multilateral	Binding	Adopted
1994	Protocol of Colonia for the Reciprocal Promotion and Protection of Investments in the MERCOSUR (Intra-zonal)	MERCOSUR	Regional	Binding	Adopted
1994	Recommendation of the Council on Bribery in International Business Transactions	OECD	Regional	Non-binding	Adopted
1994	Protocol on Promotion and Protection of Investments from States not Parties to MERCOSUR	MERCOSUR	Regional	Binding	Adopted
1994	APEC Non-Binding Investment Principles	APEC	Regional	Non-binding	Adopted
1994	Energy Charter Treaty	European Energy Charter Conference	Regional	Binding	Provisional application
1995	Consumer Charter for Global Business	Consumers International	Non-governmental	Non-binding	Adopted
1995	Pacific Basin Charter on International Investments	Pacific Basin Economic Council	Non-governmental	Non-binding	Adopted

Source: UNCTAD-DTCI, 1996c. The instruments listed here are reproduced in whole or in part in the source publication.

[a]   Bilateral investment treaties and directives of the European Union are not included in the table.

[b]   Dates given relate to original ratification. Subsequent revisions of instruments are not included.

[c]   The OECD Declaration on International Investment and Multinational Enterprises is a political undertaking supported by legally-binding Decisions of the Council. The Guidelines on Multinational Enterprises are non-binding standards.

Table V.3. Main elements in key international FDI instruments

Element	Bilateral	Regional / interregional						
	Bilateral investment treaties	Investment Agreement between ASEAN countries	MERCOSUR: Protocol of Colonia on Investment (Intrazone)	APEC Non-Binding Investment Principles	Islamic Conf.: Agreement on Investment	Arab League: Unified Agreement for Investment of Arab Capital among Arab States	CoMESA: Treaty Est. the Common Market for Eastern and Southern Africa [a]	NAFTA: North American Free Trade Agreement
Legally binding	✓	✓	✓		✓	✓	✓	✓
Definition of FDI:								
a) Investment	✓	✓	✓		✓	✓	✓	✓
b) Investor	✓	✓	✓		✓	✓		✓
Investment measures that affect the entry and operations of foreign investors								
1. Restrictions								
a) Entry and establishment	✓(some)	✓	✓	✓	✓	✓	✓	✓
b) Ownership and control								
c) Operational conditions	✓	✓		✓		✓		✓
d) Authorization and reporting	✓(some)	✓	✓		✓		✓	
2. Incentives				✓	✓	✓	✓	✓
3. Standards of treatment								
a) National treatment	✓		✓	✓	✓(in part)	✓		✓
b) Most favoured nation treatment (MFN)	✓	✓	✓	✓	✓	✓		✓
c) Fair and equitable treatment	✓	✓	✓			✓	✓	✓

Regional / interregional (cont'd)			Multilateral			
	OECD		World Trade Organization		World Bank	United Nations
Energy Charter Treaty	Codes of Liberalisation of Capital Movements and Current Invisible Transactions	Declaration on International Investment and Multinational Enterprises and related Decisions	General Agreement on Trade in Services	Agreement on Trade-related Investment Measures	Convention on the Settlement of Investment Disputes between States and Nationals of Other States; Convention Establishing the Multilateral Investment Guarantee Agency; Guidelines on the Treatment of Foreign Direct Investment	ILO Tripartite Declaration of Principles Concerning Multinational Enterprises and Social Policy; UNCTAD Multilaterally Agreed Set of Principles and Rules for the Control of Restrictive Business practices; Guidelines for Consumer Protection
✓	✓	✓(Decisions)	✓	✓	✓(ICSID, MIGA)	
✓	✓		✓			
✓		✓	✓			
✓	✓	✓	✓		✓(Guidelines)	
					✓(Guidelines)	
✓		✓		✓	✓(Guidelines)	
					✓(Guidelines, MIGA)	
✓		✓		✓	✓(Guidelines)	
✓		✓	✓		✓(Guidelines)	
✓			✓	✓	✓(Guidelines)	
✓		✓			✓(Guidelines)	

/...

(Table V.3, cont'd)

Element	Bilateral	Regional / interregional						
	Bilateral investment treaties	Investment Agreement between ASEAN countries	MERCOSUR: Protocol of Colonia on Investment (Intrazone)	APEC Non-Binding Investment Principles	Islamic Conf.: Agreement on Investment	Arab League: Unified Agreement for Investment of Arab Capital among Arab States	CoMESA: Treaty Est. the Common Market for Eastern and Southern Africa [a]	NAFTA: North American Free Trade Agreement
4. <u>Transfer of funds</u>	✓	✓	✓	✓	✓	✓	✓	✓
5. <u>Protection standards</u>								
a) Minimum international standard of protection	✓	✓	✓		✓			✓
b) Expropriation	✓	✓	✓	✓	✓	✓	✓	✓
c) Recourse to international means for settlement of investment disputes	✓	✓	✓	✓	✓	✓	✓	✓
6. <u>Transparency</u>				✓				✓
7. <u>Measures dealing with broader concerns</u>								
a) Restrictive business practices					✓			✓
b) Consumer protection and health safety standards								
c) Labour standards								
d) Corporate behaviour				✓				

Regional / interregional (cont'd)			Multilateral			
	OECD		World Trade Organization		World Bank	United Nations
Energy Charter Treaty	Codes of Liberalisation of Capital Movements and Current Invisible Transactions	Declaration on International Investment and Multinational Enterprises and related Decisions	General Agreement on Trade in Services	Agreement on Trade-related Investment Measures	Convention on the Settlement of Investment Disputes between States and Nationals of Other States; Convention Establishing the Multilateral Investment Guarantee Agency; Guidelines on the Treatment of Foreign Direct Investment	ILO Tripartite Declaration of Principles Concerning Multinational Enterprises and Social Policy; UNCTAD Multilaterally Agreed Set of Principles and Rules for the Control of Restrictive Business practices; Guidelines for Consumer Protection
✓	✓				✓(Guidelines)	
✓		✓			✓(Guidelines, MIGA)	
✓					✓(Guidelines, MIGA)	
✓					✓(Guidelines, ICSID)	
✓	✓	✓	✓	✓	✓(Guidelines, MIGA)	
✓		✓	✓		✓	✓(RBP, GCP)
		✓				✓(RBP, GCP)
		✓				✓(ILO)
		✓			✓(Guidelines)	

Source: UNCTAD, based on annex table 13.

Key: ✓ means the issue is dealt with in the instrument; it does not indicate, however, whether the provisions is in the direction of more liberalization and protection, or in the direction of more controls; for more detailed information on these aspects see annex table 13; an empty space means the issue is not dealt with in the instrument.

a   Most of CoMESA provisions reflected in this table relate to investment into CoMESA.

Table V.4. Examples of differences in clauses in bilateral investment treaties

1. Admission of investments

Peru/Thailand (1991)	Germany/State of Papua Guinea (1980)	Kuwait/Poland (1990)	Argentina/United States (1991)
Art. 2	**Art. 2**	**Art. 2** Promotion and Protection of Investments	**Article II**
1. The benefits of this agreement shall apply only in cases where the investment of capital by the nationals and companies of one Contracting Party in the territory of the other Contracting Party has been specifically registered or otherwise approved in writing by the competent authority in accordance with the law and regulations of the respective Contracting Parties. 2. Nationals and companies of either Contracting Party shall be free to apply for such registration or approval in respect of any investment of capital whether made before or after the entry into force of this Agreement. 3. When granting approval in respect of any investment the Approving Contracting Party shall be free to lay down appropriate conditions.	Each Contracting Party shall in its territory promote as far as possible the investment of capital by nationals or companies of the other Contracting Party and admit such investments in accordance with its legislation.	1. Each Contracting State undertakes to provide and maintain a favourable environment for existing or new investments and reinvested returns of investors of the other Contracting State and shall, in applying its laws, regulations, administrative practices and procedures, permit such investments to be established and acquired in its territory on terms and conditions that accord treatment not less favourable than the treatment it accords to investments of its own investors of any third State, whichever is the most favourable.	1. Each Party shall permit and treat investment, and activities associated therewith, on a basis no less favourable than that accorded in like situations to investment or associated activities of its own nationals or companies, or of nationals or companies of any third country, whichever is the more favourable, subject to the right of each Party to make or maintain exceptions falling within one of the sectors or matters listed in the Protocol to this Treaty. Each Party agrees to notify the other Party before or on the date of entry into force of this Treaty of all such laws and regulations of which it is aware concerning the sectors or matters listed in the Protocol. Moreover, each Party agrees to notify the other of any future exception with respect to the sectors or matters listed in the Protocol, and to limit such exceptions to a minimum. Any future exception by either party shall not apply to investment existing in that sector or matter at the time the exception becomes effective. The treatment accorded pursuant to any exceptions shall, unless specified otherwise in the Protocol, be no less favourable than that accorded in like situations to investments and associated activities of nationals or companies of any third country.

2. Most-favoured-nation treatment

Singapore/Sri Lanka (1980)	Belgium/Luxembourg/Cameroon (1980)	China/Sweden (1982)	Hungary/Netherlands (1987)
Art. 4 Most-Favoured-Nation Treatment Provisions		**Art. 2**	**Art. 3**
1. Subject to paragraph (2) of this Article and to Article 5, neither Contracting Party shall in its territory subject investments admitted in accordance with the provisions of Article 2 or returns of nationals and companies of the other Contracting Party to treatment less favourable than that which it accords to investments or returns of nationals and companies of any third State.	3. The treatment and protection guaranteed in paragraphs 1 and 2 of this Article shall be at least equal to the treatment and protection enjoyed by the natural persons and bodies corporate of a third party State, and may in no case be less favourable than safety and protection granted under international law.	2. Investments by investors of either Contracting State in the territory of either Contracting State shall not be subject to a treatment less favourable than that accorded to investments by investors of third States.	2. More particularly, each Contracting Party shall accord to such investments full physical security and protection which in any case shall not be less than that accorded either to investments of its own nationals or to investments of investors of any third State, whichever is more favourable to the investor.

(Table V.4, cont'd)

Singapore/Sri Lanka (cont'd)	China/Sweden (cont'd)	Hungary/Netherlands (cont'd)
2. Investments of nationals and companies of either Contracting Party and the returns therefrom shall not be entitled to any treatment or privilege which is not available, on a reciprocal basis, to investments or returns of nationals and companies of the other Contracting Party. **Art. 5** Exceptions 1. The provisions of this Agreement relating to the grant of treatment no less favourable than that accorded to the nationals and companies of any third State shall not be construed so as to oblige one Contracting Party to extend to the nationals and companies of the other the benefit of any treatment, preference or privilege resulting from any regional arrangement for customs, monetary, tariff or trade matters or any agreement designed to lead in future to such a regional arrangement. 2. The provisions of this Agreement shall not apply to matters of taxation in the territory of either Contracting Party. Such matters shall be governed by any Avoidance of Double Taxation Treaty between the two Contracting Parties and the domestic laws of each Contracting Party.	3. Notwithstanding the provisions of paragraph (2) of this Article, a Contracting State, which has concluded with one or more other States, an agreement regarding the formation of a customs union or a free trade area, shall be free to grant a more favourable treatment on investments by investors of the State or States, which are also parties to the said agreement, or by investors of some of these States. A Contracting State shall also be free to grant a more favourable treatment to investment by investors of other States, if this is stipulated under bilateral agreements concluded with such States before the date of the signature of this Agreement.	3. If a Contracting Party has accorded special advantages to investors of any third State by virtue of agreements establishing customs unions, economic unions or similar institutions, or on the basis of interim agreements leading to such unions or institutions, that Contracting Party shall not be obliged to accord such advantages to investors of the other Contracting Party. 4. The treatment granted under the present Article shall not extend to taxes, fees, charges and to fiscal deductions and exemptions granted by either Contracting Party to investors of third States by virtue of a double taxation agreement or other agreement regarding matters of taxation, or on the basis of reciprocity with a third State.

/...

(Table V.4, cont'd)

	3. National treatment		
China/Japan (1988)	**France/Guinea (1982)**	**Pakistan/Republic of Korea (1988)**	**United Kingdom/USSR (1989)**
The treatment accorded by either Contracting Party within its territory to nationals and companies of the other Contracting Party with respect to investments, returns and business activities in connection with the investment shall not be less favourable than that accorded to nationals and companies of the (first mentioned) Contracting Party.	**Art. 4** Chaque Partie contractante applique sur son territoire et dans ses zones maritimes, aux nationaux ou sociétés de l'autre Partie, en ce qui concerne leurs investissements et activités liées à ces investissements, le traitement accordé a ses nationaux ou sociétés, ou le traitement accordé aux nationaux ou sociétés de la Nation la plus favorisée, si celui-ci est plus avantageux. A ce titre les nationaux autorisés à travailler sur le territoire et les zones maritimes de l'une des Parties contractantes doivent pouvoir benéficier des facilités matérielles appropriées pour l'exercice de leurs activités profesionnelles.	(b) Each Contracting Party shall in its territory accord to nationals or companies of the other Contracting Party as regards the management, use, enjoyment or disposal of their investments, treatment which is fair and equitable and not less favourable than that which it accords to its own nationals and companies or to the nationals and companies of any third State.	**Art. 3** (3) Each Contracting Party shall, to the extent possible, accord, in accordance with its laws and regulations, the same treatment, as mentioned in paragraphs (1) and (2) of this Article and in Article 4 of this Agreement, to the investments and returns of investors of the other Contracting Party as it accords to the investments and returns of its own investors.

Source: UNCTAD.

Note: The clauses shown in this table do not necessarily reflect the most common BITs practice.

Intended to promote investment between the treaty partners through the protection of investment, BITs are considered important signals concerning a country's investment climate (Salacuse, 1990). At the same time, BITs entered into by developing countries do not disregard the special development needs of individual treaty partners: they emphasize the importance of FDI for economic development; they generally recognize the effect of national law on FDI; and they contain exceptions or qualifications to some general principles (e.g., exceptions for balance-of-payments considerations in relation to the principle of free transfer of funds).

The network of BITs is expanding constantly. Some two-thirds of the nearly 1,160 treaties concluded up to June 1996 were concluded in the 1990s (172 in 1995 alone), involving 158 countries.[11] Originally concluded between developed and developing countries, more and more BITs are between developed countries and economies in transition, between developing countries and between developing countries and transition economies (figures V.2 and V.3 and annex table 13).

Other important principles developed at this level, but separately from BITs, relate to the avoidance of double taxation.[12] Double taxation occurs when income and capital of firms operating (broadly defined) in more than one tax jurisdiction are considered as taxable in more than one jurisdiction (Muchlinski, 1995). To avoid or resolve such conflicts, bilateral treaties for the avoidance of double taxation have been concluded in great numbers between countries from all regions and at different levels of development. For example, the member States of the European Union had concluded over 740 double taxation treaties (table V.5) as of June 1996 (IBFD, 1996). In the treaties, the parties agree to observe certain rules for the allocation of tax revenue between the jurisdictions involved and seek to address instances of taxable income that is not taxed in either jurisdiction. Most treaties are based on two model conventions, one prepared by the United Nations and the other by the OECD. The OECD model has generally been used in treaties concluded between developed countries, while the United Nations model serves as a model for agreements involving developing countries.

Recently, some developed countries have also completed cooperation, notification and information-exchange agreements in the area of competition policy with their principal trading partners (e.g., Germany with France; Australia with New Zealand; Australia, Canada, the European Union, Germany and Japan, each with the United States). They deal with notification and enforcement issues, but do not establish common substantive principles, standards or obligations. They could, nevertheless, be taken as a preliminary step towards the development of broader cooperation efforts to enforce national rules dealing with international business transactions (European Commission, 1995b).

Figure V.2. Growth of bilateral investment treaties, 1959-1996[a]

(Percentage)

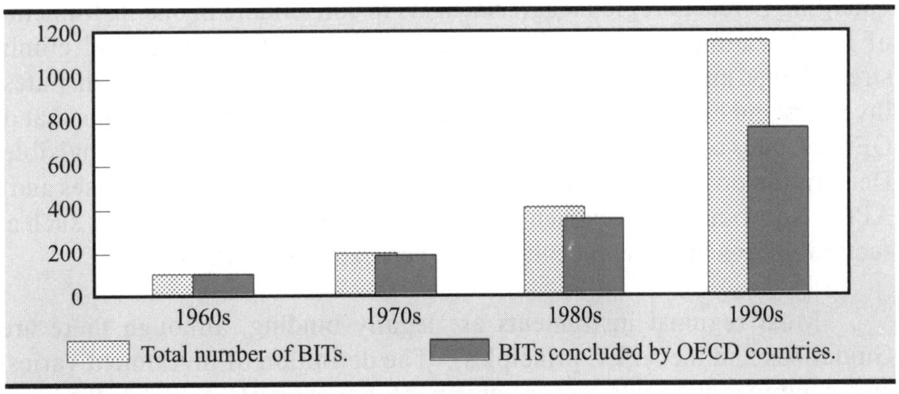

Source: UNCTAD, based on national sources.

a   Up to June 1996.

Bilateral investment treaties do not address investment-trade interrelations, with the principal exception being provisions that deal with performance requirements.   These interrelations, however, are reflected in some bilateral free trade and integration agreements concluded by a number of countries in the 1980s, notably between Australia and New Zealand, as well as between Canada and the United States (which later was renegotiated to include Mexico and became the NAFTA).

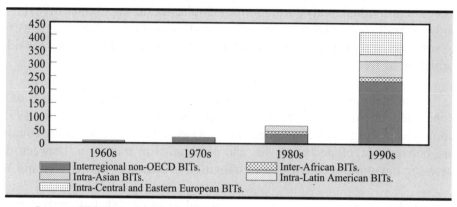

Figure V.3. Bilateral investment treaties among developing countries and economies in transition, by region, 1959 to 1996[a]

Source: UNCTAD, based on national sources.

a   Up to June 1996.

2. Regional level

At the regional level, the mix of investment issues covered is broader than that found at the bilateral level, and the operational approaches to deal with them are less uniform, reflecting, among other things, differences in interests and needs, levels of development and perspectives on future development.

The main objective typically pursued at this level -- and the first to be tackled -- is the liberalization of restrictions to entry and establishment of FDI, followed by the elimination of discriminatory operational conditions. Protection aspects have been added more recently. At this level, FDI liberalization proceeds mainly with a gradual elimination of existing restrictions, a system of reporting on existing regulations and changes to ensure transparency of measures and monitoring mechanisms to follow up on the implementation of schedules for further liberalization. A pattern emerging in recent regional agreements is to consolidate in one instrument an expanded set of issues of liberalization and protection, while procedures for the gradual elimination of restrictions are strengthened and provision is made for the settlement of investment disputes, including those between investors and host States. But there are also a number of agreements that do not go that far, e.g., the OECD Codes of Liberalisation of Capital Movements and Current Invisible Operations,[13] the OECD Declaration on International Investment and Multinational Enterprises and related decisions, and the APEC Non-binding Investment Principles. Some important aspects such as insurance, shipping and sectoral issues have been dealt with in separate instruments.[14]

Most regional instruments are legally binding, although there are exceptions (the OECD Guidelines and the APEC principles). The definition of investment varies considerably, depending on the purpose and context of an agreement. For example, NAFTA, the Investment Agreement among ASEAN countries and the Protocol on intra-MERCOSUR Investment contain broad definitions of investment and investors similar to those used in BITs. The OECD Codes, on the other hand, cover most international financial transactions.

Right of entry and establishment is increasingly being granted in many regional agreements (table V.3). In particular, the OECD Code of Liberalisation of Capital Movements and NAFTA contain such provisions, although signatory countries have typically exempted a number of industries or activities. Exceptions are dealt with through the use of negative lists which identify measures that are contrary to the core liberalising provisions in the agreement. At the other end of the spectrum are the APEC principles, which call for best efforts in this respect.

In terms of operational conditions, performance requirements have received limited attention at this level (table V.3), although NAFTA goes beyond most bilateral or other regional instruments by prohibiting some performance requirements, whether imposed on NAFTA or non-NAFTA investors (Gestrin and Rugman, 1994). Admission of foreign senior personnel in relation to an investment is now increasingly addressed (table V.3). Incentives have also been covered under some regional agreements, notably in the OECD Declaration and related Decision; sometimes they are addressed indirectly, either under performance requirements related to the conferral of benefits (NAFTA), or under competition rules (e.g., in the European Union).

With respect to standards of treatment and protection after entry, most regional agreements that contain them (table V.3), follow very closely the content and structure of BITs: they prescribe general standards (typically national treatment, MFN, fair and equitable treatment and treatment in accordance with international law), as well as specific high protection commitments, mainly on expropriation. In addition, most regional agreements dealing with either liberalization or protection standards, or with

Table V.5. Tax treaties of the European Union members, June 1996[a]

Members	Developed countries	Developing countries		Latin America and the Caribbean	Central and Eastern Europe[b]	Total
		Africa	Asia			
Austria	24	2	9	2	5	42
Belgium	23	4	11	1	7	46
Denmark [c]	22	9	12	3	10	56
Finland [c]	20	5	10	2	11	48
France	27	24	24	7	7	89
Germany	25	11	14	8	7	65
Greece	15	0	1	0	4	20
Ireland	22	1	2	0	2	27
Italy	24	8	12	6	7	57
Luxembourg	19	1	4	1	5	30
Netherlands	22	7	13	4	9	55
Portugal	12	1	0	1	0	14
Spain	19	2	4	4	7	36
Sweden [c]	20	12	13	8	11	64
United Kingdom	29	20	18	13	11	91
Total European Union	323	107	147	60	103	740

Source: International Bureau of Fiscal Documentation, 1996.

[a]   Income and capital tax treaties.

[b]   Treaties with the former Soviet Union have not been counted as separate treaties for all newly independent states.

[c]   The Nordic Tax Treaty, between Denmark, Faroe Islands, Finland, Iceland, Norway and Sweden, is not reflected in this list.

both, now include the free transfer of all investment-related funds, subject to some standard exceptions (e.g., related to bankruptcy laws and balance-of-payments safeguards). As with BITs, compliance with these standards and principles can generally be enforced in local courts, or through international arbitration. Provisions on investor-State settlement of disputes are now being increasingly included in regional agreements (table V.3). These are designed to permit arbitration proceedings, either through the International Convention on the Settlement of Investment Disputes between States and Nationals of other States (ICSID) (Broches, 1972) or other mechanisms and rules, generally after trying to settle the dispute amicably.

Other important issues dealt with in some regional instruments are transfer of technology, competition, environmental protection, taxation, conflicting requirements, and standards for the conduct of TNCs in relation to, e.g., disclosure of information, employment and labour relations, science and technology and illicit payments.

Moreover, the structure of the most advanced regional free trade and integration agreements (NAFTA, European Union) reflects increasingly the interrelations between investment, trade, services, intellectual property rights and competition policy. In particular, the NAFTA provisions on services reflect the continuum that exists between activities conducted on a cross-border basis and those carried out through an established presence (Gestrin and Rugman, 1994). NAFTA provisions on FDI go a step further than OECD in addressing more advanced integration issues; but they fall short of those of the European Union (Brewer and Young, 1995a). These variations among regional instruments partly reflect the fact that negotiations that address a wide range of issues also allow for trade-offs across issues.

The countries involved in most regional agreements share similar levels of development and outlooks on FDI, even though this may well conceal divergent needs and interests. Still, the question of providing for special treatment to certain partners on account of different levels of development arises less often than in the case of bilateral or multilateral arrangements. When it does, as in the case of NAFTA and ECT, the approach to development tends to be similar to that followed at the multilateral level, i.e., through exceptions, derogations, safeguards and the phasing of commitments. APEC -- which also involves developed and developing countries -- is somewhat different. The principles stated there are not legally binding commitments and only require best efforts. That in itself allows for discretionary application while keeping within the spirit that inspires them.

Finally, some regional groups have also developed common regimes for investment in and from third countries. The European Union, for example, has formulated investment principles aimed at promoting European Union investment in the ACP States in the Lomé IV Convention. Also, provisions for the free movement of capital, right of establishment and common competition rules are now included in association agreements with Central European countries; the bilateral agreements that are being negotiated with the former republics of the Soviet Union and the Mediterranean countries also include some of these provisions. Another example of a common regional approach to third-country FDI is the Protocol on Protection and Promotion of Investments Originating in Non-member States of MERCOSUR, which follows the structure and substance of BITs.

3. Multilateral level

At the multilateral level, most pertinent agreements relate to sectoral or to specific issues, moving in, as it were, on central FDI concerns from the outside. These include:

- **Services.** Foreign investment in this sector is now regulated in the General Agreement on Trade in Services (GATS), which covers the supply of markets through the presence of foreign service suppliers. Some general principles (transparency and, subject to a once-off list of temporary derogations, MFN treatment) are applicable to all services industries. Market-access and national treatment obligations depend on specific commitments contained in national schedules, which are to be progressively enlarged in coverage and depth through further negotiations. The Agreement also contains a number of annexes providing for additional rules in specific industries (Croome, 1995; Sauvé, 1994, 1995a, 1995b; UNCTAD and World Bank, 1994; UNCTAD, 1994a, ch. VII).

- **Performance requirements** are dealt with in the Agreement on Trade-related Investment Measures (TRIMs). However, this Agreement deals only with investment measures related to trade in goods. It forbids performance requirements inconsistent with Articles III (National Treatment) and XI (General Elimination of Quantitative Restrictions) of the GATT, including both mandatory restrictions and those linked to incentives. The Agreement contains an illustrative list of TRIMs deemed to be inconsistent with these articles, including local content requirements, trade-balancing requirements and export restrictions (UNCTC-UNCTAD, 1991; Low and Subramanian, 1995; Sauvé, 1994a; UNCTAD, 1994a, ch. VI).

- **Intellectual property rights**. The most comprehensive framework dealing with the protection at the multilateral level of intellectual property rights in trade and investment is the Agreement on Trade-related Aspects of Intellectual Property Rights (TRIPS Agreement). Building on the existing groundwork of intellectual property conventions, this Agreement lays down general provisions and basic principles regarding the protection of intellectual property rights, including national treatment and MFN requirements, as well as rules on substantive standards for the protection of specific categories of intellectual property rights, domestic enforcement procedures and international dispute settlement (Sauvé, 1994; UN-TCMD, 1993; UNCTAD, 1994a).

- **Insurance coverage** for political risks in developing countries is available for foreign investors under the Multilateral Investment Guarantee Agency (MIGA), an organization belonging to the World Bank Group. As a precondition for issuing a guarantee, the Agency must be satisfied that the investor complies with the laws of the host country and that these laws meet basic international standards (Shihata, 1992).

- **Settlement of disputes.** The issue of the settlement of investment disputes between private investors and host countries is specifically addressed in the Convention on the Settlement of Investment Disputes between States and Nationals of other States. Over the years, the International Centre on Settlement of Investment Disputes (ICSID), another World Bank Group institution, which administers the system of conciliation and arbitration established by the Convention, has increased its country membership substantially and has had a number of cases before it (table V.6). References to the ICSID Convention or to other arbitration rules and facilities (e.g., UNCITRAL, ICC) can be found in various international instruments (Gray, 1990; Broches, 1991; Shihata, 1992).

Table V.6. Investment disputes registered by ICSID, July 1996

Case	Year of registration	Status
Holiday Inns S.A., Occidental Petroleum Corporation et al. v. Government of Morocco	1972	Amicable settlement
Adriano Gardella S.p.A. v. Government of Côte d'Ivoire	1974	Arbitration award
Alcoa Minerals of Jamaica, Inc. v. Government of Jamaica	1974	Amicable settlement
Kaiser Bauxite Company v. Government of Jamaica	1974	Amicable settlement
Reynolds Jamaica Mines Limited and Reynolds Metals Company v. Government of Jamaica	1974	Amicable settlement
Government of Gabon v. Société Serete S.A.	1976	Amicable settlement
AGIP S.p.A. v. Government of the People's Republic of the Congo	1977	Arbitration award
S.A.R.L. Benvenuti & Bonfant v. Government of the People's Republic of the Congo	1977	Arbitration award
Guadalupe Gas Products Corporation v. Federal Military Government of Nigeria	1978	Amicable settlement
Amco Asia Corporation, Pan American Development Limited and P.T. Amco Indonesia v. Republic of Indonesia	1981	Arbitration award
Kloeckner Industrie-Anlagen GmbH, Klockner Belge S.A. and Klockner Handelmaatschappij B.V. v. United Republic of Cameroon and Société Camerounaise des Engrais	1981	Arbitration award
Société Ouest Africaine des Bétons Industriels v. State of Senegal	1982	Arbitration award
SEDITEX Engineering Beratungsgesellschaft fur die Textilindustrie m.b.H. v. Government of the Democratic Republic of Madagascar	1982	Conciliation
Swiss Aluminium Limited and Icelandic Aluminium Company Limited v. Government of Iceland	1983	Amicable settlement
Liberian Eastern Timber Corporation v. Government of the Republic of Liberia	1983	Arbitration award
Tesoro Petroleum Corporation v. Government of Trinidad and Tobago	1983	Conciliation
Atlantic Triton Company Limited v. People's Revolutionary Republic of Guinea	1984	Arbitration award
Colt Industries Operating Corporation, Firearms Division v. Government of the Republic of Korea	1984	Amicable settlement
Southern Pacific Properties (Middle East) Limited v. Arab Republic of Egypt	1984	Arbitration award

/...

(Table V.6, cont'd)

Case	Year of registration	Status
Maritime International Nominees Establishment v. Government of the Republic of Guinea	1984	Arbitration award
Gaith R. Pharaon v. Republic of Tunisia	1986	Amicable settlement
Société d'Etudes de Travaux et de Gestion SETIMEG S.A. v. Republic of Gabon	1987	Amicable settlement
Mobil Oil Corporation, Mobil Petroleum Company Inc. and Mobil Oil New Zealand Limited v. New Zealand Government	1987	Amicable settlement
Asian Agricultural Products Limited v. Democratic Socialist Republic of Sri Lanka	1987	Arbitration award
Occidental of Pakistan, Inc. v. Islamic Republic of Pakistan	1987	Amicable settlement
Manufacturers Hanover Trust Company v. Arab Republic of Egypt and General Authority for Investment and Free Zones	1989	Amicable settlement
Vacuum Salt Products Limited v. Government of the Republic of Ghana	1992	Arbitration award
Scimitar Exploration Limited v. Bangladesh Oil, Gas and Mineral Corporation	1992	Arbitration award
American Manufacturing & Trading, Inc. v. Republic of Zaire	1993	Pending
Philippe Gruslin v. Government of Malaysia	1994	Amicable settlement
SEDITEX Engineering Beratungsgesellschaft für die Textilindustrie m.b.H. v. Government of Madagascar	1994	Pending
Tradex Hellas S.A. v. Republic of Albania.	1994	Pending
Leaf Tobacco A. Michaelides S.A. and Greek-Albanian Leaf Tobacco & Co. S.A. v. Republic of Albania	1995	Pending
Cable Television of Nevis, Ltd. and Cable Television of Nevis Holdings, Ltd. v. Federation of St. Kitts and Nevis	1995	Pending
Antoine Goetz and others v. Republic of Burundi	1995	Pending
Compañia del Desarrollo de Santa Elena S.A. v. Government of Costa Rica	1996	Pending
Misma Mines Pty. Ltd. v. Independent State of Papua Guinea	1996	Pending
Fedax N.V. v. Republic of Venezuela	1996	Pending

Source: ICSID.

- **Employment and labour relations**. This issue is covered by the Tripartite Declaration of Principles Concerning Multinational Enterprises and Social Policy. It contains principles recommended to governments, employers' and workers' organizations and to TNCs on employment, training, conditions of work and life, and industrial relations. In all these areas, TNCs are called upon to assume a leading role in applying the best standards, usually those applying in their home countries, to labour conditions and relations in host countries.

Finally, the treatment of FDI is dealt with in the Guidelines on the Treatment of Foreign Direct Investment, developed by the World Bank. They are based on an exhaustive analysis of existing instruments and best practices. While they are not formally binding, the Guidelines represent a serious effort to reconcile the concerns of developing countries with the need to meet investors' demands to increase and maintain investment flows (World Bank, 1992a; 1992b).

Some issues covered at this level deal with the proper functioning of the market. Thus, for example, multilateral competition rules are established in UNCTAD's Set of Multilaterally Agreed Equitable Principles and Rules for the Control of Restrictive Business Practices; provisions on specific competition policy issues are also contained in the WTO agreements on trade in services and the protection of intellectual property. The WTO Agreement on Subsidies and Countervailing Measures deals with subsidies including, in principle, those that apply to FDI operations involving trade in goods. Non-discriminatory access to procurement by some government entities is provided by the Agreement on Government Procurement which is one of the WTO's plurilateral trade agreements. And United Nations standards for consumer protection have been developed in the Guidelines for Consumer Protection.

It is at the multilateral level that concern for development is most apparent. This is particularly so in the case of the GATS (box V.1), TRIPS and TRIMs agreements, as well as the Restrictive Business Practices Set, where transitional arrangements are made that take into account the needs of developing countries. The World Bank Guidelines, too, are sensitive to development concerns, while insurance under MIGA is available, particularly for projects in developing countries.

B. Lessons learned

The future elaboration of FDI rules should take into account the lessons of the past. At the same time, it is difficult to draw definite conclusions, because many instruments -- especially many of those advancing the process of liberalization -- are relatively recent, are not always fully implemented and the real effect of their application is not always clear yet. Still, on the basis of the evolution and the present status of international FDI arrangements, a number of lessons may be drawn:

- **The evolution of international arrangements for FDI has followed and interacted with developments at the national level and reflects the priorities and concerns of a particular period**. After the Second World War, FDI concerns related mainly to natural resources and key industries. With decolonization, the principal concern for host developing countries became how to regain control over their economies and natural wealth, in order to consolidate their political independence. These efforts were epitomized in the principle of permanent sovereignty over natural wealth and resources which, eventually, became widely accepted (Gess, 1964; Kemper, 1976; Rosenberg, 1983). For foreign investors and their home countries, the main preoccupation was to protect their investments from political risks, especially from nationalization. In this climate, standards for protection of investment emerged, albeit on a bilateral basis and at the initiative of the capital exporting countries. Issues of entry and establishment were generally left to be regulated by national laws by both developed and developing countries. Such laws in many cases established restrictions, controls and conditions on the entry and establishment of FDI and on its operations, including on the repatriation of profits and capital; in many cases, they also dealt with issues related to the need to ensure access to and transfer of technology. At the multilateral level, developing countries used their rising influence to assert their economic independence and sought to elaborate standards of behaviour for TNCs (Asante, 1989; Horn, 1980; Fatouros, 1993).

In the 1980s, these trends were reversed, mainly as a result of the debt crisis in many developing countries (which made FDI a more desirable alternative to bank lending) and of the changing perceptions in these countries as to the role that FDI could play in the growth and development of their economies. As a result, laws and policies began to change dramatically

---

Box V.1. The development dimension in the GATS

An important objective of the GATS is to promote development of developing countries. The second preambular paragraph reads as follows: "wishing to establish a multilateral framework of principles and rules for trade in services with a view to the expansion of such trade under conditions of transparency and progressive liberalization and as a means of promoting the economic growth of all trading partners and the development of developing countries", and the fifth preambular paragraph states: "desiring to facilitate the increasing participation of developing countries in trade in services and the expansion of their service exports including, *inter alia*, through the strengthening of their domestic services capacity and its efficiency and competitiveness".

Countries agreed during the Uruguay Round that participation of developing countries should be based on the principle of relative reciprocity/development compatibility, and should not be seen as "special treatment" along the lines of GATT Part IV. Article IV of GATS commits members to facilitate the participation of developing countries in trade in services through negotiated specific commitments relating to the strengthening of their domestic services capacity, including through access to technology on a commercial basis, improved distribution channels and information networks and the liberalization of market access in sectors and modes of supply of export interest to them. Article IV also provides for the establishment of contact points to facilitate access to information on commercial and technical aspects of the supply of services, registration, recognition and obtaining of professional qualification, and the availability of service technology.

Article XIX of GATS calls for successive rounds of negotiations, aimed at achieving a progressively higher level of liberalization. Article XIX:2 provides that the process of liberalization will take place with due respect for national policy objectives and the level of development of individual parties, both overall and in individual industries. Appropriate flexibility is foreseen for individual developing countries for opening fewer industries, liberalizing fewer types of transactions, progressively extending market access in line with their development situation and, when making access to their markets available to foreign service suppliers, attaching to it conditions aimed at achieving the objectives referred to in Article IV.

Article XIX:3 provides for an assessment of trade in services in overall terms and on a sectoral basis with reference to the objectives of GATS, including those set out in paragraph 1 of Article IV for the purposes of establishing negotiating guidelines.

Finally, by covering all factors of production, including the temporary movement of natural persons, the GATS opens opportunities for increased services exports from developing countries, an innovation of considerable importance to these countries. Furthermore, by using a positive-list approach (i.e. market access and national treatment are subject to specific negotiations), each country can strategically negotiate the individual service industries or transactions that it is ready to open up (subject to specific conditions and limitations), in pursuance of long-term progressive liberalization.

Source: UNCTAD.

---

in the direction of liberalization, protection and promotion of FDI, and continue to do so. Liberalization efforts in developed countries were also expanded and deepened. At the same time, a shift in development strategies pursued by governments, from highly protective import-substitution models (which are not inconsistent with openness to inward FDI) to outward-looking policies emphasizing export-led growth, stressed the opportunities offered by FDI to establish linkages with globally-integrated production, distribution and marketing networks and led to a more coherent policy approach towards trade and investment. These changes are now being reflected in regional instruments, and in sectoral or issue-specific multilateral agreements.

Two lessons can be drawn from past swings in FDI policies: one is that progress in the development of international investment rules is linked to the convergence of policies across countries; the other is that an approach to FDI issues that takes into account the interests of all parties, and hence is to their mutual advantage, is more likely to gain widespread acceptance and, ultimately, is more effective. In practice, this raises the question of how an appropriate balance of rights and obligations among the participants can be found. At the same time, international negotiations for FDI liberalization have further stimulated countries to introduce changes unilaterally in national laws, even before such changes were required by international commitments, thus exemplifying the interaction between the development of national and international rules.

- **Widespread recognition is emerging of the principal FDI issues that need to be addressed internationally**. With the growing appreciation of the role of FDI in development and the convergence of national attitudes in favour of market-oriented policies, a number of issues have moved from the national to the international level and have become standard items in international discussions on FDI. At the same time, the extent to which, and the manner in which, these are at present incorporated in specific international instruments at the bilateral, regional and multilateral levels varies considerably, as does the strength with which they are addressed:

  - General standards of treatment applying after FDI establishment, notably national treatment, MFN and fair and equitable treatment, are widely reflected at the bilateral and regional levels; the same is true with respect to the free transfer of funds in relation to an investment.

  - Questions of entry and establishment for FDI and certain operational conditions (such as performance requirements and also, indirectly, incentives and managerial personnel restrictions), which typically aim at increasing market access, are presently addressed in a number of regional and multilateral agreements. These issues have received limited attention at the bilateral level where the general tendency is to leave matters of admission and operational conditions to be dealt with in accordance with specific national development objectives.

  - Certain protection standards, on issues such as expropriation and investor-to-state dispute settlement, are dealt with mainly at the bilateral but increasingly also at the regional level, while machinery for dispute settlement has also been established at the multilateral level.

- Issues of corporate behaviour bearing on the proper functioning of markets, such as restrictive business practices (in the broader context of competition policy), consumer, labour and environmental standards, as well as illicit payments, are dealt with in a number of specific instruments, most of which are non-binding.

- Other issues, such as the promotion of FDI and conflicting requirements applying to foreign investors (within the broader context of conflicts of jurisdiction) have so far received limited attention in international instruments.

In a rapidly globalizing world economy, the list of substantive issues entering international FDI discussions is becoming increasingly broader -- both at the level of individual instruments and as a result of the proliferation of instruments concluded -- and may eventually include the entire range of questions concerning factor mobility. Issues that receive relatively little attention at this time may therefore acquire increased importance in the future.

- **So far, progress has been gradual, helped by increasingly greater transparency and monitoring.** As regards the functional characteristics of present arrangements, there are, with many variations, also some common features:

  - Progressive elimination of restrictions. Higher standards are being sought over time. In the case of the OECD, for example, it took 25 years from the adoption of the Liberalisation Codes until the right of establishment was confirmed.

  - Transparency of national regulation. Through the reporting of investment measures and relevant normative changes, regional and multilateral FDI instruments provide a mechanism to increase transparency of national regulations, thus contributing to a key aspect of a favourable investment climate.

  - Monitoring, follow-up and dispute-settlement mechanisms. Bilateral, regional and multilateral instruments on FDI include procedures for their implementation. These can vary considerably in their strength and the degree of authority delegated to the monitoring authorities, from the full-fledged settlement of disputes to consultation and peer reviews on issues relevant to the implementation and interpretation of an agreement. In addition, bilateral treaties and an increasing number of regional agreements address the question of investor-State dispute settlement, and reflect increased acceptance of international arbitration, often referring to ICSID. Implementation mechanisms are important to identify and resolve concrete problems and make an instrument effective.

A key lesson that emerges from these functional approaches is that implementing and strengthening standards is a lengthy process. The present regional and multilateral instruments have taken some time to be negotiated and need more time to show fully their effects. But globalization pressures and changing corporate strategies may encourage faster normative responsiveness in the future.

- **The interrelations between investment and trade are seen increasingly in a common framework.** Friendship, Commerce and Navigation treaties concluded immediately after the Second World War addressed a wide range of aspects of bilateral economic relations, including the entry and treatment of nationals of one party in the territory of another party, as well as trade, investment and exchange-control matters (UNCTC, 1988). This comprehensive approach, especially the need to integrate investment, trade and competition rules, was also manifested at the multilateral level in the Havana Charter. It was soon felt, however, that such broad agreements were difficult to negotiate. As a result, developed countries turned, in the 1960s, to specialized bilateral treaties, BITs, i.e., treaties with an almost exclusive focus on investment matters. More recently, however, driven by the logic of the requirements of firms to contest effectively international markets, the need to bring especially investment and trade matters together has asserted itself again, particularly at the regional (e.g., NAFTA) and multilateral levels (Lawrence, 1996). The Uruguay Round of Multilateral Trade Negotiations was indeed the first time investment issues were introduced as part of the disciplines of the multilateral trading system (although, indirectly, investment-related issues had been dealt with for quite some time under, for example, the Subsidies Code and the Government Procurement Agreement). Trade and investment issues converged most markedly in the negotiations of GATS which defines trade in services as including four modes of supply, including the provision of services through commercial presence. The TRIMs Agreement, in fact, focuses on one aspect of the policy interrelationship between trade and investment. Possible future work on investment policy and competition policy may lead to even deeper policy integration. A major question at this juncture is the extent to which this new trend should be accommodated or encouraged through the development of concepts designed to capture the relationships between trade and investment and, to the extent that a more comprehensive approach is pursued, how to avoid the difficulties that caused countries to move away from Friendship, Commerce and Navigation treaties in the first place.

Development issues must be and can be addressed. For international agreements to be effective and stable, they need to take into account the interests of all parties, incorporate a balance of interests and allow for mutual advantage. This applies particularly to developing countries and, more generally, to agreements between countries at different levels of development. In particular, any agreement involving developed and developing countries must take into account the special importance of development policies and objectives. In fact, economic and social development is a long-standing and fundamental goal of the international community. This has been expressly recognized in many international instruments, some of which have been dedicated exclusively to serve that end.

The development dimension can be addressed in international investment accords at all levels and in several fashions. Most FDI agreements begin with at least hortatory commitments to promote FDI flows between signatory parties. Some, notably the Lomé IV Convention between the European Union and 68 African, Caribbean and Pacific States, provide for specific commitments to promote investment into these regions to accelerate their development. The TRIPS agreement commits governments to provide incentives to promote technology transfer to the least developed countries. Tax-sparing provisions have been included in taxation treaties with developing countries.

The development dimension is further addressed in FDI agreements by structuring the contents of the instrument in a manner that takes into account the special situation of developing countries (UNCTC, 1990). Thus, provisions of an investment agreement can be negotiated or defined in such a way as to exclude from coverage certain areas or national policy instruments necessary for a country's development. Being a developing country has been a qualifying factor for being granted broad (or broader) exceptions or special treatment in a number of investment instruments (such as BITs, NAFTA and the RBP Set). Development or adjustment needs can also be addressed by granting longer transitional periods in the implementation of particular commitments (e.g., TRIMs, TRIPS, ECT, NAFTA). In fact, this device is also being used within developed country arrangements -- the OECD and the European Union, for instance -- to allow relatively less developed members time to strengthen their indigenous economic base and prepare for a greater exposure to international competition. This approach to the development dimension has facilitated the participation of developing countries in the development of international instruments, while giving them flexibility to synchronize their liberalization steps with development objectives.

* * *

Thus, there has been progress in the past fifty years in the elaboration of international arrangements for FDI. Present arrangements are reflected in a variety of instruments of different geographical scope and with significant differences as to their substantive coverage, specific content, approach and legal nature. The instruments are neither exhaustive nor mutually exclusive. Although there has been a proliferation of international instruments, covering a broadening set of issues, even taken together, they do not add up to a coherent and complete international FDI framework. Besides, even when governments are prepared to agree to certain rules at the bilateral or regional level, they are not necessarily prepared to make the same commitments at the multilateral level.

In this respect it is useful to recall that the present national, bilateral, regional and multilateral approaches to FDI emerged partly as a result of the failure to conclude comprehensive multilateral rules in this field in the past. Over the past decade or so, however, there has been a certain convergence of FDI policies in the context of convergent development strategies. The new situation provides a different environment for discussions and negotiations and creates a new set of costs and benefits for various sets of international arrangements.

Notes

[1] The Draft Convention on the Protection of Foreign Property was completed by the OECD but was never opened for signature. See Van Hecke, 1964.

[2] Key among these is the Convention for the Settlement of Investment Disputes between States and Nationals of Other States, concluded in 1965 under the auspices of the World Bank.

[3] For recent general overviews of issues relating to expropriation, see Higgins, 1982 and Mouri, 1994.

[4] Even among developed countries, considerable attention was given to national control; see Miller, 1959; Fatouros, 1961.

[5] These negotiations, however, contributed to a better understanding of the issues involved. On international codes of conduct, see UNCTC, 1986; Horn, 1980; Kline, 1985; Rubin and Hufbauer, 1984; and Metaxas, 1988.

[6] For a discussion of issues pertaining to the international framework for FDI, see Fatouros, 1994; and Hansen and Aranda, 1991; these complement a discussion of issues at the national level, contained in Rubin and Wallace, 1994.

[7] For a detailed analysis of BITs, see UNCTC, 1992b; UNCTC, 1988; and Dolzer and Stevens, 1995.

[8] In fact, BITs often make it clear that only investments that are admitted in accordance with the requirements of national laws or that are approved by the competent authority would be protected under the treaty; see, e.g., the treaties between Singapore and Switzerland (1973) and between Malaysia and Sweden (1979). For a more elaborate discussion of admission clauses in BITs, see Laviec, 1985; Akinsanya, 1987; and Sornarajah, 1985.

[9] This is reflected in the United States bilateral investment treaty prototype, which is reproduced in UNCTAD-DTCI, 1996c (vol. III).

[10] See, for example, the BITs between Germany and China (1983) and between Egypt and the United States (1982).

[11] For a comprehensive list of BITs concluded until July 1995, see UNCTAD-DTCI, 1996c (vol. III). For an update to the list until July 1996, see annex table 12.

[12] For a discussion of taxation issues in relation to TNCs, see Plasschaert, 1994. On double taxation model conventions and bilateral treaties, see Okran, 1989; and United Nations, 1979.

[13] The history of the Codes has recently been presented in OECD, 1995a.

[14] For an analysis of specific regional investment instruments, see Brewer 1995b; Brewer and Young, 1995a, 1996a, 1996b; Bora 1995; Bora and Graham, 1995; Gestrin and Rugman, 1994; Graham, 1995; Green and Brewer, 1995; OECD, 1993a, 1993b, 1993c and 1994a; Parra, 1995; UNCTAD-DTCI, 1996a, introduction; and Waelde, 1995.

Chapter VI

Policy approaches, key issues and fora

A. Policy approaches

The purpose of this section is to explore basic approaches regarding the future evolution of international arrangements for foreign direct investment (FDI). For analytical purposes, two basic approaches, two ideal types, are distinguished, and the principal arguments advanced by their proponents are presented. One approach involves allowing current arrangements to evolve organically, while actively deepening and expanding them, as appropriate. The other approach involves the construction, through negotiations, of a comprehensive multilateral framework for FDI.

1. Arguments for improving current arrangements

The overarching rationale for restricting international policy action to the elaboration and improvement of current arrangements is that these arrangements are working well in providing an enabling framework that allows FDI to contribute to growth and development and in supporting high and growing volumes of FDI. Moreover, such arrangements allow for groups of countries to enter into agreements having the degree of "strength" (box VI.1) that is suitable to their particular circumstances. As regards "policy coherence" (box VI.2), while there are certainly substantial economic gains to be derived from ensuring that trade and investment policies fully support a country's economic objectives, this can be adequately addressed at the national level. At the level of international arrangements, there may be costs to lack of "coherence" between trade and investment regimes, but such costs are difficult to assess, and may be no greater than the costs of lack of "coherence" between trade and exchange-rate regime, or between trade and immigration policies. Further, bilateral, regional and multilateral arrangements are moving policies rapidly in the direction of liberalization and are beginning to introduce policy "coherence" at the international level.

At the national level, many governments have undertaken, autonomously (or in the context of bilateral, regional or multilateral arrangements), major policy-liberalization programmes that have allowed substantially increased FDI flows to many countries, including developing countries. Having recognized the importance of FDI for development, and in the absence of a backlash caused by imprudent action or lack of a proper balance, governments would not easily reverse their policies and risk damaging development prospects. But the liberalization of FDI regimes in such circumstances is one thing; to bind multilaterally the liberalization measures undertaken at a particular time and under particular circumstances, is another.

Box VI.1. What does business mean by "strong" rules?

In discussions on investment frameworks, reference is often made to the "strength" or "weakness" of a particular instrument. For example, the NAFTA investment provisions are described as "strong" while the APEC investment principles are described as "weak". These characterizations normally reflect the concerns of business. While no precise definition of what constitutes strong or weak rules exists, several key features common to most investment instruments underpin these distinctions:

- *Binding versus non-binding instruments.* Strong instruments are those that are binding legal agreements. This implies that signatories are bound to apply the agreement under a legal obligation that is enforceable in a court of law. Non-binding instruments only carry the weight of the political commitments made by the signatory governments (which can be considerable) but are not enforceable.

- *Liberalization commitments.* Many instruments not only involve the establishment of new rules governing the treatment of foreign investors and their investments, but introduce a stand-still and reduce, or roll-back, existing restrictions. To the extent that they do so successfully, an instrument is considered strong.

- *Dispute-settlement mechanisms.* Strong investment instruments include both state-to-state and investor-to-state dispute-settlement mechanisms. These mechanisms are considered particularly strong when the decisions of arbitral tribunals (or whatever other judicial bodies are used to resolve disputes) are binding upon the parties to the dispute.

- *Definition of investment.* The definition of investment in a particular instrument determines the extent of its coverage. A strong definition is therefore typically asset based and covers all types of assets, i.e., covers both FDI and portfolio investments, real estate holdings, intellectual property rights, other financial flows particular between companies and a broad range of intangible assets.

- *National treatment and most-favoured-nation (MFN) treatment.* An instrument is generally considered strong when it contains both unqualified national treatment and MFN. The two concepts combine to offer international investors particularly strong protection from discrimination since any derogation from national treatment (e.g., for national security purposes) still leaves MFN, which ensures that foreign investors will nonetheless be competing on an equal footing with other foreign investors in that market.

- *Performance requirements.* Performance requirements tend to distort investment patterns (and trade patterns in the case of TRIMs) and inhibit efficiency. Strong investment instruments are therefore those that prohibit performance requirements, both as a condition for establishment and the conferral of benefits. The longer the list of prohibited performance requirements, the stronger an investment instrument.

- *Exceptions.* The flip side of liberalization commitments are the exceptions that governments maintain or "grandfather" after the adoption of an investment instrument. The number and economic significance of these exceptions are an important consideration in any evaluation of the strength or weakness of a particular investment instrument.

While this is by no means an exhaustive list of the elements that give an investment instrument its strong or weak characteristics as far as the business community is concerned, they are nonetheless among the more important factors.

Sources: Messing, 1996; USCIB, 1995; BIAC, 1994a, 1994b; ICC, 1996.

Moreover, despite the growing convergence of national FDI policies, there are significant differences in national characteristics and conditions. These call for differentiated approaches to regulatory frameworks for FDI, reflecting a country's development strategy. International disciplines that are too restrictive of national initiatives, thus reducing the "degrees of freedom" countries need to pursue development objectives, are therefore not helpful (Third World Network, 1996). More generally, some countries prefer an approach in which the starting point is not the foreign investor's right to invest but the host country government's permission to allow them to do so. The principal reason is that national policies developed without multilateral constraints would allow more carefully calibrated approaches to policy issues in the area of FDI (UNCTAD-DTCI, 1995a, chapter VI).

This applies also, at least partly, to regional approaches. Thus, while the OECD governments can negotiate a "high-standards" agreement, developing countries can be just as ambitious in negotiating common investment regimes within their regional contexts.

Within the context of globalization and international production, governments have, indeed, recognized that international cooperation is desirable. They have, therefore, concluded bilateral, regional and multilateral agreements dealing with FDI. These have created a more favourable policy environment for FDI by raising practices and norms most important to foreign investors to the level of international commitments. Commitments negotiated between like-minded governments, or on specific issues, are often "stronger" than those achievable for a broad range of issues at the multilateral level (box VI.1). The present array of international arrangements for FDI has been expanding and deepening at a fast pace, indicating that governments are responding to the internationalization of markets and production. Bilateral treaties, in particular, can be concluded easily and rapidly because it is easier for two countries to reach agreement and because prototypes are available for both developed and developing countries. Some two-thirds of the more than 1,100 BITs were concluded since 1990.

In fact, allowing countries and regions to develop their own approaches fosters policy competition, which leads to the relatively rapid spread of best practices in FDI policy in relation to countries' development objectives. Since transnational corporations (TNCs) are flexible and experienced in operating in diverse policy frameworks, they can adapt to regulatory differences among countries.

The present network of bilateral and regional arrangements covers already most of the principal home countries and increasingly most of the main host countries, as well as most of the issues of interest to investors. At the same time, through MFN clauses in bilateral agreements, the highest standards in them can be extended to other countries, covering more and more countries and regions, and establishing a level playing field for foreign investors. A similar process takes place through regional arrangements. Any gaps, overlaps and even conflicting rules applying to global investors in different locations could be mitigated in a number of ways. For example, a global model bilateral investment treaty could be helpful in this respect,[1] an approach followed in the area of taxation through the OECD and the United Nations model conventions. And, of course, it is part of the nature of regional agreements to harmonize policies; in the process, they also provide a testing ground for rule-making in this area.

In any event, the momentum for further international agreements to liberalize FDI policies and to promote and protect investment is currently at the bilateral and regional levels. It may be counter-productive if this momentum were disturbed, if not disrupted, by multilateral negotiations on investment issues in which countries might take strong positions that could become divisive. The risk of this increases with the length and the level of complexity of negotiations, and the extent to which

Box VI.2. What is market contestability, modal neutrality and policy coherence?

The priorities and objectives of governments and TNCs differ, but their interaction is one of the fundamental dynamics underpinning economic growth and development. One of the principal challenges faced by policy makers is to identify and implement policies that promote the objectives of government and which encourage (or at least do not inhibit) the pursuit by firms -- the principal wealth creators -- of their objectives: increased efficiency and competitiveness in the interest of profitability. While the objectives of governments are more complex than those of firms (and include security and social welfare considerations), the overarching government objective of economic growth and development constitutes the nexus of governments' and firms' interests and objectives.

One of the characteristics of this nexus concerns the achievement, maintenance and promotion of "contestable markets" that are open to entry by domestic and foreign firms. "Market contestability" goes beyond the traditional notion of "access to markets". It embodies the idea that firms can contest markets through a number of modalities. For example, whereas a market might be characterized by low tariffs for a particular product, restrictions on FDI can reduce contestability (even though access is relatively open with respect to the trade modality), and, hence, also reduce competition and economic efficiency. In addition, the concept of "contestability" also relates to the degree to which firms have access to, and can compete for, factors of production. In this important respect, market contestability is broader than "market access", which has traditionally meant only access to product markets (UNCTAD-DTCI, 1995a, chapter IV). The inclusion of factor markets in the notion of market contestability gives rise to a much more encompassing range of policy issues. For instance, policies that limit participation in real estate markets, or restrict visas, or restrict grants of government research-and-development contracts on the basis of the nationality of ownership of firms, inhibit the contestability of factor markets, respectively, in land, labour and technology.

Furthermore, maintaining conditions of market contestability, particularly in international production (which often involves firms with strong financial, marketing, distribution and other forms of leverage) requires that governments enact competition policies aimed at scaling back the contestability-impairing effects of various private restraints to trade and investment. In this context, governments risk reducing contestability through their presence in markets if, and when, state enterprises and discriminatory procurement policies reduce the scope for international competition.

The concept of "modal neutrality" is used to describe policies that leave to firms the decision as to how markets will be served (be it through trade or FDI) in the interest of their competitiveness. In other words, a policy regime that is characterized by modal neutrality will not be biased towards either trade or FDI (Julius, 1994).

Modal neutrality increases the efficiency of firms and can increase the contestability of markets. However, modal neutrality and market contestability must be pursued in the context of development and social considerations. These considerations provide the anchor for coherent policies.

"Policy coherence" relates to the level of consistency between government objectives and policies across a broad spectrum of issues, including fiscal and monetary policies. A high level of policy coherence is desirable, as it will increase the likelihood that government objectives are achieved. In some instances, achieving policy coherence is straightforward -- lower infant mortality will require higher expenditures on better use of child health-care programmes, or both. With respect to economic development, however, especially in an economy that is taking part in global production, the objective of policy coherence can be much more difficult to achieve or maintain. For example, policy coherence can refer to the relationships between investment and trade policies, which, where economic efficiency is a consideration, need to be consistent and complementary. An investment policy that facilitates the establishment of final assembly facilities in combination with a trade policy that discourages capital equipment imports is an example of policy incoherence. The objective of policy coherence, therefore, is consistency between government objectives and the policies implemented to achieve these -- it acts, therefore, as a filter for appropriate policies (see accompanying figure).

/...

the negotiating body has already a broad range of responsibilities. This consideration aside, prolonged negotiations on a multilateral framework could create uncertainties that might lead TNCs to defer investments; and negotiations could be expected to be long because a multilateral agreement would be more than a simple amalgamation of existing BITs since, presumably, it would go beyond the issues covered in such treaties (especially by dealing with issues related to market access).

In fact, given that world economic conditions are changing rapidly, regulatory responsiveness is particularly important. As the Uruguay Round has shown, there were suggestions for work on new issues even before the Round was completed, and they could not be addressed. The Uruguay Round also showed that the world was not yet ready for an investment agreement. Witness the fact that some participants had at the outset an ambitious investment agenda but eventually settled on a narrow set of trade-related investment measures. Indeed, many developing countries have not yet adjusted to the impact that liberalization measures agreed in the Uruguay Round have on their economies. They are in transition, and it may simply be too early for many to contemplate another multilateral undertaking that may include substantial liberalization obligations, including such important issues as right of establishment. (Even the GATS Agreement, which addresses this issue, does not create a "right of establishment" but rather a "permission of establishment".)

A careful approach to the construction of a broader framework through the further development of regional agreements is a prudent and effective way to move along the route towards a more

---

(Box VI.2. cont'd)

Modal neutrality and policy coherence are of particular relevance to a discussion of a framework for FDI. As the global economy becomes more transnationalized, trade and FDI become increasingly intertwined. Consequently, the need to treat trade and FDI policies as inherently intertwined has also increased, as have the potential costs of "modal bias" and "policy incoherence". Furthermore, globalization has not only complicated policy formulation and implementation with respect to trade and FDI but has also constrained the autonomy of policy makers in so far as greater exposure to international market forces now means that policy "mistakes" carry much higher penalties than they did when national markets were more segmented. The potential gains from policy coherence have increased because the lines between domestic and international policy spheres are blurring.

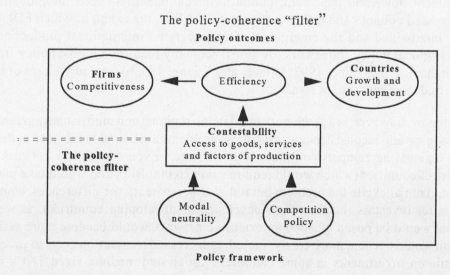

The policy-coherence "filter"

Source: UNCTAD.

---

comprehensive framework. Some countries are members of various regional agreements, thus facilitating cross-regional harmonization and common learning. And, if a multilateral framework were ultimately deemed desirable, the WTO's TRIMs Agreement contains provisions for a review of the operation of the Agreement around the year 1999. If an investment agreement were desirable, it could be considered in the context of this review, together with competition policy. But even then, the question remains whether all the issues that need to be considered would pass the trade-relatedness filter that, in the past, has guided the choice of issues addressed in the world's premier trade organization.

Multilateral negotiations, moreover, may be dominated by the agenda of the strongest economies. This has led some developing countries to doubt that their priorities -- especially restrictive business practices, technology transfer, standards for the behaviour of TNCs vis-à-vis host countries and, indeed, labour mobility -- would receive sufficient attention in multilateral negotiations, especially since there would be an asymmetry in multilateral investment negotiations between countries that are only host countries and those that are both home and host countries. This is in marked contrast to trade, where all countries are both importers and exporters; thus, many of the analogies that are sometimes made about multilateral trade and investment negotiations are not always compelling.

Still, there is one element that is common to both investment and trade: ultimately FDI flows -- like trade flows -- are *not* determined primarily by regulatory factors, once an enabling framework is in place. While the regulatory framework can be crucial in preventing or hindering FDI flows, economic and other determinants become dominant once an enabling framework exists. The regulatory framework can be permissive; it is not causal as far as FDI flows are concerned. In many instances, indeed, TNCs are willing and able to undertake FDI in promising markets, despite difficult national policy frameworks. On the other hand, many countries, and especially many least developed countries, have liberal FDI frameworks in place, but barely attract any FDI. The relative importance of basic economic factors and regulatory frameworks must, therefore, be kept in mind.

2. Arguments in favour of a comprehensive multilateral framework

The overarching rationale for a comprehensive multilateral investment framework is that it would create a stable, predictable and transparent enabling framework, which would facilitate the growth of investment flows and their contribution to development. In fact, the globalization of business, the increased volumes and growing importance of FDI, the extent to which FDI and trade are inextricably intertwined and the emergence of an integrated international production system require a similarly global policy framework. A global economy requires a global policy framework (Bergsten and Graham, 1992; Kline, 1993; Brewer and Young, 1995b), including a set of rules that is consistent for trade and investment issues.

What exists now, however, is a patchwork of bilateral, regional and multilateral agreements that contains overlaps, gaps and inconsistencies. And these problems are bound to increase as the number of bilateral and regional agreements continues to proliferate. Even a complete network of BITs covering all pairs of countries (which would require some 20,000 BITs and would take many years to negotiate) would not alleviate the problem but rather exacerbate it: the differences, complexities and uncertainties for investors (be they from developed or developing countries), as well as for governments, that would be posed by such an extensive network would become more serious, and dealing with them would become more costly, including increased transaction costs to investors and higher risk premia on investments in some countries. Small and medium-sized TNCs would be particularly disadvantaged. More generally, the sensitivity of firms to cost factors, including risks, is one of the principal motivating forces behind business' demand for a multilateral framework.

Indeed, the recent changes in the world economy have been so extensive that some studies (emphasizing efficiency concerns) (Julius, 1990, 1994; Lawrence, 1996; Sauvé and Zampetti, 1996; OECD, 1996a) explore new concepts to guide analysis and the formulation of economic policy. These concepts include market contestability, modal neutrality and policy coherence (box VI.2). The motivation behind these new concepts has been the view that traditional trade-oriented analytical frameworks are becoming anachronistic given the globalization of markets and production processes. Not only has FDI assumed much greater prominence in global economic relations -- both in absolute terms and relative to trade -- but FDI and trade have become inextricably linked in international production. Therefore, whereas traditional approaches focused mainly on the degree of trade access to particular markets enjoyed by firms, the new broader concepts focus more on the degree of freedom firms enjoy in contesting markets, irrespective of the modality used to contest them. Some policy arrangements at the regional level partly reflect this new approach in so far as they address FDI and trade in a more integrated manner; while they are called free trade agreements, they are increasingly becoming free trade and investment agreements.

Independently of broader considerations of this kind, a comprehensive multilateral investment framework is seen by its proponents as the appropriate response to the need for a global policy framework:

- *Governments* expect increased FDI flows to contribute to development, directly as well as indirectly (as they increase trade). They also expect that conflicts arising from FDI are more likely to be subject to an effective dispute-settlement process in the context of a rule-based, not power-based, framework; smaller countries, in particular, benefit from a rule-based system, not only because they are more protected but also because they can participate in policy formulation and implementation.

- *Firms* -- large and small -- expect that a multilateral investment framework should remove impediments to investment, establish high and coherent standards, provide protection for investment and put in place a mechanism for resolving disputes. A stable, predictable and transparent framework is particularly important for large-scale, long-term infrastructure projects and for internationally integrated production networks (ICC, 1996; USCIB, 1995; Messing, 1996; UNICE, 1995; EACC, 1995).

- *Trade unions* expect effective rules on FDI which would incorporate the principles of the ILO Tripartite Declaration, thus alleviating the danger of downward pressure on basic labour standards resulting from policy competition and contributing to a stable labour regime, which is essential for integrating TNCs in development strategies (ICFTU, 1996).

- *Other groups*, in particular the consumer movement, expect a rule-based system for international economic relations, which would also include effective consumer, competition and environment policies, and which would not marginalize some groups of countries but rather complement global liberalization.

Beyond that, it is expected that the existing multilateral economic institutions would benefit because they would be able to function more effectively if FDI were brought into the purview of the multilateral system governing international economic relations.

A comprehensive multilateral agreement, especially if it is linked to the international trade framework, would contribute more to increasing international investment flows. Not only would it entail a worldwide reciprocal lowering of barriers to the inflow and outflow of investment, but the consolidation of the commitment of countries to an open investment regime would give greater credibility to such policies in the eyes of investors. It should thus enable countries to attract greater inflows of investment at a lower cost, and subscribing to it would become a "good housekeeping" seal of approval. The stronger the agreement, and the higher the standards, the more it would contribute to investment flows and hence development.

Linked to this is the expectation that a comprehensive multilateral investment agreement could play the same "constitutional" role in investment as the GATT has played in trade. In particular, it would help national governments resist pressure from sectional interest groups aimed at capturing national investment policies in their narrow interests and thus contribute to offsetting the asymmetry in the political process whereby domestic producer interests predominate over wider national interests and consumer interests.

To achieve the benefits sought, the proponents of a comprehensive multilateral investment framework seek: to lock in policy changes that have occurred at the national and regional levels; to set minimum standards for government policies (to prevent, among other things, a "race to the bottom" as governments or regional organizations may be tempted to adopt "beggar-thy-neighbour" policies to attract FDI); to provide direction for further liberalization; and to establish procedures for monitoring and enforcing compliance with such an agreement and settling disputes. As more firms from developing countries become outward investors, furthermore, the interests and concerns of more and more countries converge with respect to the issues dealt with in a multilateral framework.

There is already momentum at the multilateral level, stemming from the Uruguay Round agreements and including the WTO's built-in agenda to address investment-related issues during the next few years, particularly with regard to the TRIMs and GATS agreements (Ruggiero, 1996; Brewer and Young, 1995c). There exists a half-century of experience in addressing FDI issues in multilateral fora, and there are some building blocks in place. A multilateral framework therefore does not have to be created "from scratch", unlike the services framework during the Uruguay Round. Moreover, multilateral negotiations offer opportunities for compromises among countries across issues as they make trade-offs and exchanges with one another, and as they negotiate and resolve simultaneously their differing positions on multiple issues (Nymark, 1996). Continuing this momentum at the multilateral level -- without being diverted or possibly even hindered by regional arrangements -- is seen as the best way to create a broader framework that covers both trade and investment.

In doing so, a multilateral framework can be responsive to the differing circumstances of countries and their place in the international system of sovereign states. In particular, a multilateral system can be sensitive to the differing levels of development, for instance, by allowing for different schedules for phasing in new rules. Indeed, recent experiences with multilateral agreements have shown that they have the capacity to deal with such issues, and that investment rule-making at the multilateral level can contribute to a better enabling framework without constraining unduly the fundamental rights of governments to formulate policies and strategies appropriate to their countries' development.

3. Observations

These two policy approaches have been presented for expositional purposes as stylized alternatives, to highlight differences, even at the risk of oversimplification. In reality, even the proponents of each option seldom make such a clear distinction. Those in favour of an approach that allows current arrangements to evolve organically include a diverse range of governments -- including from developed and developing countries -- and others. Their support for this approach, however, does not necessarily preclude support for an eventual multilateral framework.

Among developing countries, there are many that prefer maintaining or improving the current arrangements because this gives them more freedom to pursue development objectives according to their priorities and policy traditions and because they are sceptical about their ability to shape the FDI agenda in wider multilateral fora. At the same time, a rapidly increasing number of governments -- including from developing countries and economies in transition -- are concluding BITs. Governments are also actively deepening and expanding regional and interregional investment ties, typically supported by the private sector. As to the most prominent and recent of these efforts, both the business and labour advisory groups at the OECD have endorsed negotiations on a Multilateral Agreement on Investment in that Organization (in the case of trade unions, conditional on the inclusion of the existing OECD Guidelines for Multinational Enterprises) (ICC, 1996; USCIB, 1995; UNICE, 1995; Messing, 1996; EACC, 1995; BIAC, 1994a and 1994b).

There appears, indeed, to be a consensus among diverse governmental and non-governmental participants in the international community that greater cooperation on FDI issues is desirable. This underlying consensus is reflected in both of the policy approaches. The differences among governments and others in their support for either -- or some combination of the two -- lie more in opinions on how best to achieve greater cooperation. In this perspective, the two approaches can be seen as coexisting and, indeed, developing in a complementary manner.

This has not, however, prevented the international business community (ICC, 1996; PBEC, 1996; UNICE, 1995; EACC, 1995) and the international trade-union movement (ICFTU, 1996, p. 63; and box VI.3) from calling for work to begin on a comprehensive multilateral framework for FDI, an objective that is shared by a range of governments which, simultaneously, seek to improve actively existing arrangements at the bilateral and regional levels. The position of the European Commission (European Commission, 1995a; Brittan, 1995) is characteristic of such attitudes. Similarly, the OECD Council at the ministerial level resolved to "begin an examination of trade and investment in the WTO and work towards a consensus which might include the possibility of negotiations" (OECD, 1996b, p. 5).

There are also variations across groups of countries in their support for regional initiatives. There is considerable support to strengthen cooperation on FDI matters in the Western Hemisphere. In the Asia and Pacific region, work continues on investment issues in the context of APEC's non-binding investment agreement. In Western Europe, FDI integration has proceeded farthest, while individual member governments continue to enter into many BITs with countries outside the region.

Thus, there is support for particular bilateral and regional agreements by many governments, firms and trade unions, apart from any views they may have about the larger issues represented by the two policy approaches.

This suggests that the basic approaches to the strengthening of international FDI arrangements represent only clusters of options on a complex continuum that ranges from doing little at one end to constructing a comprehensive binding convention at the other. The first alternative alternative allows -- and even seeks -- continuing improvement of the current arrangements, for instance through the negotiation of new BITs and regional arrangements, and, therefore, is by no means necessarily less proactive than the second alternative. The second approach is, in many respects, incremental, in that it would build on existing agreements. In any event, it would be neither an easy nor a quick process to create a multilateral investment framework, let alone a framework that incorporates high FDI standards. It may be instructive in this regard to recall that it required fifty years of evolution to reach the multilateral trade framework as it now exists.

There have been many attempts in the past to strengthen international arrangements on FDI. Some did not get far because of opposition by developed countries, while others failed because of opposition by developing countries. By their nature, FDI issues are complex, and any effective effort to strengthen the international FDI arrangements will necessarily have to address the diverse and changing interests of all parties.

Box VI.3. The trade-union perspective on international FDI rules

Trade unions have played an important role in introducing labour issues into the current international FDI framework. The trade-union agenda has been pursued through a number of organizations. Several instruments bring together FDI and labour issues, including the International Confederation of Free Trade Unions' Multinational Charter of Trade Union Demands for the Legislative Control of Multinational Companies (1975), the OECD's Guidelines for Multinational Enterprises (1976) and, most importantly, the International Labour Organization's (ILO) Tripartite Declaration of Principles concerning Multinational Enterprises and Social Policy (1977). Both the OECD Guidelines and the ILO Declaration recognize unequivocally the right of employees to be represented by trade unions. The ILO has also adopted a number of conventions that are central to trade union concerns, including, inter alia, Convention No. 87, concerning Freedom of Association and Protection of the Right to Organize and Convention No. 98, concerning the Application of the Principles of the Right to Organize and Bargain Collectively.

The globalization of production has heightened concerns among trade unions over labour and employment issues. Some concerns deal with inadequate information disclosure; inadequate access to decision makers; and problems arising out of the ability of TNCs to transfer all or part of their operations to other countries. Other concerns -- and much more fundamental ones -- relate to the perceived tendency of governments, in their quest to attract FDI, to avoid certain obligations of ILO Conventions 87 and 98.

The ILO Declaration deals with all of these issues. Trade unions, however, expect that globalization will require ongoing cooperation between TNCs and themselves. In seeking comprehensive multilaterally agreed rules on FDI, trade unions emphasize that one of the most important elements of a stable environment for FDI is employment relations. As foreign managers of a domestic work force, TNCs need a broad political consensus to reinforce their prominent role. Various International Trade Secretariats (international trade-union organizations grouped by industry or sector) have begun to deal directly with TNCs.

The most significant international instrument addressing industrial relations since the adoption of the ILO Declaration is the European Union's 1994 Directive establishing European Works Councils (UNCTAD-DTCI, 1994a). Trade unions in Europe are now negotiating Europe-wide information and consultation agreements with TNCs. In this process, some TNCs have voluntarily expanded these arrangements to a world-wide level. Trade unions would want a multilateral investment framework to address the issue of world-wide information and consultation mechanisms or at least provide that national legislation should not prevent companies and trade unions making such arrangements.

The most basic trade-union objective is to have the provisions of the ILO Declaration included as an integral part of the international FDI framework; and, of course, trade unions, like the business community, would want the opportunity to be consulted in the drafting and eventual implementation of any future multilateral FDI framework. Trade unions believe that, while progress at the national level is critical, there is a growing need for international cooperation and coordination. As expressed by the Director-General of the ILO in 1994, "the balance between State, market and society...can no longer be the sole responsibility of the Nation-State. It will indeed be difficult to promote social justice if we do not very quickly identify ways and means of regulating the world economy satisfactorily" (TUAC, 1994, p. 2).

Source: ICFTU, 1996 and other sources.

B. Key issues

Since the further development of international arrangements for FDI is being pursued at all levels, it is important to identify and analyse issues that need to be considered in this connection, especially their implications for development. Investment issues can be classified in various ways, e.g., a distinction can be drawn between issues already subject to disciplines in the context of trade agreements or otherwise directly related to trade (most-favoured-nation treatment, commercial presence) and those that are not covered (e.g., proprietary rights). An examination of investment instruments provides a listing of key issues that one would reasonably expect to be addressed in these discussions. For the purpose of this analysis, they can usefully be organised as follows (UNCTAD-DTCI, 1994a, chapter VII):

- Investment measures that affect the entry and operations of foreign investors.

- The application, with respect to FDI, of certain positive standards of treatment.

- Measures dealing with broader concerns, including setting appropriate standards of behaviour for investors and ensuring the proper functioning of the market.

- The elimination (or reduction) of non-business risks through provisions on investment protection and settlement of disputes.

Since FDI is a domain in which international norms function largely in reference to national ones, one needs to begin with a brief analysis of the interplay between them, especially also as it concerns the relationship between FDI and trade. And, of course, one needs to consider the types of activities and transactions involved -- which define the scope of any framework -- before dealing with the four elements listed above.

1. The interplay of national and international norms in trade and investment

In matters of economic policy, international norms are generally developed by reference to national policies and measures. International norms seek to allow or strengthen, or to restrict or channel, national action. Where state jurisdiction is recognized by international law, other states are normally bound to recognize the validity of measures taken by a State in accordance with and within the limits established by the applicable norms of international law. Going one step farther, international rules may encourage a state to act by requiring that other states cooperate. On the other hand, international norms may limit state action; they may even prohibit some government measures. Other states may then be entitled to treat such measures as violations of international legal obligations.

The effectiveness of this formal interplay is based on the fundamental fact that international norms on FDI are normally established by States through direct or indirect consensual action. The constraints created in international affairs by the realities of economic or political power relationships cannot be disregarded; yet, in matters relating to FDI, acceptance by each state of limitations on its ability to act is based on the realization that this, when coupled with the acceptance by other states of similar limitations on their power to act, is in its own interest. In a world in which countries are at considerably different levels of development, international rules, to obtain wide consensus and support, also need to differentiate when it comes to applicability. It is characteristic that international norms and policies on FDI have closely followed the movements of national ones. In the 1970s, efforts at the international level to legitimize national controls over FDI paralleled national restrictive action. More recently, international trends towards the liberalization of investment policies have followed corresponding national trends.

While the formal interplay of binding international norms and equally binding national ones is at the centre of the discussion, less definite categories of norms should not be disregarded. Legal rules may vary in their normative intensity, i.e., in the degree of their binding force. Certain prescriptions may lack full binding force, whether because they are issued as declarations or recommendations or because, although adopted in formally binding form, they are formulated in language that allows a wide margin of freedom of action for those to whom the norms are directed. This is a phenomenon that, under the rubric of "soft law", has been extensively studied in international economic and environmental law and, while the topic was extensively discussed with respect to the proposed codes of conduct of the late 1970s and similar instruments, it retains its importance in the context of international treaties, the normative intensity of whose provisions may vary widely. In reality, states and other interested parties have more choices than formal considerations allow, when drafting and adopting an international instrument. When adopted with the full consent of all parties concerned, such "soft law" prescriptions may still express potentially important policy preferences and may exert formative influence on national legal norms (Horn, 1980; Kline, 1985; Rubin and Hufbauer, 1984; Handl, et al., 1988; Seidl-Hohenveldern, 1989).

The proper formulation of international norms thus requires a clear and comprehensive picture of the national measures they seek to deal with (Rubin and Wallace, 1994) and of the ways in which they will address them.

In respect to trade and investment, an additional consideration has to be kept in mind: the prominence, historically, of the regulation of border measures in trade instruments, as compared with the emphasis on internal measures in international investment instruments. However, as international trade instruments increasingly deal with a range of domestic policy issues, these differences are now becoming less and less marked.

More specifically, international rules on trade dealt traditionally with a relatively limited range of possible national measures. Their initial concerns were the reduction or elimination of customs duties, direct quantitative and other restrictions at the border as well as the avoidance of discrimination among states (the MFN principle). It is only after the first steps towards trade liberalization were taken and the obvious obstacles removed that concern moved to more diffuse and more domestically oriented issues. These were at first domestic measures directly concerned with trade, e.g., subsidies, internal measures discriminating between foreign and domestic products (application of the national treatment standard) and various other non-tariff barriers. Then measures that concern trade in a more indirect manner came into play, e.g., technical standards, government procurement and performance requirements. As became evident in the European Community integration process, once customs duties and quantitative restrictions at the borders had been eliminated, attention shifted to the obstacles to trade created by differing domestic legislation, whether intended to discriminate against foreign goods and services or not.

In the past, international rules addressed a limited range of FDI issues, mainly expropriation. For the rest, national law and policy were recognized as governing. Today, international FDI rules address many more issues, starting with obstacles at the border (the functional equivalent of customs duties): restrictions on entry, screening, and so on. Beyond this, they deal with issues of domestic economic policy and with the conditions of operation of firms, domestic and foreign, thereby becoming more intrusive into the domestic policy fabric. They deal with these topics from the start, not at a later point as in the case of trade. Moreover, the kind of differentiation (discrimination) that is at the heart of the matter is that between domestic and foreign firms. (Discrimination between foreign firms of different origin or nationality -- that is to say, discrimination in violation of the MFN principle -- is rarely a primary concern in FDI matters.)

Another important difference between international rules on trade and on investment has to do with the different role that reciprocity plays in the two domains. In trade, progress in the elimination of restrictions and the application of treatment standards has relied extensively in the past on reciprocity, both with respect to the undertaking of liberalization obligations ("reciprocal concessions") and the implementation of such commitments (possibilities of countermeasures or retaliation). This was partly because the national origin of goods was normally clearly determinable. While more frequent in the past, the application of the principle of reciprocity is less common today in investment. Reciprocity is important, however, with respect to particular issues, e.g., financial services or national treatment in research and development.

Reflecting these differences, the traditional approach to international rule making in FDI and trade was much informed by the differences that characterize the relationship of independent economic operators selling goods and services to each other, as compared to the relationship between investors and foreign affiliates. The central fact of continuing control of the affiliates by investors, combined with the fact that production and operation takes place in host countries, contrasts with the international trade situation that normally proceeds through a series of transactions in which ownership over the goods and services changes after sale.[2]

International rule making is beginning to come to grips with these differences, as the evolution of GATT shows, reflecting the increasing integration of the two policy areas in international economic relations. Whereas originally the GATT was primarily concerned with the treatment at the border of imports of foreign goods, it subsequently found it had to deal increasingly with internal policy instruments that can distort the conditions of international trade. In the most recent development, the rules of the multilateral trading system have entered directly into the area of FDI, establishing rules that govern the treatment of foreign companies operating within a country's territory. This is most evident in the agreements in the areas of services (GATS) and intellectual property (TRIPS) negotiated in the Uruguay Round.

The shift in emphasis in the multilateral trading system from the negotiation of specific concessions to rule making has also been reflected in a declining role for the traditional concept of reciprocity and its substitution by the concepts of mutual advantage and increased benefits to all participants as the motors for reaching international rules.

2. Scope

In any international normative instrument on FDI, the forms and types of transactions and operations to which it applies need to be determined. Definitions, whether of investment, investors or other key concepts, are important because they are not mere descriptions but form part of an instrument's normative substance. It is only at the end of a negotiation that a definitive answer to such questions can be given, since it is only then that the actual substance and nature of the rules, as eventually agreed, is clear. Keeping in mind recent experience with instruments on related issues, some basic questions can be identified.

Key is the delineation of the scope of an investment instrument. If an approach is taken that aims at covering factors of production in general, not only capital movements but also movements of natural persons would be addressed; existing international instruments on FDI can not be characterized as taking such an approach. When it comes to capital movement, the key question is how broad or narrow the definition of investment should be. Recent investment agreements (e.g., many BITs, NAFTA, the Energy Charter Treaty) have tended to include broad definitions (Dolzer and Stevens, 1995; Parra, 1995), so as to extend treaty protection to all assets of an enterprise, including movable and immovable property rights, equity in companies, claims to money and contractual rights, copyrights and industrial property rights, concessions, licences and similar rights; moreover, provisions aimed at the protection of an investment have tended to cover all aspects of an investment's operations inside the host country. In this connection, the question of whether or not portfolio investment should be covered is receiving increasing attention. This reflects recognition of the fact that contributions of foreign investors to the firms they control or in which they participate assume various forms. Definitions in instruments directed at the liberalization of FDI entry and establishment (e.g., the OECD Liberalisation Codes), on the other hand, have tended to be narrower, focusing on the transfer of capital and technology and exercise of control, since it was restrictions at the border that they sought to remove (Ley, 1996).

Any international FDI instrument needs, therefore, to address the question to what extent it should cover, e.g., non-equity forms or contractual rights concerning the transfer of technology, intangible assets and such administrative rights as licences and permits that are prerequisites for the actual operation of foreign affiliates, or even portfolio investment (which is generally left out of definitions of direct investment but has increasingly come to be covered in international investment instruments). One needs to take into account that the broader the coverage of assets, the higher the likelihood that exceptions are taken and safeguards built into an instrument to protect host countries; for example, the inclusion of portfolio investment would make a balance-of-payments safeguard all the more important.

The definition of "investment" is, of course, only one of the parameters determining the scope of an investment instrument. Other questions that are highly relevant in this regard include the definition of "investor" (which raises, among other things, the question of corporate nationality), the application in time of the instrument and its territorial scope.

Difficult questions as to scope also arise as regards the interconnections between the several modalities of economic operations. To the extent that investment, trade, transfer of technology and financial transactions are increasingly interconnected and part of the same overall transaction or operation, common or at least interconnected definitions may be appropriate, so as to avoid treating closely linked situations differently.

3. Substantive provisions

(a)   *Investment measures that affect the entry and operations of foreign investors*

Governments impose measures that affect or restrict FDI for a number of reasons. Some measures apply to all private investment and reflect national policies regarding the structure of an economy and the proper apportionment of resources between the public and the private sectors. Some industries may be closed to private ownership (e.g., natural resources or public utilities); such restrictions were common in the past, particularly in centrally planned economies; they are now generally becoming less important. In many countries, special conditions of operation are imposed on firms operating in industries considered as particularly sensitive or important (natural resources, energy, utilities, banking). These conditions can also reflect the importance attached to economic and social objectives, including the proper functioning of the market and protection of consumers.

Other restrictions concern FDI specifically. They are typically meant to maintain a government's freedom of action to take measures intended to enhance the country's economic development (although other concerns also play a role, e.g., national security). Host countries may also wish to retain control of natural resources and key industries, or allow foreign investors in such industries subject to certain conditions. Investment may be allowed in a country only after approval by the competent agencies. Such "screening" of investments may take different forms and serve various purposes, from relatively non-interventionist ones (such as the registration of an investment to help collect statistical information, or the determination of the amount of capital invested to permit its eventual repatriation), to more prescriptive ones (such as authorization aimed at encouraging investment in certain industries and discouraging it in others).

The purposes behind the latter type of restrictions on FDI are often similar to those behind restrictions on trade, in particular when it comes to the protection of local producers. And regardless of the reasons for which they are imposed, they affect the operation of the market. In particular, they help national firms that are not competitive otherwise by keeping more competitive foreign firms out of the market or by imposing additional costs on them. In developing countries, in particular, some restrictions of this kind on FDI may be needed, at least sometimes, to allow domestic firms to build up capacities and prepare for the rigours of international competition. It is central here to distinguish which measures are really needed for development purposes, and which are not -- a task that is certainly not easy -- and to ensure that costly and inefficient production structures are not protected for prolonged or indefinite periods. Some countries have pursued this approach successfully, while others have allowed it to stifle both investment and development. Other countries have pursued successfully different approaches, partly in recognition of the contribution that FDI can make to development, by encouraging foreign investors to participate in establishing local industries. In the past, in fact, a number of countries combined a relaxation of admission controls on FDI with the erection of tariff barriers against foreign goods and services to encourage import substitution. Also, this suggests that developing countries may need some freedom to promote development in a manner they consider most appropriate. Considerations of this kind are central to any international FDI instrument involving developing countries. They are the core of its development dimension and need to be taken into account when dealing with investment measures.

Beyond that, it needs to be kept in mind that there are many other government measures that affect the operation of the market, and which are needed to ensure the proper functioning of the market. One should avoid the conceptual trap of treating all national or other measures of legal regulation (of investment or otherwise) as actual or potential discriminatory restrictions. It is part of the function of government to establish and maintain a legal framework for the economy, a framework that serves public purposes, including the promotion of development. It is for this reason that the role and appropriateness of governmental policy intervention in the market must be seen in relation to a country's particular circumstances, including its level of development and special developmental needs.

i.   Admission and establishment

States have traditionally exercised control over the admission of aliens, foreign goods, services and firms. Multilateral agreements on trade of goods and services have significantly reduced and in some cases eliminated border barriers to trade. Despite the powerful current trend towards elimination, however, controls remain in many cases where investment is concerned. They are intended to serve various purposes, and their scope and strictness vary widely (table VI.1).

Recent bilateral and regional instruments deal with admission restrictions and requirements in a variety of ways. "Soft law" hortatory clauses expressing a favourable attitude to the promotion and admission of foreign investment serve to commit governments, if only in political rather than legal terms, to a policy favourable to FDI. But even provisions that are not overly strict but contain extensive negative lists of excluded industries, can improve transparency.

An effort to eliminate those restrictions aimed at FDI is made in recent United States BITs which provide that investors seeking admission are to be accorded the better of national and MFN treatment (Vandevelde, 1992). This presumably means that they are not to be excluded from industries that are

Table VI.1. Measures relating to admission and establishment[a]

- Closing certain sectors, industries or activities to FDI.

- Quantitative restrictions on the number of foreign companies admitted in specific sectors, industries or activities.

- Minimum capital requirements.

- Subsequent additional investment or reinvestment requirements.

- Screening, authorization and registration of investment.

- Conditional entry upon investment meeting certain development or other criteria (e.g. environmental responsibility).

- Investment must take certain legal form (e.g., incorporated in accordance with local company law requirements).

- Restrictions on forms of entry (e.g., mergers and adquisitions may not be allowed, or must meet certain additional requirements).

- Special requirements for non-equity forms of investment (e.g., build-operate-transfer (BOT) agreements, licensing of foreign technology).

- Investment not allowed in certain zones or regions within a country.

- Restrictions on import of capital goods needed to set up an investment (e.g., machinery, software).

- Investors required to deposit certain guarantees (e.g., for financial institutions).

- Admission to privatization bids restricted or conditional on additional guarantees, for foreign investors.

- Admission fees (taxes) and incorporation fees (taxes).

- Investors required to comply with norms related to national security, policy, customs, public morals requirements as conditions to entry.

Source: UNCTAD.

[a]   These measures may apply to all FDI or to investment in specific sectors, industries or activities, or to investors of a certain nationality. Some measures listed in this table could also be relevant to ownership and control and operation of TNCs (tables VI.2 and VI.3).

open to local investors (or on the basis of procedures different from those that are applicable to nationals). But they typically also contain a list of excepted industries. Still, there are some conceptual and practical difficulties in the application of such a standard. One particular problem is that, in several countries, a national legal framework for investment, domestic as well as foreign, for the entire economy or for particular industries, does not exist. As a result, relative standards such as national treatment cannot always be applied easily, because they depend by implication on the existence of a consistent investment regime, so that comparisons can be made. While applicable to treatment after admission as well as at the time of admission, this kind of problem is particularly relevant to the latter.

ii. Ownership and control

There are many different kinds of ownership-and-control restrictions (table VI.2). Perhaps most importantly, comprehensive restrictions of this type, establishing compulsory majority or minority shareholdings for foreign investors, are less common now than in the past (UNCTAD-DTCI, 1994a). They are increasingly limited to particular industries, mostly services and natural resources. Even their relatively more frequent utilization in the context of privatization programmes may reflect in many cases the special conditions obtaining in particular industries (e.g., public utilities).

Table VI.2. Measures relating to ownership and control[a]

- Restrictions on foreign ownership (e.g., no more than 50 per cent of foreign owned capital allowed).

- Compulsory joint ventures, either with State participation or with local private investors.

- Mandatory transfers of ownership to local firms, usually over a period of time (fade-out requirements).

- Nationality restrictions on the ownership of the company or shares thereof.

- Restrictions on the use of long-term (5 years or more) foreign loans (e.g., bonds).

- Restrictions on the type of shares or bonds held by foreign investors (e.g., shares with non-voting rights).

- Restrictions on the free transfer of shares or other proprietory rights over the company held by foreign investors (e.g., shares cannot be transferred without permission).

- Restrictions on foreign shareholders rights (e.g., on payment of dividends, reimbursement of capital upon liquidation; on voting rights; denial of information disclosure on certain aspects of the running of the investment).

- "Golden" shares to be held by the host government allowing it, e.g., to intervene if the foreign investor captures more than a certain percentage of the investment.

- Government reserves the right to appoint one or more members of the board of directors.

- Restrictions on the nationality of directors, or limitations on the number of expatriates in top managerial positions.

- Government reserves the right to veto certain decisions, or requires that important board decisions be unanimous.

- Government must be consulted before adopting certain decisions.

- Management restrictions on foreign-controlled monopolies or upon privatization of public companies.

- Restrictions on land or immovable property ownership and transfers thereof.

- Restrictions on industrial or intellectual property ownership or insuficient ownership protection.

- Restrictions on the licensing of foreign technology.

Source: UNCTAD.

[a]   These measures may apply to all FDI or, more often, to investment in specific sectors, industries or activities. Some measures listed in this table could also be relevant to admission and establishment and operation of TNCs (tables VI.1 and VI.3).

iii.   *Operational and other measures*

Even after admission, foreign firms may be confronted by a range of restrictive measures (table VI.3) aimed at their operations and seeking to influence their various side-effects, such as on employment and the use of technology. Restrictions and special measures can be found across the board and tend to be less sectorally oriented.

Some measures that have received special attention in some recent investment agreements concern the issue of the right of temporary entry for key personnel in connection with the development or operation of a foreign affiliate and the right of a foreign investor to hire key personnel legally resident in the host country without regard to nationality. Another category of such measures concerns performance requirements, i.e., conditions imposed on foreign firms, at the time of entry or later, concerning their export policies, the local content of their products, training of local labour and other such matters. While these requirements were initially seen as a substitute for more restrictive measures, their trade and market-distorting effects have led to the prohibition of some of them in some bilateral and regional agreements, as well as the Uruguay Round's agreement on TRIMs (see chapter V).

While a broad consensus on the benefit of reducing certain restrictions on FDI has been reached in recent years (and, indeed, restrictions are being reduced unilaterally by many countries), for many developing countries the problem remains of replacing such restrictions by other measures serving in part the same ends, including, to defend themselves against restrictive business practices of TNCs, to promote the development of particular industries and to induce foreign investors to increase their contributions in technology. Restrictions are a relatively convenient, if often ineffective and market-distorting, instrument. Promoting a country's development through other means, generally more indirect and without restrictive effects, is more difficult and requires more effective use of administrative and other human resources.

iv.   *Incentives* [3]

The flip side of the conditions governments impose on FDI consists of the incentives they offer to attract FDI. Such incentives are diverse (table VI.4). The most common incentives are fiscal incentives; financial incentives; and other measures, such as subsidized infrastructure, preferential treatment in government contracts and tariff protection. Incentives may be granted unconditionally or conditionally (by linking them to performance requirements); they may be granted automatically to certain categories of investments (e.g., in specific industries); or the administering authorities may have considerable discretion to decide on whether to grant them or not. Moreover, for large or important FDI projects, *ad hoc* incentives are often granted as part of project negotiations. Incentives competition (including between sub-national authorities) has increased considerably in the past decade.

The rationale for some investment incentives is to capture the wider benefits arising from externalities in production. Positive externalities can result from such factors as economies of scale, the creation of widely diffused new knowledge, or the upgrading of skills of workers who are mobile. In addition, individual investments can lead to associated investments by other TNCs, thus creating agglomeration effects, and they can lead to backward and forward linkages. Moreover, in the more dynamic context of growth and development, incentives can correct for the failure of markets, and they can compensate investors for other government interventions, such as performance requirements.

Table VI.3. Measures relating to operations[a]

- Restrictions on employment of foreign key professional or technical personnel, including restrictions associated with granting of visas, permits, etc..

- Performance requirements, such as sourcing/local content requirements, manufacturing requirements; technology transfer requirements, employment requirements, regional and/or global product mandates, training requirements, export requirements, trade- balancing requirements, import restrictions, local sales requirements, linking export quotas to domestic sales, export/foreign exchange earning requirements.

- Public procurement restrictions (e.g., foreign investors excluded as government suppliers or subject to providing special guarantees).

- Restrictions on imports of capital goods, spare parts, manufacturing imputs.

- Restrictions/conditions on access to local raw materials, spare parts and inputs.

- Restrictions on long-term leases of land and real property.

- Restrictions to relocate operations within the country.

- Restrictions to diversify operations.

- Restrictions on access to telecommunications networks.

- Restrictions on the free flow of data.

- Operation restrictions relating to monopolies or participation in public companies (e.g., obligation to provide a public service at a certain price).

- Restrictions on access to local credit facilities.

- Restrictions on access to foreign exchange (e.g., to pay for foreign finance, imports of goods and services or remitting profits).

- Restrictions on repatriation of capital and profits (case by case approval, additional taxation or remittances, phase out of transfers over a number of years).

- "Cultural" restrictions, mainly in relation to educational or media services.

- Disclosure of information requirements (e.g., on the foreign operations of a TNC).

- Special operational requirements on foreign firms in certain sectors/activities (e.g., on branches of foreign banks).

- Operational permits and licences (e.g., to transfer funds).

- Special requirements on professional qualifications, technical standards.

- Advertising restrictions for foreign firms.

- Ceilings on royalties and technical assistance fees or special taxes.

- Limits on the use of certain technologies (e.g., territorial restrictions), brand names, etc., or case-by-case approval and conditions.

- Rules of origin, tracing requirements.

- Linking local production to access or establishment of distribution facilities.

- Operational restrictions related to national security, public order, public morals, etc..

Source: UNCTAD.

[a] These measures may apply to all FDI or, more often, to investment in specific sectors, industries or activities. Some measures listed in this table could also be relevant to admission and establishment and ownership and control (tables VI.1 and VI.2).

Table VI.4. Main types of incentive measures offered to foreign investors

1. *Fiscal incentives, including:*

    •   Reduction of the standard corporate income-tax rate.
    •   Tax holidays.
    •   Allowing losses incurred during the holiday period to be written off against future profits.
    •   Accelerated depreciation allowances on capital taxes.
    •   Investment and reinvestment allowances.
    •   Reductions in social security contributions.
    •   Deductions from taxable earnings based on the number of employees or on other labour-related expenditures.
    •   Corporate income-tax deductions based on, for example, expenditures relating to marketing and promotional activities.
    •   Value-added based incentives, including:
        •   Corporate income-tax reductions or credits based on the net local content of outputs.
        •   Granting of income-tax credits based on net value earned.
    •   Import-based incentives, including:
    •   Exemption from import duties on capital goods, equipment or raw materials, parts and inputs related to the production process.
    •   Tax credits for duties paid on imported materials or supplies.
    •   Export-based incentives, including:
        •   Exemptions from export duties.
        •   Preferential tax treatment of income from exports.
        •   Income-tax reduction for special foreign-exchange-earning activities or for manufactured exports
        •   Tax credits on domestic sales in return for export performance.
        •   Duty drawbacks.
        •   Income-tax credits on net local content of exports.
        •   Deduction of overseas expenditures and capital allowance for export industries.

2. *Financial incentives, including:*

    •   "Direct subsidies" to cover (part of) capital, production or marketing costs in relation to an investment project.
    •   Subsidized loans.
    •   Loan guarantees.
    •   Guaranteed export credits.
    •   Publicly funded venture capital participating in investments involving high commercial risks.
    •   Government insurance at preferential rates, usually available to cover certain types of risks such as exchange-rate volatility, currency devaluation, or non-commercial risks such as expropriation and political turmoil (often provided through an international agency).

3. *Other incentives, including:*

    •   Subsidized dedicated infrastructure.
    •   Subsidized services, including assistance in identifying sources of finance, implementing and managing projects, carrying out pre-investment studies, information on markets, availability of raw materials and supply of infrastructure, advice on production processes and marketing techniques, assistance with training and retraining, technical facilities for developing know-how or improving quality control.
    •   Preferential government contracts.
    •   Closing the market to further entry or the granting of monopoly rights.
    •   Protection from import competition.
    •   Special treatment with respect to foreign exchange, including special exchange rates, special foreign debt-to-equity conversion rates, elimination of exchange risks on foreign loans, concessions of foreign exchange credits for export earnings, and special concessions on the repatriation of earnings and capital.

Source: UNCTAD-DTCI (1996b).

There have been some efforts internationally to limit incentives -- for instance, in the Uruguay Round agreement on Subsidies and Countervailing Measures, in the Decision on Incentives and Disincentives that is part of the OECD Declaration on Multinational Enterprises, in the Caribbean Common Market agreement on the harmonization of fiscal incentives and in the European Union measures to limit incentives as part of its competition rules. The effect of these efforts has, however, been limited.

Experience suggests that incentives do not rank high among the determinants of FDI, although their impact on FDI locational choices is sometimes apparent at the margin. Impact typically also varies across types of incentives, depending on investors' strategies. Many incentive packages for foreign investors more than cover the wedge between the private and social benefits to correct for market failures, they can introduce distortions in the production structure similar to those caused by restrictions on trade. In any case, incentives involve direct financial costs in the form of cash outlays or lost revenues (whose alternative use for development purposes may well have been more effective), and they also involve complex policies that lack transparency and that are difficult to administer. In many instances, therefore, incentives can be a waste of resources -- something most countries can ill-afford -- and, when they are successful, can be distortional.

v. Investment-related trade measures

Apart from incentives, the symbiotic relationship between FDI and trade creates the potential for the volume, sectoral composition and geographical distribution of FDI to be affected by various trade measures. It is possible, therefore, to identify -- in the same spirit underlying the discussion of TRIMs -- investment-related trade measures (IRTMs) (table VI.5). Even though some of them may not be specifically intended to affect FDI flows, all of them do (UNCTC, 1992a).

To the extent that international investment agreements seek to reduce the distorting effects of some government measures, IRTMs may deserve some attention.

Table VI.5. Investment-related trade measures

Trade measure	Possible impact on FDI
Tariffs and quantitative restrictions on imports	Induces import-substituting FDI
Sectorally managed trade, including voluntary export restraints	Induces import-substituting FDI
Regional free trade agreements	Promotes FDI in the member countries
Rules-of-origin policies	Induces FDI in component production
Export-processing zones	Induces export-oriented FDI
Export controls (security and foreign policy)	Induces export-replacing FDI
Export financing	Increases export-oriented FDI
Non-monetary trade arrangements (coproduction; buy-back)	Depends on the nature of specific arrangements
Safety, health, environment, privacy and other national standards	Induces import-substituting FDI

Source: UNCTC, 1992a.

(b) Standards of treatment

Legal standards may be distinguished from rules in that they do not contain clear and specific prescriptions (in the way rules are supposed to), but refer instead to a body of law or to broad terms, whose exact content is to be determined at the time (and occasion) of application. Standards of treatment are "relative" (or contingent) when they refer to treatment according to a body or system of rules; the national treatment standard, for instance, calls for the application of the same rules (or rules no less favourable than those) that are applied to a country's nationals. The content of the rules is not specified; there is only the general reference to the rules applicable to nationals. Standards are "absolute" (or noncontingent) when they state the treatment to be accorded, although in terms whose exact content will be determined by reference to the concrete circumstances of application; "reasonableness" (or "reasonable treatment") and "proportionality" are such standards. Absolute standards may often involve an implied reference to a third-party decision-maker who will apply the terms to the specific facts.

With respect to FDI, three standards, two relative and one absolute, are in general use and may apply to different phases or aspects of an investment. All three are based, in slightly differing ways, on treaty practice, some of it old and some recent.

- The two relative standards, primarily intended to ensure nondiscrimination, are the "national treatment" standard, according to which the foreign investor is to be treated in a manner no less favourable than that in which local nationals are treated; and the "most-favoured-nation treatment" standard, according to which foreign investors are to be treated in a manner not less favourable than that in which other alien investors are treated. Both these standards were used in bilateral commercial treaties. The MFN standard was the principal instrument through which multilateral (non-discriminatory) trade of goods and services evolved before the GATT multilateral treaty framework was established, and it continues to enjoy pride of place within that framework. It was further applied to the treatment of aliens in Establishment (and Friendship, Commerce and Navigation) treaties, as well as in bilateral and regional investment instruments. The national treatment standard was first applied to the general treatment of aliens, through parallel unilateral measures based on reciprocity that dealt in the main with private law matters, such as property or contract; the standard soon found its way into commercial treaty practice with respect to the economic and other activities of aliens, and then into bilateral and regional investment-related agreements.

- The third standard, that of "fair and equitable treatment", is more recent and it is absolute. It is generally considered that the aim of including a "fair and equitable treatment" clause is to provide a basic standard detached from the host country's law which an investor (or the home state) may invoke (Dolzer and Stevens, 1995). Its precise contents depend on judgments to be made in concrete cases, either by third-party decision makers or by the parties in their consultations. Its current use in investment matters originated with its inclusion in the 1967 Convention on the Protection of Foreign Property prepared by the OECD, even though that Convention was never opened for signature. The standard was subsequently included in BITs and, more recently, in regional and interregional agreements (table V.3). A more definite understanding of the contents of that last standard is still developing; it can be expected that it will develop in the future through diplomatic and arbitral (or judicial) practice.

To a considerable extent, all three standards aim at the elimination of discrimination that would be detrimental to foreign investors. This is the principal function of the two relative standards and one of the functions of the third. At the same time, none of them (and in particular the national treatment standard currently in use) is usually intended to provide *equality* of treatment between domestic and foreign investors. The privileged treatment of foreign firms, i.e., discrimination to their advantage, is *not* excluded (as the usual language "treatment no-less-favourable-than" makes clear). The provisions calculated to provide special protection to foreign investors are an obvious illustration of such treatment, but they are not the only possibilities the standard allows.

Even as regards detrimental discrimination, in no case is nondiscrimination the sole function of these standards. They also serve to provide an indication of the broader legal regime that is applicable to investors. This is particularly true of national treatment, through which the entire body of law applicable to domestic enterprise becomes applicable to foreign firms. It is characteristic in this respect that many BITs contain, in addition to the provisions on general standards of treatment, explicit clauses forbidding discrimination, which would have been unnecessary if that were the only role of the general provisions. The "fair-and-equitable-treatment" standard as well, while often associated with the explicit nondiscrimination clauses, aims at far more than mere equality of treatment.

Some questions remain, however, concerning the exact limits of application of these standards, in particular the relative ones, and they tend to appear when it is attempted to apply the standards to particular cases. Both standards are generally made applicable where the situation of the enterprises concerned (i.e., domestic and foreign ones, in the one case, foreign ones of different national origin, in the other) are similar or comparable. This is often spelled out expressly (e.g., in the BITs practice of the United States and NAFTA, where terms such as "in like situations" are used), but it is understood in less definite terms as applying in other cases -- this is indeed implicit in the very notion of a relative standard. Such comparisons are, however, difficult to make in concrete terms. In many respects, whether to its advantage or its detriment, a foreign firm is not entirely comparable to a domestic one. Moreover, the emergence of integrated international production systems created by TNCs from more and more countries diminishes the distinction between host and home country and, ultimately, blurs the distinction between domestic and foreign firms.

What has in fact happened is that the exact functions of these standards have changed when their application has shifted from matters of trade to investment. Their relative importance is not the same in the two cases. In trade, the MFN standard (or even "principle") is of fundamental significance, not only in theory but in practice as well: it is the foundation of the prevailing multilateral trade regime. In matters of investment, this standard was important as long as special commercial relationships persisted, whether colonial or post-colonial preferences or other kinds of arrangements. Today, discrimination as between firms of different national origins is rather rare and may arise solely by virtue of special circumstances. The MFN standard appears to operate chiefly with respect to the relationships between several BITs. Given the several, usually small, differences among their provisions, the question of a possible extension of their application through the MFN clause they contain raises problems. The standard may also be relevant to relations arising out of regional and multilateral agreements, although the cases of regional integration arrangements -- where the question arises whether regional economic integration organizations should be allowed to deviate from the MFN principle in order to preserve their ability to move ahead with internal investment liberalization at a faster pace than other states (Karl, forthcoming; Graham, 1996a, p.112) -- are of a different, although controversial, nature.

The reverse situation exists with respect to national treatment. This standard was in use in trade agreements, but traditionally was not of primary significance. As a result of the Uruguay Round negotiations, however, the national treatment principle has acquired more importance in the trade area (especially in services and intellectual property rights). It is only in cases of deeper integration (as with respect to regional integration arrangements) that problems arise, because national treatment may not suffice where differences in national trade legislation create obstacles to the movement of goods. In matters of investment, of course, national treatment is more important, despite the difficulties of application.

The national treatment standard serves a dual function for investments: it enhances predictability on the one hand, and nondiscrimination on the other. By referring to an entire body of law, rather than to specific laws or measures, the standard reduces the possibilities for uncertainties and gaps, especially with respect to routine operation. This aim may not be fully served where the situation of a foreign firm is too novel or different to be adequately covered by existing national law. Still, a frame of reference is provided as well as a standard for the evaluation of whatever actual treatment is accorded. Non-discrimination, on the other hand, involves a degree of equality of treatment with local enterprises, at the very least the absence of privileged (essentially protectionist) treatment for these firms. Such equality has policy problems of its own that are reflected in the exceptions and exclusions common in the application of the national treatment standard.

The application of the MFN and national treatment standards in investment agreements is frequently qualified by provisions that limit their scope, by granting a temporary or indefinite exception or by excluding certain areas from the applicability of the agreement. First, some investment instruments apply these standards to both the establishment of an investment and the post-establishment treatment, while others provide for their application only to the post-establishment. Second, a number of investment instruments contain limitations of the scope of the MFN and national treatment clauses in regard to particular subjects; for example, qualifications of these principles as applied to taxation and prudential measures in the financial services sector are common. Third, there may be exemptions from these obligations for specific key industries. Finally, general exceptions are at times included to allow for limitations for reasons of national security, international peace and security and public order. A particularly important question in this context is how far a general exception can also be made for reasons of national economic development. Exclusion is motivated by the desire by host governments to retain control over part of their national economic development policies as well as the ability to change them when needed. A host country's desire to choose and control its economic policies, especially where its economic development is concerned, does not necessarily run counter to the application of positive, non-discriminatory standards; for instance, regional development incentives may be offered to both domestic and foreign firms. Still, to the extent that the objective is to assist in the development of local enterprise, the promotion of technological capacity or structural change, temporary exceptions may be needed, so as to allow differential treatment for a period, in line with a country's level of development and special developmental needs.

(c)   Measures addressing broader concerns

In an increasingly liberalized world economy, structures and mechanisms of prudential supervision to ensure the orderly functioning of economic activity acquires increased significance. It would be too much to expect international FDI agreements to ensure the proper functioning of national legal and administrative systems so as to guarantee the necessary predictability and legal security for economic operators. This is a difficult task that the national governments must discharge. It remains for the international community, however, to establish the appropriate cooperative mechanisms to assist states to create and administer an appropriate legal framework for the operation of the market, taking into account broader concerns. In fact, a growing number of issues arising from the internationalization of firms can increasingly be expected to require a multilateral approach on issues ranging from international insolvency (UNCTAD-DTCI, 1993a) to the supervision of financial markets.

Such cooperation is particularly important in areas of close interaction between states as well as between states and TNCs, where the efforts of a single state would not be sufficient and a degree of international cooperation is indispensable -- and this is without prejudice to the requirement that foreign investors respect the laws of host countries. Prominent among them are those of restrictive business practices, transfer pricing and taxation, technology transfer, employment, the protection of the environment, illicit payments, consumer protection and information disclosure -- many of which are elements of good corporate citizenship or, indeed, corporate responsibility (UNCTAD-DTCI, 1994a; Asante, 1989).

i.   Restrictive business practices

Restrictive business practices are anti-competitive practices by enterprises, that aim at monopolizing markets, creating or abusing a dominant position of market power, or both. There are two main types of restrictive practices: horizontal agreements or cartels (involving cooperation between competitors so as to raise prices or allocate markets and, to this end, engage in collusive tendering, exclusion of outsiders and other such practices) and vertical restraints (where a dominant firm exploits its market power in order to impose restraints on its suppliers or distributors through, e.g., exclusive dealing, refusal to deal and resale-price maintenance).

Such practices are found to hamper both domestic and international markets. Conscious of this, all developed countries and a growing number of economies in transition and developing countries, have adopted national legislation on competition.[4] Competition policy is expected to foster competition, thereby increasing efficiency in the markets, which should optimize resource allocation in the economy. With the impetus of competition, enterprises are forced to perform in the most cost-effective way, to offer the lowest prices for the best quality, to be innovative and to offer the best choice of goods and services for the benefit of consumers, including user-enterprises, and, hence, of the economy. Moreover, countries which secure domestic competition and are able to have competitive firms domestically, are expected to be competitive in international trade as well. Given its economic impact, competition policy is a tool to accelerate growth and development. Governments sometimes utilize investment restrictions, such as performance requirements, to counteract restraints to competition (restrictive business practices).

Apart from the European Community Treaty, which provides for supranational enforcement of common competition rules (van Miert, 1996), existing international instruments exist mainly at a bilateral level in the form of agreements on cooperation on procedural aspects of the enforcement of competition policy. The only comprehensive multilateral instrument in existence is the United Nations Set of Equitable Principles and Rules for the Control of Restrictive Business Practices adopted by the General Assembly in 1980 (Brusick, 1996). Agreements negotiated in the Uruguay Round on trade in services and intellectual property also contain provisions on specific competition-policy issues. Thus, the WTO Agreement on TRIPS addresses the interface between technology transfer and restrictive business practices issues by specifying that "some licensing practices or conditions pertaining to intellectual property rights which restrain competition may have adverse effects on trade and may impede the transfer and dissemination of technology" (Article 40.1). The liberalization of economic policies and globalization of economic activity have raised complex issues in relation to firms' dominant positions in international markets, which have led to a renewed interest in exploring options for strengthening international cooperation in competition policy. Proposals made range from improvements to existing bilateral cooperation procedures to the establishment of a common set of substantive standards and dispute-settlement mechanisms at a multilateral level.[5]

ii.   Transfer pricing

"Transfer pricing" refers to the pricing of intra-enterprise transactions between units of the same TNC. The terms of these transactions (prices in particular, but also delivery and payment conditions etc.) are determined on the basis of internal calculations which may or may not fully reflect the corresponding terms in the arm's-length market. Firms sometimes abuse the possibilities offered by such transactions to avoid income or other taxes, import duties or exchange controls. Transfer pricing and related transactions can also be used as a restrictive business practice to eliminate competition.

The issue is of considerable importance to national fiscal authorities because of the effects of such practices on the allocation of income and, hence, on tax revenues (UNCTAD-DTCI, 1993a). The broader economic effects of such practices are not easily determinable, in view of the lack of systematic information. Evidence exists, however, that abusive transfer pricing occurs (UNCTAD, 1996). National tax laws generally prescribe methods for the determination of the prices and terms that would have been negotiated if the transaction were conducted at arm's length; but the application of the arm's length principle is not without difficulties. In many cases, the final adjustments are made on the basis of bargaining between tax authorities and enterprises. In recent years, the methodologies acceptable to the tax authorities have become more flexible. Thus, in specified circumstances, comparisons of profit performance among TNCs in similar circumstances have occurred. In addition, advance transfer-pricing agreements between TNCs and tax authorities are becoming more common.

Provisions on cooperation between tax authorities with respect to transfer pricing are generally found in bilateral double taxation agreements, and the United States Internal Revenue Service administers a "simultaneous examination programme" that involves the coordination between governments of audits of TNCs in different tax jurisdictions. The main objective of the programme is to make audits of firms with international operations more complete and efficient. Simultaneous examinations usually fall under the authority of double taxation treaties. There is also a set of guidelines on international tax issues prepared by the OECD.

iii.   Transfer of technology

The process of technology transfer involves movements of knowledge, be it embodied in goods (e.g., capital equipment) or in the form of ideas, information and skills (e.g., soft technologies) across borders. Technology transfer can take place either at arm's length, as in the case of the export of capital equipment, or of licensing agreements between unaffiliated firms, or it can be internalized, as in the case of a TNC transferring a new production technique to its foreign affiliates. Over two-thirds of global research and development is estimated to take place in the United States, Japan and the European Union; developing countries account for only 6 per cent and, without China, probably for less than 4 per cent (Freeman and Hagendoorn, 1992). Advanced industrial countries are, therefore, net exporters of technology to developing countries. It is partly due to the concentration of technology-development capacity in the advanced countries and partly to the central importance of technology for economic growth that the process of technology transfer has received attention in international rule-making.

For firms, the issues of technology development and diffusion have also become more pressing because of the escalation of research-and-development costs in recent years, due to increased international competition and the shortening of lead-time as "new generation" technologies become available much faster. As a result, cooperation (including strategic partnerships) in research and development between firms has increased significantly. This trend has in turn made national policies -- relating to technology- transfer issues and the national treatment of foreign capital -- an increasingly important matter for TNCs.

So far, international rule-making in technology has focused more on the protection of the proprietary rights of producers of technology and less on the terms and conditions of technology transfer. The issue of property rights has been dealt with successfully in a number of conventions (e.g., the Paris Convention) and most recently in the WTO Agreement on Trade-Related Aspects of Intellectual Property Rights. However, international rule-making on matters relating to the international market for technology and, more generally, the advantages to host countries from the transfer of technology -- have not met with similar success. The most ambitious effort -- the UNCTAD Code of Conduct on the Transfer of Technology -- was never completed, although subsequent efforts have produced significant results.[6] The Energy Charter Treaty, for example, calls upon signatories "to promote access to and transfer of energy technology on a commercial and non-discriminatory basis" and states that "the Contracting Parties shall eliminate existing and create no new obstacles to the transfer of technology in the field of Energy Material and Products" (ECT, Article 8). Likewise, the WTO General Agreement on Trade in Services states that "Developed country Members...shall establish contact points....to facilitate the access of developing country Members' service suppliers to information, related to their respective markets, concerning...the availability of services technology" (GATS, Art. IV.2(c) --III). Finally, the WTO Agreement on TRIPS states that "Developed country Members shall provide incentives to enterprises and institutions in their territories for the purpose of promoting and encouraging technology transfer to least-developed country Members in order to enable them to create a sound and viable technological base" (Article 66.2) and "shall provide...technical and financial cooperation in favour of developing and least-developed country Members" (Article 67). Similarly, all major treaties on environmental protection contain provisions dealing with the transfer of environmentally sound technologies to developing countries and the financial and technical assistance necessary to realize that objective (UNCTAD-DST, 1996b, forthcoming).

iv. Employment

Employment and related issues are of great importance in the context of FDI (UNCTAD-DTCI, 1994a). They involve aspects such as the role and responsibilities of governments and TNCs regarding employment promotion, equality of opportunity and treatment, security of employment, training, wages, benefits, work conditions, safety and health, freedom of association and the right to organize, information disclosure, collective bargaining, consultation, examination of grievances and settlement of industrial disputes. They were among the earliest to be addressed at the international level, in particular in the OECD Guidelines on Multilateral Enterprises and, most importantly, in the ILO Tripartite Declaration of Principles concerning Multinational Enterprises and Social Policy, which provides a widely accepted set of standards covering most key labour issues. These instruments, developed with the direct involvement of labour and business representatives, provides a key reference standard for international investment accords that seek to address the relationship between FDI and labour issues.

More recently, broader issues relating to minimum international labour standards have been raised, with the discussion focusing particularly on freedom of association, forced labour, discrimination and child labour. While traditionally these issues have been mainly associated with increased trade linkages, the growing importance of FDI in linking economies at the level of production complicates this issue further because the worldwide affiliate networks of TNCs open up new possibilities to influence labour standards globally (UNCTAD-DTCI, 1994a, ch. IX).

v.   *Environmental issues*

Protection of the environment is an obvious area of concern but national action has often proved inadequate. Many environmental impacts cannot be contained within national boundaries, assuring international interest and involvement when national measures fail to preclude serious environmental degradation. Transnational corporations are often involved in environmentally significant activities in host countries; are visible on environmental performance measures; and generally have superior resources to provide leadership on environmental protection issues, which they often actually do (UNCTC, 1992a). At the same time, differences in environmental protection rules and practices in host countries can influence investment decisions to the detriment of sustainable development. A variety of international conventions exists dealing with specific environmental issues (UNCED, 1993). In addition, provisions on protection of the environment have been introduced in various international investment instruments, such as the OECD Guidelines and NAFTA, while a number of documents issued by the United Nations (e.g., Criteria for Sustainable Development Management), the ICC (Business Charter for Sustainable Development) and other non-governmental organizations (the CERES Principles) have sought to influence the impact of FDI on the environment, including by promoting the use of best practices by foreign affiliates. The question of environmental protection is thus increasingly seen as part of a framework of rules that seek to promote the orderly operation of economic activity.

vi.   *Illicit payments*

The meaning of "illicit payments", "bribery" or "corruption" is generally understood, although no single definition is universally accepted. Definitions often restrict recipients to public officials, but the growing privatization of the economy makes this restriction less and less relevant. Illicit payments concern FDI flows for a number of reasons. There is some evidence that it lowers investment. It can also reduce the efficiency of any given investment in so far as an investment decision may depend more on the incidental return to particular decision-makers than to the investment project. Corruption can also influence the sectoral composition of investment, possibly involving a shift in investment from industries with a high rate of internal return to others with a lower rate of return. Apart from the effect of corruption on the efficiency of investment, it constitutes a distortion in the investment market including by blocking the transparency essential to the working of a free competitive market.

International instruments concerning illicit payments are beginning to emerge. The Recommendation on Bribery in International Business Transactions adopted by the Council of the OECD in May 1994 is a case in point, and there is also a draft international agreement on illicit payments negotiated in the framework of the United Nations.

* * *

Transnational corporations are not formally recognised "legal persons" in international law. For international norms in any of these areas to be established, states would have to follow one of several legal techniques: they might recognize the competence of States to legislate on the topic, while at the same time setting international standards for cooperation among States; they might prescribe the content of norms and impose on States the duty to legislate and enforce them; they might direct their prescriptions to TNCs, possibly providing for some procedure or machinery for implementation at the international level; or the norms may take the form of recommendations, addressed to TNCs, possibly with some institutional machinery for further implementation, although not strictly speaking "enforcement". The first approach is in use in some areas (e.g., in some environmental treaties), while the second is by far the one that is best established and most convenient (e.g., the ILO Conventions); for its success, however, it requires the continuing cooperation of the States involved. The third method is the most difficult and unlikely to be adopted, since, while legally possible, it runs counter to the general practice and the usual habits in such matters. The last method was the one followed in the 1970s, when codes of conduct for various aspects of TNC behaviour were negotiated; but experience has shown that this approach does not command sufficient consensus to deal with the issues at hand.

Overall, the question of the legal personality of TNCs under international law is a complex one and one that is at the forefront of change. The full dimensions of this issue cannot be dealt with in this chapter; suffice it to say that, to the extent to which any of these matters and the pertinent techniques might be addressed in future international instruments, they require careful consideration.

(d)   Investment protection and dispute settlement

Specific rules on the protection of investments are generally deemed necessary for the creation of a favourable investment climate. As a result, such rules can be found in many recent international instruments. However, theoretically at least, investment protection is covered by the other elements already discussed.[7] The elimination of restrictions, the application of positive standards of treatment and the operation of a properly functioning legal system should provide an adequate framework for FDI. If restrictive measures were eliminated, including exchange restrictions, there would be no need for rules on transfer of funds; if standards of treatment were generally perceived to be applied in the framework of a well functioning legal system (be it in developed or developing countries, or economies in transition), there would be no need for specific rules to prevent, for example, discriminatory treatment. It is mainly because investors remain apprehensive of the political and other conditions in a number of host countries; because the imposition (or re-imposition) of restrictions cannot be reasonably excluded; because, given political and economic conditions, arbitrary governmental measures are not out of the question; that they, and their home countries, insist on the inclusion of investment-protection provisions in international agreements. On the other hand, it is because they do not expect (or wish) to take the kinds of measures involved that the governments of capital-importing, especially developing countries and economies in transition, have accepted such provisions for a long time now in bilateral agreements and more recently in regional ones. The expansion of these instruments has meant, of course, that an increasing number of countries are now bound by such provisions.

In contrast to most provisions on standards of treatment, most investment-protection provisions are "absolute" and not relative in character, i.e., they do not refer to another body of rules (e.g., rules of domestic law, in the case of the national treatment standard) but expressly state the conduct that is expected. In particular, they spell out the conditions under which an expropriation is lawful and the manner in which compensation is to be assessed and paid. The approach they follow reflects concerns of investors, not only that they may be treated in a discriminatory manner, but that the national law rules on such issues applicable to local nationals and firms may not be adequate, may be very hard to determine and apply or may be too easily and too frequently changed.

Investment-protection provisions may then be understood as provisions concerning the specific, detailed and non-contingent treatment of investors. On the other hand, the possible effects of the behaviour of investors on the protection afforded to them by international rules may have to be taken into consideration. In fact, in some instances, the availability of some elements of investment protection are made conditional on investors having met certain criteria: the Overseas Private Investment Corporation (OPIC) of the United States, for example, requires that a FDI project meet some criteria as far as impact on host and home countries is concerned (e.g., positive developmental effects and absence of negative environmental effects on the host country; and absence of deterimental effect on the economy of the home country). Depending on the form of bilateral agreement under which its programmes operate in a given country, OPIC also requires either specific approval of the project by the host government, or assurance that the project has received such host government approval as is required in the ordinary course. Similarly, before MIGA insures a project, it must undergo a review during which an assessment is made of, among other things, the contribution of the project to the host country's development (including job creation, technology transfer and export generation); in addition, MIGA must obtain the host government's approval to offer insurance to an investor.

Typically, however, investment-protection provisions complement the general grant of national, MFN and fair and equitable treatment. Indeed, they go beyond the first two of these standards, in that the treatment they accord may in fact, under present conditions, discriminate in favour of FDI. From another angle, protection provisions may be understood as transitional measures, designed to provide assurances and guarantees to investors for a certain time or with respect to particular countries (even though such limitations in no way appear in their formulation or indeed in the intent of their drafters), in the expectation that the assurances will largely create the "investment climate" needed and that there will be no need for the provisions to be invoked in practice. Their occasional invocation by the home country (or the investor) is thus to be considered as an exception rather than the rule. Such an understanding of investment-protection provisions may help to explain the continuing support for such clauses by investors and home countries, despite the relative absence of recent formal practice on the matter, in particular with respect to formal recourse in diplomatic practice to the protection provisions of BITs.

Investment protection (and pertinent provisions) involve issues, not necessarily closely related one to another, at least in legal terms. There are two broad categories:

- Government measures, such as expropriations, nationalizations or abrogations of contracts with foreign investors, which generally cause major disruptions to an investor's operations or even put an end to an investor's presence in a host country.

- Other measures, such as excessive and discriminatory taxation, refusal to allow repatriation of funds and unfair treatment by administrative and judicial authorities, which, although by definition detrimental to an investor's interests, do not normally endanger the continuation of operations in the host country. While such measures are smaller in scale and do not amount to a total disruption of an investment, they may cause major damage to the investor and, whether because of the scale of injury or the intent of the measures, may amount to "indirect" expropriation.

The principal elements of investment-protection provisions fall under the following headings:

- expropriations and property takings in general;
- abrogation (or unilateral amendment) of state contracts with investors;
- transfer of funds;
- other specific treatment issues;
- settlement of disputes.

i. Takings of property

The problems arising from takings of foreign property by the state have been on the international agenda since the nineteenth century. They acquired increasing saliency this century, in the period between the two world wars and especially in the decades after the Second World War. The political focus shifted over the years, from the ideological conflict of the first post-war decades to decolonization and developing countries' efforts to assert control over natural resources in subsequent decades. The government actions involved were in most cases large-scale measures, in the context of general sociopolitical change and decolonization. The historical and ideological context has today changed and, while the possibility of individual measures of property deprivation cannot be excluded, the actual risk of large-scale action of this sort is considerably diminished.

Relevant international law norms have been the object of considerable debate both in diplomatic correspondence and in scholarly writings. Developed countries have insisted that takings of foreign property are unlawful in international law unless they meet certain requirements, most important of which is the payment of full compensation. Developing countries have asserted that property takings are subject to the exclusive jurisdiction of the host country, which also determines how compensation is to be assessed and paid (see, e.g., Higgins, 1982; Asante, 1988; Mouri, 1994; Sornarajah, 1994). In practice, it was the requirement of compensation and the modalities for its assessment and payment that have been at the centre of the debate. Debate ranged over a wide field, from the assertion of a need for "full, adequate and effective" compensation to numerous qualifications of varying effect, such as "fair" or "appropriate" compensation (Lillich, 1974-1987; Schachter, 1984). Despite the doctrinal debate, the practice of arbitral tribunals and diplomatic settlements has tended to take into account to varying extent numerous pertinent factors arising in each particular case.

Nowadays, host countries are increasingly willing to provide to investors assurances of fair treatment, generally including undertakings against expropriation, promises of full compensation in case of property taking and acceptance of dispute-settlement procedures. Bilateral investment treaties, as well as some recent regional instruments (e.g., NAFTA, Energy Charter Treaty), include elaborate provisions setting strict conditions for the legality of expropriations and specifying standards for the compensation to be paid. Future problems are likely to relate to compensation for new forms of property interests of investors, such as administrative licences and permits, under which a foreign affiliate operates in a host country.

Bilateral treaties and some other instruments also deal with a related topic, that of losses due to war, civil strife or other such catastrophe. Related provisions, however, establish a relative standard, essentially that of national (and MFN) treatment and accord to foreign investors in such cases the same treatment that host nationals (or nationals from other countries) receive.

ii.   State contracts

In recent years, the abrogation (or modification) of contracts that host states have concluded with investors has largely been dealt with along the same lines as property takings. In earlier times, the international law aspects of the repudiation of external public debt were at the centre of attention. Recently, however, and despite the problems of excessive indebtedness, the issue has been dealt with on a consensual basis, through the renegotiation of public debt. Concession agreements for natural resources (especially hydrocarbons) received much attention for a time, and the scope of pertinent rules was extended to cover the many contractual and quasi-contractual instruments used by countries in the implementation of investment-screening statutes and incentive measures. While investors have long insisted on the application of unqualified "sanctity-of-contract" principles to state agreements of these kinds, international arbitral practice has approached the topic carefully, seeking to reconcile respect for contractual obligations with the public interest (Fatouros, 1980; Leboulanger, 1985; Kuusi, 1979; Paasivirta, 1990).

iii.   Transfer of funds

It is chiefly because this particular topic is generally treated in specific and absolute terms, as part of the provisions on protection of investments, that it is dealt with here. Otherwise, it would have been treated along with other measures affecting investment operations, since, after all, the issue arises solely because many host countries still retain foreign exchange controls. Moreover, restrictions of this kind are usually measures of a general character, i.e., they are not specifically directed at foreign investors. However, this is an issue of central importance to foreign investors because such restrictions tend particularly to affect them, far more indeed than they affect local firms, since foreign affiliates have close ties with firms in other countries and normally belong to an enterprise, a TNC, whose profit centre is located outside the host country. For this reason, foreign investors are particularly interested in receiving assurances concerning their ability to transfer funds abroad. Such assurances were provided with considerable difficulty in past decades, but they are now invariably found in recent international instruments and national laws. At the same time, they contain often a number of limitations, linked especially to a country's economic (and particularly balance-of-payment) situation.

iv.   Other treatment issues

Some other issues of less significance, but still of practical importance to investors, are normally dealt with in this context. One category concerns particular aspects of the day-to-day operations of foreign firms, including, in particular, their ability to employ foreign key personnel of their choice; the possibility of keeping their books in the language and the currency most convenient to them; and their right to full access to local courts (which, of course, might also be considered as covered in part by the national treatment provisions).

Another issue flows from the fact that many home countries have created and administer agencies for investment insurance to cover non-business risks that private insurers might not. It is thus necessary to provide that a state or state agency that has paid investors on investment-insurance contracts will be recognized as subrogated to their rights and claims, usually against the host state.

v.   Settlement of disputes

In international instruments on FDI, a special role is played by provisions on the settlement of possible disputes on investment matters between home and host states, on the one hand, and between host states and investors, on the other. It is generally understood that many, probably most, legal and other problems arising from the operation of foreign firms will be avoided, in the first place, through good business and legal planning on each side, and resolved, in the second place, through consultations and bargaining between the parties concerned. Nevertheless, experience from business operations suggests that it is likely that some problems will remain. These may involve disputes between states, parties to the pertinent instruments, between states and investors and between private investors (Brewer, 1995a).

The normal method for the resolution of disputes between private parties is through recourse to the courts of the state that has jurisdiction over the dispute or to commercial arbitration proceedings. It is usually the host state that has jurisdiction to adjudicate such disputes, although other states may also be competent, depending on the dispute, including contractual arrangements between the parties. Recourse to commercialization, again on the basis of contractual undertakings, is quite common.

On the other hand, provisions on state-to-state disputes and on investor-to-state disputes have become more common in recent instruments relating to investments. The former involve disputes concerning the application or interpretation of the instrument, and they follow the usual pattern of dispute-settlement clauses in international agreements. Their main distinguishing characteristic is that they often place special emphasis on consultations and other procedures before recourse to arbitration. Otherwise, their provisions on the constitution and functioning of the arbitral tribunal are similar to those found in other international agreements.

Investor-to-state disputes involve a state and a private person. In the absence, therefore, of any related provision in bilateral, regional or multilateral instruments, in national legislation or in contracts between a state and an investor, they would normally come before national courts, most frequently the courts of the host country. Nowadays, recourse to arbitration is common. While not all legal differences between investors and the host State are amenable to direct arbitral proceedings, the parties concerned often agree to submit disputes to arbitration, whether through an agreement between them or, more recently, through international treaties between home and host States. Investors prefer to avoid the delays and elaborate procedures that they fear to encounter in national courts, and to rely instead on the expertise and impartiality of arbitrators. Host states on their part have often -- and increasingly so -- found it convenient to accept recourse to arbitration, to speed up the disposition of economic disputes and to persuade investors of their willingness to carry out the arrangements involved.

One advantage of direct investor-to-state proceedings is that, through them, it is possible for the parties concerned to avoid recourse to the more complicated and political process of formal diplomatic protection, where the home State, invoking a violation of international law, espouses the investor's claim, and the dispute becomes an inter-state one (Gray, 1990). A number of possible models for investor-to-state arbitral proceedings are now available. The World Bank-sponsored Convention on the Settlement of Investment Disputes between States and Nationals of Other States is the best-known and widely accepted relevant instrument. It provides a permanent machinery and established procedures for such disputes. Other institutions (UNCITRAL, the International Chamber of Commerce, the Permanent Court of Arbitration) have prepared arbitration rules, and some provide facilities that may be utilized in such cases (Craig, et al., 1990; Toope, 1990). The availability of several dispute-settlement mechanisms provides a significant element of flexibility, although it may also lead, at least in theory, to a situation in which several mechanisms might be used in the same dispute and reach differing results.

* * *

Investment-protection provisions go beyond liberalization measures. In a way, they move along another plane. Although they are primarily directed at possible measures of host governments, they may best be understood as efforts to counteract the perceived uncertainties of current international economic relations. Through legal commitments, they seek to establish a degree of stability, transparency and predictability that circumstances do not provide. The extent to which the governments of host countries have in their large majority accepted to provide assurances in the directions desired by investors suggests that they, too, understand the process in these terms. They seek to bind themselves with respect to actions and measures that they do not wish to take, with the twin purpose of creating a favourable investment climate that will attract FDI and make it more difficult for such measures to be taken in the future.

It is possible therefore to see, to a certain extent, the investment-protection category as the mirror image of the development-exception category: provisions and arrangements intended to be temporary (although not necessarily short-term) to take care of current conditions, with the expectation that after considerable progress in the international economy, such provisions may become unnecessary. Restrictions will have been largely eliminated, the fear of arbitrary action will no longer be present and several of the international norms of protection will have been "internalized" in the law of all countries concerned. If this appears too distant a vision, it should be compared to that concerning the time when no special development provisions (or exceptions) will be necessary, because development will have advanced to such an extent that other considerations become more important.

4. Procedural approaches

Other important questions relating to an international instrument involve its legal character and the approach adopted to the mechanisms used to give effect to its provisions, including those related to the liberalization of investment restrictions. In the latter regard, there are several basic models, with a number of variations.

One basic pattern (as, for instance, in the case of the OECD) starts with a standstill clause, prohibiting the imposition of new restrictions, and proceeds to establish strict, advanced undertakings by the parties concerning the elimination of restrictions. Parties are, however, allowed to qualify these undertakings with extensive reservations, exceptions and exclusions. These are gradually removed primarily through regular reviews and examinations of individual states in the organization's intergovernmental committees; only occasionally is there collective bargaining for the amendment of the initial texts. The whole process functions on the basis of shared perspectives and informal persuasion or "peer pressure". Member states are continuously exposed to this process, and they gradually accept to remove their reservations and exceptions. Some (big or small) states, as well as the organization (especially through its secretariat), can take a lead role in promoting the acceptance of high standards. Along more or less the same lines, one finds another pattern which also starts with extensive liberalization commitments, but commitments that are limited by negative lists of existing measures, sectoral exceptions and a broad national security exemption.

Another pattern (as, for instance, in the case of the WTO) starts with an initial agreement that contains a few general obligations and definitions; it also provides the benchmarks towards which the parties agree to proceed. Each member makes an offer and negotiates on the obligations it will undertake in its "schedules". Thus, the parties retain control of the extent of their possible obligations and the pace at which they are committed to move towards the elimination of restrictions in particular industries. At regular intervals, collective negotiations are conducted during which the parties exchange their offers for further advances towards the elimination of restrictions.

The actual patterns are, of course, more complex than these rough descriptions suggest. One important variant is the possibility of allowing certain countries, whether developing ones or countries in transition, to benefit from transitional arrangements, i.e., exceptions for a specific time. Another variant involves the selective use of "best-efforts" clauses, to cover some issues of special difficulty.

All these arrangements are aimed at setting in motion a dynamic process, whereby they will achieve their ends. The impossibility of implementing an ambitious agenda at the time of conclusion of an agreement is realized, and procedures are established, with the help of institutional mechanisms as well as various informal processes, which are intended to ensure the future implementation of the agreement by the states party to it.

5. Concluding observations

The purpose of this section was to identify key issues that arise as regards the further development of international arrangements governing FDI, with special attention being given to their implication for development. Although extensive, the list of key issues considered is by no means exhaustive. Altogether, these issues are of central importance to the future of the global economy, as well as its principal actors, including developed and developing countries, the private sector and other interested parties. The relative importance of particular issues varies, of course, for different actors. While investment protection and liberalization, for instance, are especially important to TNCs, the implications for sustainable growth and development of all these issues are of particular significance for governments. Social policy questions, meanwhile, are special concerns of other groups, in particular, trade unions and consumer groups.

It is particularly important to analyse carefully the implications for development of all efforts to strengthen current international arrangements for investment. The importance of the development dimension cannot be overemphasized: if it is desired that a framework be effective, it needs to take into account the interests of all parties, so that it is to their advantage and, therefore, is more likely to gain widespread acceptance and application. Broadly speaking, the development objective needs to be:

- *safeguarded* by allowing developing countries in need of a transition period -- through exclusions, exemptions and temporary measures -- the time to adjust to more stringent standards of investment liberalization, it being recognized that many developing countries have gone already far on their own initiative;

- *advanced* by agreeing that developing countries can take appropriate measures to increase the benefits that they can reap from FDI, without infringing on the essential interests of foreign investors; and

- *supported* by home country governments committing themselves to help developing countries attract FDI, in particular FDI that is most consonant with their developmental needs (e.g., because it embodies appropriate technology or is export-oriented). Governments of home countries can promote FDI flows to developing countries, e.g., through the provision of information and technical assistance; direct financial support and fiscal incentives; and investment insurance and tax-sparing provisions (UNCTAD-DTCI, 1995a, ch. VII). While many home countries have already many measures in place in this respect (table VI.6), and some international instruments address this issue (e.g., the Lomé Convention -- box VI.4), not all do, and those that do, can be strengthened.

Experience has shown that development objectives can not only be accommodated but actually be promoted by international agreements. The further development of international arrangements for FDI needs to keep this objective at the centre of its attention.

C. Fora

A distinction has already been made between the gradual evolution of existing international arrangements governing FDI on the one hand, and the creation of a comprehensive multilateral framework on the other, as two basic approaches towards future international rule-making in this area. This section provides a brief overview of significant current international initiatives towards the establishment of international rules on FDI matters. Leaving aside the rapidly evolving network of bilateral investment agreements, the focus is on key initiatives undertaken at the regional and interregional levels, and on recent suggestions for the creation of a multilateral framework for FDI.

Table VI.6. Outward FDI promotion programmes of OECD member countries, early 1990s

| Country | Information and technical assistance | | | | | Financing | | Insurance |
	Information	Matchmaking	Missions	Feasibility studies [a]	Project development and start-up [a]	Equity	Loans	Guarantees
Australia	*	*	*	*				
Austria	*					*	*	*
Belgium	*	*				*	*	*
Canada	*	*	*	*	*	*		
Denmark						*	*	*
Finland	*		*	*	*	*	*	*
France	*			*	*	*	*	
Germany	*	*	*	*	*	*	*	*
Italy	*	*	*	*	*	*	*	*
Japan	*	*	*	*	*	*	*	*
Netherlands	*	*	*	*		*	*	*
New Zealand	*	*		*		*		
Norway	*	*	*	*	*		*	*
Portugal	*	*	*				*	
Spain	*	*	*			*	*	*
Sweden	*	*		*		*	*	
Switzerland	*	*	*	*	*	*	*	*
United Kingdom						*	*	*
United States	*	*	*	*	*		*	*

Source: UNCTAD-DTCI, 1995a.

[a]   May include some financial support.

1. Regional and interregional

Investment issues are currently the subject of discussion or negotiation in a number of regional and interregional fora. One important recent initiative was the launching, in May 1995, by OECD members of negotiations aimed at the conclusion of a Multilateral Agreement on Investment by the time of the OECD ministerial meeting of 1997 (OECD, 1995b, 1996b). The main aim of these negotiations is to eliminate discrimination between foreign and domestic investors. The agreement is intended to provide a broad framework for international investment, with high standards for the liberalization of investment regimes and the protection of investment, and with effective dispute-settlement procedures (Witherell, 1995, 1996; OECD, 1995c). Evidently, in the negotiations on a Multilateral Agreement on Investment, as indeed in any further elaboration of international rules on FDI, account needs to be taken of interrelationships with existing arrangements, to avoid inconsistent outcomes, e.g., with respect to WTO provisions in areas such as GATS, TRIMs and TRIPS and with bilateral investment agreements.

The OECD undoubtedly possesses important advantages with respect to the matter at hand: most FDI activity takes place within the OECD area, and member countries are the main sources of FDI for developing countries and economies in transition. Moreover, it is the first organization to have concluded and administered a set of FDI rules, and, over the years, the OECD Secretariat and OECD committees have acquired considerable expertise in FDI matters. The OECD also has a well-tested institutional structure for consulting business and trade unions.

While this agreement is negotiated among OECD members only, the negotiation mandate provides that it will be a "free-standing international treaty open to all OECD Members and the

---

Box VI.4. Measures to promote FDI flows to ACP countries in Lomé IV

To encourage private investment flows and the development of enterprises, the Fourth Lomé Convention between the European Union and African, Caribbean and Pacific (ACP) States prescribes, among other things, that the ACP States and the Union "shall":

- "(a) support efforts aimed at promoting European private investments in the ACP States by organizing discussions between any interested ACP States and potential investors on the legal and financial framework that ACP States might offer to investors;

- (b) encourage the flow of information on investment opportunities by organizing investment promotion meetings, providing periodic information on existing financial or other specialized institutions, their facilities and conditions and encouraging the establishment of focal points for such meetings;

- (c) encourage the dissemination of information on the nature and availability of investment guarantees and insurance mechanisms to facilitate investment in ACP States;

- (d) provide assistance to small and medium-sized enterprises in ACP States in designing and obtaining equity and loan financing on optimal terms and conditions;

- (e) explore ways and means of overcoming or reducing the host-country risk for individual investment projects which could contribute to economic progress;

- (f) provide assistance to ACP States in:

  - (i) creating or strengthening the ACP States' capacity to improve the quality of feasibility studies and the preparation of projects in order that appropriate economic and financial conclusions might be drawn;

  - (ii) producing integrated project management mechanisms covering the entire project development cycle within the framework of the development programme of the State."

Source: Fourth Lomé Convention, Article 259, contained in UNCTAD-DTCI, 1996a.

European Communities, and to accession by non-OECD Member countries, which will be consulted as the negotiations progress"(OECD, 1995c, p.3). To facilitate the future expansion of the agreement, the OECD has established an outreach programme, so that a dialogue with non-member states can be maintained throughout the negotiations (OECD, 1995c). At the same time, it is an open question how many non-OECD member countries will want to adhere to such an important agreement without having participated in its negotiation and helped shape its provisions. This may be important for developing countries, some of whose concerns differ from those of the highly developed countries that are the majority of OECD membership. Even so, the Multilateral Agreement on Investment, once concluded, will reflect the policy consensus among the OECD countries on the treatment of FDI.

Other regional and interregional fora are considering investment issues, too. There are the non-binding investment principles adopted in 1994 by APEC members, as well as further work on investment undertaken in the context of APEC's "Action Agenda" (Brewer, 1995b); the decision by ASEAN in December 1995 to study an ASEAN free investment area; the examination of cooperation in investment policy in the context of the Free Trade Area for the America's initiative; and negotiations under the European Energy Charter treaty on a supplementary treaty which would extend the coverage of its investment provisions to the admission of investment.

2. Multilateral

Although multilateral rules on FDI could be established in an independent agreement, recent proposals aim at negotiating such rules in the framework of international organizations with global or potentially global membership. In particular, the WTO has been mentioned as an appropriate forum for such negotiations (Brittan, 1995).[8] An important consideration underlying this suggestion is that the growing complementarity of investment and trade in the world economy requires a more integrated approach to international rule-making. This has already manifested itself in the work of the GATT and the WTO. Thus, the WTO already deals with some investment issues in the agreements on trade in services, trade-related aspects of intellectual property rights and trade-related investment measures, and an agenda exists for the expansion and deepening of these rules: negotiations on liberalisation through the expansion of the GATS schedules of commitments are scheduled to take place before 1999, and the TRIMs Agreement provides for consideration of competition and investment issues by the same year (Ruggiero, 1996). One issue is, therefore, whether the scope of the Organization should be broadened to take a more comprehensive approach which would encompass all aspects of FDI or whether it is desirable and feasible to deal only with those FDI issues that fit into a concept of trade-relatedness.

Members of the WTO are currently discussing a proposal for a decision to be taken at the WTO's first Ministerial Conference in Singapore in December 1996 to create a body to conduct a work programme on trade and investment. If such a decision were taken, it is likely to provide for work of an exploratory nature rather than the immediate launching of negotiations on a set of investment rules.

A major theme in any work on investment that might be launched in the WTO is likely to be the examination of the economic interrelationships between investment and trade and their evolution in recent years, with a view towards reaching a common understanding about the extent to which trade and investment have become inseparable policy issues. Beyond that, it would be expected to address issues of scope; investment measures that affect the entry and operations of foreign investors; standards of treatment; measures dealing with broader concerns; and investment protection and dispute settlement. It might also be that the impact that trade policy measures can have on FDI flows needs to be addressed. Finally, a matter that might need to be examined would be whether, in addition to providing an enabling framework, positive action to facilitate FDI by developed country enterprises in developing, and in particular least-developed, countries should be envisaged.

Above all, the development dimension -- the implications of all provisions for developing countries -- would need to permeate any such work in the WTO framework, as would the importance of ensuring mutual advantage and increased benefits to all. A further horizontal issue is the need for coherence between different policy areas, including investment, trade, technology and competition, and also between initiatives at the bilateral, regional and multilateral levels, guided by the principle of non-discrimination. A prominent consideration would also be the importance of guaranteeing that no countries or groups of countries were marginalized in, or excluded from, the evolving international framework for investment. A further theme could be the desirability of maximizing cooperation and minimizing duplication with other intergovernmental organizations and benefiting from their experience.

An important question arising in connection with possible future negotiations on investment in the WTO is the manner in which an agreement -- should one be negotiated in this forum -- would be incorporated into the WTO's institutional framework. In the present structure of the WTO, multilateral agreements, which are integral parts of the WTO Agreement and bind all WTO members, are distinguished from plurilateral agreements, which are part of the WTO Agreement only for those WTO members that have accepted them. The possibility of a wholly separate, "stand-alone" agreement, while novel in the WTO context, cannot be excluded either.

While there are advantages in incorporating any future investment agreement into the multilateral WTO framework, thus establishing close internal relationships between its provisions and its implementation and those of other WTO multilateral agreements as well as with the entire WTO institutional machinery, such an approach also raises a number of issues that would have to be taken into consideration. One is that obligations undertaken by WTO members in the area of investment might come within the scope of the WTO dispute-settlement mechanism and thus ultimately be enforceable through the suspension of trade concessions, in the context of what is usually called "cross-retaliation". While possible with respect to trade in goods, retaliation in the context of dispute settlement in GATT/WTO has been virtually unknown. Only once was it authorised (in the 1950s), and even then it was not carried out. It is moreover possible, at least *in abstracto*, to include in the pertinent investment instrument specific provisions excluding the possibility of cross-retaliation with respect to trade (in goods or services).[9]

The question of a possible future multilateral framework on investment was addressed at the 1996 UNCTAD IX Conference at which it was agreed that, as part of its activities on investment, enterprise development and technology, UNCTAD should identify and analyze implications for development of issues relevant to a possible multilateral framework on investment, beginning with an examination and review of existing agreements, taking into account the interests of developing countries and bearing in mind the work undertaken by other organizations. The areas of policy analysis and consensus-building, with a particular focus on the development dimension, are, indeed, areas in which UNCTAD can make a contribution.

Notes

[1]   The Afro-Asian Legal Consultative Committee has prepared three different model treaties which are recommended to its members, and the OECD has a draft Convention on the Protection of Foreign Property which serves as a model for a number of BITs.

[2]   Traditional trade theory is, in fact, based on the assumption that trade between states is arm's length; it has had difficulties to take into account that a good part of international trade consists of intra-firm trade, i.e., where prices typically are administered as opposed to being set in the market.

[3]   For a detailed examination of issues related to investment incentives, see UNCTAD-DTCI, 1996b. See also Guisinger, 1985; Lecraw, 1991; Graham, 1994b; Brewer and Young, 1996b.

[4]   For a discussion of RBPs and competition policy, see Davidow and Chiles, 1978; Davidow, 1980; Green and Rosenthal, 1996; Scherer, 1994; Warner and Rugman, 1994; and Graham, 1994b.

[5]   For a discussion of the latter approach, see Brittan and van Miert, 1996.

[6]   Agenda 21 adopted at the United Nations Conference on Environment and Development (UNCED) has devoted a full chapter (34) on cooperation for the transfer of environmentally sound technologies and capacity building. See, UNCED, 1993; UNCTAD, forthcoming. For a synthesis of some of the policy options for the transfer of environmentally sound technologies, see UNCTAD-DST (1996a, forthcoming).

[7]   See the discussion of the nature of the liberalization process in UNCTAD-DTCI, 1994a, pp. 303-309, where several of the items here discussed under "investment protection" are dealt with under "Standards of treatment".

[8]   While the WTO enjoys wide membership (123 members as of July 1996, with 36 observers), it has yet to achieve universal membership, the largest non-members being China and Russia.

[9]   In this regard it may be noted that the plurilateral WTO agreement on government procurement contains a provision ruling out cross-retaliation in regard to other WTO agreements (Art. XXII.7).

References

Akinsanya, Adeoye (1987). "International protection of direct foreign investment in the Third World", *International and Comparative Law Quarterly*, 36, pp. 58-75.

Amerasinghe, C.F. (1992). "Issues of compensation for the taking of alien property in the light of recent cases and practice", *International and Comparative Law Quarterly*, 41, pp. 22-65.

Anayiotos, Andrea (1994). "Infrastructure investment funds", *Private Sector,* December, pp. 29-32.

Asante, Samuel K.B. (1988). "International law and foreign investment: a reappraisal", International and Comparative Law Quarterly, 37, pp.588-628.

_____ (1989). "Concept of the good corporate citizen in international business", *ICSID Review*, 4, 1 (Spring), pp. 1-38.

Bergsten, C.F., T. Horst and T.H. Moran (1978). *American Multinationals and American Interests* (Washington, DC: The Brookings Institution).

Bergsten, F. and Graham, E. M. (1992). "Needed: new international rules for foreign direct investment", *The International Trade Journal*, 7, pp. 15-44.

Blomström, M. (1990). *Transnational Corporations and Manufacturing Export from Developing Countries* (New York: United Nations), ST/CTC/101.

_____ and R.E. Lipsey (1993). "Foreign firms and structural adjustment in Latin America: lessons from the debt crisis", Working Paper 1856, National Bureau of Economic Research.

_____ and K. Kulchyck (1988). "US and Swedish Direct Investment and Exports", in R.E. Baldwin, ed., *Trade Policy Issues and Empirical Analysis* (Chicago: University of Chicago Press), pp.259-97.

Bora, B. K. (1995). "APEC's non-binding investment principles: a step forward?", in Carl J. Green and Thomas L. Brewer, eds., *International Investment Issues in the Asia Pacific Region and the Role of APEC* (Dobbs Ferry: Oceana).

_____ and Graham, E. M. (1995). "Nonbinding investment principles in APEC", *CAPA Report* (San Francisco: The Asia Foundation's Centre for Asian Pacific Affairs), January.

Brainard, S. Lael (1992). "A simple theory of multinational corporations and trade with a trade-off between proximity and concentration", Working Paper 4269, National Bureau of Economic Research.

Brash D.T. (1966). *American Investment in Australian Industry* (Canberra: Australian University Press).

Brewer, Thomas L. (1995a). "International investment dispute settlement procedures: the evolving regime for foreign direct investment", *Law and Policy in International Business*, 26, 3, pp. 633-673.

_____ (1995b). "Investment issues in the WTO and implications for APEC", in Carl J. Green and Thomas L. Brewer, eds., *International Investment Issues in the Asia Pacific Region and the Role of APEC* (Dobbs Ferry: Oceana).

_____ and Stephen Young (1995a). "European Union policies and the problems of multinational enterprises", *Journal of World Trade*, 29, 1, pp. 32-52.

_____ (1995b). "Towards a multilateral framework for foreign direct investment: issues and scenarios", *Transnational Corporations*, 4, 1, pp. 69-83.

_____ (1995c). "The multilateral agenda for foreign direct investment: problems, principles and priorities for negotiations at the OECD and WTO", *World Competition*, 18, 4, pp. 67-83.

_____ (1996a). "Investment policies in regional and multilateral agreements: a comparative analysis", *Transnational Corporations*, 5, 1, forthcoming.

_____ (1996b). "Global and regional agreements on investment incentives: constraints on the international competition for FDI". Paper presented for the World Conference on Globalization and Regionalization of Trade and International Investment, Paris, 29-30 May 1996, mimeo..

Brittan, Sir Leon (1995). "Investment liberalization: the next great boost to the world economy", *Transnational Corporations*, 4, 1, pp. 1-10.

_____ and Karel van Miert (1996). "Towards an international framework of competition rules", Communication to the Council (Brussels: European Commission), mimeo.

Broches, A. (1972). "The Convention on the Settlement of Investment Disputes between States and Nationals of other States", *Hague Academy Recueil des Cours*, 130, pp. 331-410.

_____ (1991). *Arbitration under the ICSID Convention* (Washington, D.C.: ICSID).

Bronz, G. (1969). "The International Trade Organization Charter", *Harvard Law Review*, 62, pp. 1089-1125.

Brusick, Philippe (1996). "The United Nations Code and policy on restrictive business practices". Paper presented at the Oslo Conference: Competition Policies for an Integrated World Economy (Oslo: Norwegian Competition Authority), mimeo.

Buck, F. (1987). "Some basic roots of the J. Walter Thompson company", unpublished paper (New York: J. Walter Thompson archives).

Buckley, Peter J. and Pervez Ghauri, eds., *The Internationalization of the Firm* (London: Academic Press).

Business and Industry Advisory Committee to the OECD (BIAC) (1994a). "The OECD Multilateral Investment Agreement-BIAC views on specific elements of an eventual instrument" (Paris: BIAC), mimeo.

_____ (1994b). "Supplementary BIAC recommendation for the OECD Multilateral Investment Agreement" (Paris: BIAC), mimeo.

Cantwell, J.A. (1987a). "The role of foreign direct investment in development in Africa", mimeo, Reading University, Economic Department.

_____ (1987b). "The reorganisation of European industries after integration: selected evidence on the role of multinational enterprise activities", *Journal of Common Market Studies*, 26, 2, pp. 127-151.

_____ (1992), "The effects of integration on the structure of multinational corporation activity in the EC", in M.W. Klein and P.J.J. Welfens, eds., *Multinationals in the New Europe and Global Trade* (Berlin: Springer-Verlag).

_____ (1994). "The relationship between International Trade and International Production", in David Greenaway and L. Alan Winters, eds., *Survey in International Trade* (Oxford, UK, Cambridge, MA: Blackwell), pp. 303-328.

_____ (1995). "The globalisation of technology: what remains of the product cycle model?", *Cambridge Journal of Economics*, 19, 1, pp. 155-174.

Casson, Mark et al. (1982). *Multinationals and World Trade: Vertical Integration and Division of Labour in World Industries* (London: Allen & Unwin)

CEPAL (1993). *Directorio sobre inversión extranjera en América Latina y el Caribe, 1993, marco legal e información estatisca* (Santiago: United Nations publication).

_____ (1995). "La inversion extranjera en América Latina y el Caribe", (LG/G.1890) (Santiago: United Nations publication).

Chen, E.K.Y. (1983). *Multinational Corporations, Technology and Employment* (New York: St. Martin's Press).

Craig, William, William Park and Jean Paulsson (1990). *International Chamber of Commerce Arbitration* (Dobbs Ferry: Oceana).

Croome, J. (1995). *Reshaping the World Trading System: A History of the Uruguay Round* (Geneva: World Trade Organization).

Davidow, Joel (1980). "The UNCTAD Restrictive Business Practices Code", in N. Horn, ed., *Legal Problems of Codes of Conduct for Multinational Enterprises* (Dewenter: Kluwer), pp. 193-210.

_____ and Lisa Chiles (1978). "The United States and the issue of the binding or voluntary nature of international codes of conduct regarding restrictive business practices", *American Journal of International Law*, 72, pp. 247-271.

Diebold, W. (1952). "The End of the ITO", *Essays in International Finance*, 16 (Princeton: Princeton University Press).

Dolzer, Rudolf and Margrete Stevens (1995). *Bilateral Investment Treaties* (Washington, D.C.: ICSID).

Doz, Y. (1986). *Strategic Management in Multinational Companies* (Oxford: Pergamon Press).

Dunning J.H. (1958). *American Investment in British Manufacturing Industry* (London: George Allen and Unwin; reprinted by Arno Press, New York, 1976).

_____ (1976). *US Industry in Britain* (London: Wilton House).

_____ (1985). "The United Kingdom", in J.H. Dunning, ed., *Multinational Enterprises, Economic Structure and International Competitiveness* (Chichester and New York: John Wiley and Sons).

_____ (1989). *Transnational Corporations and the Growth of Services: Some Conceptual and Theoretical Issues,* UNCTC Current Studies Series A, No. 9 (New York: UNCTC).

_____ (1993). *Multinational Enterprises and the Global Economy* (Wokingham: Addison-Wesley Publishing Company).

_____ (1994). "Re-evaluating the benefits of foreign direct investment", in *Transnational Corporations,* 3, 1 (February), pp. 23-52.

_____ (1995). "What's wrong–and right–with trade theory?", *The International Trade Journal*, IX, 2, (Summer), pp. 163-202

_____ (1996). *The European Internal Market Program and Inbound Foreign Direct Investment,* forthcoming.

Economist Intelligence Unit (EIU) (1996). *Economies in Transition. Eastern Europe and the Former Soviet Union* (London: EIU), country forecast, 1st quarter.

Ethier, Wilfred J. (1986). "The multinational firm". *Quarterly Journal of Economics*, 101, pp. 805-833.

European Commission (1995a). "A level playing field for direct investment world-wide", COM (95) 42 (Brussels: European Commission), mimeo..

_____ (1995b). "Competition policy in the new trade order: strengthening international cooperation and rules". Report of the group of experts established by Commissioner van Miert (Brussels: European Commission).

European-American Chambers of Commerce (EACC) (1995). "Securing an agreement on investment rules: the European-American Chamber of Commerce's proposal for a trans-Atlantic consensus", mimeo.

European Bank for Reconstruction and Development (1994). *Transition Report 1994* (London: EBRD).

_____ (1995). *Transition Report 1995: Investment and Enterprise Development* (London: EBRD)

Export-Import Bank of Japan, 1996. "EXIM Japan questionnaire on foreign direct investment in fiscal 1995", mimeo.

Fatouros, Arghyrios A. (1961). "An international code to protect private investment: proposals and perspectives", *University of Toronto Law Journal*, 14, pp. 77-102.

_____ (1962). *Government Guarantees to Foreign Investors* (New York: Columbia University Press).

_____ (1980). "International law and the internationalized contract", *Amerian Journal of International Law*, 74, pp. 134-141.

_____ (1993). "Les principes directeurs de l'OCDE à l'intention des entreprises multinationales: perspectives actuelles et possibilités futures", in Chr. Dominicé, R. Patry and Cl. Reymond, eds., *Etudes de droit international en l'honneur de Pierre Laline* (Basel: Helbing and Lichtenhahn).

_____ (1994). "Introduction: the evolving international framework for foreign direct investment", in A. A. Fatouros, ed., *Transnational Corporations: The International Legal Framework. United Nations Library on Transnational Corporations*, 20 (London and New York: Routledge, for the United Nations), pp. 1-37.

Felix, David (1964). "Monetarists, structuralists and import-substituting industrialization: a critical appraisal", in Werner Baer and Isaac Kerstenetzky, eds., *Inflation and Growth in Latin America* (Homewood, Illinois: Richard D. Irvin), pp. 393-394.

Freeman and Hagendoorn (1992). *Globalization of Technology,* Report for the FAST Programme, Directorate General Science, research and Development (Brussels: European Commission).

GATT (1994a). "News of the Uruguay Round of Multilateral Trade Negotiations" (Geneva: GATT), mimeo.

_____ (1994b). *The Results of the Uruguay Round of Multilateral Trade Negotiations* (Geneva: GATT).

Gess, K. (1964). "Permanent sovereignty over natural resources: analytical review of the United Nations Declaration and its genesis", *International and Comparative Law Quarterly*, 13, pp. 398-449.

Gestrin, Michael and Rugman, Alan M. (1994). "The North American Free Trade Agreement and foreign direct investment", *Transnational Corporations*, 3, 1, pp. 77-95.

_____ (1996). "The NAFTA investment provisions: prototype for multilateral investment rules?" in OECD, *Market Access After the Uruguay Round: Investment, Competition and Technology Perspectives* (Paris: OECD), pp. 63-78.

Goldberg, Paul and Charles P. Kindleberger (1970). "Towards a GATT for investment: a proposal for supervision of the international corporation", *Law and Policy in International Business*, 2, pp. 295-325.

Graham, E. M. (1994a). "Toward an Asia Pacific Investment Code", in Carl J. Green and Thomas L. Brewer, eds., *International Investment Issues in the Asia Pacific Region and the Role of APEC* (Dobbs Ferry: Oceana). Reprinted from *Transnational Corporations*, 3, 2, pp. 1-27.

_____ (1994b). "Competition policy and the new trade agenda". Paper presented at "New dimensions of market access in a globalizing world economy" (Paris: OECD).

_____ (1996a). *Global Corporations and National Governments* (Washington, D.C.: Institute for International Economics).

_____ (1996b). "Investment and the new multilateral trade context", in OECD, Market Access After the Uruguay Round: Investment, Competition and Technology Perspectives (Paris: OECD), pp. 35-62.

Gray, C. (1990). *Judicial Remedies in International Law* (Oxford: Clarendon Press).

Green, C. J. and Thomas L. Brewer, eds. (1995). *International Investment Issues in the Asia Pacific Region and the Role of APEC* (Dobbs Ferry: Oceana).

Green, C. J. and D. E. Rosenthal (1996). *Competition Regulation Among the APEC Countries: Convergence and Divergence* (Dobbs Ferry: Oceana).

Grigera Naon, H.A. (1980). "Transnational enterprises under the Pacto Andino and national laws of Latin America", in N. Horn, ed.,*Legal Problems of Codes of Conduct for Multinational Enterprises* (Deventer: Kluwer), pp. 237-273.

Grubel, Herbert (1988). "Direct and embodied trade in services," in C. Lee and S. Naya, eds., *Trade and Investment in Services in the Asia and Pacific Region* (Boulder: Westview Press), pp. 65-66.

Guisinger, Stephen and associates (1985). *Investment Incentives and Performance Requirements* (New York: Praeger).

Hamill, James (1993). "Cross-border mergers, acquisitions and strategic alliances", in Bailey, P., A. Parisotto and G. Renshaw, eds., *Multinationals and Employment: The Global Economy of the 1990s* (Geneva: ILO).

Hamilton, G. (1983). "International codes of conduct for multinationals", *Multinational Business*, 1, pp. 1-10.

Handl, Gunther F., et al. (1988). "A hard look at soft law",*American Society of International Law Proceedings*, 82, pp. 371-395.

Hansen, Peter and Victoria Aranda (1991). "An emerging international framework for transnational corporations", *Fordham International Law Journal*, 14, pp. 881-891.

Hansen, Michael W. (1996). *Danish Foreign Direct Investment in Less Developed Countries and Eastern Europe: A Survey of the International Operations of Danish Companies*, Working paper series 9 (Copenhagen: Department of Intercultural Communication and Management, Copenhagen Business School).

Hart, Michael (1995). "Doing the right thing: regional integration and the multilateral trade regime". Paper presented at a Trinational Symposium (Canada, Mexico and the United States) on Border Demographics and Regional Interdependency, Western Washington University (February).

Hatem, Fabrice (1996). *International Investment Towards the Year 2000* (Paris: Arthur Andersen).

Hedlund, G. and A. Kverneland (1983). "Are entry strategies for foreign markets changing? The case of Swedish investments in Japan", Stockholm School of Economics. Included in Peter J. Buckley and Pervez Ghauri, eds., The Internationalization of the Firm (London: Academic Press), pp. 106-123.

Helpman, Elhanan (1981). "International trade in the presence of product differentiation, economics of scale and monopolistic competition: a Chamberlin-Hecksher-Ohlin Approach":*Journal of International Economics*, 11, pp. 305-340.

_____ (1984). "A simple theory of international trade with multinational corporations". Journal of Political Economy, 92, pp. 451-471.

_____ and Paul R. Krugman (1985). *Market Structure and Foreign Trade* (Cambridge: MIT Press).

Henderson H. (1960). "A short history of the J. Walter Thompson company", unpublished paper (New York: J. Walter Thompson archives).

Higgins, R. (1982). "The taking of property by the State", *Hague Academy Recueil des Cours*, 176, pp. 259-392.

Hipple, Steb F. (1990). "The measurement of international trade related to multinational companies", *American Economic Review,* 80, pp. 1263-70.

Horn, N., ed. (1980). *Legal Problems of Codes of Conduct for Multinational Enterprises* (Deventer: Kluwer).

Horstmann, Ignatius J. and James R. Markusen (1987). "Licensing versus direct investment: a model of internalization by the multinational enterprise". *Canadian Journal of Economics*, 20, pp. 464-481.

_____ (1992). "Endogenous market structures in international trade", *Journal of International Economics*, 32, pp. 109-129

Hymer, S. (1976). *The International Operations of National Firms: a Study of Direct Investment* (Cambridge, Mass.: MIT Press).

IDB and IRELA (1996). *Foreign Direct Investment in Latin America in the 1990s* (Madrid: IDB).

IMF (1995). *Direction of Trade Statistics Yearbook 1995* (Washington: IMF).

International Bureau of Fiscal Documentation (IBFD) (1996). *Tax Treaties Data Base* (Amsterdam: International Bureau of Fiscal Documentation).

International Chamber of Commerce (ICC) (1996). "Multilateral rules for investment", (Paris: ICC), document 103/179, Rev., of 30 April 1996, mimeo.

International Confederation of Free Trade Unions (ICFTU) (1996). *The Global Market: Trade Unionism's Greatest Challenge* (Brussels: ICFTU).

Japan, Institute for Overseas Investment (1993). "Higashi Ajia ni okeru infura kensetsu heno chokusetsu Toshi no katsuyo", *Kaigai Toyushi,* 2, 3 (May), pp. 3-17.

Japan, Ministry of Foreign Affairs (1995). *Japan's ODA Annual Report 1994* (Tokyo: Association for Promotion of International Cooperation).

JETRO (1994). *JETRO Hakusho: Toshi-hen 1994* (Tokyo: JETRO).

_____ (1995). *JETRO Hakusho: Toshi-hen 1995* (Tokyo: JETRO).

_____ (1996). *JETRO Hakusho: Toshi-hen 1996* (Tokyo: JETRO).

Johanson, J. and Finn Wiedersheim Paul (1993). "The internationalization of the firm - four Swedish cases", in Peter J. Buckley and Pervez Ghauri, eds., *The Internationalization of the Firm* (London: Academic Press).

Johanson J. and J.E. Vahnle (1993). "The internationalization process of the firm - a model of knowledge development and increasing foreign market commitments", in Peter J. Buckley and Pervez Ghauri, eds., *The Internationalization of the Firm* (London: Academic Press).

Jones, Geoffry (1996). *The Evolution of International Business* (London: Routledge).

Juhl P. (1985). "The Federàl Republic of Germany", in J.H. Dunning, ed., *Multinational Enterprises, Economic Structure and International Competitiveness* (Chichester and New York: John Wiley and Sons).

Julius, DeAnne (1990). *Global Companies and Public Policy* (London: Pinter Publishers).

_____ (1994). "International direct investment: strengthening the policy regime", in Peter B. Kenen, ed., *Managing the World Economy: Fifty Years after Bretton Woods* (Washington D.C.: Institute for International Economics), pp. 269-286.

Karl, Joachim (1996). "Multilateral investment agreements and regional integration", *Transnational Corporations,* 5, 2, forthcoming.

Kemper, R. (1976). *Nationale Verfuegung ueber natuerliche Ressourcen und die neue Weltwirtschaftsordnung der Vereinten Nationen* (Berlin: Duncker und Humblot).

Kim, Jooheon (1996). "Internationalization strategies of Korean MNEs: the case of the three major consumer electronics companies" (Seoul: Sookmyung Women's University), mimeo.

Kline, John M. (1985). *International Codes and Multinational Business* (Westport: Greenwood Press).

_____ (1991). "The inverse relationship between nation-states and global corporations", in S. Belous and Kelly L. McClenahan, eds., *Global Corporations and Nation-States: Do Companies or Countries Compete* (Washington D.C.: National Planning Association), pp. 26-31.

_____ (1993). "Intenational regulation of transnational business: providing the missing leg of global investment standards", *Transnational Corporations*, 2, 1, pp. 153-164.

Kobrin, Stephen (1984). "Expropriation as an attempt to control foreign firms in LDCs", *International Studies Quarterly*, 28, p. 337.

Kojima, Kiyoshi and Terutomo Ozawa, 1984. *Japan's General Trading Companies: Merchants of Economic Development* (Paris: OECD Development Centre).

Koo, B.Y. (1985). "Korea", in J.H. Dunning (ed.), *Multinational Enterprises, Economic Structure and International Competitiveness* (Chichester: John Wiley).

KPMG (1996). *Dealwatch* (Amsterdam: KPMG), various issues.

Krugman, Paul (1986). *Strategic Trade Policy and the New International Economics* (Cambridge: MIT Press).

Kuusi, Juha (1979). *The Host State and the Transnational Corporation: An Analysis of Legal Relationships* (Westmead: Saxon House).

Lall, S. (1994). "Industrial policy: the role of government in promoting industrial and technological development", *UNCTAD Review*, pp. 65-89.

Langhammer R.J. (1992). "The developing countries and regionalism", *Journal of Common Market Studies* June, 30, 2, pp. 211-231

Laviec, Jean-Pierre (1985). *Protection et promotion des investissements: etude de droit international économique* (Paris: PUF).

Lawrence, Robert (1996). "Towards globally contestable markets", in OECD, *Market Access after the Uruguay Round: Investment, Competition and Technology Perspectives* (Paris: OECD), pp. 25-34.

Leamer, Edward E. (1984). *Sources of International Comparative Advantages: Theories and Evidence* (Cambridge, Mass.: MIT Press).

Leboulanger, Philippe (1985). *Les Contrats entre États et Entreprises Étrangères* (Paris: Economica).

Lecraw, D.J. (1990). "Factors influencing FDI in LDCs", in Jeremy Clegg and Peter Budkley, eds., *Multinational Enterprises in Developing Countries* (London: Macmillan Press).
_____ (1991). "Transnational corporations-host country relations: a framework for analysis", South Carolina Essays in International Business, No.9

Ley, Robert (1996). "Multilateral rules to promote the liberalization of investment regimes" in OECD, *Towards Multilateral Investment Rules* (Paris: OECD).

Lillich Richard B., ed. (1972,1973,1975,1987). *The Valuation of Nationalized Property in International Law* (Charlottesville, Virginia: University Press of Virginia), vol. 1-4.

Lipsey, Robert E. (1988). "Changing patterns of international investment in and by the United States", in Martin Feldstein, ed., *The United States in the World Economy* (Chicago: University of Chicago Press), pp. 475-545.

_____ (1995). "Outward direct investment and the U.S. economy", Working Paper 2020, National Bureau of Economic Research.

_____ (1996). "Natural resource FDI", unpublished note.

_____, I.B. Kravis and R.R. Roldan (1982). "Do multinational firms adapt factor proportions to prices?", in A.O. Krueger,ed., *Trade and Employment in Developing Countries: Factor Supply and Substitution* (Chicago: University of Chicago Press).

Lipsey R.E. and M.Y. Weiss (1981). "Foreign production and exports in manufacturing industries", *Review of Economics and Statistics,* 63, pp. 488-94.

_____ (1984). "Foreign production and exports of individual firms", *Review of Economics and Statistics,* 66, pp. 304-8

Lipsey, Robert E. and Zbigniew Zimny (1993). "The impact of transnational service corporations on developing countries: competition, market structure and unique services", in Karl P. Sauvant and Padma Mallampally, eds., *Transnational Corporations in Services. United Nations Library on Transnational Corporations* (London: Routledge), pp. 316-332.

Low, Patrick and Arrind Subramanian (1995). "TRIMs in the Uruguay Round: an unfinished business?", paper presented at the World Bank conference, 26-27 January 1995, mimeo.

Low, Linda, Eric D. Ramstetter and Henry Wai-Chung Yeung (forthcoming). "Accounting for outward direct investment from Hong Kong and Singapore: who controls what?", NBER Working Paper, mimeo.

Mann, Michael A. and Sylvia A. Bargas (1995). "U.S. international sales and purchases of private services", *Survey of Current Business,* 75, 9 (September), pp. 68-105.

Markusen, James R. (1984). "Multinational, multi-plant economies, and the gains from trade", *Journal of International Economics*, 16, pp. 205-226.

_____ (1995). "The boundaries of multinational firms and the theory of international trade", *Journal of Economic Perspectives*, 9, pp. 169-189.

_____ and Anthony J. Venables (1995). "Multinational firms and the new trade theory", Working Paper 5036, National Bureau of Economic Research.

Markusen, James R., Anthony J. Venables, Denise Eby Konan and Kevin H. Zhang (1996). "A unified treatment of horizontal direct investment, vertical direct investment, and the pattern of trade in goods and services", mimeo.

Martin J. (1996). "Tunisia: a new era of trade", *The Middle East,* May, pp. 17-18

Mataloni, Raymond and Lee Goldberg (1994). "Gross product of U.S. multinational companies, 1977-91", *Survey of Current Business*, 74, 2 (February), pp. 42-63.

Maun, Michael A. and Sylvie E. Berges (1995). "United States international sales and purchases of private services", *Survey of Current Business*, 75, 9 (September), pp. 68-105.

McKern, Bruce (1993). "Introduction", in Bruce McKern, ed., *TNCs and the Exploitation of Natural Resources. United Nations Library on Transnational Corporations,* volume 10 (London: Routledge).

Merron, J. L. (1991). "American culture goes abroad: J. Walter Thompson and the General Motors export account, 1927-1933", unpublished Ph.D dissertation (Chapel Hill, North Carolina: University of North Carolina).

Messing, Joel (1996). "Towards a Multilateral Agreement on Investment", *Transnational Corporations,* forthcoming.

Metaxas, S. (1988). *Enterprises Transnationales et Codes de Conduite* (Zürich: Schulthess).

Michalet C.A. and Chevallier T. (1985). "France", in J.H. Dunning, ed., *Multinational Enterprises, Economic Structure and International Competitiveness* (Chichester and New York: John Wiley and Sons).

Miller, A. S. (1959). "Protection of private foreign investment by multilateral convention", *American Journal of International Law*, 53, pp. 371-378.

Ministry of International Trade and Industry (MITI) (1994). *Dai 5-kai Kaigai Jigyo Katsudo Kihon Chosa: Kaigai Toshi Tokei Soran* (Tokyo: Ministry of Finance Printing Bureau).

_____ (1995). *Dai 24-kai Wagakuni Kigyo no Kaigai Jigyo Katsudo* (Tokyo: Ministry of Finance Printing Bureau).

_____ (1996). "Dai 25-kai kaigai Jigyo katsudo doko chosa gaiyo", mimeo.

Mody, Ashoka and Fang Yi Wang (1994). "Explaining industrial growth in coastal China: economic reforms ...and what else?" (Washington, D.C.: World Bank), mimeo.

Motta, M. (1993). "Le motivazione oligopolistiche e strategiche degli IDE. Una rassegna della letteratura ed il ruolo dei modelli di teoria dei giochi", *Il Circolo Virtuoso Trilaterale*, (Bologna, Il Mulino).

Mouri, A. (1994). *The International Law of Expropriation as Reflected in the Work of the Iran-U.S. Claims Tribunal* (Dordrecht: Nijhoff).

Muchlinski, P. (1995). *Multinational Enterprises and the Law* (Oxford: Blackwell).

Mundell, R.A. (1957). "International trade and factor mobility", *American Economic Review,* 47 (June), pp. 321-335.

Nicholas, S.J. (1982). "British multinational investment before 1939", *Journal of European Economic History*, 11, 3, pp. 605-630

Nymark, Alan (1996). "Foreign direct investment in a globalizing world economy". Paper presented at the UNCTAD ("Divonne II") conference, Divonne, 27 February, mimeo.

Okran, T.M. (1989). "Double taxation treaties and transnational investment", *Transnational Lawyer*, 2, pp. 131-178.

Organisation for Economic Co-operation and Development (OECD) (1992). "Intra-firm trade study", Working Party of the Trade Committee (Paris:OECD), 29-30 October.

_____ (1993a). *National Treatment for Foreign-Controlled Enterprises* (Paris: OECD).

_____ (1993b). *Code of Liberalisation of Capital Movements* (Paris: OECD).

_____ (1993c). *Code of Current Invisible Operations* (Paris: OECD).

_____ (1994a). *The OECD Guidelines for Multinational Enterprises* (Paris: OECD).

_____ (1994b). *The New World Trading System: Readings* (Paris: OECD).

_____ (1994c). *Globalisation of Industrial Activities: Sector Case Study of Globalisation in the Automobile Industry* (Paris: OECD).

_____ (1995a). *Introduction to the OECD Codes of Liberalisation* (Paris: OECD).

_____ (1995b). Meeting of the OECD Council at the ministerial level: communiqué, 24 May 1995 (Paris: OECD), SG/Press (95) 41.

_____ (1995c). *A Multilateral Agreement on Investment: Progress Report by the Committee on International Investment and Multinational Enterprises (CIME) and the Committee on Capital Movements and Invisible Transactions (CMIT)* (Paris: OECD).

_____ (1995d). *International Direct Investment Statistical Yearbook 1995* (Paris: OECD).

_____ (1995e). *OECD Economic Outlook* (Paris: OECD), December.

_____ (1996a). *Market Access after the Uruguay Round: Investment Competition and Technology Perspectives* (Paris: OECD).

_____ (OECD) (1996b). *Multilateral Agreement on Investment: Progress Report by the MAI Negotiating Group* (Paris: OECD), OECD/GD (96) 78.

Ozawa T. (1985). "Japan", in J.H. Dunning, ed., *Multinational Enterprises, Economic Structure and International Competitiveness* (Chichester and New York: John Wiley and Sons).

_____ (1992). "Foreign direct investment and economic development", *Transnational Corporations*, 1, 1, pp. 27-54.

Paasivirta, E. (1990). *Participation of States in International Contracts* (Helsinki: Finnish Lawyers' Publishing Co.).

Pacific Basin Economic Council (PBEC) (1996). "Implementing free trade and investment in the Pacific region", mimeo.

Parra, Antonio (1995). "The scope of new investment laws and international instruments", *Transnational Corporations,* 4, 3, pp. 27-48. Also forthcoming in R. Pritchard, ed., *Development, Investment and the Law.*

Patel, P. and Pavitt, K.L.R. (1991), "Large firms in the production of the world's technology: an important case of 'non-globalisation'", *Journal of International Business Studies*, 22, 1, pp. 1-21.

Pearce R.D. (1990). "Overseas production and exporting performance: some further investigations", University of Reading Discussion Papers in International Investment and Business Studies, 135.

Pellet, Alain (1988). "A new internaitonal legal order: what legal tools for what changes?" in F Snyder and P. Slim, eds., *International Law of Development: Comparative Perspectives* (Abingdon: Professional Books), pp. 117-135.

Plasschaert, S., ed. (1994). *Transnational Corporations, Transfer Pricing and Taxation. United Nations Library on Transnational Corporations* (London: Routledge).

Price, Daniel M. (1996). "Investment rules and high technology: towards a multilateral agreement on investment", in OECD, *Market Access after the Uruguay Round: Investment, Competition and Technology Perspectives* (Paris: OECD), pp. 171-186.

Pugel, T.A. (1981). "The determinants of foreign direct investment: an analysis of US manufacturing industries", *Managerial and Decision Economics,* 2, pp. 220-28.

_____ (1985). "The United States", in John H. Dunning, ed., *Multinational Enterprises, Economic Structure and International Competitiveness* (Chichester and New York: John Wiley and Sons).

Ramstetter, Eric D. (forthcoming). "Estimating economic activities by Japanese transnational corporations: how to make sense of the data", *Transnational Corporations.*

Read, Robert (1986). "The banana industry: oligopoly and barriers to entry", in M.C. Casson et al., *Multinationals and World Trade* (London: Allen and Unwin).

Robertson, David (1996). "The OECD investment mandate of 1995: catching up with the market", in OECD, *Towards Multilateral Investment Rules* (Paris: OECD), pp. 75-84.

Rosenberg, D. (1983). *Le Principe de Souveraineté des Etats sur leurs Resources Naturelles* (Paris: LGDJ).

Rubin, Seymour J. (1948). "Private foreign investment: the ITO Charter and the Bogota Economic Agreement", American Foreign Law Association, *Proceedings*, No. 31.

_____ and G.C. Hufbauer (1984). "Lessons from the codes", in S.J. Rubin and G.C. Hufbauer, eds., *Emerging Standards of International Trade and Investment. Multinational codes and Corporate Conduct* (Totowa, New Jersey: Rowman and Allanheld)

Rubin, Seymour J. and Donald Wallace, Jr., eds. (1994). *Transnational Corporations and National Law: United Nations Library on Transnational Corporations*, 19 (London and New York: Routledge).

Rùggiero, Renato (1996). "Foreign direct investment and the multilateral trading system", *Transnational Corporations*, 5, 1, forthcoming.

Safarian A.E. (1966). *Foreign Ownership of Canadian Industry* (Toronto: University of Toronto Press).

_____ (1996). *The Performance of Foreign Owned Firms in Canada* (Montreal and Washington: Private Association of Canada).

Salacuse, Jeswald W. (1990). "BIT by BIT: the growth of bilateral investment treaties and their impact on foreign direct investment in developing countries", *International Law Review*, 24, p. 655.

Sauvant, Karl P. (1990). "The tradability of services", in Patrick A. Messerlin and Karl P. Sauvant, eds., *The Uruguay Round, Services in the World Economy* (Washington, D.C.: The World Bank and UNCTC), pp. 114-122.

_____ and Victoria Aranda (1993). "The international legal framework for transnational corporations", in A.A. Fatouros, ed., *Transnational Corporations: The International Legal Framework. United Nations Library on Transnational Corporations*, 20 (London: Routledge), pp. 83-115.

Sauvant, Karl P. and Zbigniew Zimny (1987). "Foreign direct investment in services: the neglected dimension in international service negotiations", *World Competition*, 31 (October), pp. 27-55.

Sauvé, Pierre (1994). "A first look at investment in the Final Act of the Uruguay Round", *Journal of World Trade*, 28, 5 (October), pp. 5-16.

_____ (1995a). "Market access through market presence: new directions in investment rule making". Paper presented at the Annual Meeting of the Canadian Economics Association, Montreal, 3 June, mimeo.

_____ (1995b). "Assessing the General Agreement on Trade in Services: half full or half empty?", *Journal of World Trade*, 29, 4 (August), pp. 125-145.

_____ and A. B. Zampetti (1996). "Onwards to Singapore: the international contestability of markets and the new trade agenda", forthcoming in *World Economy*.

Schachter, Oscar (1984). "Compensation for expropriation", *American Journal of International Law,* 78, pp.121-130.

Scherer, F. M. (1994). *Competition Policies for an Integrated World Economy* (Washington, D.C.: The Brookings Institution).

Seidl-Hohenveldern, Iguaz (1989). *International Economic Law* (The Hague: Nishoff).

Services of the European Commission and UNCTAD-DTCI (1996). *Investing in Asia's Dynamism: European Union Direct Investment in Asia,* interim version, Brussels and Geneva, March.

Shihata, Ibrahim (1992). *Towards a Greater Depoliticization of Investment Disputes: The Roles of ICSID and MIGA* (Washington, D.C.:ICSID).

Simoes V.C. (1985). "Portugal", in J.H. Dunning, ed., *Multinational Enterprises, Economic Structure and International Competitiveness* (Chichester and New York: John Wiley and Sons).

Sirtaine, Sophie (1994). "Financing infrastructure in Asian developing countries: attracting Asian capital market investors in BOT schemes," London School of Economics, Development Economics Research Programme Working Paper No. 52 (January), mimeo.

Smith, Alister (1996). "The development of a Multilateral Agreement on Investment at the OECD: a preview", in OECD, *Towards Multilateral Investment Rules* (Paris: OECD), pp. 31-40.

Sornarajah, M. (1985). "The new international economic order, investment treaties and foreign investment laws", *Malaya Law Review* (ASEAN), 27, p. 440.

_____ (1994). *The International Law on Foreign Investment* (Cambridge: Cambridge University Press).

Southard, Frank A., Jr. (1931). *American Industry in Europe* (Boston and New York: Houghton Mifflin Co.).

Steuer M.D. (1973). *The Impact of Foreign Direct Investement on the United Kingdom* (London:HMSO).

Stubenitsky F. (1970). *American Direct Investement in Netherlands Industry* (Rotterdam University Press).

Swedenborg, Birgitta (1979).*The Multinational Operations of Swedish Firms: An Analysis of Determinants and Effects* (Stockholm: Industriens Utredningsinstitut).

_____ (1985). "Sweden", in John H. Dunning, ed., *Multinational Enterprises, Economic Structure and International Competitiveness* (Chichester and New York: John Wiley and Sons).

Tejima, Shigeki (1995). "Future trends in Japanese foreign direct investment",*Transnational Corporations*, 4, 1, pp. 84-96.

Terpstra, V. and Yu C. M. (1988). "Determinants of foreign investment of U.S. advertising agencies",*Journal of International Business Studies*, 19, Spring, pp. 33-46.

Third World Network (1996). "The WTO and the proposed foreign investment treaty: implications for developing countries and proposed positions" (Penang: Third World Network), mimeo.

Thisen, K.J. (1994). "The European single market and its possible effects on African external trade", UNCTAD Discussion papers no 78, January.

Toope, S.J. (1990). Mixed International Arbitration: Studies in Arbitration between States and Private Parties (Cambridge, Massachusetts: Grotius).

Toyo Keizai (1996). *Kaigai Shinshutsu Kigyo Soran, 1996* (Tokyo: Toyo Keizai Shimposha).

Trade Union Advisory Committee to the OECD (TUAC) (1994). "TUAC room document" (Paris: OECD), mimeo.

United Nations (1979). *Manual for the Negotiation of Bilateral Tax Treaties Between Developed and Developing Countries* (New York: United Nations), United Nations publication, Sales No. E.79.XVI.3.

_____ (1995). *National Accounts Statistics: Main Aggregates and Detailed Tables, 1992, Volumes I and II* (New York: United Nations), United Nations publication, Sales No. E.95.II.D.

_____ (1996). *World Economic and Social Survey 1996* (New York: United Nations), forthcoming.

United Nations Conference on Environment and Development (UNCED) (1993). "Report of the United Nations Conference on Environment and Development", Rio de Janeiro, 3-14 June 1992, 2, resolutions adopted by the Conference. (New York: United Nations), United Nations publication.

United Nations Center on Transnational Corporations (UNCTC) (1979). *Transnational Corporations in Advertising* (New York: United Nations).

_____ (1986). The United Nations Code of Conduct on Transnational Corporations (New York: United Nations), Current Studies, Series A, No. 4, United Nations publication, Sales No. E.86.II.A.15.

_____ (1988). *Bilateral Investment Treaties* (New York: United Nations), United Nations publication, Sales No. E.88.II.A.1.

_____ (1989). *Foreign Direct Investment and Transnational Corporations in Services* (New York: United Nations), United Nations publication, Sales No. E.89.II.A.9.

_____ (1990). "Key concepts in international investment arrangements and their relevance to negotiations or international transactions in services", Current Studies, Series A (New York: United Nations), United Nations publication, Sales No. E.90.II.A.3.

_____ (1992a). *World Investment Report 1992: Transnational Corporations as Engines of Growth* (New York: United Nations), United Nations publication, Sales No. E.92.II.A.24.

_____ (1992b). *The Determinants of Foreign Direct Investment: A Survey of the Evidence* (New York: United Nations), United Nations publication, Sales No. E.92.II.A.2.

_____ (1992c). *Foreign Direct Investment and Industrial Restructuring in Mexico* (New York: United Nations), United Nations publication, Sales No. E.92.II.A.9.

_____ (1993). "Transnational service corporations and developing countries: areas of impact", in Karl P. Sauvant and Padma Mallampally, eds., *Transnational Corporations in Services* (London: Routledge), pp. 275-299.

_____ and International Chamber of Commerce (ICC) (1992). *Bilateral Investment Treaties 1959-1991* (New York: United Nations), United Nations publication, Sales No. E.92.II.A.16.

UNCTC and United Nations Conference on Trade and Development (UNCTAD) (1991). *The Impact of Trade-related Investment Measures on Trade and Development* (New York: United Nations), United Nations publication, Sales No. E.91.II.A.19.

United Nations, Transnational Corporations and Management Division (UN-TCMD) (1993). *Foreign Direct Investment and Trade Linkages in Developing Countries* (New York: United Nations), United Nations publication, Sales No. E.93.II.A.12.

United Nations Conference on Trade and Development (UNCTAD) (1993). "Fostering competitive services sectors. A comparative analysis of services sectors in developing countries" (Geneva: United Nations), mimeo.

_____ (1994a). *Trade and Development Report, 1994* (Geneva: United Nations), United Nations publication, Sales No. E.94.II.D.26.

_____ (1994b). "Transnational service corporations and developing countries: impacts and policy options", mimeo.

_____ (1995a). *Handbook of International Trade and Development Statistics, 1994* (Geneva: United Nations), United Nations publication, sales No. E/F.95.II.D.15.

_____ (1995b). "Ways of enhancing access to and use of information networks and distribution channels" (Geneva: United Nations), mimeo.

_____ (1996). "Transfer pricing regulations and transnational corporation practices: guidance for developing countries" (Geneva: United Nations), mimeo.

_____ and Economic Commission for Africa (UNCTAD/ECA) (1995). *Japanese Foreign Direct Investment in Africa* (Addis Abeba: ECA), mimeo.

UNCTAD, Division on Science and Technology (UNCTAD-DST) (1996a). "Policies for promoting the use of environmentally sound technologies", 12, forthcoming.

_____ (1996b). *Fostering Technological Dynamism: Evolution of Thought on Technological Development Process and Competitiveness: A Review of the Literature* (Geneva: United Nations), United nations publication, Sales No. E.95.II.D.21.

UNCTAD, Division on Transnational Corporations and Investment (UNCTAD-DTCI) (1993a). *World Investment Report 1993: Transnational Corporations and Integrated International Production* (New York: United Nations), United Nations publication, Sales No. E.93.II.A.14.

_____ (1993b). *Small and Medium-sized Transnational Corporations: Role, Impact and Policy Implications* (New York: United Nations), United Nations publication, Sales No. E.93.II.A.15.

_____ (1993c). *Explaining and Forecasting Regional Flows of Foreign Direct Investment* (New York: United Nations), United Nations publication, Sales No. E.94.II.A.5.

_____ (1994a). *World Investment Report 1994: Transnational Corporations, Employment and the Workplace* (Geneva: United Nations), United Nations publication, Sales No. E.94.II.A.14.

_____ (1994b). *Tradability of Banking Services: Impact and Implications* (Geneva: United Nations), United Nations publication, Sales No. E.94.II.A.12.

_____ (1995a). *World Investment Report 1995: Transnational Corporations and Competitiveness* (Geneva: United Nations), United Nations publication, Sales No. E.95.II.A.9.

_____ (1996a). *World Investment Directory, Volume 5: Africa* (Geneva: United Nations), United Nations publication, forthcoming.

_____ (1996b). *International Investment Instruments: A Compendium*, vols. I, II and III, (Geneva: United Nations), United Nations publication, Sales No. E.96.II.A.12.

_____ (1996c). *Incentives and Foreign Direct Investment* (Geneva: United Nations), United Nations publication, Sales No. E.96.II.A.6.

_____ (forthcoming a). *Transnationalization of Economic Activity* (Geneva: United Nations).

_____ (forthcoming b). *Sharing Asia's Dynamism: Asian Direct Investment in the European Union,* interim version, Geneva, July.

_____ and World Bank (1994). *Liberalizing International Transactions in Services: A Handbook* (New York and Geneva: United Nations), United Nations publication, Sales No. E.94.II.A.11.

Union of Industrial and Employers' Confederation of Europe (UNICE) (1995). "UNICE Preliminary Comments on Trade and Investment" (Brussels: UNICE), mimeo.

United Kingdom, Department of Trade and Industry (1996). *Competitiveness White Paper: Study on Outward Investment* (London: HMSO).

United States, Department of Commerce (1942). *American Direct Investments in Foreign Countries, 1940* (Washington, D.C.: USGPO).

_____ (1975). *U.S. Direct Investment Abroad, 1966, final data.* (Washington D.C.: U.S. Government Printing Office).

_____ (1981). *U.S. Direct Investment Abroad, 1977* (Washington D.C.: U.S. Government Printing Office).

_____ (1985). *U.S. Direct Investment Abroad, 1982, Benchmark Survey Data* (Washington D.C.: U.S. Government Printing Office).

_____ (1986a). *U.S. Direct Investment Abroad: Operations of U.S. Parent Companies and Their Foreign Affiliates. Revised 1983 estimates* (Washington D.C.: U.S. Government Printing Office).

_____ (1986b). *Foreign Direct Investment in the United States: Operations of U.S. Affiliates of Foreign Companies. Revised 1993 estimates* (Washington D.C.: U.S. Government Printing Office).

_____ (1988). *U.S. Direct Investment Abroad: Operations of U.S. Parent Companies and Their Foreign Affiliates. Revised 1985 estimates* (Washington D.C.: U.S. Government Printing Office).

_____ (1989). *U.S. Direct Investment Abroad: Operations of U.S. Parent Companies and Their Foreign Affiliates. Revised 1986 estimates* (Washington D.C.: U.S. Government Printing Office).

_____ (1992). *U.S. Direct Investment Abroad, 1989 Benchmark Survey. Final Results* (Washington D.C.: U.S. Government Printing Office).

_____ (1995a). *U.S. Direct Investment Abroad: Operations of U.S. Parent Companies and Their Foreign Affiliates. Preliminary 1993 estimates* (Washington D.C.: U.S. Government Printing Office).

_____ (1995b). "U.S. direct investment abroad: detail for historical-cost position and related capital and income flows, 1994", *Survey of Current Business*, 75, 8 (August).

_____ (1995c). *U.S. Direct Investment Abroad: Operations of U.S. Parent Companies and Their Foreign Affiliates. Revised 1992 estimates* (Washington D.C.: U.S. Government Printing Office).

_____ (1995d). *Foreign Direct Investment in the United States: Operations of U.S. Affiliates of Foreign Companies. Preliminary 1993 estimates* (Washington D.C.: U.S. Government Printing Office).

United States Council for International Business (USCIB) (1995). "Statement of the United States Council for International Business on the Multilateral Investment Agreement (MIA)", mimeo.

Van den Bulke D. (1985). "Belgium", in J.H. Dunning, ed., *Multinational Enterprises, Economic Structure and International Competitiveness* (Chichester and New York: John Wiley and Sons).

Van Miert, Karel (1996). "EU competition policy in the new trade order", paper presented at the Oslo Conference: Competition Policies for an Integrated World Economy (Oslo: Norwegian Competition Authority), mimeo.

Van Hecke, G. (1964). "Le projet de convention de l'OCDE sur la protection des biens etrangers", *Revue Générale de Droit International Public*, 68, pp. 641-664.

Vandevelde, Kenneth J. (1992). *United States Investment Treaties: Theory and Practice* (Deventer: Kluwer).

_____ (1993). "United States bilateral investment treaties: the second wave", *Michigan Journal of International Law,* 11, p. 259.

Vernon, Raymond (1966). "International investment and international trade in the product cycle", *Quarterly Journal of Economics*, 80, pp. 190-207.

_____ and B. Levy (1982). "State-owned enterprises in the world economy: the case of iron ore", in L.P. Jones, ed., *Public Enterprise in Less Developed Countries* (Cambridge, MA: Cambridge University Press).

Waelde, T. (1995). "Introductory note", in "European Energy Charter Conference: Final Act", *International Legal Materials*, 34, 2, pp. 360-454.

Warner, M. and Rugman, A. M. (1994). "Competitiveness: an emerging strategy of discrimination in U.S. Antitrust and R & D Policy", *Law and Policy in International Business,* 25, 3 (Spring), pp. 945-982.

Weinstein, A. K. (1974). "The international expansion of U.S. multinational advertising agencies", *MSU Business Topics*, Summer, pp. 29-35.

Weisskoff, R. and Edward Wolff (1977). "Linkages and leakages: industrial tracking in an enclave economy", *Economic Development and Cultural Change*, 4, pp. 607-628.

Welch, L.S. and R. Luostarinen (1988). "Internationalization: evolution of a concept", Journal of General Management, 14, 2, pp. 36-64. Included in Peter J. Buckley and Pervez Ghauri, eds., The Internationalization of the Firm (London: Academic Press), pp. 106-123.

Wells, Louis T. and Eric S. Gleason (1995). "Is foreign infrastructure investment still risky?", *Harvard Business Review,* 73 (September-October), pp. 44-55.

West, D. (1987). "From T-square to T-plan: the London office of the J. Walter Thompson advertising agencies, 1919-1970", *Business History*, April, pp. 199-217.

Wheeler, David and Ashoka Mody (1992). "International investment location decisions: the case of U.S. firms", *Journal of International Economics*, 33 (August), pp. 57-76.

Wilcox, C. (1949). *A Charter for World Trade* (New York: Macmillan).

Wilkins, Mira (1970). *The Emergence of Multinational Enterprise: American Business Abroad from the Colonial Era to 1914* (Cambridge, MA: Harvard University Press).

_____ (1974). *The Maturing of the Multinational Enterprise: American Business Abroad from 1914 to 1970*, (Cambridge, Massachusetts: Harvard University Press).

Wilson, Mark (1992). "The office farther back: business services, productivity and the offshore back office" (Michigan: State University), mimeo..

Witherell, William H. (1995). "The OECD Multilateral Agreement on Investment", *Transnational Corporations*, 4, 2, pp. 1-14.

_____ (1996). "Toward an international set of rules for investment", in OECD, *Towards Multilateral Investment Rules* (Paris: OECD).

World Bank (1992a). *Legal Framework for the Treatment of Foreign Investment, Volume I: Survey of Existing Instruments* (Washington, D.C.: The World Bank).

_____ (1992b). *Legal Framework for the Treatment of Foreign Investment, Volume II: Guidelines* (Washington, D.C.: The World Bank).

_____ (1994). *World Development Report 1994: Infrastructure for Development* (New York and Oxford: Oxford University Press).

_____ (1995a). *The Emerging Asian Bond Market* (Washington, D.C.: World Bank).

_____ (1995b). *Infrastructure Development in Asia and the Pacific* (Washington, D.C.: World Bank).

_____ (1996). *World Debt Tables 1996* (Washington, D.C.: World Bank).

World Trade Organization (1995). *International Trade. Trends and Statistics* (Geneva: WTO).

Yachir (1988). *Mining in Africa Today: Strategies and Prospects* (London: Zea Books).

Zhan, James Xiaoning (1993). "The role of foreign direct investment in market-oriented reforms and economic development: the case of China", *Transnational Corporations*, 2, 3, pp. 121-148.

_____ (1995). "Transnationalization and outward investment: the case of Chinese firms", *Transnational Corporations*, 4, 3, pp. 67-100.

Zimny, Zbigniew (1993). "The impact of transnational corporations in services on trade of developing countries" (Geneva: UNCTAD), mimeo..

ANNEXES

DEFINITIONS AND SOURCES

A. General definitions

1. Transnational corporation

Transnational corporations are incorporated or unincorporated enterprises comprising parent enterprises and their foreign affiliates. A *parent enterprise* is defined as an enterprise that controls assets of other entities in countries other than its home country, usually by owning a certain equity capital stake. An equity capital stake of 10 per cent or more of the ordinary shares or voting power for an incorporated enterprise, or its equivalent for an unincorporated enterprise, is normally considered as a threshold for the control of assets.[1] A *foreign affiliate* is an incorporated or unincorporated enterprise in which an investor, who is resident in another economy, owns a stake that permits a lasting interest in the management of that enterprise (an equity stake of 10 per cent for an incorporated enterprise or its equivalent for an unincorporated enterprise). In the *World Investment Report*, subsidiary enterprises, associate enterprises and branches are all referred to as *foreign affiliates* or *affiliates*.

- *Subsidiary:* an incorporated enterprise in the host country in which another entity directly owns more than a half of the shareholders voting power and has the right to appoint or remove a majority of the members of the administrative, management or supervisory body.

- *Associate:* an incorporated enterprise in the host country in which an investor owns a total of at least 10 per cent, but not more than a half, of the shareholders' voting power.

- *Branch:* a wholly or jointly owned unincorporated enterprise in the host country which is one of the following: (i) a permanent establishment or office of the foreign investor; (ii) an unincorporated partnership or joint venture between the foreign direct investor and one or more third parties; (iii) land, structures (except structures owned by government entities), and /or immovable equipment and objects directly owned by a foreign resident; (iv) mobile equipment (such as ships, aircraft, gas or oil-drilling rigs) operating within a country other than that of the foreign investor for at least one year.

2. Foreign direct investment

Foreign direct investment (FDI) is defined as an investment involving a long-term relationship and reflecting a lasting interest and control of a resident entity in one economy (foreign direct investor or parent enterprise) in an enterprise resident in an economy other than that of the foreign direct investor (FDI enterprise or affiliate enterprise or foreign affiliate).[2] Foreign direct investment implies that the investor exerts a significant degree of influence on the management of the enterprise resident in the other economy. Such investment involves both the initial transaction between the two entities and all subsequent transactions between them and among foreign affiliates, both incorporated and unincorporated. Foreign direct investment may be undertaken by individuals as well as business entities.

Foreign-direct-investment inflows and *outflows* comprise capital provided (either directly or through other related enterprises) by a foreign direct investor to a FDI enterprise, or capital received from a FDI enterprise by a foreign direct investor. There are three components in FDI: equity capital, reinvested earnings and intra-company loans.

- *Equity capital* is the foreign direct investor's purchase of shares of an enterprise in a country other than its own.

- *Reinvested earnings* comprise the direct investor's share (in proportion to direct equity participation) of earnings not distributed as dividends by affiliates or earnings not remitted to the direct investor. Such retained profits by affiliates are reinvested.

- *Intra-company loans* or *intra-company debt transactions* refer to short- or long-term borrowing and lending of funds between direct investors (parent enterprises) and affiliate enterprises.

Foreign-direct-investment stock is the value of the share of their capital and reserves (including retained profits) attributable to the parent enterprise, plus the net indebtedness of affiliates to the parent enterprise.[3] Foreign-direct-investment flow and stock data used in the *World Investment Report* are not always defined as above, because these definitions are often not applicable to disaggregated FDI data. For example, in analysing geographical and industrial trends and patterns of FDI, data based on approvals of FDI may also be used because they allow a disaggregation at the country or industry level. Such cases are denoted accordingly.

3. Non-equity forms of investment

Foreign direct investors may also obtain an effective voice in the management of another business entity through means other than acquiring an equity stake. These are non-equity forms of FDI, and they include, *inter alia*, subcontracting, management contracts, turnkey arrangements, franchising, licensing and product sharing. Data on transnational corporate activity through these forms are usually not separately identified in balance-of-payments statistics. These statistics, however, usually present data on royalties and licensing fees, defined as "receipts and payments of residents and nonresidents for: (i) the authorized use of intangible non-produced, non-financial assets and proprietary rights such as trade-marks, copyrights, patents, processes, techniques, designs, manufacturing rights, franchises, etc., and (ii) the use, through licensing agreements, of produced originals or prototypes, such as manuscripts, films, etc."[4]

B. Availability and limitations of foreign-direct-investment data presented in the *World Investment Report*

Data on FDI flows in annex tables 1 and 2, as well as some tables in the text, are on a net basis (capital transactions' credits less debits between direct investors and their foreign affiliates). Net decreases in assets or net increases in liabilities are recorded as credits (recorded with a positive sign in the balance of payments), while net increases in assets or net decreases in liabilities are recorded as debits (recorded with a negative sign in the balance of payments). In the annex tables, as well as in the tables in the text, the negative signs are deleted for practical use. Hence, FDI flows with a negative sign in the *World Investment Report* indicate that at least one of the three components of FDI (equity capital, reinvested earnings or intra-company loans) is negative and not offset by positive amounts of the remaining components. These are instances of reverse investment or disinvestment.

Not all countries record every component of FDI flows. Table 1 summarizes the availability of each component of FDI during 1980-1995, the period covered in the *World Investment Report*. Comparison of data among countries should therefore be made bearing these limitations in mind.

1. Inflows

The most reliable and comprehensive data on FDI flows that are readily available from international sources and follow the above definition are reported by the International Monetary Fund (IMF). For the purpose of assembling balance-of-payments statistics for its member countries, IMF collects and publishes data annually on FDI inflows and outflows in the *Balance of Payments Statistics Yearbook*. The same data are also available in IMF's *International Financial Statistics* for certain countries. Therefore, data from IMF used in the *World Investment Report* were obtained directly from IMF's computer tape containing balance-of-payments statistics or international financial statistics. In those cases in which economies do not report to IMF (e.g., Taiwan Province of China), or their reporting does not cover the entire 1980-1995 period that is used in the *World Investment Report*, data from UNCTAD Division on Transnational Corporations and Investment, FDI database, which contains published or unpublished national official FDI data obtained from central banks, statistical offices or national authorities, were used. These data were also supplemented with data of the Organisation for Economic Co-operation and Development, *Geographical Distribution of Financial Flows to*

Developing Countries (retrieved by OECD from a computer tape). Data reported by OECD are based on FDI outflows to developing countries from the member countries of the Development Assistance Committee of OECD.[5] Inflows of FDI to developing countries reported by OECD are therefore underestimated. Those countries and territories for which OECD data, or estimates based on OECD data, were used for the 1980-1995 period, or part of that period, are listed below.

1980-1994	Guinea-Bissau
1980-1993	Afghanistan, Cayman Islands, Gibraltar, Hong Kong, Macau, Qatar, United States Virgin Islands, (former) Yugoslavia,
1980-1991	Djibouti, United Republic of Tanzania, Uraguay
1980-1990	Iraq, United Arab Emirates,
1980-1989	Bermuda, Cuba, Ethiopia, India, Islamic Republic of Iran, Kuwait, Lebanon, Nepal, Syrian Arab Republic, Yemen, Viet Nam, Zaire
1980-1988	Equatorial Guinea, Madagascar, Myanmar, Western Samoa
1980-1985	Guinea, Maldives, Mozambique,
1980-1984	Angola, Burundi,
1980-1982	Belize
1981-1989	Benin
1982-1993	Sudan
1982-1986 and 1990	Gambia
1984-1993	Malawi
1984-1989	Namibia
1985-1990	Uganda
1985-1991	Nicaragua
1986-1993	Guyana
1986-1989	Niger, Somalia
1987-1989	Democratic Poeple's Republic of Korea
1988-1993	Liberia
1989-1993	Congo, Senegal
1991-1993	Burkina Faso

As of 1 June 1996, data on FDI inflows for 1995 were available for Canada, Germany, Italy, Japan, Netherlands, Sweden, Taiwan Province of China and the United Kingdom (from UNCTAD Division on Transnational Corporations and Investment, FDI database) and for Albania, Australia, Brazil, France, Nicaragua, Republic of South Africa, Slovenia, Spain and the United States (from IMF's international-financial-statistics tape).

Table 1. List of economies for which at least one component of foreign direct investment is not available [a]

Equity investment	Reinvested earnings	Intra-company loans
Developed countries:		
Denmark, Iceland[b], Ireland, Israel, Italy, Spain, Sweden[c], United Kingdom	Austria[b], Belgium, Canada[d], Denmark, France[e], Greece[f], Iceland, Ireland, Japan, Norway, South Africa, Spain, Sweden[c]	Austria[b], Denmark, Ireland, Italy, Spain, Sweden[c]
Developing economies:		
Africa:		
Algeria, Angola[f], Benin, Botswana[g], Burundi, Cape Verde, Chad, Comoros, Djibouti, Egypt, Equitorial Guinea, Ghana[h], Gambia, Lesotho, Liberia, Libyan Arab Jamahiriya, Madagascar, Malawi, Mali[i], Mauritania, Mozambique, Namibia[j], Nigeria, Seychelles, Somalia, Uganda, Zaire, Zambia[l], Zimbabwe	Algeria, Angola[f], Benin, Burundi, Cameroon[k], Cape Verde, Libyan Arab Jamahiriya[l], Chad[m], Comoros, Congo[n], Djibouti[m], Egypt, Equitorial Guinea, Ghana[h], Gambia, Guinea-Bissau, Lesotho, Liberia[k], Madagascar, Malawi, Mali, Mauritania, Mauritius[o], Mozambique, Namibia[o], Nigeria, Senegal[p], Somalia, Togo[q], Tunisia, Uganda, Zambia[i], Zimbabwe[h]	Algeria, Angola, Benin, Burundi, Cape Verde, Chad, Comoros, Djibouti, Egypt, Equitorial Guinea, Ghana[h], Gambia, Guinea, Lesotho, Libyan Arab Jamahiriya[l], Madagascar, Malawi, Mali, Mauritania, Mauritius[o], Mozambique, Namibia, Nigeria, Somalia, Uganda, Zaire, Zambia[i]
Latin America and the Caribbean:		
Antigua and Barbuda[b], Aruba, Barbados, Chile, Dominican Republic, Grenada, Netherlands Antilles, Saint Kitts and Nevis[b], Saint Lucia[b], Saint Vincent and the Grenadines[b], Suriname, Paraguay, Peru, Uraguay, Venezuela	Antigua and Barbuda[b], Aruba, Belize[r], Chile[r], Dominica[s], Grenada[s], Saint Kitts and Nevis[b], Saint Lucia[o], Saint Vincent and the Grenadines[b], Paraguay[j], Uruguay	Argentina, Antigua and Barbados, Aruba, Bolivia, Chile, Colombia, Dominican Republic, Ecuador, El Salvador, Grenada, Guatemala[o], Netherlands Antilles, Paraguay, Saint Kitts and Nevis[b], Saint Lucia[b], Saint Vincent[b], Surinam, Uruguay[b], Venezuela
West Asia:		
Bahrain, Cyprus, Islamic Republic of Iran, Iraq, Kuwait, Lebanon, Qatar, Saudi Arabia, Syrian Arab Republic, Turkey, United Arab Emirates, Yemen	Bahrain, Islamic Republic of Iran, Iraq, Jordan, Kuwait, Lebanon, Qatar, Saudi Arabia, Syrian Arab Republic, Turkey, United Arab Emirates, Yemen	Bahrain, Islamic Republic of Iran, Iraq, Jordan, Kuwait, Lebanon, Qatar, Saudi Arabia, Syrian Arab Republic, Turkey, United Arab Emirates, Yemen
South, East and South-East Asia:		
Bangladesh, Cambodia, China, Republic of Korea, Lao People's Democratic Republic, Malaysia, Myanmar, Pakistan, Singapore, Sri Lanka, Taiwan Province of China	Bangladesh, Indonesia, Republic of Korea[i], Lao People's Democratic Republic[o], Malaysia, Maldives, Myanmar, Pakistan, Philippines, Singapore, Sri Lanka, Thailand	Bangladesh, Cambodia, China, Indonesia, Republic of Korea, Lao People's Democratic Republic, Malaysia, Maldives, Myanmar, Pakistan, Singapore, Sri Lanka
The Pacific:		
Kiribati, New Caledonia, Solomon Islands, Tonga, Vanuatu	Kiribati, New Caledonia, Tonga	Kiribati, New Caledonia, Solomon Islands, Tonga

/...

For those countries for which FDI data were not available up to 1995, data have been estimated by UNCTAD, Division on Transnational Corporations and Investment. The economies for which FDI data was estimated are listed below:

1995: Antigua and Barbuda, Aruba, Armenia, Austria, Azerbaijan, Bahamas, Bahrain, Bangladesh, Belgium and Luxembourg, Belarus, Belize, Bolivia, Botswana, Brunei Darussalam, Bulgaria, Cambodia, Central African Republic, Chile, China, Colombia, Congo, Costa Rica, Côte d'Ivoire, Cyprus, Czech Republic, Denmark, Dominica, Dominican Republic,Ecuador, Egypt, Estonia, Gabon, Gambia, Ghana, Guinea, Guinea-Bissau, Greece, Grenada, Guatemala, Hong Kong, Hungary, Iceland, Indonesia, Ireland, Israel, Jamaica, Jordan, Kazakhstan, Kyrgystan, Republic of Korea, Latvia, People's Democratic Republic of Lao, Lithuania, Lesotho, Macau, Madagascar, Malaysia, Mali, Malta, Mauritania, Mauritius, Mexico, Republic of Moldova, Morocco, Namibia, Netherlands Antilles, New Caledonia, New Zealand, Nigeria, Norway, Panama, Paraguay, Peru, Philippines, Poland, Portugal, Romania, Russian Federal Republic, Saint Kitts and Nevis, Saint Lucia, Saint Vincent and the Grenadines, Saudi Arabia, Senegal, Seychelles, Singapore, Slovakia, Sri Lanka, Surinam, Swaziland, Switzerland, Tajikistan, Thailand, Trinidad and Tobago, Tunisia, Turkey, Uganda, Ukraine, Uzbekistan, Vanuatu, Venezuela and Yemen.

1994-1995: Angola, Argentina, Barbados, Burkina Faso, Burundi, Cameroon, Chad, Djibouti, El Salvador, Fiji, Guyana, Honduras, Kenya, Maldives, Malawi, Oman, Pakistan, United republic of Tanzania, Tonga and Zimbabwe.

1993-1995: Mozambique, Rwanda, Sierra Leone and Solomon Islands,

1992-1995: Algeria, Comoros, Equatorial Guinea, Mongolia, Papua New Guinea, Uruguay and Zambia.

1991-1995: Iraq, Libyan Arab Jamahiriya and United Arab Emirates.

1990-1995: Benin, Bermuda, Cuba, Ethiopia, Haiti, India, Islamic Republic of Iran, Democratic People's Republic of Korea, Kuwait, Lebanon, Myanmar, Nepal, Niger, Western Samoa, Somalia, Syrian Arab Republic, Viet Nam and Zaire.

(Table 1, cont'd)

Equity investment	Reinvested earnings	Intra-company loans
Central and Eastern Europe:		
Albania, Belarus, Bulgaria, Czech Republic, Czechoslovakia (former), Hungary, Latvia, Lithuania, Republic of Moldova, Romania, Russian Federation, Slovakia, Ukraine	Albania, Belarus, Bulgaria, Czech Republic, Czechoslovakia (former), Latvia, Lithuania, Republic of Moldova, Poland,[j] Romania, Russian Federation, Ukraine	Albania, Belarus, Bulgaria, Czech Republic, Czechoslovakia (former), Hungary, Latvia, Lithuania, Republic of Moldova, Romania, Russian Federation, Slovakia, Ukraine

Source: UNCTAD, Division on Transnational Corporations and Investment, based on International Monetary Fund, balance-of-payments tape, retrieved in May 1996, and official national sources.

a	Countries not available at least one year are all reported in the table.		
b	Started reporting since 1986.	k	Stopped reporting since 1985.
c	Started reporting since 1982.	l	Stopped reporting since 1983.
d	Started reporting since 1983.	m	Started reporting since 1993.
e	Stopped reporting since 1981.	n	Stopped reporting since 1987.
f	Reported only in 1991.	o	Started reporting since 1988.
g	Stopped reporting since 1991.	p	Stopped reporting since 1988.
h	Stopped reporting since 1984.	q	Stopped reporting since 1989.
i	Started reporting since 1989.	r	Started reporting since 1987.
j	Started reporting since 1990.	s	Started reporting since 1985.

For the remaining economies, estimates based on an annual average of the last available three years are used (Cape Verde for 1993, 1994 and 1995; Afghanistan, Cayman Islands, Gibraltar, Liberia, Qatar, Sudan, Togo and Virgin Islands for 1994 and 1995; and Croatia for 1995).

2. *Outflows*

In the case of FDI outflows, IMF was the principal source. However, for a number of developing economies, including large outward investors such as Argentina (IMF data available only until 1983), Hong Kong, India, Malaysia, Mexico, Nigeria and Thailand, IMF does not report outward flows. For China, Malaysia and Nigeria, as well as Taiwan Province of China (which is not a member of IMF), the FDI data base of UNCTAD Division on Transnational Corporations and Investment was used. This FDI database was also used to supplement gaps in IMF data for Ireland and Greece (1984-1988) and for New Zealand (1987-1995). In the case of countries for which FDI outflows were unavailable from national authorities, inflows to large recipient economies were used as a proxy. Thus, for India, Indonesia and the Philippines, inflows to the European Union and the United States were used as a proxy. In the case of Hong Kong, inflows to China, the European Union and the United States are used as a proxy. For Angola (1991-1994), Argentina (1984-1994), Bahamas (for all years), Bahrain (for all years), Bangladesh (for all years), Bermuda (for all years), Cape Verde (1991-1994), Cuba (1990-1994), Dominican Republic (1990-1994), Ethiopia (1991-1994), Greece (1991-1994), Guyana (1991-1994), Iraq (1991-1994), Kenya (1991-1993), Lebanon (for all years), Liberia (for all years), Malawi (1991-1994), Mexico (for all years), Oman (for all years), Panama (for all years), Peru (1991-1993), Saudi Arabia (for all years) and United Arab Emirates (for all years), Uruguay (1989-1994), inflows into the United States were used as a proxy of their outflows.

The United States data on FDI outflows and outward stocks were adjusted for the financial sector of the Netherlands Antilles. This is because considerable intra-company loans between United States parent enterprises and their financial affiliates in the Netherlands Antilles are in many respects more akin to portfolio investment than to FDI. For 1995 data, however, the financial sector of the Netherlands and Antilles is included as a geographical breakdown of the data was not available at the time when this volume was prepared.

As of 1 June 1996, FDI outflows for 1995 were available for Canada, Denmark, Germany, Italy, Japan, Netherlands, Sweden, the United Kingdom and the United States only (from UNCTAD, Division on Transnational Corporations and Investment, FDI database). For Australia, Austria, Brazil, Estonia, Finland, France, Israel, Jordan, Republic of Korea, Latvia, Lithuania, Portugal, Slovenia, Slovakia, Spain and Turkey, the 1995 data are estimated by annualizing the first quarter of 1995 (data from IMF, balance-of-payments and international-financial-statistics tapes).

For the remaining countries, estimates for 1995 are either an average annual growth for the last three available years (Chile, Malaysia, Singapore, Taiwan Province of China and Thailand) or an average of FDI outflows for the last three available years (Ireland since 1989; Albania and Nigeria since 1993, Barbados, Belize, Cameroon, Chad, Fiji and Pakistan since 1994). The 1995 FDI outward flows for Hong Kong are based on the Division's own estimates.

3. *Stocks*

Various tables in the *World Investment Report* present data on FDI stocks at book value or historical cost, reflecting prices at the time when the investment was made. For a large number of countries (as indicated in annex tables 3 and 4), FDI stocks are estimated by cumulating FDI flows over a period of time. For a number of countries (indicated in annex tables 3 and 4), estimates of FDI stocks are obtained by adding cumulated flows to a FDI stock estimate that has been obtained for a particular year. All estimates of FDI stocks for 1995 are obtained by adding FDI flows for 1995 to the stock figures of 1994.

All data, unless otherwise indicated, are expressed in United States dollars. Data reported in national currencies or Special Drawing Rights are converted to United States dollars by using the period's average exchange rate for flow data and the end-of-the-period exchange rate for stock data.

All FDI data and estimates in the *World Investment Report* are continuously revised. Because of the on-going revision, FDI data reported in the *World Investment Report* may differ from those reported in earlier *Reports* or other publications of the Division on Transnational Corporations and Investment. In particular, recent FDI data are being revised in many countries according to the fifth edition of the IMF's balance-of-payments manual.

C. Definitions and sources of the data in annex tables 5-11

Annex tables 5 and 6

These two annex tables show the ratio of inward and outward FDI flows to gross fixed capital formation (annex table 5) and inward and outward FDI stock to GDP (annex table 6), respectively. All of these data are in current prices. The data on both gross fixed capital formation and GDP were obtained from the IMF's international-financial-statistics tape, retrieved on 1 June 1996. For some economies such as Taiwan Province of China, the data are supplemented from national sources. Data on FDI are from annex tables 1-4.

Annex tables 7, 8 and 9

Data on cross-border M&As are obtained from the KPMG International Research Desk. This consulting firm collects information through a variety of secondary sources including newspapers and other periodicals, and a quarterly meeting of the 42-member KPMG Corporate Finance Network. All data in the text refer to only cross-border M&A transactions which result in the equity holding of more than 50 per cent (unless otherwise indicated). Data on minority investments are not included in the discussion on the assumption that portfolio investments account for the bulk of minority-held investments. However, in annex tables 7, 8 and 9, all M&As (including minority-held investments) are also presented for information. (For comparison of the data between FDI and M&As, see box I.1.) Cross-border M&As are recorded in both directions of transactions; i.e., when a cross-border M&A takes place, it registers as both a sale in the country of the target firm, and as a purchase in the home country of the acquiring firm. Data showing cross-border M&A activities on an industrial basis refer to only sales figures (annex table 9). Thus, if a food company acquires a chemical company, this transaction is recorded in the chemical industry.

Annex tables 10 and 11

Data on FDI in infrastructure are mainly taken from UNCTAD, Division on Transnational Corporations and Investment, FDI database. Supplemented sources include *International Direct Investment Statistics Yearbook 1995* by the Organisation for Economic Co-operation and Development and "Statistical survey of recent trends in foreign investment in East European countries" by Economic Commission for Europe (Trade/R.636, November 1995). The data are collected for the infrastructure industries for which the data are commonly available throughout countries, i.e., construction, telecommunication, and transport and storage. Flow data are annual average of the most recent three years, while stock data are obtained for a year in the mid-1980s (in most cases) and for the most recent available year.

Notes

[1]   In some countries such as Germany and the United Kingdom, a stake of 20 per cent or more is a threshold.

[2]   This general definition of FDI is based on OECD, *Detailed Benchmark Definition of Foreign Direct Investment*, second edition (Paris, OECD, 1992) and International Monetary Fund, *Balance of Payments Manual*, fifth edition (Washington, D.C., IMF, 1993).

[3]   There are, however, some exceptions. For example, in the case of Germany, loans granted by affiliate enterprises to their parent enterprises are not deducted from the stock.

[4]   International Monetary Fund, op. cit., p. 40.

[5]   Includes Austria, Belgium, Canada, Denmark, Finland, France, Germany, Italy, Japan, Netherlands, Norway, Spain, Sweden, United Kingdom and United States.

Annex table 1. FDI inflows, by host region and economy, 1984-1995
(Millions of dollars)

Host region/economy	1984-1989 (Annual average)	1990	1991	1992	1993	1994	1995 [a]
Total inflows	115370	203812	157773	168122	207937	225660	314933
Developed countries	93117	169777	114001	114002	129302	132758	203168
Western Europe	39755	103393	80567	81879	77484	68401	115630
European Union	37702	97387	77715	79812	74467	64017	111920
Austria	318	653	360	891	770	1309	1040
Belgium and Luxembourg	2793	8047	9363	11286	10750	7464	9107
Denmark	323	1132	1553	1017	1713	5006	3360
Finland	314	812	-233	396	864	1496	897
France	5364	13183	15153	21840	20752	17136	20124
Germany	1833	2689	4071	2370	277	-2993	8996
Greece	624	1005	1135	1144	977	981	890
Ireland	85	99	97	102	89	90	90
Italy	2560	6411	2401	3105	3749	2199	4347
Netherlands	3787	12349	6316	7656	6521	4369	9850
Portugal	639	2610	2448	1873	1502	1270	1386
Spain	4535	13984	12493	13276	8144	9359	8250
Sweden	982	1982	6351	-79	3885	6247	13672
United Kingdom	13545	32430	16208	14934	14475	10085	29910
Other Western Europe	2052	6006	2852	2068	3016	4384	3710
Gibraltar	23	36	37	89	107	77	91
Iceland	1	6	35	14	8	-	14
Norway	408	1003	-398	716	2003	623	1313
Switzerland	1620	4961	3178	1249	899	3684	2292
North America	48656	55773	24760	22097	46125	55803	71418
Canada	4718	7855	2740	4517	4997	6043	11182
United States	43938	47918	22020	17580	41128	49760	60236
Other developed countries	4706	10612	8674	10026	5693	8554	16120
Australia	4306	7077	4903	4912	2687	4423	13094
Israel	147	101	351	539	580	421	501
Japan	81	1753	1730	3490	234	908	39
New Zealand	176	1686	1698	1090	2200	2796	2483
South Africa	-3	-5	-8	-5	-8	6	4
Developing countries	22195	33735	41324	50376	73135	87024	99670
Africa	2728	2303	2809	2987	3300	5084	4657
North Africa	1260	1166	925	1495	1496	2102	1762
Algeria	6	-	12	12	15	18	5
Egypt	1085	734	253	459	493	1256	1000
Libyan Arab Jamahiriya	5	159	160	150	160	80	90
Morocco	73	227	375	503	590	555	417
Sudan	5	-31	-1	-	-	-	-
Tunisia	86	76	126	371	238	194	250
Other Africa	1468	1137	1884	1491	1804	2982	2895
Angola	172	-335	665	288	302	350	400
Benin	-	1	13	7	10	5	1
Botswana	64	96	-8	-2	-287	-48	70

/...

(Annex table 1, cont'd)

Host region/economy	1984-1989 (Annual average)	1990	1991	1992	1993	1994	1995 [a]
Other Africa (cont'd)							
Burkina Faso	2	1	1	-	-	1	1
Burundi	1	1	1	1	1	1	2
Cameroon	61	-113	-15	29	5	105	102
Cape Verde	-	-	1	-1	-	-	-
Central African Republic	4	1	-5	-11	-10	4	3
Chad	20	..	4	2	15	7	7
Comoros	2	-	3	1	2	2	2
Congo	21	7	5	4	3	4	1
Côte d'Ivoire	47	48	16	-231	40	18	45
Djibouti	-	-	-	2	3	3	4
Equatorial Guinea	2	10	42	20	23	26	20
Ethiopia	1	12	1	6	6	7	7
Gabon	54	74	-55	127	-114	-103	135
Gambia	2	-	10	6	11	10	10
Ghana	6	15	20	23	125	233	245
Guinea	9	18	39	20	3	-	35
Guinea-Bissau	1	2	2	6	-2	-	1
Kenya	29	57	19	6	2	4	20
Lesotho	8	17	8	3	15	19	23
Liberia	165	225	8	-11	30	9	10
Madagascar	7	22	14	21	15	6	18
Malawi	14	23	18	2	3	1	1
Mali	2	-7	4	-8	-20	45	15
Mauritania	5	7	2	8	16	2	5
Mauritius	16	41	19	15	15	20	25
Mozambique	2	9	23	25	30	33	36
Namibia	2	29	121	79	32	30	45
Niger	8	-1	1	-	1	1	1
Nigeria	624	588	712	897	1345	1959	1340
Rwanda	17	8	5	2	3	1	1
Senegal	4	-3	22	1	1	8	1
Seychelles	17	20	19	9	26	31	26
Sierra Leone	-21	32	8	-6	-7	39	41
Somalia	-5	6	-	3	2	1	1
Swaziland	38	39	79	69	49	46	54
Togo	7	18	7	-2	1	2	-
Uganda	-	-6	1	3	3	5	7
United Republic of Tanzania	1	-3	3	12	20	-	27
Zaire	-4	-12	15	1	1	1	1
Zambia	71	203	34	50	55	60	66
Zimbabwe	-8	-12	3	15	28	35	40
Latin America and the Caribbean	7739	8900	15362	17698	19456	25302	26560
South America	3396	4627	6755	8824	10808	12421	14993
Argentina	653	1836	2439	4179	6305	1200	3900
Bolivia	-2	11	25	35	25	20	50
Brazil	1416	989	1103	2061	1292	3072	4859
Chile	614	590	523	699	841	2518	3021
Colombia	563	500	457	790	960	1667	1200
Ecuador	105	126	160	178	469	531	400
Guyana	-	8	13	-	7	3	3
Paraguay	6	76	84	137	111	180	200
Peru	9	41	-7	145	371	2326	900

/...

(Annex table 1, cont'd)

Host region/economy	1984-1989 (Annual average)	1990	1991	1992	1993	1994	1995 [a]
South America (cont'd)							
Suriname	-67	-43	10	-30	-47	-30	15
Uruguay	29	42	32	1	102	170	200
Venezuela	71	451	1916	629	372	764	245
Other Latin America	4343	4273	8607	8873	8648	12881	11566
Antigua and Barbuda	27	61	55	20	15	25	25
Aruba	-	131	185	-37	-18	-73	-80
Bahamas	4	-17	..	7	27	27	27
Barbados	7	11	7	14	9	10	12
Belize	7	17	15	18	11	14	15
Bermuda	1144	819	2489	3321	2960	2923	2900
Cayman Islands	224	49	-9	27	-18	-	3
Costa Rica	82	163	178	226	247	87	265
Cuba	-	1	10	5	4	5	7
Dominica	9	13	15	21	13	22	25
Dominican Republic	77	133	145	180	183	190	250
El Salvador	16	2	25	15	16	20	19
Grenada	9	13	15	23	20	19	24
Guatemala	121	48	91	94	143	38	160
Haiti	6	8	14	8	8	2	2
Honduras	36	44	52	48	35	70	77
Jamaica	16	138	133	142	78	117	154
Mexico	2436	2549	4742	4393	4389	7978	6984
Netherlands Antilles	-23	8	33	40	11	22	10
Nicaragua	-1	1	11	15	39	40	70
Panama	36	-147	138	173	-658	549	-18
Saint Kitts & Nevis	16	49	21	13	14	15	40
Saint Lucia	17	45	58	41	34	32	63
Saint Vincent & the Grenadines	6	8	9	19	31	51	15
Trinidad & Tobago	57	109	169	178	379	516	274
Virgin Islands	14	18	5	-131	675	183	242
Developing Europe	33	113	195	172	281	271	296
Bosnia and Herzegovina	..	..	..	..	..	..	..
Croatia	..	..	..	..	74	98	86
Malta	30	46	77	-3	69	89	60
Slovenia	..	..	..	111	113	84	150
TFYR Macedonia	..	..	..	..	..	..	..
Yugoslavia (former)	3	67	118	64	25	..	..
Asia	11540	22122	22694	29114	49979	56266	68051
West Asia	1688	2319	1919	1800	3303	2383	2468
Bahrain	96	-4	-7	-9	-5	-31	6
Cyprus	64	127	83	93	83	76	80
Iran, Islamic Republic of	-62	-362	23	-170	-50	-10	-30
Iraq	2	-	-3	-1	1	-	-
Jordan	31	38	-12	41	-34	3	43
Kuwait	-	-6	1	35	13	16	15
Lebanon	4	6	2	4	6	7	35
Oman	116	141	149	87	99	130	150
Qatar	-6	5	43	40	29	37	35
Saudi Arabia	1084	1864	160	-79	1369	1341	890

/...

(Annex table 1, cont'd)

Host region/economy	1984-1989 (Annual average)	1990	1991	1992	1993	1994	1995 [a]
West Asia (cont'd)							
Syrian Arab Republic	50	71	62	67	70	76	77
Turkey	245	684	810	844	636	608	1037
United Arab Emirates	56	-116	26	130	183	113	110
Yemen	7	-131	583	719	903	17	20
Central Asia	..	..	..	140	195	263	549
Armenia	..	..	..	..	..	8	10
Azerbaijan	..	..	..	..	..	..	110
Georgia	..	..	..	..	..		
Kazakhstan	..	..	..	100	150	185	284
Kyrgyzstan	..	..	..	..	..	10	15
Tajikistan	..	..	..	..	..	10	15
Uzbekistan	..	..	..	40	45	50	115
South, East and South-East Asia	9852	19803	20775	27174	46481	53619	65033
Afghanistan	-	..	-	-	-	-	-
Bangladesh	1	3	1	4	14	11	125
Brunei Darussalam	-	3	1	4	14	6	7
Cambodia	..	..	..	33	54	69	80
China	2282	3487	4366	11156	27515	33787	37500
Hong Kong	1422	1728	538	2051	1667	2000	2100
India	133	162	141	151	273	620	1750
Indonesia	406	1093	1482	1777	2004	2109	4500
Korea, Democratic People's Republic	106	-	-	-	-	-	1
Korea, Republic of	592	788	1180	727	588	809	1500
Lao, People's Democratic Republic	1	6	8	9	60	60	75
Macau	-	1	3	2	3	3	2
Malaysia	798	2333	3998	5183	5006	4348	5800
Maldives	3	6	7	7	7	8	9
Mongolia	..	..	2	8	8	10	10
Myanmar	1	5	-	3	4	4	10
Nepal	1	6	2	4	6	7	8
Pakistan	136	244	257	335	354	422	639
Philippines	326	530	544	228	1025	1457	1500
Singapore	2239	5575	4879	2351	5016	5588	5302
Sri Lanka	36	43	48	123	195	166	195
Taiwan Province of China	691	1330	1271	879	917	1375	1470
Thailand	676	2444	2014	2116	1726	640	2300
Viet Nam	2	16	32	24	25	100	150
The Pacific	155	297	264	405	119	101	107
Fiji	17	80	15	50	49	35	35
Kiribati	-	-	..	..	..	..	
New Caledonia	2	31	3	17	20	10	10
Papua New Guinea	123	155	203	291	1	4	15
Solomon Islands	5	10	15	14	15	17	17
Tonga	-	-	-	1	2	2	2
Vanuatu	8	13	25	26	27	30	25
Western Samoa	-	7	3	5	5	3	3
Central and Eastern Europe	59	300	2448	3744	5500	5878	12095
Albania	..	..	-1	20	58	53	70
Belarus	..	..	..	7	10	15	20
Bulgaria	-	4	56	42	55	106	135

/...

(Annex table 1, cont'd)

Host region/economy	1984-1989 (Annual average)	1990	1991	1992	1993	1994	1995 [a]
Central and Eastern Europe (cont'd)							
Czech Republic	..	..	..	..	568	862	2500
Czechoslovakia (former)	43	207	600	1103		..	
Estonia	..	..	..	82	162	214	188
Hungary	..	..	1462	1479	2350	1144	3500
Latvia	..	..	..	29	45	215	250
Lithuania	..	..	..	10	30	31	50
Moldova, Republic of	..	..	..	17	14	23	32
Poland	16	89	291	678	1715	1875	2510
Romania	..	..	40	77	94	340	373
Russian Federation	..	..	..	..	..	637	2017
Slovakia	..	..	..	..	199	203	250
Ukraine	..	..	..	200	200	159	200
Memorandum:							
Least developed countries[b] in	533	154	1582	1283	1636	869	1120
Africa	499	221	925	451	533	640	746
Latin America and the Caribbean	6	8	14	8	8	2	2
Asia	14	-105	601	779	1048	176	327
West Asia	7	-131	583	719	903	17	20
South, East and South-East Asia	7	26	18	60	145	159	307
The Pacific	13	30	43	45	47	50	45
Oil-exporting countries[c] in	7270	9389	14748	14747	16744	21732	22760
Africa	2114	1190	1864	2337	2447	3864	3323
Latin America and the Caribbean	2667	3246	7012	5413	5634	9809	7953
Asia	2490	4952	5872	6997	8663	8059	11483
West Asia	1286	1523	391	33	1639	1596	1176
South, East and South-East Asia	1204	3429	5481	6964	7024	6463	10307
All developing countries minus China	19912	30248	36958	39220	45620	53237	62170

Source: UNCTAD, based on the International Monetary Fund balance-of-payments and International Financial Statistics tapes, retrieved in May 1996; data provided by the Organisation for Economic Co-operation and Development Secretariat; official national sources; and own estimates.

[a]   Estimates. For details see definitions and sources.

[b]   Least developed countries include: Afghanistan, Angola, Bangladesh, Benin, Bhutan, Burkina Faso, Burundi, Cambodia, Cape Verde, Central African Republic, Chad, Comoros, Djibouti, Equatorial Guinea, Eritrea, Ethiopia, Gambia, Guinea, Guinea-Bissau, Haiti, Kiribati, Lao People's Democratic Republic, Lesotho, Liberia, Madagascar, Malawi, Maldives, Mali, Mauritania, Mozambique, Myanmar, Nepal, Niger, Rwanda, Western Samoa, Sierra Leone, Solomon Islands, Somalia, Sudan, Togo, Tuvalu, Uganda, United Republic of Tanzania, Vanuatu, Yemen, Zaire and Zambia.

[c]   Oil exporting countries include: Algeria, Angola, Bahrain, Bolivia, Brunei Darussalam, Cameroon, Congo, Ecuador, Egypt, Gabon, Indonesia, Islamic Republic of Iran, Iraq, Kuwait, Libyan Arab Jamahiriya, Malaysia, Mexico, Nigeria, Oman, Qatar, Saudi Arabia, Trinidad and Tobago, Tunisia, United Arab Emirates and Venezuela.

Annex table 2. FDI outflows, by home region and economy, 1984-1995

(Millions of dollars)

Host region/economy	1984-1989 (Annual average)	1990	1991	1992	1993	1994	1995 [a]
Total outflows	121630	240253	210821	203115	225544	230014	317849
Developed countries	113995	222450	201930	181387	192366	190852	270546
Western Europe	67961	139809	115176	115702	101131	113249	141887
European Union	62641	132959	106842	108716	91488	101070	132285
Austria	325	1701	1293	1947	1396	1247	716
Belgium and Luxembourg	2561	6314	6271	11407	4904	588	5633
Denmark	776	1482	1852	2236	1373	4162	2851
Finland	1424	3313	-120	-757	1402	4354	1512
France	8828	34823	23932	31269	20403	22802	17554
Germany	9599	24214	23723	19698	13176	14653	35302
Greece	..	..	-2	-44	29	-4	-6
Ireland	297	499	634	510	547	564	540
Italy	2775	7585	7222	5891	7409	5106	3210
Netherlands	7052	15388	13565	14294	10934	11510	12431
Portugal	31	163	463	687	116	289	762
Spain	722	3522	4442	2192	2652	3831	3574
Sweden	4969	14629	7262	404	1476	6634	10367
United Kingdom	23283	19327	16304	18982	25671	25334	37839
Other Western Europe	5320	6850	8334	6986	9643	12179	9603
Gibraltar	..	..	..	..	..	..	..
Iceland	2	9	11	5	4	3	4
Norway	1152	1471	1782	411	876	1628	972
Switzerland	4165	5370	6541	6571	8763	10548	8627
North America	21511	31900	39111	42613	74803	50421	100291
Canada	4664	4725	5655	3635	5825	4781	4782
United States [b]	16847	27175	33456	38978	68978	45640	95509
Other developed countries	24523	50741	47644	23071	16432	27182	28368
Australia	3338	186	3126	113	1611	5842	5372
Israel	53	166	424	651	721	778	400
Japan	20793	48024	42619	21916	15471	18521	21286
New Zealand	276	2365	1475	392	-1370	2041	1310
South Africa	63	..	..	..	..	..	..
Developing countries	7621	17765	8853	21629	32981	38612	47001
Africa	1031	1408	975	337	731	592	553
North Africa	55	121	139	41	23	73	46
Algeria	7	5	50	..	..	..	..
Egypt	13	12	62	4	..	43	16
Libyan Arab Jamahiriya	36	105	..	..	..	..	..
Morocco	..	..	23	32	23	24	26
Sudan	..	..	..	..	..	..	..
Tunisia	-	-1	3	5	..	6	4

/...

(Annex table 2, cont'd)

Host region/economy	1984-1989 (Annual average)	1990	1991	1992	1993	1994	1995 [a]
Other Africa	976	1287	836	296	708	519	508
Angola	-	1	-	-	2	-2	-
Benin	..	..	..	..	..	..	..
Botswana	-	-	1	1	-	-	-
Burkina Faso	..	..	..	..	..	..	..
Burundi	..	..	..	..	..	..	..
Cameroon	17	15	22	33	22	26	27
Cape Verde	-	-	-	-	-	1	-
Central African Republic	2	4	4	6	5	7	6
Chad	6	..	11	14	11	12	12
Comoros	..	1	..	..	..	..	-
Congo	..	..	..	..	..	..	..
Côte d'Ivoire	..	..	..	..	..	..	..
Djibouti	..	..	..	..	..	..	..
Equatorial Guinea	..	..	..	..	..	..	..
Ethiopia	..	..	..	..	1	-1	..
Gabon	7	29	15	26	3	1	10
Gambia	..	..	..	..	..	..	..
Ghana	..	..	..	..	..	..	..
Guinea	..	..	..	..	..	..	..
Guinea-Bissau	..	..	..	..	..	..	..
Kenya	9	..	-1	-2	2	..	..
Lesotho	..	..	..	..	..	..	..
Liberia	49	13	348	-30	-4	47	4
Madagascar	..	..	..	..	..	..	..
Malawi	..	..	1	-1	1	..	..
Mali	..	..	..	..	..	..	..
Mauritania	..	..	..	..	..	..	..
Mauritius	..	1	11	43	33	1	26
Mozambique	..	..	..	..	..	..	..
Namibia	..	1	7	-2	9	5	4
Niger	..	..	..	..	..	..	..
Nigeria	875	1213	390	176	593	386	385
Rwanda	..	..	..	..	..	..	..
Senegal	2	..	..	..	..	..	..
Seychelles	5	1	1	1	1	1	1
Sierra Leone	..	..	..	..	..	..	..
Somalia	..	..	..	..	..	..	..
Swaziland	7	8	28	31	29	34	32
Togo	..	..	..	..	..	..	..
Uganda	..	..	..	..	..	..	..
United Republic of Tanzania	..	..	..	..	..	..	..
Zaire	..	..	..	..	..	..	..
Zambia	..	..	..	..	..	..	..
Zimbabwe	-4	..	..	..	..	..	..
Latin America and the Caribbean	597	4536	-425	2612	2231	3873	3815
South America	383	1114	1313	738	2075	2625	2722
Argentina	31	50	-41	46	-26	36	19
Bolivia	1	1	2	2	-2	-2	-1
Brazil	184	665	1014	137	491	1037	1384
Chile	8	8	123	378	431	883	644
Colombia	27	16	24	50	240	152	147
Ecuador	..	..	..	..	..	..	..

/...

(Annex table 2, cont'd)

Host region/economy	1984-1989 (Annual average)	1990	1991	1992	1993	1994	1995 [a]
South America (cont'd)							
Guyana	..	..	..	-2	2	..	..
Paraguay	..	..	..	..	..	..	..
Peru	..	..	..	-1	21	..	7
Suriname	..	..	..	..	..	..	..
Uruguay	3	-1	3	-28	32	-6	-1
Venezuela	129	375	188	156	886	525	522
Other Latin America	213	3422	-1738	1874	156	1249	1093
Antigua and Barbuda	-	..	..	-2	..	..	-1
Aruba	-	..	..	..	..	..	-
Bahamas	6	1573	-2533	1359	646	-146	620
Barbados	2	1	1	1	3	2	2
Belize	..	..	2	2	2	2	2
Bermuda	5	741	28	-471	-35	479	-9
Cayman Islands	..	..	..	..	..	..	..
Costa Rica	4	2	6	4	2	6	4
Cuba	..	..	..	..	..	-3	-1
Dominica	..	..	..	..	..	..	..
Dominican Republic	..	..	..	-1	7	..	2
El Salvador	..	..	..	..	..	..	..
Grenada	..	..	1	..	..	..	..
Guatemala	..	..	..	..	..	..	..
Haiti	..	8	14	..	..	..	..
Honduras	..	..	..	..	..	..	..
Jamaica	..	..	..	..	..	..	..
Mexico	128	224	167	730	16	1045	597
Netherlands Antilles	1	2	1	2	-2	1	..
Nicaragua	..	..	..	..	..	..	..
Panama	64	870	576	250	-486	-141	-126
Saint Kitts & Nevis	..	..	..	..	..	..	..
Saint Lucia	..	..	..	..	..	..	..
Saint Vincent & the Grenadines	..	..	..	..	..	..	..
Trinidad & Tobago	3	..	..	..	3	5	3
Virgin Islands	..	..	..	..	..	..	..
Developing Europe	..	..	..	-2	2	..	7
Bosnia and Herzegovina	..	..	..	..	..	..	..
Croatia	..	..	..	..	..	..	..
Malta	..	..	..	..	1	1	1
Slovenia	..	..	..	-2	1	-3	7
TFYR Macedonia	..	..	..	..	..	..	..
Yugoslavia (former)	..	..	..	..	..	..	..
Asia	5984	11816	8307	18680	30013	34145	42623
West Asia	837	-459	-344	1301	749	1143	1096
Bahrain	12	-21	-8	..	-20	6	-5
Cyprus	1	5	15	15	11	10	12
Iran, Islamic Republic of	..	..	..	..	..	..	..
Iraq	..	..	-	-	-	-8	-3
Jordan	4	-32	14	-3	-53	-23	-32
Kuwait	443	239	-186	1211	848	1075	1044
Lebanon	8	-7	-6	-7	-6	-7	-7
Oman	..	-1	-2	-1	-4	7	1

/...

(Annex table 2, cont'd)

Host region/economy	1984-1989 (Annual average)	1990	1991	1992	1993	1994	1995 [a]
West Asia (cont'd)							
Qatar	..	..	..	..	..	..	..
Saudi Arabia	359	-613	-198	5	-49	82	13
Syrian Arab Republic	..	..	..	..	..	..	..
Turkey	2	-16	27	65	14	49	80
United Arab Emirates	9	-13	1	17	8	-48	-8
Yemen	..	..	..	..	..	..	..
Central Asia	..	..	..	..	..	..	..
Armenia	..	..	..	..	..	..	..
Azerbaijan	..	..	..	..	..	..	..
Georgia	..	..	..	..	..	..	..
Kazakhstan	..	..	..	..	..	..	..
Kyrgyzstan	..	..	..	..	..	..	..
Tajikistan	..	..	..	..	..	..	..
Uzbekistan	..	..	..	..	..	..	..
South, East and South-East Asia	5147	12276	8651	17379	29263	33003	41527
Afghanistan	..	..	..	..	..	..	..
Bangladesh	-	-	2	-1	-	-	-
Brunei Darussalam	.	..	..	..	..	..	..
Cambodia	..	..	..	..	..	..	..
China	581	830	913	4000	4400	2000	3467
Hong Kong	1833	2448	2825	8254	17713	21437	25000
India	5	6	-11	24	41	49	38
Indonesia	16	-11	13	52	-31	15	12
Korea, Democratic People's Republic	..	..	..	..	..	..	..
Korea, Republic of	137	1056	1500	1208	1361	2524	3000
Lao, People's Democratic Republic	..	..	..	..	..	..	..
Macau	..	..	..	..	..	..	..
Malaysia	233	532	389	514	1325	1817	2575
Maldives	..	..	..	..	..	..	..
Mongolia	..	..	..	..	..	..	..
Myanmar	..	..	..	..	..	..	..
Nepal	..	..	..	..	..	..	..
Pakistan	10	2	-4	-12	-2	-6	-6
Philippines	4	-5	-26	5	-7	28	9
Singapore	286	2034	1024	1317	1784	2177	2799
Sri Lanka	1	1	5	2	7	8	6
Taiwan Province of China	1999	5243	1854	1869	2451	2460	3822
Thailand	41	140	167	147	221	493	904
Viet Nam	..	..	..	..	..	..	..
The Pacific	9	5	-4	2	5	1	3
Fiji	11	5	-4	2	5	1	3
Kiribati	..	..	..	..	..	..	..
New Caledonia	..	..	..	..	..	..	..
Papua New Guinea	-2	..	..	..	..	..	..
Solomon Islands	..	..	..	..	..	..	..
Tonga	..	..	..	..	..	..	..
Vanuatu	..	..	..	..	..	..	..
Western Samoa	..	..	..	..	..	..	..
Central and Eastern Europe	14	38	37	99	197	550	301
Albania	..	..	..	20	7	9	12
Belarus	..	..	..	..	..	..	..

/...

(Annex table 2, cont'd)

Host region/economy	1984-1989 (Annual average)	1990	1991	1992	1993	1994	1995 [a]
Central and Eastern Europe (cont'd)							
Bulgaria	..	..	..	..	..	..	-
Czech Republic	..	..	..	..	90	116	69
Czechoslovakia (former)	..	20	14	30	..	..	..
Estonia	..	..	..	2	8	2	6
Hungary	..	..	27	28	11	49	29
Latvia	..	..	..	2	-4	-65	16
Lithuania	..	..	..	..	..	..	2
Moldova, Republic of	..	..	..	..	..	..	-
Poland	14	..	-7	13	18	29	20
Romania	..	18	3	4	7	1	4
Russian Federation	..	..	..	..	..	386	129
Slovakia	..	..	..	..	61	14	12
Ukraine	..	..	..	..	..	8	3
Memorandum:							
Least developed countries[c] in	58	27	379	-12	16	64	23
Africa	58	19	363	-11	16	64	23
Latin America and the Caribbean	..	8	14	..	..	..	..
Asia	-	-	2	-1	-	-	-
West Asia	..	..	..	..	..	..	..
South, East and South-East Asia	..	..	2	-1	..	..	..
The Pacific	..	..	..	..	..	..	..
Oil-exporting countries[d] in	2286	2091	908	2930	3600	4978	5192
Africa	954	1378	542	243	619	460	441
Latin America and the Caribbean	261	600	357	888	903	1573	1121
Asia	1072	112	9	1798	2078	2946	3629
West Asia	823	-409	-393	1232	783	1114	1043
South, East and South-East Asia	246	512	403	567	1294	1832	2587
All developing countries minus China	7039	16935	7940	17629	28581	36612	43535

Source: UNCTAD, based on the International Monetary Fund balance-of-payments and International Financial Statistics tapes, retrieved in May 1996; data provided by the Organisation for Economic Co-operation and Development Secretariat; official national sources; and own estimates.

[a] Estimates. For details see definitions and sources.

[b] Excluding FDI in the financial sector of the Netherlands Antilles, except for 1995. For details, see definitions and sources.

[c] Least developed countries include: Afghanistan, Angola, Bangladesh, Benin, Bhutan, Burkina Faso, Burundi, Cambodia, Cape Verde, Central African Republic, Chad, Comoros, Djibouti, Equatorial Guinea, Eritrea, Ethiopia, Gambia, Guinea, Guinea-Bissau, Haiti, Kiribati, Lao People's Democratic Republic, Lesotho, Liberia, Madagascar, Malawi, Maldives, Mali, Mauritania, Mozambique, Myanmar, Nepal, Niger, Rwanda, Western Samoa, Sierra Leone, Solomon Islands, Somalia, Sudan, Togo, Tuvalu, Uganda, United Republic of Tanzania, Vanuatu, Yemen, Zaire and Zambia.

[d] Oil exporting countries include: Algeria, Angola, Bahrain, Bolivia, Brunei Darussalam, Cameroon, Congo, Ecuador, Egypt, Gabon, Indonesia, Islamic Republic of Iran, Iraq, Kuwait, Libyan Arab Jamahiriya, Malaysia, Mexico, Nigeria, Oman, Qatar, Saudi Arabia, Trinidad and Tobago, Tunisia, United Arab Emirates and Venezuela.

Annex table 3. FDI inward stock, by host region and economy, 1980, 1985, 1990, 1994 and 1995

(Millions of dollars)

Host region/economy	1980	1985	1990	1994	1995 [a]
World	481907	734928	1716850	2342182	2657859
Developed countries	373548	537984	1373328	1728840	1932742
Western Europe	200287	244830	758682	971964	1087594
European Union	184960	226493	712190	916151	1028070
Austria	4459	6122	10765	12994	14034 [b]
Belgium and Luxembourg	7306	8840	36635 [c]	75498 [c]	84605 [c]
Denmark	4193	3613	9192	18481 [d]	21841 [d]
Finland	540	1339	5132	5713 [e]	6610 [e]
France	22617	33392	86514	142299 [e]	162423 [e]
Germany	36630	36926	111231	125006 [e]	134002 [e]
Greece	4524	8309	14016 [c]	18253 [c]	19143 [c]
Ireland	3749	4649	4974 [f]	5352 [f]	5442 [f]
Italy	8892	18976	57985	60349	64696 [b]
Netherlands	19167	24952	73664	92748 [g]	102598 [g]
Portugal	1102	1339	5132	5487 [e]	6873 [e]
Spain	5141	8939	66276	120609 [h]	128859 [h]
Sweden	3626	5071	12461	19133 [e]	32805 [e]
United Kingdom	63014	64028	218213	214231	244141 [b]
Other Western Europe	15327	18337	46492	55814	59523
Gibraltar [i]	..	32	197	506	597
Iceland [i]	123	226	201	257	271
Norway	6698 [j]	8020 [j]	12402	14267 [k]	15580 [k]
Switzerland	8506	10058	33693	40783 [e]	43075 [e]
North America	137209	249272	507965	610007	681425
Canada	54163	64657	113054	105606	116788 [b]
United States	83046	184615	394911	504401	564637 [b]
Other developed countries	36053	43882	106681	146869	163723
Australia	13173	25049	75752	91082	104176 b
Israel [i]	727	1131	1962	3852	4353
Japan	3270	4740	9850	17792 e	17831 e
New Zealand	2363	2043	8065	23106	26322
South Africa	16519 [l]	0919	11052 [l]	11038 [l]	11041 [l]
Developing countries	108271	196764	341675	593621	693300
Africa	20816	26971	41573	54999	59565
North Africa	4429	8988	16230	21698	23370
Algeria [i]	1320	1281	1315	1372	1377
Egypt [i]	2256	5700	11039	13500	14500
Libyan Arab Jamahiriya	..	..	..	..	..
Morocco [i]	305	557	1155	3178	3595
Sudan [i]	..	28	12	11	11
Tunisia	548	1422	2709 [l]	3638 [l]	3888 [l]
Other Africa	16387	17984	25343	33300	36195
Angola [i]	61	675	1024	2629	3029
Benin [i]	32	34	36	71	72
Botswana [i]	266	515	877	532	602
Burkina Faso [i]	18	25	31	32	33

/...

(Annex table 3, cont'd)

Host region/economy	1980	1985	1990	1994	1995 [a]
Other Africa (cont'd)					
Burundi [i]	7	23	29	32	34
Cameroon [i]	330	1125	1042	1166	1268
Cape Verde [i]	..	..	3	3	3
Central African Republic [i]	50	77	96	74	77
Chad [i]	123	186	243	271	278
Comoros [i]	..	-	15	23	25
Congo [i]	309	479	564	580	581
Côte d'Ivoire	650	550	1087 [c]	930 [c]	975 [c]
Djibouti [i]	3	3	5	13	17
Equatorial Guinea [i]	..	5	23	134	154
Ethiopia [i]	110	114	116	136	143
Gabon [i]	511	833	1208	1064	1199
Gambia [i]	21	21	36	73	83
Ghana	288	312	375	776 [d]	1021 [d]
Guinea [i]	2	3	70	131	166
Guinea-Bissau [i]	..	4	8	14	15
Kenya	666	368	393	423 [d]	443 [d]
Lesotho	9	15	69	113 [d]	136 [d]
Liberia	1230	1334 [m]	2527 [m]	2564 [m]	2574 [m]
Madagascar [i]	36	47	103	159	177
Malawi [i]	100	138	210	235	236
Mali [i]	13	35	29	50	65
Mauritania [i]	..	33	51	80	85
Mauritius [i]	20	37	162	231	256
Mozambique [i]	15	17	42	153	189
Namibia	..	1943 [n]	2060 [n]	2123 [n]	2168 [n]
Niger [i]	188	203	260	264	265
Nigeria [i]	2404	4405	8022	12935	14275
Rwanda [i]	54	133	213	223	224
Senegal	360	194	304 [o]	337 [o]	338 [o]
Seychelles [i]	37	87	186	271	297
Sierra Leone [i]	77	66	-3	30	71
Somalia [i]	29	4	-7	-1	-
Swaziland [i]	149	184	435	678	732
Togo [i]	182	216	249	257	258
Uganda [i]	9	7	4	16	23
United Republic of Tanzania	154	72	11	46 [d]	73 [d]
Zaire [i]	440	351	277	290	291
Zambia	414	99	593 [l]	792 [l]	858 [l]
Zimbabwe	7023	3013	2267 [c]	2348 [c]	2388 [c]
Latin America and the Caribbean	48031	76311	121330	199181	225805
South America	29330	42131	64289	103197	118175
Argentina	5344	6563	8778 [c]	22901 [c]	26801 [c]
Bolivia	420	592	806	911 [d]	961 [d]
Brazil	17480	25665	37143	44671 [d]	49530 [d]
Chile	886	2321	6175	10756 [d]	13777 [d]
Colombia	1061	2231	3500	7374 [d]	8574 [d]
Ecuador	719	982	1370	2708 [d]	3108 [d]
Guyana [i]	1	14	18	41	44
Paraguay [i]	218	298	401	913	1113
Peru	898	1152	1254	4091 [d]	4991 [d]
Suriname	..	..	..	..	..

/...

(Annex table 3, cont'd)

Host region/economy	1980	1985	1990	1994	1995 [a]
South America (cont'd)					
Uruguay [i]	700	767	980	1285	1485
Venezuela	1604	1548	3865	7546 [d]	7791 [d]
Other Latin America	18701	34180	57041	95984	107630
Antigua and Barbuda [i]	23	94	299	414	439
Aruba	..	..	..	..	..
Bahamas [i]	298	294	336	398	425
Barbados [i]	102	123	169	210	222
Belize [i]	12	10	72	130	145
Bermuda [i]	5132	8053	13850	25543	28443
Cayman Islands [i]	223	1479	1749	1750	1754
Costa Rica	672	957	1447	2186 [d]	2451 [d]
Cuba [i]	-	1 [n]	3 [n]	26 [n]	33 [n]
Dominica [i]	..	6 [n]	67 [n]	138 [n]	163 [n]
Dominican Republic	239	265	572	1269 [d]	1519 [d]
El Salvador	154	181	212	289 [d]	308 [d]
Grenada [i]	1	13	70	147	171
Guatemala [i]	44	71	743	1109	1269
Haiti [i]	79	112	149	181	183
Honduras [i]	93	172	383	588	665
Jamaica [i]	501	458	690	1161	1315
Mexico [i]	8992	19200	32836	54338	61322
Netherlands Antilles [i]	569	56	207	313	323
Nicaragua [i]	109	109	105	200	270
Panama	387	533	345 [c]	547 [c]	529 [c]
Saint Kitts & Nevis [i]	1	32	160	224	264
Saint Lucia [i]	94	197	315	479	542
Saint Vincent & the Grenadines [i]	1	9	46	156	171
Trinidad & Tobago	976	1719	2093	3335 [d]	3609 [d]
Virgin Islands [i]	..	38	124	856	1099
Developing Europe	297 4	65	722	1642	1474
Bosnia and Herzegovina	..	..	..	..	..
Croatia	..	..	..	172 [k]	258 [k]
Malta [i]	156	286	465	697	757
Slovenia	..	..	..	308 [p]	458 [p]
TFYR Macedonia	..	..	..	..	..
Yugoslavia (former) [i]	141	179	257	465	..
Asia	37961	91846	175925	334786	403336
West Asia	5714	27461	29837	39243	41711
Bahrain	..	281	610 [q]	559 [q]	565 [q]
Cyprus	310	520	970 [q]	1305 [q]	1385 [q]
Iran, Islamic Republic of	1214	857	284 [q]	76 [q]	46 [q]
Iraq	153	149	167 [c]	164 [c]	164 [c]
Jordan	155	455	344 [c]	342 [c]	385 [c]
Kuwait	348	342	343 [c]	408 [c]	423 [c]
Lebanon	12	11	7	26 [d]	61 [d]
Oman	266	985	1407	1872 [d]	2022 [d]
Qatar	174	167	157	305 [d]	340 [d]
Saudi Arabia	2200	22422	22829 [c]	25620 [c]	26510 [c]
Syrian Arab Republic [i]	-	37	374	650	727
Turkey	107	360	1320	4218 [c]	5255 [c]
United Arab Emirates	719	792	1060 [q]	1511 [q]	1621 [q]
Yemen	56	83	-35 [r]	2187 [r]	2207 [r]

/...

(Annex table 3, cont'd)

Host region/economy	1980	1985	1990	1994	1995 [a]
Central Asia	..	..	..	598	1147
Armenia	..	..	..	8 [s]	18 [s]
Azerbaijan	..	..	..	..	110 [t]
Georgia	..	..	..	..	..
Kazakhstan	..	..	..	435 [p]	719 [p]
Kyrgyzstan	..	..	..	10 [s]	25 [s]
Tajikistan	..	..	..	10 [s]	25 [s]
Uzbekistan	..	..	..	135 [p]	250 [p]
South, East and South-East Asia	32248	64385	146087	294945	360478
Afghanistan [i]	11	12	12	13	13
Bangladesh	63	112	148 [q]	178 [q]	303 [q]
Brunei Darussalam [i]	19	33	30	55	62
Cambodia	..	..	..	156 [p]	236 [p]
China	..	3444	14135 [c]	90959 [c]	128959 [c]
Hong Kong	1729	3520	13413 [c]	19669 [c]	21769 [c]
India	1177	1075	1593 [q]	2778 [q]	4528 [q]
Indonesia	10274	24971	38883	46255 [d]	50755 [d]
Korea, Democratic People's Republic	..	..	633 [o]	633 [o]	634 [o]
Korea, Republic of	1140	1806	8424	12536 [e]	14036 [e]
Lao, People's Democratic Republic [i]	2	1	13	150	225
Macau [i]	2	11	12	23	25
Malaysia	6078	8510	14117	32653	38453
Maldives	5	3	25	53	62
Mongolia	..	..	..	28	38
Myanmar	5	6	17	28	38
Nepal	1	2	12	31	39
Pakistan	690	1079	1708 [q]	3096 [q]	3735 [q]
Philippines	1225	1302	2098 [c]	5352 [c]	6852 [c]
Singapore	6203	13016	32355 [c]	50189 [c]	55491 [c]
Sri Lanka	231	517	681 [q]	1213 [q]	1408 [q]
Taiwan Province of China	2405	2930	9735 [q]	14177 [q]	15647 [q]
Thailand	981	1999	7980 [c]	14475 [c]	16775 [c]
Viet Nam [i]	7	38	66	247	397
The Pacific	1167	1171	2125	3014	3121
Fiji	358	393	390 [c]	540 [c]	575 [c]
Kiribati	..	..	.. ..	..	
New Caledonia	..	..	40 [l]	90 [l]	100 [l]
Papua New Guinea	748	683	1508 [c]	2007 [c]	2022 [c]
Solomon Islands [i]	28	32	69	130	147
Tonga	..	..	..	5 [p]	7 [p]
Vanuatu [i]	33	62	110	218	243
Western Samoa [i]	1	1	8	24	27
Central and Eastern Europe	87	180	1846	19722	31817
Albania	..	..	..	130 [u]	200 [u]
Belarus	..	..	..	32 [p]	52 [p]
Bulgaria	..	..	4 [v]	263 [v]	398 [v]
Czech Republic	..	..	1055 [w]	3558 [w]	6058 [w]
Czechoslovakia (former)	..	..	464 [w]	..	..
Estonia	..	..	..	458 [p]	646 [p]
Hungary [i]	1	3	3	6438	9938
Latvia	..	..	..	289 [p]	539 [p]
Lithuania	..	..	..	71 [p]	121 [p]
Moldova, Republic of	..	..	..	54 [p]	86 [p]
Poland [i]	86	177	320	4879	7389

/...

(Annex table 3, cont'd)

Host region/economy	1980	1985	1990	1994	1995 [a]
Central and Eastern Europe (cont'd)					
Romania	..	..	..	551 [p]	924 [p]
Russian Federation	..	..	..	2037 [p]	4054 [p]
Slovakia	..	..	..	402 [k]	652 [k]
Ukraine	..	..	..	559 [p]	759 [p]
Memorandum:	..	..	..		
Least developed countries[y] in	3657	4393	6899	12265	13385
Africa	3373	3969	6372	8918	9663
Latin America and the Caribbean	79	112	149	181	183
Asia	144	218	191	2795	3122
West Asia	56	83	-35	2187	2207
South, East and South-East Asia	88	135	226	608	915
The Pacific	61	95	187	372	417
Oil-exporting countries[z] in	41895	99467	147780	215199	237869
Africa	7739	15919	26923	36883	40116
Latin America and the Caribbean	12712	24040	40969	68838	76791
Asia	21444	59508	79888	109479	120962
West Asia	5073	25995	26858	30516	31693
South, East and South-East Asia	16370	33513	53030	78963	89270
All developing countries minus China	108271	193320	327540	502662	564341

Source: UNCTAD FDI database, based on official national sources, the International Monetary Fund balance-of-payments and International Financial Statistics tapes, retrieved in May 1996; and own estimates.

a	Estimates. For details, see definitions and sources.
b	Estimated by adding flows to the stock of 1994.
c	Estimated by adding flows to the stock of 1989.
d	Estimated by adding flows to the stock of 1990.
e	Estimated by adding flows to the stock of 1993.
f	Estimated by adding flows to the stock of 1986.
g	Estimated by adding flows to the stock of 1992.
h	Estimated by adding flows to the stock of 1991.
i	Estimated by accumulating flows since 1970.
j	Estimated by subtracting flows from 1987 stock.
k	Estimated by accumulating flows since 1993.
l	Estimated by accumulating flows since 1988.
m	Estimated by accumulating flows since 1981.
n	Estimated by accumulating flows since 1984.
o	Estimated by accumulating flows since 1987.
p	Estimated by accumulating flows since 1992.
q	Estimated by adding flows to the stock of 1988.
r	Estimated by adding flows to the stock of 1987.
s	Estimated by accumulating flows since 1994.
t	Estimated by accumulating flows since 1995.
u	Estimated by accumulating flows since 1991.
v	Estimated by accumulating flows since 1990.
w	Estimated by accumulating flows since 1989.

y Least developed countries include: Afghanistan, Angola, Bangladesh, Benin, Bhutan, Burkina Faso, Burundi, Cambodia, Cape Verde, Central African Republic, Chad, Comoros, Djibouti, Equatorial Guinea, Eritrea, Ethiopia, Gambia, Guinea, Guinea-Bissau, Haiti, Kiribati, Lao People's Democratic Republic, Lesotho, Liberia, Madagascar, Malawi, Maldives, Mali, Mauritania, Mozambique, Myanmar, Nepal, Niger, Rwanda, Western Samoa, Sierra Leone, Solomon Islands, Somalia, Sudan, Togo, Tuvalu, Uganda, United Republic of Tanzania, Vanuatu, Yemen, Zaire and Zambia.

z Oil exporting countries include: Algeria, Angola, Bahrain, Bolivia, Brunei Darussalam, Cameroon, Congo, Ecuador, Egypt, Gabon, Indonesia, Islamic Republic of Iran, Iraq, Kuwait, Libyan Arab Jamahiriya, Malaysia, Mexico, Nigeria, Oman, Qatar, Saudi Arabia, Trinidad and Tobago, Tunisia, United Arab Emirates and Venezuela.

Annex table 4. FDI outward stock, by home region and economy, 1980, 1985, 1990, 1994 and 1995

(Millions of dollars)

Home region/economy	1980	1985	1990	1994	1995 [a]
Total outward stock	513740	685549	1684136	2412219	2730146
Developed countries	507494	664228	1614569	2243766	2514317
Western Europe	236593	312457	853866	1190565	1332458
European Union	213157	286485	777227	1076547	1208838
Austria	747	1908	4656	11295	12011 [b]
Belgium and Luxembourg	6037	4688	28965 [c]	52135 [c]	57768 [c]
Denmark	2065	1801	7342	16965 [d]	19816 [d]
Finland	743	1829	11227	13789 [e]	15301 [e]
France	23604	37077	110126	183348 [e]	200902 [e]
Germany	43127	59909	151581	199701 [e]	235003 [e]
Ireland	..	202 [f]	2284 [f]	4539 [f]	5079 [f]
Italy	7319	16301	56102	83462	86672 [b]
Netherlands	42116	47772	109124	146182 [g]	158613 [g]
Portugal [h]	130	200	517	2072	2834
Spain	1226	2076	14987	30697 [i]	34271 [i]
Sweden	5611	12408	49491	51194 [e]	61561 [e]
United Kingdom	80434	100313	230825	281170	319009 [b]
Other Western Europe	23435	25973	76640	114017	123620
Iceland	..	..	21 [j]	44 [j]	48 [j]
Norway	1944	4623	10888	14347 [e]	15319 [e]
Switzerland	21491	21350	65731	99626 [e]	108253 [e]
North America	242750	291981	514072	715667	815958
Canada	22572	40947	78853	105606	110388 [b]
United States [k]	220178	251034	435219	610061	705570 [b]
Other developed countries	28151	59789	246630	337535	365901
Australia	2260	6653	30108	35925	41296 [b]
Israel [h]	28	510	913	3487	3887
Japan	18833	44296	204659	284259	305545 [b]
New Zealand	1308	1826	3320	6234	7542
South Africa	5722	6504	7630 [l]	7630 [l]	7630 [l]
Developing countries	6167	21222	69369	167358	214453
Africa	500	6582	12091	14718	15271
North Africa	389	647	1459	1737	1783
Algeria [h]	99	157	185	235	235
Egypt [h]	7	59	131	240	255
Libyan Arab Jamahiriya [h]	39	121	447	451	451
Morocco [h]	76	102	164	266	292
Sudan [h]	162	206	526	526	526
Tunisia [h]	6	2	6	20	24
Other Africa	111	5935	10632	12981	13488
Benin [h]	-	2	2	2	2
Botswana [h]	3	3	3	5	5
Cameroon [h]	-	30	128	231	258

/...

(Annex table 4, cont'd)

Home region/economy	1980	1985	1990	1994	1995 [a]
North Africa (cont'd)					
Central African Republic [h]	2	3	20	42	48
Chad [h]	1	1	36	84	96
Gabon [h]	-	25	87	132	142
Kenya [h]	18	60	66	65	65
Liberia [m]	48	361	453	813	817 [b]
Mauritius	..	..	..	80 [n]	106 [n]
Namibia	..	..	1 [o]	20 [o]	24 [o]
Nigeria	..	5334	9652	11197 [g]	11582 [g]
Senegal [h]	8	45	52	52	52
Seychelles [h]	14	44	61	65	66
Swaziland [h]	18	28	72	194	226
Latin America and the Caribbean	2910	7207	12654	20817	24631
South America	930	2251	4698	11010	13732
Argentina [m]	70	280	420	431	450 [b]
Bolivia [h]	1	1	7	7	7
Brazil	652	1361	2397	5076 [d]	6460 [d]
Chile	42	102	178	2027 [g]	2671 [g]
Colombia	137	301	402	868 [d]	1016 [d]
Peru	3	38	63	63 [d]	70 [d]
Uruguay [m]	3	2	9	17	16 [b]
Venezuela	23	165	1221	2520 [e]	3042 [e]
Other Latin America	1980	4956	7956	9807	10900
Bahamas [m]	285	154	1535	1038	1658 [b]
Barbados [h]	5	12	23	30	31
Belize	..	..	..	8 [n]	10 [n]
Bermuda [m]	727	2002	1550	1921	1912 [b]
Costa Rica [h]	6	26	44	62	66
Mexico [m]	136	533	575	2084	2681 [b]
Netherlands Antilles [h]	10	10	21	23	23
Panama [m]	811	2204	4188	4613	4487 [b]
Trinidad and Tobago	..	16 [p]	21 [p]	29 [p]	31 [p]
Developing Europe	..	..	..	2	3
Malta	..	..	..	2 [q]	3 [q]
Asia	2737	7383	44519	131723	174447
West Asia	1066	1728	5884	8739	9835
Bahrain [m]	-1	-3	46	25	20 [b]
Cyprus	..	..	9 [r]	60 [r]	72 [r]
Jordan [h]	103	121	111	46	14
Kuwait [h]	568	930	3663	6611	7655
Lebanon [m]	1	40	-16	-42	-49 [b]
Oman [n]	1	40	7	-1	- [b]
Saudi Arabia [m]	228	420	1811	1673	1686 [b]
Turkey [h]	161	161	154	309	389
United Arab Emirates [m]	5	19	99	59	51 [b]
Central Asia	..	..	..	..	..
South, East and South-East Asia	1671	5656	38636	122984	164612
Bangladesh [m]	..	..	-	1	1 [b]
China	..	131	2489 [c]	13802 [c]	17268 [c]
Hong Kong [s]	148	2345	13242	60156	85156 [b]

/...

(Annex table 4, cont'd)

Home region/economy	1980	1985	1990	1994	1995 [a]
South, East and South-East Asia (cont'd)					
India [m]	4	19	30	86	94 [b]
Indonesia [m]	-1	49	25	98	110 [b]
Korea, Republic of	142	526	2095	8079	11079 [b]
Malaysia	414	749	2283 [l]	6328	8903 [l]
Pakistan	31	127	282 [l]	258 [l]	251 [l]
Philippines	171	171	155 [l]	155 [l]	164 [l]
Singapore [h]	652	1320	4741	11043	13842
Sri Lanka	..	1 [t]	8 [t]	30 [t]	36
Taiwan Province of China	97	204	12888 [l]	21522 [l]	24344 [l]
Thailand	13	14	398 [c]	1426 [c]	2333 [c]
The Pacific	21	50	105	98	100
Fiji [h]	10	23	83	87	90
Papua New Guinea	10	22	7 [c]	7 [c]	7 [c]
Vanuatu	..	5 [p]	15 [p]	4 [p]	4 [p]
Central and Eastern Europe	79	100	199	1094	1377
Albania	..	..	..	36 [q]	48 [q]
Czech Republic	..	..	..	206 [u]	275 [u]
Czechoslovakia (former)	..	..	11 [o]	..	..
Estonia	..	..	..	12 [q]	18 [q]
Hungary	..	..	..	115 [n]	144 [n]
Poland [h]	79	100	170	223	243
Romania	..	..	18 [o]	33 [o]	37 [o]
Russian Federation	..	..	..	386 [v]	515 [v]
Slovakia	..	..	..	75 [u]	87 [u]
Ukraine	..	..	..	8 [v]	11 [v]
Memorandum:					
Least developed countries [w] **in**	212	578	1052	1472	1495
Africa	212	573	1037	1467	1490
Latin America and the Caribbean	..	..	..	..	..
Asia	-	-	-	1	1
West Asia	..	..	..	..	..
South, East and South-East Asia	..	..	-	1	1
The Pacific	..	5	15	4	4
Oil-exporting countries [x] **in**	1525	8646	20393	31938	37130
Africa	151	5728	10636	12506	12946
Latin America and the Caribbean	160	715	1824	4640	5761
Asia	1214	2204	7934	14793	18423
West Asia	801	1406	5626	8367	9410
South, East and South-East Asia	413	798	2308	6426	9013
All developing countries minus China	6167	21091	66880	153557	197184

Source: UNCTAD FDI database, based on official national sources, the International Monetary Fund balance-of-payments and International Financial Statistics tapes, retrieved in May 1996; and own estimates.

- [a] Estimates.
- [b] Estimated by adding flows to the stock of 1994.
- [c] Estimated by adding flows to the stock of 1989.
- [d] Estimated by adding flows to the stock of 1990.
- [e] Estimated by adding flows to the stock of 1993.
- [f] Estimated by accumulating flows since 1984.

g   Estimated by adding flows to the stock of 1992.
h   Estimated by accumulating flows since 1970.
i   Estimated by adding flows to the stock of 1991.
j   Estimated by adding flows to the stock of 1986.
k   Excluding FDI in the financial sector of the Netherlands Antilles, except for 1995. For details, see definitions and sources.
l   Estimated by adding flows to the stock of 1988.
m   Estimated by using the country's inward stock in the United States.
n   Estimated by accumulating flows since 1991.
o   Estimated by accumulating flows since 1990.
p   Estimated by accumulating flows since 1983.
q   Estimated by accumulating flows since 1992.
r   Estimated by accumulating flows since 1987.
s   Estimated by using the country's inward stock in the United States and China.
t   Estimated by accumulating flows since 1985.
u   Estimated by accumulating flows since 1993.
v   Estimated by accumulating flows since 1994.
w   Least developed countries include: Afghanistan, Angola, Bangladesh, Benin, Bhutan, Burkina Faso, Burundi, Cambodia, Cape Verde, Central African Republic, Chad, Comoros, Djibouti, Equatorial Guinea, Eritrea, Ethiopia, Gambia, Guinea, Guinea-Bissau, Haiti, Kiribati, Lao People's Democratic Republic, Lesotho, Liberia, Madagascar, Malawi, Maldives, Mali, Mauritania, Mozambique, Myanmar, Nepal, Niger, Rwanda, Western Samoa, Sierra Leone, Solomon Islands, Somalia, Sudan, Togo, Tuvalu, Uganda, United Republic of Tanzania, Vanuatu, Yemen, Zaire and Zambia.
x   Oil exporting countries include: Algeria, Angola, Bahrain, Bolivia, Brunei Darussalam, Cameroon, Congo, Ecuador, Egypt, Gabon, Indonesia, Islamic Republic of Iran, Iraq, Kuwait, Libyan Arab Jamahiriya, Malaysia, Mexico, Nigeria, Oman, Qatar, Saudi Arabia, Trinidad and Tobago, Tunisia, United Arab Emirates and Venezuela.

Annex table 5. Share of inward and outward FDI flows to gross fixed capital formation, by region and economy, 1984-1994

(Percentage)

Region/economy	1984-1989 (Annual average)	1990	1991	1992	1993	1994
World						
inward	3.1	4.0	3.1	3.2	3.8	3.9
outward	3.3	4.7	4.2	3.9	4.2	4.0
Developed countries						
inward	3.9	4.9	3.3	3.1	3.5	3.3
outward	4.7	6.5	5.8	5.0	5.2	4.8
Western Europe						
inward	4.6	7.0	5.4	5.4	5.7	4.8
outward	7.8	9.4	7.8	7.6	7.5	8.0
European Union						
inward	4.7	7.0	5.5	5.5	5.8	4.8
outward	7.7	9.5	7.6	7.5	7.2	7.6
Austria						
inward	1.4	1.7	0.9	1.9	1.8	2.7
outward	1.4	4.4	3.1	4.2	3.2	2.6
Belgium and Luxembourg						
inward	13.0	19.4	22.8	25.0	26.7	17.5
outward	12.0	15.2	15.3	25.3	12.2	1.4
Denmark						
inward	2.0	5.0	7.3	4.7	8.4	23.0
outward	4.8	6.6	8.7	10.3	6.8	19.1
Finland						
inward	1.6	2.2	-0.9	2.0	6.9	10.7
outward	7.1	9.1	-0.4	-3.9	11.2	31.2
France						
inward	3.5	5.2	5.9	8.2	8.9	7.1
outward	5.8	13.6	9.4	11.8	8.8	9.4
Germany						
inward	1.0	0.9	1.2	0.6	0.1	-0.9
outward	5.2	7.7	7.0	5.2	3.9	4.2
Greece						
inward	7.9	7.7	8.7	8.1	7.7	7.5
outward	-	..	-	-0.3	0.2	..
Ireland						
inward	1.8	1.2	1.3	1.3	1.3	1.1
outward	6.2	6.2	8.4	6.4	7.7	7.2
Italy						
inward	2.0	2.8	1.0	1.3	1.6	0.9
outward	2.1	3.3	3.1	2.5	3.2	2.2
Netherlands						
inward	9.9	20.8	10.7	11.9	10.8	6.8
outward	18.5	26.0	22.9	22.2	18.2	17.9
Portugal						
inward	8.0	16.6	13.7	8.5	8.1	6.5
outward	0.4	1.0	2.6	3.1	0.6	1.5
Spain						
inward	8.1	11.6	10.0	10.6	8.6	9.9
outward	1.3	2.9	3.5	1.7	2.8	4.0

/...

(Annex table 5, cont'd)

Region/economy	1984-1989 (Annual average)	1990	1991	1992	1993	1994
Sweden						
inward	3.4	4.0	13.7	-0.2	14.7	23.1
outward	17.3	29.6	15.7	1.0	5.6	24.6
United Kingdom						
inward	11.5	17.0	9.4	9.1	10.2	6.6
outward	19.8	10.1	9.5	11.6	18.1	16.5
Other Western Europe						
inward	3.6	6.9	3.4	2.5	4.0	5.2
outward	9.2	7.9	9.8	8.4	12.7	14.4
Iceland						
inward	0.1	0.5	2.7	1.2	0.8	-
outward .	0.2	0.8	0.8	0.4	0.4	0.3
Norway						
inward	2.0	4.0	-1.6	2.8	8.7	2.5
outward	5.6	5.9	7.3	1.6	3.8	6.5
Switzerland						
inward	4.5	8.2	5.4	2.2	1.7	6.3
outward	11.5	8.8	11.1	11.5	16.8	17.9
North America						
inward	5.8	6.1	2.9	2.5	4.7	4.9
outward	2.6	3.5	4.6	4.8	7.6	4.4
Canada						
inward	5.4	6.5	2.4	4.2	5.0	5.9
outward	5.3	3.9	4.9	3.4	5.8	4.7
United States						
inward	5.8	6.0	3.0	2.2	4.7	4.8
outward	2.2	3.4	4.5	4.9	7.8	4.4
Other developed countries						
inward	0.7	1.0	0.7	0.8	0.4	0.6
outward	3.5	4.8	4.1	1.9	1.2	1.9
Australia						
inward	8.6	10.6	8.1	8.4	4.7	6.4
outward	6.6	0.3	5.1	0.2	2.8	8.5
Israel						
inward	2.3	1.0	2.5	3.5	3.9	2.5
outward	0.8	1.7	3.0	4.3	4.9	4.6
Japan						
inward	-	0.2	0.2	0.3	-	0.1
outward	3.4	5.1	4.0	2.0	1.2	1.4
New Zealand						
inward	2.5	20.4	20.6	16.2	27.4	36.4
outward	3.9	28.6	17.9	5.8	-17.1	26.6
South Africa						
inward	-	-	-	-	-	-
outward	0.4	..	-	..	..	..
Developing countries						
inward	2.8	3.2	4.0	4.8	6.3	7.5
outward	1.0	1.7	0.9	2.2	3.0	3.4

/...

(Annex table 5, cont'd)

Region/economy	1984-1989 (Annual average)	1990	1991	1992	1993	1994
Africa						
inward	3.6	2.7	4.2	4.4	4.9	7.5
outward	1.4	1.7	1.5	0.5	1.1	0.9
North Africa						
inward	2.4	2.1	2.3	3.5	3.6	5.0
outward	0.1	0.2	0.3	0.1	0.1	0.2
Algeria						
inward	-	-	0.1	0.1	0.1	0.1
outward	-	-	0.4	..	..	..
Egypt						
inward	5.5	4.3	2.8	5.3	6.4	14.8
outward	0.1	0.1	0.7	0.0	..	0.5
Libyan Arab Jamahiriya						
inward	0.1	1.7	1.8	1.7	1.8	0.9
outward	0.4	1.1	..	..	..	..
Morocco						
inward	1.9	3.7	6.1	7.5	9.3	8.6
outward	..	..	0.4	0.5	0.4	0.4
Sudan						
inward	0.5	-1.5	-0.1	-	-	-
outward	..	..	..	..	..	..
Tunisia						
inward	4.0	2.5	4.0	8.9	5.7	4.7
outward	-	-	0.1	0.1	..	0.1
Other Africa						
inward	6.4	3.9	7.2	5.9	7.0	11.3
outward	4.2	4.5	3.2	1.2	2.7	2.0
Angola						
inward	31.3	-52.7	107.5	..	48.0	55.8
outward	..	0.1	..	..	0.3	-0.3
Benin						
inward	0.1	0.3	5.1	3.0	4.1	2.0
outward	-	..	..	..	..	..
Botswana						
inward	13.4	18.0	-0.6	-0.2	-20.2	-3.4
outward	-	0.1	0.1	0.1	-	-
Burkina Faso						
inward	0.5	0.1	0.1	-	0.1	0.2
outward	..	..	..	..	..	
Burundi						
inward	0.6	0.7	0.5	0.3	0.4	0.9
outward	-	..	..	0.1	0.1	
Cameroon						
inward	2.2	-3.3	-0.8	2.5	0.5	9.6
outward	0.6	0.4	1.1	2.9	2.0	2.4
Cape Verde						
inward	0.5	-0.1	1.0	-	0.1	0.1
outward	0.2	0.2	..	..	..	0.8
Central African Republic	0.0					
inward	3.5	0.4	-2.8	-7.0	-9.4	3.3
outward	1.8	2.2	2.0	3.7	5.0	6.8

/...

(Annex table 5, cont'd)

Region/economy	1984-1989 (Annual average)	1990	1991	1992	1993	1994
Chad						
inward	24.8	..	3.0	1.8	13.3	6.2
outward	7.3	..	7.6	12.4	9.7	10.4
Comoros						
inward	5.5	0.7	5.4	2.1	4.0	4.0
outward	..	1.9	..	..	..	..
Congo						
inward	4.3	1.5	1.8	0.9	0.8	1.2
outward	..	..	..	..	..	..
Côte d'Ivoire	..					
inward	4.5	5.2	1.8	-24.5	4.3	1.9
outward	..	..	..	..	..	..
Djibouti						
inward	0.3	-	-	1.8	2.2	2.3
outward	..	..	..	..	..	..
Equatorial Guinea						
inward	8.9	17.4	140.1	53.3	55.6	71.5
outward	0.1	0.2	0.4	..	..	..
Ethiopia						
inward	0.1	1.6	0.1	2.5	0.9	1.0
outward	..	..	..	..	0.1	-0.1
Gabon						
inward	4.7	6.6	-5.1	10.5	-9.7	-8.7
outward	0.6	2.6	1.4	2.1	0.2	0.1
Gambia	0.0					
inward	6.2	-0.4	20.0	8.8	19.2	16.8
outward	..	..	..	..	..	..
Ghana						
inward	1.1	1.9	2.3	2.5	9.4	22.6
outward	..	..	..	..	..	
Guinea						
inward	2.2	4.5	7.8	4.0	0.5	-
outward	..	..	..	..	..	..
Guinea-Bissau	0.0					
inward	1.4	3.5	3.3	10.0	-2.6	..
outward	..	..	..	..	..	..
Kenya						
inward	2.1	3.2	1.2	0.5	0.2	0.3
outward	0.6	-	-0.1	-0.1	0.2	..
Lesotho						
inward	4.6	3.8	1.7	0.5	2.6	3.3
outward	-	..	..	..	..	..
Liberia						
inward	133.0	239.6	8.2	-11.1	31.1	9.4
outward	39.3	13.8	341.1	-30.7	-4.1	47.4
Madagascar						
inward	2.4	4.2	6.3	6.2	4.0	1.8
outward	..	..	..	..	..	..
Malawi						
inward	7.7	7.8	4.9	0.8	1.6	0.7
outward	..	..	0.3	-0.3	0.5	..
Mali						
inward	0.8	-1.4	0.7	..	-4.2	10.4
outward	..	..	..	..	..	..

/...

(Annex table 5, cont'd)

Region/economy	1984-1989 (Annual average)	1990	1991	1992	1993	1994
Mauritania						
inward	2.3	3.3	0.9	3.0	6.7	0.9
outward	0.2	..	..	..	..	..
Mauritius						
inward	4.3	5.1	2.4	1.7	1.6	1.9
outward	-	0.1	1.4	4.9	3.7	0.1
Mozambique						
inward	0.4	1.1	2.6	3.2	3.2	3.3
outward	..	..	..	..	..	..
Namibia						
inward	1.2	6.2	34.0	14.5	6.5	5.8
outward	..	0.3	1.8	-0.3	1.7	1.1
Niger						
inward	3.5	-0.4	0.5	0.2	0.4	0.5
outward	0.2	..	..	..	..	..
Nigeria						
inward	16.5	15.2	19.8	26.3	36.5	50.5
outward	23.2	31.3	10.8	5.2	16.1	10.0
Rwanda						
inward	5.6	2.5	2.0	0.9	1.1	0.4
outward	..	..	..	..	..	..
Senegal						
inward	0.9	-0.5	3.0	0.1	0.1	1.1
outward	0.4	..	..	..	..	..
Seychelles						
inward	32.7	23.8	24.3	9.9	21.0	31.3
outward	10.0	1.4	1.4	1.3	0.9	1.3
Sierra Leone						
inward	-25.2	47.0	13.9	-11.1	-14.6	81.3
outward	..	..	..	..	..	..
Somalia						
inward	-1.6	2.6	-0.1	1.2	0.8	0.4
outward	..	..	..	..	..	..
Swaziland						
inward	31.1	21.6	49.5	41.4	29.0	27.8
outward	6.0	4.3	17.5	18.6	17.2	20.8
Togo						
inward	1.5	1.6	0.6	..	0.1	0.2
outward	..	..	..	..	..	..
Uganda						
inward	-	-1.1	0.2	0.6	0.6	0.7
outward	..	..	..	..	..	..
United Republic of Tanzania						
inward	0.1	-0.2	0.3	1.1	2.0	..
outward	..	..	..	..	..	..
Zaire						
inward	-0.4	-0.8	2.7	0.1	0.1	0.1
outward	..	..	..	..	..	..
Zambia						
inward	28.4	40.2	8.9	14.3	26.7	19.1
outward	..	..	..	..	..	..
Zimbabwe						
inward	-0.9	-1.1	0.2	1.2	2.2	2.7
outward	-0.4	..	..	..	..	..

/...

(Annex table 5, cont'd)

Region/economy	1984-1989 (Annual average)	1990	1991	1992	1993	1994
Latin America and the Caribbean						
inward	4.2	4.0	6.4	7.2	6.3	8.6
outward	0.4	2.0	-0.2	1.5	0.9	1.3
South America						
inward	3.1	3.4	5.2	7.4	6.6	7.4
outward	0.3	0.8	1.0	0.6	1.3	1.6
Argentina						
inward	3.8	24.2	15.1	41.7	56.1	9.6
outward	0.2	0.7	-0.3	0.5	-0.2	0.3
Bolivia						
inward	-0.4	2.2	3.1	4.3	3.0	2.4
outward	0.1	0.2	0.2	0.2	-0.2	-0.3
Brazil						
inward	2.3	1.0	1.4	3.0	1.3	3.0
outward	0.3	0.7	1.3	0.2	0.5	1.0
Chile						
inward	15.6	8.3	7.3	7.2	7.2	19.9
outward	0.2	0.1	1.7	3.9	3.7	7.0
Colombia						
inward	8.5	7.5	11.5	11.5	10.6	13.8
outward	0.4	0.2	0.7	0.7	2.6	1.3
Ecuador						
inward	4.8	6.4	..	7.2	16.5	15.8
outward	..	..	..	..	..	..
Guyana						
inward	0.3	4.8	10.6	..	4.9	2.2
outward	..	..	..	-1.4	1.4	..
Paraguay						
inward	0.5	6.6	5.7	9.7	7.3	10.2
outward	..	..	..	..	..	..
Peru						
inward	0.1	0.8	-0.1	3.1	4.8	30.3
outward	..	..	..	-	0.3	..
Suriname						
inward	-30.9	-11.6	2.2	-4.6	-3.4	-3.6
outward	..	..	..	..	..	..
Uruguay						
inward	4.1	4.7	2.7	0.1	5.7	8.3
outward	0.5	-0.1	0.3	-1.9	1.8	-0.3
Venezuela						
inward	0.7	6.6	19.7	4.9	3.2	6.7
outward	1.2	5.5	1.9	1.2	7.6	4.6
Other Latin America						
inward	7.3	5.7	8.8	7.0	5.7	10.8
outward	0.5	4.8	-2.7	2.9	0.2	0.9
Bahamas						
inward	0.7	-2.5	-	1.1	4.1	4.1
outward	1.1	229.6	-395.1	206.4	97.7	-22.3
Barbados						
inward	2.8	3.4	2.7	8.3	4.3	4.7
outward	0.9	0.4	0.5	0.5	1.2	0.7

/...

(Annex table 5, cont'd)

Region/economy	1984-1989 (Annual average)	1990	1991	1992	1993	1994
Belize						
inward	12.3	16.3	11.9	12.9	7.0	10.6
outward	..	..	1.2	1.6	1.3	1.5
Costa Rica						
inward	9.5	12.8	16.0	16.1	14.1	5.2
outward	0.5	0.2	0.5	0.3	0.1	0.3
Dominica						
inward	23.7	18.5	19.8	30.1	18.1	30.4
outward	..	..	..	..	..	..
Dominican Republic						
inward	5.3	7.5	8.8	9.2	8.3	8.1
outward	..	..	..	-0.1	0.3	..
El Salvador						
inward	2.5	0.3	3.1	..	1.3	1.3
outward	..	..	..	..	..	..
Grenada						
inward	17.7	16.5	18.2	32.6	26.2	25.1
outward	..	..	1.5	..	..	..
Guatemala	0.0					
inward	12.0	4.8	7.9	5.8	7.8	1.9
outward	..	..	..	..	..	..
Haiti						
inward	2.0	2.3	4.0	2.3	2.3	0.6
outward	..	2.2	4.0	..	..	..
Honduras						
inward	5.4	7.1	8.9	6.3	3.5	7.4
outward	..	..	..	..	..	..
Jamaica						
inward	2.4	11.8	13.6	16.0	5.9	11.0
outward	..	..	..	..	..	..
Mexico						
inward	7.8	5.6	8.5	6.4	6.0	10.4
outward	0.4	0.5	0.3	1.1	-	1.4
Nicaragua						
inward	-0.2	0.2	3.5	4.2	9.6	8.6
outward	..	..	..	..	..	..
Panama						
inward	5.2	-31.1	14.9	13.6	-41.0	43.4
outward	9.4	183.8	62.3	19.7	-30.3	-11.1
Saint Kitts & Nevis						
inward	35.9	55.3	30.3	18.3	18.3	20.6
outward	..	..	..	..	..	..
Saint Vincent & the Grenadines						
inward	15.7	13.1	14.1	33.5	52.2	85.7
outward	..	..	..	..	..	..
Trinidad & Tobago						
inward	5.5	16.9	23.6	27.4	64.1	79.1
outward	0.3	..	..	..	0.5	0.8
Developing Europe						
inward	0.2	0.5	8.1	8.1	13.2	12.1
outward	..	..	..	..	0.1	..
Malta						
inward	7.6	6.2	10.4	-0.4	9.7	12.1
outward	..	..	..	..	0.1	0.1

/...

(Annex table 5, cont'd)

Region/economy	1984-1989 (Annual average)	1990	1991	1992	1993	1994
Yugoslavia (Former)						
inward	-	0.3	0.5	..	..	..
outward	..	..	..	..	..	..
Asia						
inward	2.3	3.1	3.4	4.1	6.5	7.2
outward	1.2	1.6	1.2	2.6	3.9	4.3
West Asia						
inward	1.3	1.2	1.7	1.5	2.1	1.8
outward	0.7	-0.2	-0.3	1.1	0.5	0.9
Bahrain						
inward	8.8	-0.3	-0.6	-0.6	-0.4	-2.1
outward	1.1	-2.1	-0.7	..	-1.4	0.4
Cyprus						
inward	7.3	9.3	5.9	5.2	5.6	5.1
outward	0.1	0.3	1.1	0.8	0.7	0.7
Iran, Islamic Republic of						
inward	-0.1	-0.3	0.1	-0.7	-0.1	-
outward	..	..	..	..	..	..
Iraq						
inward	-	..	..	..	..	..
outward	..	..	..	..	..	..
Jordan						
inward	2.6	3.6	-1.2	2.6	-1.8	0.2
outward	0.3	-3.1	1.4	-0.2	-2.8	-1.2
Kuwait						
inward	-	-0.2	0.0	1.0	0.4	0.4
outward	12.2	8.3	-4.6	35.0	24.5	29.4
Lebanon						
inward	1.3	1.3	0.2	0.4	0.3	0.4
outward	2.5	-1.4	-0.7	-0.6	-0.3	-0.4
Oman						
inward	6.0	10.2	8.7	4.4	4.7	6.8
outward	-	-0.1	-0.1	-0.1	-0.2	0.4
Qatar						
inward	-0.6	0.4	4.1	3.6	2.6	3.4
outward	..	..	..	..	..	..
Saudi Arabia						
inward	5.7	9.5	0.7	-0.3	5.2	5.4
outward	1.9	-3.1	-0.9	0.0	-0.2	0.3
Syrian Arab Republic						
inward	1.1	1.8	1.2	0.9	0.8	1.0
outward	..	..	..	..	..	..
Turkey						
inward	1.4	2.0	2.3	2.3	1.4	1.6
outward	..	..	0.1	0.2	-	0.1
United Arab Emirates						
inward	0.9	-1.8	0.4	1.6	2.5	1.5
outward	0.1	-0.2	0.0	0.2	0.1	-0.6
Yemen						
inward	1.0	-10.8	34.9	33.1	36.1	0.7
outward	-	..	..	..	..	..

/...

(Annex table 5, cont'd)

Region/economy	1984-1989 (Annual average)	1990	1991	1992	1993	1994
South, East and South-East Asia						
inward	2.6	3.7	3.7	4.7	7.6	8.2
outward	1.4	2.3	1.5	2.9	4.7	5.0
Afghanistan						
inward	-	-	-	-	-	-
outward	..	..	..	..	..	..
Bangladesh						
inward	0.1	0.1	0.1	0.1	0.4	0.3
outward	..	..	0.1	-	..	..
China						
inward	1.8	2.6	3.3	7.8	20.0	24.5
outward	0.5	0.6	0.7	2.8	3.2	1.5
Hong Kong						
inward	12.2	8.5	2.3	7.7	7.1	8.2
outward	15.6	11.7	11.6	28.7	74.5	86.3
India						
inward	0.2	0.2	0.3	0.3	0.5	1.1
outward	-	-	-	-	-	-
Indonesia						
inward	1.6	2.8	3.6	3.9	3.8	3.6
outward	0.1	-	-	0.1	-	-
Korea, Republic of						
inward	1.4	0.8	1.0	0.6	0.5	0.6
outward	0.3	1.1	1.3	1.1	1.1	1.9
Malaysia						
inward	8.8	23.8	23.8	26.0	22.5	16.1
outward	2.6	3.8	2.3	2.6	5.9	6.7
Maldives						
inward	7.7	..	11.3	10.9	11.3	13.4
outward	..	..	..	..	..	..
Myanmar						
inward	0.1	0.2	-	0.1	0.2	0.2
outward	..	..	..	..	..	..
Nepal						
inward	0.2	1.1	0.7	0.7	1.1	1.2
outward	..	..	..	..	..	..
Pakistan						
inward	2.0	2.8	3.3	3.5	3.5	4.7
outward	0.1	-	-	-0.1	-	-0.1
Philippines						
inward	5.1	5.2	6.0	2.1	7.9	9.6
outward	..	..	-0.3	0.1	-	0.2
Singapore						
inward	28.3	47.1	33.5	13.3	24.6	23.5
outward	3.6	17.2	7.0	7.4	8.8	9.2
Sri Lanka						
inward	2.3	2.5	2.4	5.4	7.5	5.3
outward	0.1	-	0.2	0.1	0.3	0.3
Taiwan Province of China						
inward	3.3	3.8	3.0	2.4	2.4	3.5
outward	9.6	15.0	4.4	5.1	6.5	6.3
Thailand						
inward	4.4	7.1	4.9	4.8	3.5	1.1
outward	0.3	0.4	0.4	0.3	0.5	0.9

/...

(Annex table 5, cont'd)

Region/economy	1984-1989 (Annual average)	1990	1991	1992	1993	1994
The Pacific						
inward	17.9	23.8	20.0	30.4	7.5	6.8
outward	1.1	0.4	-0.3	0.1	0.4	0.1
Fiji						
inward	9.7	37.0	8.3	27.0	22.0	17.8
outward	6.2	2.2	-2.4	0.9	2.2	0.4
Papua New Guinea						
inward	20.0	19.1	19.1	28.5	0.1	0.4
outward	-0.3	..	..	..	..	..
Solomon Islands						
inward	12.6	..	..	..	..	..
outward	..	..	..	..	..	..
Vanuatu						
inward	25.9	21.2	53.1	52.2	54.0	61.3
outward	..	..	..	..	..	..
Central and Eastern Europe						
inward	-	-	0.4	0.6	0.9	0.9
outward	-	-	-	-	-	0.1
Bulgaria						
inward	-	-	2.8	2.0	2.5	4.9
outward	..	..	-	-	-	-
Czech Republic						
inward	..	..	..	-	7.9	9.1
outward	..	..	..	-	1.1	1.2
Czechoslovakia (former)						
inward	0.7	3.4	21.8	..	..	..
outward	-	0.3	0.5	..	..	..
Estonia						
inward	..	..	..	..	43.1	-
outward	..	..	..	..	2.1	-
Hungary						
inward	..	..	21.2	20.2	32.7	13.9
outward	..	..	0.4	0.4	0.1	0.6
Poland						
inward	0.1	0.7	2.0	5.0	12.8	13.5
outward	0.1	..	-	0.1	0.1	0.2
Romania						
inward	..	..	1.0	2.7	2.8	9.9
outward	..	0.2	0.1	0.1	0.2	-
Russian Federation						
inward	..	..	..	..	-	0.1
outward	..	..	..	..	-	0.1
Slovakia						
inward	..	..	..	..	6.3	9.8
outward	..	..	..	..	1.9	0.7
Memorandum:						
Least developed countries[a] in						
inward	1.1	0.2	2.1	1.6	1.8	0.9
outward	0.1	-	0.5	-	-	0.1
Africa						
inward	4.9	1.5	7.8	3.6	4.2	5.2
outward	0.6	0.1	3.1	-0.1	0.1	0.5

/...

(Annex table 5, cont'd)

Region/economy	1984-1989 (Annual average)	1990	1991	1992	1993	1994
Latin America and the Caribbean						
inward	2.0	2.3	4.0	2.3	2.3	0.6
outward	-	2.2	4.0	-	-	-
Asia						
inward	-	-0.2	0.9	1.2	1.3	0.1
outward	-	-	-	-	-	-
West Asia						
inward	1.0	-10.8	34.9	33.1	36.1	0.7
outward	-	-	-	-	-	-
South, East and South-East Asia						
inward	-	-	-	-	-	-
outward	-	-	-	-	-	-
The Pacific						
inward	18.5	38.0	83.9	80.7	84.0	96.0
outward	-	-	-	-	-	-
Oil-exporting countries[b] in						
inward	3.0	3.1	6.3	5.7	5.6	7.3
outward	1.0	0.7	0.4	1.1	1.2	1.7
Africa						
inward	3.7	2.1	4.5	5.6	6.0	9.4
outward	1.7	2.5	1.3	0.6	1.5	1.1
Latin America and the Caribbean						
inward	5.8	5.9	10.1	6.4	6.3	10.6
outward	0.6	1.1	0.5	1.0	1.0	1.7
Asia						
inward	1.8	2.5	4.8	5.3	5.1	5.0
outward	0.8	0.1	-	1.4	1.2	1.8
West Asia						
inward	1.3	1.1	0.6	-	1.7	2.1
outward	0.8	-0.3	-0.6	1.8	0.8	1.5
South, East and South-East Asia						
inward	3.5	6.6	9.4	10.6	9.4	7.5
outward	0.7	1.0	0.7	0.9	1.7	2.1
All developing countries minus China						
inward	3.0	3.3	4.1	4.3	4.4	5.1
outward	1.1	1.8	0.9	2.1	3.0	3.7

Source: UNCTAD, based on the Division's FDI database and data provided by the UNCTAD Secretariat.

[a]   Least developed countries include: Afghanistan, Angola, Bangladesh, Benin, Bhutan, Burkina Faso, Burundi, Cambodia, Cape Verde, Central African Republic, Chad, Comoros, Djibouti, Equatorial Guinea, Eritrea, Ethiopia, Gambia, Guinea, Guinea-Bissau, Haiti, Kiribati, Lao People's Democratic Republic, Lesotho, Liberia, Madagascar, Malawi, Maldives, Mali, Mauritania, Mozambique, Myanmar, Nepal, Niger, Rwanda, Western Samoa, Sierra Leone, Solomon Islands, Somalia, Sudan, Togo, Tuvalu, Uganda, United Republic of Tanzania, Vanuatu, Yemen, Zaire and Zambia.

[b]   Oil exporting countries include: Algeria, Angola, Bahrain, Bolivia, Brunei Darussalam, Cameroon, Congo, Ecuador, Egypt, Gabon, Indonesia, Islamic Republic of Iran, Iraq, Kuwait, Libyan Arab Jamahiriya, Malaysia, Mexico, Nigeria, Oman, Qatar, Saudi Arabia, Trinidad and Tobago, Tunisia, United Arab Emirates and Venezuela.

Annex table 6. Share of inward and outward FDI stock in gross domestic product, by region and economy, 1980, 1985, 1990, and 1994

(Percentage)

Region/economy	1980	1985	1990	1994
World				
inward	4.6	6.3	8.3	9.4
outward	4.9	5.9	8.1	9.7
Developed countries				
inward	4.8	6.0	8.4	8.6
outward	6.5	7.5	9.8	11.2
Western Europe				
inward	5.7	8.4	11.0	13.0
outward	6.7	10.7	12.3	15.9
European Union				
inward	5.5	8.2	10.8	12.9
outward	6.3	10.4	11.8	15.1
Austria				
inward	5.8	9.4	6.8	6.6
outward	1.0	2.9	2.9	5.7
Belgium and Luxembourg				
inward	6.0	10.6	18.2	31.7
outward	4.9	5.6	14.4	21.9
Denmark				
inward	6.3	6.2	7.1	12.6
outward	3.1	3.1	5.7	11.6
Finland				
inward	1.1	2.5	3.8	5.9
outward	1.4	3.4	8.3	14.2
France				
inward	3.4	6.4	7.2	10.7
outward	3.6	7.1	9.2	13.8
Germany				
inward	4.5	6.0	7.4	6.8
outward	5.3	9.7	10.1	10.9
Greece				
inward	11.3	24.9	21.1	23.5
outward	..	..	..	..
Ireland				
inward	19.5	24.5	11.1	10.3
outward	..	1.1	5.1	8.7
Italy				
inward	2.0	4.5	5.3	5.9
outward	1.6	3.8	5.1	8.2
Netherlands				
inward	11.3	19.5	26.0	27.7
outward	24.9	37.3	38.5	43.7
Portugal				
inward	4.4	6.5	8.5	6.6
outward	0.5	1.0	0.9	2.5
Spain				
inward	2.4	5.4	13.5	25.0
outward	0.6	1.3	3.0	6.4

/...

(Annex table 6, cont'd)

Region/economy	1980	1985	1990	1994
Sweden				
inward	2.9	5.0	5.4	9.7
outward	4.5	12.3	21.5	26.0
United Kingdom				
inward	11.7	14.0	22.3	20.9
outward	14.9	21.9	23.6	27.5
Other Western Europe				
inward	9.4	11.9	13.4	14.4
outward	14.4	16.9	22.0	29.5
Gibraltar				
inward	..	..	..	..
outward	..	..	..	..
Iceland				
inward	3.8	7.8	3.2	4.2
outward	..	..	0.3	0.7
Norway				
inward	11.6	13.8	10.8	11.6
outward	3.4	7.9	9.4	11.6
Switzerland				
inward	8.4	10.8	14.9	15.9
outward	21.1	23.0	29.1	38.7
North America				
inward	4.6	5.7	8.3	8.4
outward	8.2	6.7	8.4	9.8
Canada				
inward	20.4	18.5	19.7	19.2
outward	8.5	11.7	13.7	19.2
United States				
inward	3.1	4.6	7.2	7.5
outward	8.1	6.2	7.9	9.1
Other developed countries				
inward	2.7	2.7	3.1	2.7
outward	2.1	3.7	7.2	6.5
Australia				
inward	8.7	15.6	25.7	28.3
outward	1.5	4.1	10.2	11.1
Israel				
inward	3.3	4.7	3.8	5.2
outward	0.1	2.1	1.7	4.7
Japan				
inward	0.3	0.4	0.3	0.4
outward	1.8	3.3	7.0	6.2
New Zealand				
inward	10.5	9.0	18.5	31.6
outward	4.7	7.0	7.6	8.9
South Africa				
inward	21.3	19.8	10.4	9.1
outward	7.4	11.8	7.2	6.3
Developing countries				
inward	4.3	7.7	8.3	12.5
outward	0.2	0.8	1.7	3.5

/...

(Annex table 6, cont'd)

Region/economy	1980	1985	1990	1994
Africa				
inward	5.8	8.0	10.8	14.6
outward	0.1	2.0	3.1	3.9
North Africa				
inward	3.2	5.7	7.5	10.2
outward	0.3	0.4	0.7	0.8
Algeria				
inward	3.1	2.2	2.2	2.9
outward	0.2	0.3	0.3	0.5
Egypt				
inward	9.6	12.0	23.0	26.2
outward	-	0.1	0.3	0.5
Libyan Arab Jamahiriya				
inward	..	..	..	..
outward	0.1	0.5	1.0	1.0
Morocco				
inward	1.6	4.3	4.0	10.4
outward	0.4	0.8	0.6	1.0
Sudan				
inward	..	0.4	-	-
outward	2.0	3.1	2.2	2.2
Tunisia				
inward	6.3	17.2	22.0	23.2
outward	0.1	-	-	0.1
Other Africa				
inward	7.4	10.1	15.0	20.4
outward	-	3.3	6.3	8.0
Angola				
inward	1.7	11.1	12.4	30.2
outward	..	..	..	..
Benin				
inward	2.7	3.1	2.0	4.5
outward	..	0.2	0.1	0.1
Botswana				
inward	27.4	45.3	26.6	13.8
outward	0.3	0.2	0.1	0.1
Burkina Faso				
inward	1.4	2.4	1.1	1.1
outward	..	..	..	..
Burundi				
inward	0.7	2.0	2.5	3.0
outward	..	..	..	..
Cameroon				
inward	4.4	13.8	8.5	18.8
outward	..	0.4	1.0	3.7
Cape Verde				
inward	..	..	0.8	0.9
outward	..	..	..	..
Central African Republic				
inward	6.2	11.0	6.3	8.4
outward	0.2	0.4	1.3	4.8
Chad				
inward	13.0	27.9	19.8	35.3
outward	0.1	0.2	3.0	10.9

/...

(Annex table 6, cont'd)

Region/economy	1980	1985	1990	1994
Comoros				
inward	..	0.2	6.3	8.3
outward	..	..	..	..
Congo				
inward	18.1	22.1	19.8	24.3
outward	..	..	..	..
Côte d'Ivoire				
inward	6.4	7.9	10.1	8.9
outward	..	..	..	..
Djibouti				
inward	0.9	0.9	1.1	3.0
outward	..	..	..	..
Equatorial Guinea				
inward	..	6.4	15.7	73.2
outward	..	..	..	..
Ethiopia				
inward	2.7	2.4	1.9	2.9
outward	..	..	..	..
Gabon				
inward	11.9	22.7	22.0	27.2
outward	..	0.7	1.6	3.4
Gambia				
inward	8.7	9.4	11.9	24.3
outward	-	-	-	-
Ghana				
inward	1.8	4.9	6.0	12.8
outward	..	..	..	..
Guinea				
inward	0.1	0.1	2.3	4.2
outward	..	..	..	..
Guinea-Bissau				
inward	..	0.8	3.3	6.0
outward	..	..	..	..
Kenya				
inward	9.4	6.0	4.6	6.1
outward	0.2	1.0	0.8	0.9
Lesotho				
inward	2.4	6.2	11.0	14.5
outward	..	..	..	..
Liberia				
inward	134.1	124.8	211.7	214.8
outward	5.2	33.8	37.9	68.1
Madagascar				
inward	1.1	1.7	3.3	5.3
outward	..	..	..	..
Malawi				
inward	8.1	12.2	11.6	18.3
outward	..	..	..	..
Mali				
inward	0.9	2.8	1.2	2.9
outward	..	..	..	..
Mauritania				
inward	..	4.8	4.9	8.2
outward	..	..	..	..
Mauritius				
inward	1.8	3.5	6.3	6.7
outward	..	..	..	2.3

/...

(Annex table 6, cont'd)

Region/economy	1980	1985	1990	1994
Mozambique				
inward	0.6	0.7	2.9	10.6
outward	..	..	..	..
Namibia				
inward	..	151.7	89.5	73.6
outward	..	..	-	0.7
Niger				
inward	7.4	14.1	10.6	11.5
outward	..	..	..	..
Nigeria				
inward	2.6	5.4	24.7	31.1
outward	..	6.6	29.8	26.9
Rwanda				
inward	4.6	7.8	9.1	14.4
outward	..	..	..	..
Senegal				
inward	12.1	7.7	5.5	5.9
outward	0.3	1.8	0.9	0.9
Seychelles				
inward	24.9	51.7	50.4	58.1
outward	9.6	26.2	16.5	13.9
Sierra Leone				
inward	7.0	5.0	-0.5	3.3
outward	..	..	..	..
Somalia				
inward	1.1	0.2	-0.7	-0.1
outward	..	..	..	..
Swaziland				
inward	27.5	55.0	49.0	69.5
outward	3.3	8.4	8.1	19.9
Togo				
inward	16.1	28.7	15.2	20.3
outward	..	..	..	..
Uganda				
inward	..	0.2	0.1	0.3
outward	..	..	..	..
United Republic of Tanzania				
inward	3.0	1.1	0.3	1.3
outward	..	..	..	..
Zaire				
inward	7.1	11.8	2.5	3.5
outward	..	..	..	..
Zambia				
inward	10.7	4.4	15.8	23.9
outward	..	..	..	..
Zimbabwe				
inward	131.2	66.6	36.6	42.2
outward	..	..	..	..
Latin America and the Caribbean				
inward	6.5	10.7	11.1	12.7
outward	0.4	1.0	1.2	1.3
South America				
inward	5.8	8.9	8.2	9.2
outward	0.2	0.5	0.6	1.0

/...

(Annex table 6, cont'd)

Region/economy	1980	1985	1990	1994
Argentina				
inward	6.9	7.4	6.2	8.1
outward	0.1	0.3	0.3	0.2
Bolivia				
inward	13.7	14.7	15.1	21.5
outward	..	..	0.1	0.2
Brazil				
inward	6.9	11.3	8.1	8.0
outward	0.3	0.6	0.5	0.9
Chile				
inward	3.2	14.1	20.3	19.2
outward	0.2	0.6	0.6	4.0
Colombia				
inward	3.2	6.4	8.7	11.1
outward	0.4	0.9	1.0	1.3
Ecuador				
inward	6.1	6.2	12.8	16.4
outward	..	..	..	..
Guyana				
inward	0.1	3.1	4.4	7.6
outward	..	..	..	..
Paraguay				
inward	4.9	6.5	7.6	11.7
outward	..	..	..	..
Peru				
inward	4.3	6.7	3.7	8.2
outward	-	0.2	0.2	0.1
Suriname				
inward	..	..	..	..
outward	..	..	..	..
Uruguay				
inward	6.9	16.2	11.7	8.3
outward	..	..	0.1	0.1
Venezuela				
inward	2.7	2.6	8.0	13.0
outward	..	0.3	2.5	4.3
Other Latin America				
inward	7.8	14.2	18.7	21.3
outward	0.8	2.1	2.6	2.2
Antigua and Barbuda				
inward	24.6	54.2	89.5	106.9
outward	..	..	..	..
Aruba				
inward	..	..	..	..
outward	..	..	..	..
Bahamas				
inward	25.5	12.7	10.7	13.0
outward	24.4	6.6	48.8	33.8
Barbados				
inward	11.8	10.3	9.9	12.1
outward	0.6	1.0	1.3	1.7
Belize				
inward	6.4	5.0	17.8	23.6
outward	..	..	..	1.4

/...

(Annex table 6, cont'd)

Region/economy	1980	1985	1990	1994
Bermuda				
inward	822.0	761.1	..	..
outward	116.5	189.2	..	..
Cayman Islands				
inward	..	..	..	..
outward	..	..	..	..
Costa Rica				
inward	13.9	24.4	25.3	26.1
outward	0.1	0.7	0.8	0.7
Cuba				
inward	..	..	..	..
outward	..	..	..	..
Dominica				
inward	..	5.7	40.2	66.5
outward	..	..	..	..
Dominican Republic				
inward	3.6	5.2	7.5	12.3
outward	..	..	..	..
El Salvador				
inward	4.3	3.2	4.0	3.6
outward	..	..	..	..
Grenada				
inward	1.7	11.0	35.1	56.5
outward	..	..	..	..
Guatemala				
inward	0.6	0.6	9.7	8.6
outward	..	..	..	..
Haiti				
inward	5.7	5.6	5.3	9.5
outward	..	..	..	..
Honduras				
inward	3.6	4.7	12.6	17.6
outward	..	..	..	..
Jamaica				
inward	18.7	22.7	16.3	30.2
outward	..	..	..	..
Mexico				
inward	4.6	10.5	13.3	14.4
outward	0.1	0.3	0.2	0.6
Netherlands Antilles				
inward	57.7	4.8	13.3	20.6
outward	1.0	0.9	1.4	1.5
Nicaragua				
inward	5.1	4.1	4.7	10.8
outward	..	..	..	..
Panama				
inward	10.8	10.8	6.4	7.4
outward	22.6	44.5	77.7	62.2
Saint Kitts & Nevis				
inward	2.1	40.5	100.3	107.9
outward	..	..	..	..
Saint Lucia				
inward	95.4	105.5	94.4	94.1
outward	..	..	..	..
Saint Vincent & the Grenadines				
inward	2.0	7.5	23.3	81.2
outward	..	..	..	..

/...

(Annex table 6, cont'd)

Region/economy	1980	1985	1990	1994
Trinidad and Tobago				
inward	15.7	23.3	41.3	68.9
outward	..	0.2	0.4	0.6
Virgin Islands				
inward	..	3.8	9.2	63.7
outward	..	..	..	..
Developing Europe				
inward	0.3	1.1	31.2	10.0
outward	..	..	..	..
Bosnia and Herzegovina				
inward	..	..	..	..
outward	..	..	..	..
Croatia				
inward	..	..	..	..
outward	..	..	..	..
Malta				
inward	13.8	28.2	20.1	28.4
outward	..	..	..	0.1
Slovenia				
inward	..	..	..	2.2
outward	..	..	..	-
TFYR Macedonia				
inward	..	..	..	..
outward	..	..	..	..
Yugoslavia (former)				
inward	0.2	0.4	..	..
outward	..	..	..	..
Asia				
inward	2.9	6.3	6.7	12.1
outward	0.2	0.5	1.7	4.7
West Asia				
inward	1.2	5.8	3.1	7.2
outward	0.2	0.4	0.6	1.6
Bahrain				
inward	..	7.7	15.2	11.5
outward	..	-0.1	1.1	0.5
Cyprus				
inward	14.4	21.5	17.5	18.2
outward	..	..	0.2	0.8
Iran, Islamic Republic of				
inward	1.3	0.5	0.1	0.1
outward	0.1	0.1	-	0.1
Iraq				
inward	0.3	0.3	0.3	0.3
outward	1.1	1.9	6.4	11.0
Jordan				
inward	4.0	8.9	8.5	5.7
outward	..	0.8	-0.4	-0.7
Kuwait				
inward	1.2	1.6	1.9	1.7
outward	..	0.2	-	-

/...

(Annex table 6, cont'd)

Region/economy	1980	1985	1990	1994
Lebanon				
inward	0.3	0.7	0.3	0.5
outward	5.6	27.5	71.8	30.2
Oman				
inward	4.5	9.9	13.4	16.6
outward	2.7	1.6	1.5	2.7
Qatar				
inward	2.2	2.7	2.1	4.2
outward	0.1	0.3	1.3	0.8
Saudi Arabia				
inward	1.4	25.9	21.8	21.3
outward	..	..	..	..
Syrian Arab Republic				
inward	..	0.2	1.6	1.5
outward	..	..	..	..
Turkey				
inward	0.2	0.7	0.9	3.2
outward	..	..	..	..
United Arab Emirates				
inward	2.4	2.9	3.1	4.2
outward	..	..	..	..
Yemen				
inward	2.0	2.0	-0.5	17.3
outward	..	..	..	..
Central Asia				
inward	..	..	..	3.3
outward	..	..	..	..
Armenia				
inward	..	..	..	..
outward	..	..	..	..
Azerbaijan				
inward	..	..	..	..
outward	..	..	..	..
Georgia				
inward	..	..	..	..
outward	..	..	..	..
Kazakhstan				
inward	..	..	..	3.0
outward	..	..	..	..
Kyrgyzstan				
inward	..	..	..	0.3
outward	..	..	..	-
Tajikistan				
inward	..	..	..	..
outward	..	..	..	..
Uzbekistan				
inward	..	..	..	..
outward	..	..	..	..
South, East and South-East Asia				
inward	3.8	6.5	9.2	13.3
outward	0.2	0.6	2.4	5.6
Afghanistan				
inward	0.3	..	..	..
outward	..	..	..	..

/...

(Annex table 6, cont'd)

Region/economy	1980	1985	1990	1994
Bangladesh				
inward	0.4	0.7	0.7	0.7
outward	..	..	..	..
Brunei Darussalam				
inward	0.4	0.9	1.1	1.9
outward	..	3.8	87.4	486.3
Cambodia				
inward	..	..	..	7.8
outward	..	..	..	-
China				
inward	..	1.2	3.8	17.9
outward	..	..	..	..
Hong Kong				
inward	6.3	10.5	18.7	20.5
outward	0.5	7.0	18.5	62.7
India				
inward	0.7	0.5	0.5	0.9
outward	..	..	..	..
Indonesia				
inward	14.2	28.6	36.6	26.5
outward	..	0.1	-	0.1
Korea, Democratic People's Republic				
inward	..	..	..	..
outward	..	..	..	..
Korea, Republic of				
inward	1.8	1.9	3.3	3.3
outward	0.2	0.6	0.8	2.1
Lao, People's Democratic Republic				
inward	..	..	1.4	12.1
outward	..	..	..	..
Macau				
inward	..	0.7	..	..
outward	..	-	..	..
Malaysia				
inward	24.8	27.2	33.0	46.2
outward	1.7	2.4	5.3	8.9
Maldives				
inward	11.4	3.8	24.7	36.0
outward	..	..	..	..
Mongolia				
inward	..	..	..	2.5
outward	..	..	..	..
Myanmar				
inward	0.1	0.1	0.1	-
outward	..	..	..	..
Nepal				
inward	0.1	0.1	0.3	0.8
outward	..	..	..	..
Pakistan				
inward	2.5	3.3	4.3	6.0
outward	0.1	0.4	0.7	0.5
Philippines				
inward	3.8	4.2	4.7	8.3
outward	0.5	0.6	0.3	0.2
Singapore				
inward	52.9	73.6	86.6	72.8
outward	5.6	7.5	12.7	16.0

/...

(Annex table 6, cont'd)

Region/economy	1980	1985	1990	1994
Sri Lanka				
inward	5.7	8.6	8.5	10.4
outward	..	..	0.1	0.3
Taiwan Province of China				
inward	5.8	4.7	6.2	6.6
outward	0.2	0.3	8.2	9.9
Thailand				
inward	3.0	5.1	9.3	10.1
outward	..	..	0.5	1.0
Viet Nam				
inward	..	0.2	1.1	1.9
outward	..	..	..	..
The Pacific				
inward	26.4	31.2	40.3	40.1
outward	0.5	1.3	2.0	1.3
Fiji				
inward	29.8	34.4	28.3	32.8
outward	0.8	2.0	6.0	5.3
Kiribati				
inward	..	..	..	..
outward	..	..	..	..
New Caledonia				
inward	..	..	..	..
outward	..	..	..	..
Papua New Guinea				
inward	27.1	31.1	46.8	39.4
outward	0.4	1.0	0.2	0.1
Solomon Islands				
inward	19.2	19.9	32.8	51.8
outward	..	..	..	..
Tonga				
inward	..	..	..	3.3
outward	..	..	..	..
Vanuatu				
inward	29.0	60.0	71.8	120.3
outward	..	4.7	9.8	2.2
Western Samoa				
inward	0.4	0.9	5.4	16.1
outward	..	..	..	..
Central and Eastern Europe				
inward	..	0.1	0.8	7.4
outward	..	..	0.1	0.4
Albania				
inward	..	..	..	10.0
outward	..	..	..	2.8
Belarus				
inward	..	..	..	..
outward	..	..	..	..
Bulgaria				
inward	..	..	..	0.6
outward	..	..	..	..
Czech Republic				
inward	..	..	..	9.9
outward	..	..	..	0.6

/...

(Annex table 6, cont'd)

Region/economy	1980	1985	1990	1994
Czechoslovakia (former)				
inward	-	-	1.0	..
outward	-	-	-	..
Estonia				
inward	..	..	..	26.5
outward	..	..	..	0.7
Hungary				
inward	..	..	..	15.6
outward	..	..	..	0.3
Latvia				
inward	..	..	..	8.5
outward	..	..	..	-
Lithuania				
inward	..	..	..	1.7
outward	..	..	..	-
Moldova, Republic of				
inward	..	..	..	..
outward	..	..	..	..
Poland				
inward	0.2	0.2	0.5	5.3
outward	0.1	0.1	0.3	0.2
Romania				
inward	..	..	..	1.8
outward	..	..	..	0.1
Russian Federation				
inward	..	..	..	..
outward	..	..	..	..
Slovakia				
inward	..	..	..	3.2
outward	..	..	..	0.6
Ukraine				
inward	..	..	..	..
outward	..	..	..	..
Memorandum:				
Least developed countries[a] in				
inward	3.4	4.7	4.5	5.9
outward	0.2	0.6	0.7	0.7
Africa				
inward	4.4	6.7	6.8	10.3
outward	0.3	1.0	1.1	1.7
Latin America and the Caribbean				
inward	5.7	5.6	5.3	9.5
outward	-	-	-	-
Asia				
inward	0.5	0.7	0.3	2.3
outward	-	-	-	0.0
West Asia				
inward	2.0	2.0	-0.5	17.3
outward	-	-	-	-
South, East and South-East Asia				
inward	0.3	0.5	0.4	0.6
outward	-	-	-	0.0
The Pacific				
inward	15.4	26.9	34.2	60.1
outward	-	1.4	2.7	0.6

/...

(Annex table 6, cont'd)

Region/economy	1980	1985	1990	1994
Oil-exporting countries[b] in				
inward	4.3	9.8	10.1	17.0
outward	0.2	0.3	0.7	1.6
Africa				
inward	3.5	6.7	11.9	16.6
outward	0.1	0.2	0.4	0.6
Latin America and the Caribbean				
inward	4.6	8.9	12.9	14.9
outward	0.1	0.3	0.6	1.0
Asia				
inward	4.5	11.7	8.6	18.7
outward	0.3	0.4	0.9	2.5
West Asia				
inward	1.3	6.7	3.5	9.0
outward	0.2	0.4	0.7	2.5
South, East and South-East Asia				
inward	16.1	27.5	34.9	31.8
outward	0.4	0.7	1.5	2.6
All developing countries minus China				
inward	4.9	8.5	8.7	11.9
outward	0.3	0.9	1.8	3.6

Source: UNCTAD, based on the Division's FDI database and data provided by UNCTAD Secretariat.

[a]   Least developed countries include: Afghanistan, Angola, Bangladesh, Benin, Bhutan, Burkina Faso, Burundi,   Cambodia, Cape Verde, Central African Republic, Chad, Comoros, Djibouti, Equatorial Guinea, Eritrea, Ethiopia, Gambia, Guinea, Guinea-Bissau, Haiti, Kiribati, Lao People's Democratic Republic, Lesotho, Liberia, Madagascar, Malawi, Maldives, Mali, Mauritania, Mozambique, Myanmar, Nepal, Niger, Rwanda, Western Samoa, Sierra Leone, Solomon Islands, Somalia, Sudan, Togo, Tuvalu, Uganda, United Republic of Tanzania, Vanuatu, Yemen, Zaire and Zambia.

[b]   Oil exporting countries include: Algeria, Angola, Bahrain, Bolivia, Brunei Darussalam, Cameroon, Congo, Ecuador, Egypt, Gabon, Indonesia, Islamic Republic of Iran, Iraq, Kuwait, Libyan Arab Jamahiriya, Malaysia, Mexico, Nigeria, Oman, Qatar, Saudi Arabia, Trinidad and Tobago, Tunisia, United Arab Emirates and Venezuela.

Annex table 7. Cross-border merger and acquisition sales, 1988-1995
(Millions of dollars)

Economy	1988 Majority	1988 Total	1989 Majority	1989 Total	1990 Majority	1990 Total	1991 Majority	1991 Total	1992 Majority	1992 Total	1993 Majority	1993 Total	1994 Majority	1994 Total	1995 Majority	1995 Total
All Countries	**112544**	**112544**	**123042**	**123042**	**115371**	**159608**	**49730**	**86209**	**75382**	**122165**	**67281**	**163140**	**108732**	**196334**	**134629**	**229368**
Developed Countries	**110009**	**110006**	**120826**	**120829**	**107033**	**132664**	**46281**	**71183**	**61432**	**81305**	**54603**	**97391**	**95905**	**128531**	**120755**	**161310**
Western Europe	**30145**	**30142**	**50518**	**50521**	**48387**	**65678**	**24921**	**39421**	**44368**	**57241**	**27733**	**51623**	**41021**	**60836**	**49779**	**72822**
European Union	**29513**	**29513**	**47107**	**47107**	**43056**	**60082**	**23984**	**38163**	**42626**	**54900**	**27134**	**50965**	**38627**	**58283**	**48604**	**70781**
Austria	258	258	221	221	14	204	317	355	34	551	223	243	250	730	248	1003
Belgium	281	281	1383	1383	722	1095	1171	1699	271	803	160	2569	816	1653	1604	4971
Denmark	83	83	182	182	438	719	94	130	245	258	598	731	1860	1860	94	94
Finland	39	39	24	24	128	128	489	526	161	180	435	550	34	201	228	312
France	4175	4175	5431	5431	4494	6268	2618	4965	6679	8773	3754	5040	8858	12489	10453	12842
Germany	1338	1338	4667	4667	5994	7918	2666	4992	5271	7653	1541	5930	5987	9873	5329	6126
Greece	-	-	305	305	100	120	241	-	739	739	-	34	-	96	153	555
Ireland	550	550	173	173	459	537	144	264	229	229	1431	1588	72	274	213	845
Italy	3162	3162	1860	1860	3727	4730	1227	1971	3147	4636	2802	3215	3261	5311	2356	3136
Luxembourg	17	17	-	-	-	-	18	183	-	447	215	1254	83	503	-	40
Netherlands	2147	2147	2254	2254	1415	2029	1331	2462	5110	5976	4254	10814	1242	2348	2373	2534
Portugal	10	10	403	403	279	3580	99	232	519	834	196	414	243	855	157	300
Spain	918	918	1986	1986	3969	6240	3362	6635	3574	4390	1031	2777	2854	5153	880	1548
Sweden	310	310	953	953	1101	1508	1026	1499	1567	2685	3390	3772	2331	2468	974	1447
United Kingdom	16225	16225	27265	27265	20216	25006	9181	12250	15080	16746	7104	12034	10736	14469	23542	35028
Other Western Europe	**632**	**629**	**3411**	**3414**	**5331**	**5596**	**937**	**1258**	**1742**	**2341**	**599**	**658**	**2394**	**2553**	**1175**	**2041**
Liechtenstein																
Monaco					-	74										
Other Europe	275	272	2566	2569	231	231	-	-	-	-	-	-	-	-	-	-
Switzerland	1	1	755	755	4116	4242	679	707	120	411	455	476	1972	2131	825	1005
North America	**73221**	**73221**	**67243**	**67243**	**53130**	**59957**	**19679**	**26167**	**13895**	**19037**	**23556**	**40734**	**51670**	**62374**	**58074**	**70647**
Canada	3308	3308	10808	10808	5417	5745	1753	2277	3562	5248	3332	5573	5559	6446	9293	10625
United States	69913	69913	56435	56435	47713	54212	17926	23890	10333	13789	20224	35161	46111	55928	48781	60022
Other Developed	**6643**	**6643**	**3065**	**3065**	**5516**	**7029**	**1681**	**5595**	**3169**	**5027**	**3314**	**5034**	**3214**	**5321**	**12902**	**17841**
Australia	4728	4728	1566	1566	2137	3498	1020	2922	1015	2099	2027	3183	1460	2624	10197	12599
Israel	106	106	123	123	-	26	-	-	-	-	-	-	60	85	381	1270
Japan	95	95	133	133	23	101	84	1399	309	776	81	278	1302	1690	682	1574
New Zealand	1660	1660	1018	1018	3356	3388	577	1265	1844	2142	1182	1458	322	696	1367	1781
South Africa	54	54	225	225	-	16	-	9	1	10	24	115	70	226	275	617

/...

(Annex table 7, cont'd)

Economy	1988 Majority	1988 Total	1989 Majority	1989 Total	1990 Majority	1990 Total	1991 Majority	1991 Total	1992 Majority	1992 Total	1993 Majority	1993 Total	1994 Majority	1994 Total	1995 Majority	1995 Total
Developing Countries	**2301**	**2307**	**1956**	**1950**	**7631**	**17964**	**1084**	**9845**	**7615**	**28986**	**11660**	**53393**	**14077**	**72798**	**12752**	**63589**
Africa	-	-	**19**	**19**	-	-	-	-	**125**	**133**	**179**	**211**	**9**	**125**	-	-
North Africa	-	-	**19**	**19**	-	-	-	-	**125**	**133**	**179**	**211**	**9**	**125**	-	-
Egypt	-	-	-	-	-	-	-	-	125	133	179	211	9	125	-	-
Algeria	-	-	-	-	-	-	-	-	-	-	-	-	-	-	-	-
Libyan Arab Jamahiriya	-	-	-	-	-	-	-	-	-	-	-	-	-	-	-	-
Morocco	-	-	-	-	-	-	-	-	-	-	-	-	-	-	-	-
Tunisia	-	-	19	19	-	-	-	-	-	-	-	-	-	-	-	-
Other Africa	-	-	-	-	-	-	-	-	-	-	-	-	-	-	-	-
Gabon	-	-	-	-	-	-	-	-	-	-	-	-	-	-	-	-
Côte d'Ivoire	-	-	-	-	-	-	-	-	-	-	-	-	-	-	-	-
Mauritius	-	-	-	-	-	-	-	-	-	-	-	-	-	-	-	-
Latin America & the Caribbean	**1546**	**1546**	**106**	**106**	**6917**	**8506**	**797**	**3641**	**5285**	**10471**	**3244**	**12416**	**1957**	**12048**	**5813**	**10569**
South America	**773**	**773**	**13**	**13**	**5731**	**6131**	**500**	**2828**	**4643**	**8177**	**2661**	**7532**	**1340**	**7538**	**3582**	**6865**
Argentina	60	60	-	-	5266	5541	110	280	3917	4842	1097	2051	70	2181	1467	2271
Brazil	175	175	-	-	56	56	67	68	392	470	899	1041	8	1352	1385	2162
Chile	38	38	13	13	397	467	131	283	10	2295	81	276	817	1377	183	1865
Colombia	500	500	-	-	6	22	-	-	-	-	-	-	-	-	-	-
Peru	-	-	-	-	-	-	-	-	324	324	584	211	445	2628	547	567
Suriname	-	-	-	-	-	-	-	-	-	-	-	-	-	-	-	-
Venezuela	-	-	-	-	6	45	192	2197	-	246	-	3953	-	-	-	-
Other Latin America	**773**	**773**	**93**	**93**	**1186**	**2375**	**297**	**813**	**642**	**2294**	**583**	**4884**	**617**	**4510**	**2231**	**3704**
Bahamas	2	2	-	-	14	14	-	-	-	-	-	-	-	-	-	-
Bermuda	701	701	-	-	546	553	-	-	-	-	-	-	-	-	-	-
Others	60	60	-	-	-	44	-	-	112	1496	398	936	321	1798	1766	2691
Cayman Islands	5	5	-	-	-	-	-	-	-	-	-	-	-	-	-	-
Dominican Republic	-	-	-	-	-	-	-	-	-	-	-	-	-	-	-	-
Mexico	4	4	93	93	502	1680	297	813	530	798	185	3948	296	2712	465	1013
Panama	1	1	-	-	-	-	-	-	-	-	-	-	-	-	-	-
Puerto Rico	-	-	-	-	84	84	-	-	-	-	-	-	-	-	-	-
Trinidad & Tobago	-	-	-	-	-	-	-	-	-	-	-	-	-	-	-	-
Turks and Caicos Islands	-	-	-	-	-	-	-	-	-	-	-	-	-	-	-	-

/...

(Annex table 7, cont'd)

Economy	1988 Majority	1988 Total	1989 Majority	1989 Total	1990 Majority	1990 Total	1991 Majority	1991 Total	1992 Majority	1992 Total	1993 Majority	1993 Total	1994 Majority	1994 Total	1995 Majority	1995 Total
Asia	**803**	**803**	**1709**	**1709**	**678**	**9382**	**287**	**6204**	**1771**	**17576**	**4101**	**33248**	**3655**	**39773**	**2345**	**29450**
West Asia	**1**	**1**	**318**	**318**	**31**	**207**	**-**	**47**	**94**	**403**	**28**	**962**	**-**	**13**	**273**	**299**
Bahrain	-	-	-	-	-	-	-	-	-	-	-	-	-	-	-	-
Cyprus	-	-	-	-	-	-	-	-	-	-	-	-	-	-	-	-
Iran, Islamic Republic of	-	-	-	-	-	-	-	-	-	-	-	-	-	-	-	-
Kuwait	-	-	-	-	-	-	-	-	-	-	-	-	-	-	-	-
Lebanon	-	-	-	-	-	-	-	-	-	-	-	-	-	-	-	-
Oman	-	-	-	-	-	-	-	-	-	-	-	-	-	-	-	-
Qatar	-	-	-	-	-	-	-	-	-	-	-	-	-	-	-	-
Saudi Arabia	-	.	-	-	-	-	-	-	-	-	-	-	-	-	8	34
Turkey	-	-	318	318	31	207	-	47	94	403	28	962	-	13	265	265
United Arab Emirates	-	-	-	-	-	-	-	-	-	-	-	-	-	-	-	-
Others	1	1	-	-	-	-	-	-	-	-	-	-	-	-	-	-
Central Asia	**-**	**-**	**-**	**-**	**-**	**-**	**-**	**-**	**-**	**-**	**-**	**-**	**100**	**186**	**-**	**409**
Azerbaijan	-	-	-	-	-	-	-	-	-	-	-	-	-	-	-	-
Kazakhstan	-	-	-	-	-	-	-	-	-	-	-	-	100	186	-	409
Uzbekistan	-	-	-	-	-	-	-	-	-	-	-	-	-	-	-	-
South, East and South-East Asia	**802**	**802**	**1391**	**1391**	**647**	**9080**	**287**	**6157**	**1677**	**17165**	**4068**	**32281**	**3555**	**39574**	**2072**	**28742**
Brunei Darussalam	-	-	-	-	-	1	-	-	-	-	-	-	-	-	-	-
Cambodia	-	-	-	-	-	-	-	-	-	-	-	-	-	-	-	-
China	-	-	10	10	-	1937	16	2988	89	5201	287	15185	975	20146	637	12971
Hong Kong	527	527	772	772	190	1855	90	371	1253	3227	2880	7368	889	1768	455	878
India	20	20	-	-	-	5	52	213	13	261	105	2126	328	2880	148	3235
Indonesia	137	137	-	-	-	791	13	275	42	2288	286	1420	198	6508	125	2601
Korea, Republic of	11	11	6	6	-	223	-	712	31	122	34	60	-	827	32	167
Malaysia	-	-	203	203	71	841	57	1004	-	1197	-	541	216	396	16	821
Pakistan	-	-	-	-	-	-	-	-	-	-	-	-	-	-	-	-
Philippines	43	43	325	325	-	2576	55	123	89	577	31	678	577	1824	176	2966
Singapore	64	64	49	49	385	632	4	127	149	450	403	2073	305	1144	318	629
Taiwan Province of China	-	-	13	13	1	93	-	152	-	821	22	166	31	581	-	732
Thailand	-	-	13	13	-	116	-	145	-	2792	20	332	36	605	155	1703
Viet Nam	-	-	-	-	-	10	-	47	11	229	-	2332	-	2895	10	2039

/...

(Annex table 7, cont'd)

Economy	1988 Majority	1988 Total	1989 Majority	1989 Total	1990 Majority	1990 Total	1991 Majority	1991 Total	1992 Majority	1992 Total	1993 Majority	1993 Total	1994 Majority	1994 Total	1995 Majority	1995 Total
Other Asia	-	-	-	-	-	95	-	-	-	8	5	5	-	-	-	-
Developing Europe	-48	-42	122	116	36	76	-	-	434	806	4136	7518	8456	20852	4594	23570
Croatia	-	-	-	-	-	-	-	-	-	-	-	-	-	60	54	186
Malta	-	-	-	-	-	-	-	-	-	-	-	-	-	-	-	-
Others	-48	-42	122	116	36	76	-	-	434	806	4136	7518	8456	20792	4540	23384
Central and Eastern Europe	-	-	169	169	60	8353	557	2071	3690	5601	1100	14437	1820	4139	3272	15876
Bulgaria	-	-	-	-	-	-	-	-	-	-	-	-	-	-	-	-
Czech Republic	-	-	-	-	-	-	-	-	-	-	21	158	741	1008	113	2170
Czechoslovakia (former)	-	-	-	-	-	5159	-	-	750	1225	-	-	-	-	-	-
Hungary	-	-	169	169	60	559	145	533	370	903	299	1508	55	247	1484	1675
Latvia	-	-	-	-	-	-	-	-	-	-	-	-	-	-	-	-
Lithuania	-	-	-	-	-	-	-	-	-	-	-	-	-	-	-	-
Poland	-	-	-	-	-	521	398	746	2544	3018	730	1115	850	1168	1510	2144
Romania	-	-	-	-	-	1	14	58	-	-	-	-	-	-	-	-
Russian Federation	-	-	-	-	-	-	-	734	-	-	50	11656	174	1696	140	9730
Slovak Republic	-	-	-	-	-	-	-	-	-	-	-	-	-	-	-	-
Ukraine	-	-	-	-	-	-	-	-	-	-	-	-	-	20	25	157
USSR (former)	-	-	-	-	-	2113	-	-	26	455	-	-	-	-	-	-
Total unallocated	234	231	91	94	647	627	1808	3110	2645	6273	-82	-2081	-3070	-9134	-2150	-11407

Source: UNCTAD, based on data provided by KPMG.

Note: Majority refers to business combinations of which the investor acquires at least 50 per cent voting securities of the resulting business.

Annex table 8. Cross-border merger and acquisition purchases, 1988-1995

(Millions of dollars)

Economy	1988 Majority	1988 Total	1989 Majority	1989 Total	1990 Majority	1990 Total	1991 Majority	1991 Total	1992 Majority	1992 Total	1993 Majority	1993 Total	1994 Majority	1994 Total	1995 Majority	1995 Total
All Countries	**112544**	**112544**	**123042**	**123042**	**115371**	**159608**	**49730**	**86209**	**75382**	**122165**	**67281**	**163140**	**108732**	**196334**	**134629**	**229368**
Developed Countries	**108776**	**108776**	**115752**	**115752**	**111181**	**152189**	**47779**	**80320**	**58792**	**99372**	**57479**	**134195**	**100018**	**163367**	**126544**	**204975**
Western Europe	**74082**	**74082**	**67561**	**67561**	**71123**	**97427**	**34464**	**54214**	**35061**	**55403**	**35718**	**76808**	**65383**	**93012**	**65752**	**104068**
European Union	**64167**	**64167**	**61286**	**61286**	**65224**	**90959**	**31756**	**50691**	**30932**	**50216**	**34658**	**74389**	**51895**	**75717**	**60953**	**96155**
Austria	-	-	20	20	163	508	127	198	167	196	16	93	-	43	238	448
Belgium	817	817	2011	2011	307	659	129	629	898	1001	215	513	1253	1421	3688	7391
Denmark	223	223	476	476	541	641	353	1089	797	1063	429	613	221	706	381	1267
Finland	339	339	1362	1362	1130	1459	348	700	18	286	347	571	477	497	1133	1404
France	10739	10739	18767	18767	16841	22312	11374	16104	8857	14203	6018	9883	6141	11496	7806	12992
Germany	2868	2868	7587	7587	7037	15974	4679	7500	4105	6508	3263	7385	8521	13188	15316	21190
Greece	-	-	100	100	-	-	-	5	6	6	660	678	67	68	-	-
Ireland	1598	1598	1024	1024	773	861	483	602	427	526	576	591	2321	2433	966	1346
Italy	1147	1147	1788	1788	3673	5600	2320	4999	6034	7641	560	5891	1185	2379	2817	3640
Luxembourg	126	126	-	-	759	765	931	942	488	792	1683	2112	500	506	610	623
Netherlands	1634	1634	3707	3707	2287	4165	3754	6672	1396	6273	4696	12003	2485	4967	5419	11276
Portugal	-	-	16	16	-	-	165	165	309	309	11	162	218	242	227	247
Spain	3	3	271	271	2177	2607	353	689	675	1159	247	1392	455	2346	1254	2801
Sweden	2195	2195	1836	1836	9433	9842	839	2310	690	1090	1702	3385	1033	2068	2933	7107
United Kingdom	42478	42478	22321	22321	20103	25566	5901	8087	6065	9163	14235	29117	27018	33357	18165	24423
Other Western Europe	**9915**	**9915**	**6275**	**6275**	**5899**	**6468**	**2708**	**3523**	**4129**	**5187**	**1060**	**2419**	**13488**	**17295**	**4799**	**7913**
Liechtenstein	320	320	161	161	-	15	53	53	-	-	-	-	-	-	-	-
Monaco	-	-	-	-	-	-	-	-	-	-	-	-	-	-	-	-
Norway	687	687	570	570	1233	1472	84	228	319	1140	197	360	482	1022	174	2203
Switzerland	8741	8741	5116	5116	4666	4981	2356	3002	3809	4039	831	1870	13006	16273	4625	5710
Other Europe	167	167	428	428	-	-	215	240	1	8	32	189	-	-	-	-
North America	**17305**	**17305**	**26447**	**26447**	**19969**	**26233**	**8460**	**15697**	**16064**	**26360**	**18879**	**44257**	**28700**	**52017**	**50651**	**78286**
Canada	11215	11215	4322	4322	3955	4543	1349	2498	1679	3562	4254	6604	4185	8570	12780	14602
United States	6090	6090	22125	22125	16014	21690	7111	13199	14385	22798	14625	37653	24515	43447	37871	63684
Other Developed	**17389**	**17389**	**21744**	**21744**	**20089**	**28529**	**4855**	**10409**	**7667**	**17609**	**2882**	**13130**	**5935**	**18338**	**10141**	**22621**
Australia	5425	5425	6490	6490	1841	2084	819	1039	1594	2733	1145	2940	1400	3856	4807	5410
Israel	-	-	-	-	32	41	4	24	35	35	321	321	128	142	85	102
Japan	11117	11117	14653	14653	17341	25132	3696	8980	4187	12525	437	7193	1145	10480	4478	15907
New Zealand	764	764	593	593	664	974	128	141	429	603	328	807	-	79	409	764.
South Africa	83	83	8	8	211	298	208	225	1422	1713	651	1869	3262	3781	362	438

/..

(Annex table 8, cont'd)

Economy	1988 Majority	1988 Total	1989 Majority	1989 Total	1990 Majority	1990 Total	1991 Majority	1991 Total	1992 Majority	1992 Total	1993 Majority	1993 Total	1994 Majority	1994 Total	1995 Majority	1995 Total
Developing Countries	**2915**	**2915**	**4796**	**4796**	**4436**	**7486**	**1601**	**5159**	**14576**	**21910**	**7496**	**25848**	**8714**	**32065**	**8084**	**24073**
Africa	-	-	**40**	**40**	**140**	**140**	**104**	**155**	-	**306**	**41**	**56**	-	-	-	-
North Africa	-	-	**40**	**40**	**140**	**140**	-	**51**	-	**306**	**41**	**56**	-	-	-	-
Algeria	-	-	-	-	-	-	-	-	-	-	-	-	-	-	-	-
Egypt	-	-	40	40	-	-	-	51	-	-	-	-	-	-	-	-
Libyan Arab Jamahiriya	-	-	-	-	140	140	-	-	-	306	-	-	-	-	-	-
Morocco	-	-	-	-	-	-	-	-	-	-	5	5	-	-	-	-
Tunisia	-	-	-	-	-	-	-	-	-	-	36	51	-	-	-	-
Other Africa	-	-	-	-	-	-	**104**	**104**	-	-	-	-	-	-	-	-
Gabon	-	-	-	-	-	-	104	104	-	-	-	-	-	-	-	-
Côte d'Ivoire	-	-	-	-	-	-	-	-	-	-	-	-	-	-	-	-
Mauritius	-	-	-	-	-	-	-	-	-	-	-	-	-	-	-	-
Latin America and the Caribbean	**103**	**103**	**1600**	**1600**	**3**	**376**	**128**	**727**	**4541**	**5060**	**2155**	**2878**	**2062**	**6901**	**2009**	**2520**
South America	**7**	**7**	**719**	**719**	**0.0**	**0.0**	**16**	**186**	**184**	**531**	**1099**	**1343**	**163**	**3380**	**1616**	**1855**
Argentina	-	-	-	-	-	-	-	-	-	-	57	57	42	97	809	834
Brazil	-	-	44	44	-	-	16	16	2	29	433	446	105	3032	168	276
Chile	-	-	-	-	-	-	-	170	182	435	609	609	16	251	634	740
Columbia	-	-	-	-	-	-	-	-	-	-	-	-	-	-	-	-
Peru	-	-	-	-	-	-	-	-	-	-	-	-	-	-	5	5
Venezuela	7	7	675	675	-	-	-	-	-	67	-	228	-	-	5	5
Other Latin America	**96**	**96**	**881**	**881**	**3**	**376**	**112**	**541**	**4357**	**4529**	**1056**	**1535**	**1899**	**3521**	**393**	**665**
Bahamas	-	-	-	-	3	4	-	-	-	-	-	-	-	-	-	-
Bermuda	-	-	-	-	-	-	107	107	1500	1500	697	922	-	-	-	-
Cayman Islands	12	12	-	-	-	-	-	-	-	-	30	51	-	-	-	-
Dominican Republic	-	-	-	-	-	-	-	-	-	-	-	-	-	-	-	-
Mexico	-	-	881	881	-	-	-	79	2827	2999	329	559	1784	3064	95	170
Others	-	-	-	-	-	-	-	-	-	-	-	-	-	-	-	-
Panama	84	84	-	-	-	372	5	355	30	30	-	-	-	-	-	-
Puerto Rico	-	-	-	-	-	-	-	-	-	-	-	-	-	-	-	-
Suriname	-	-	-	-	-	-	-	-	-	-	-	3	-	-	-	-
Trinidad & Tobago	-	-	-	-	-	-	-	-	-	-	-	-	-	-	-	-

/...

(Annex table 8, cont'd)

Economy	1988 Majority	1988 Total	1989 Majority	1989 Total	1990 Majority	1990 Total	1991 Majority	1991 Total	1992 Majority	1992 Total	1993 Majority	1993 Total	1994 Majority	1994 Total	1995 Majority	1995 Total
Turks and Caicos Islands	-	8	-	-	-	6	-	-	-	-	-	-	-	-	-	-
Asia	**2812**	**2812**	**3156**	**3156**	**4293**	**6970**	**1369**	**4277**	**10035**	**16544**	**5295**	**22909**	**5974**	**22015**	**5454**	**20274**
West Asia	**1077**	**1077**	**501**	**501**	**2119**	**2178**	**563**	**1777**	**545**	**483**	**1143**	**2305**	**1258**	**2056**	**325**	**1542**
Turkey	-	-	-	-	8	17	29	-	74	-	-	9	-	-	-	7
Cyprus	-	-	-	-	-	-	34	34	-	12	-	10	-	-	-	-
Bahrain	-	-	450	450	1500	1500	-	-	402	402	745	745	-	-	-	-
Iran, Islamic Republic of	-	-	-	-	-	-	-	-	-	-	-	-	-	-	-	-
Kuwait	277	277	51	51	300	350	500	549	-	-	-	-	-	-	-	-
Lebanon	-	-	-	-	-	-	-	-	-	-	19	19	-	-	-	-
Oman	-	-	-	-	-	-	-	-	-	-	-	-	-	-	-	-
Qatar	-	-	-	-	-	-	-	-	-	-	-	-	-	-	-	-
Saudi Arabia	800	800	-	-	311	311	-	1190	32	32	177	1320	1258	2056	325	1535
Others	-	-	-	-	-	-	-	-	37	37	-	-	-	-	-	-
Central Asia	-	-	-	-	-	-	-	-	-	-	-	715	-	-	-	**6**
Azerbaijan	-	-	-	-	-	-	-	-	-	-	-	700	-	-	-	-
Kazakhstan	-	-	-	-	-	-	-	-	-	-	-	6	-	-	-	6
Uzbekistan	-	-	-	-	-	-	-	-	-	-	-	9	-	-	-	-
South, East and South-East Asia	**1735**	**1735**	**2655**	**2655**	**2174**	**4792**	**806**	**2478**	**9490**	**16061**	**4152**	**19868**	**4716**	**19959**	**5129**	**18726**
Brunei Darussalam	-	-	-	-	-	-	-	4	-	-	202	202	-	-	-	-
Cambodia	-	-	-	-	-	-	-	-	-	-	-	-	-	-	-	-
China	91	91	100	100	-	1336	-	102	786	1688	1082	5450	184	1638	54	198
Hong Kong	1304	1304	1137	1137	756	1132	426	852	7885	9558	2022	8388	719	3415	1257	3875
India	-	-	-	-	-	-	270	270	-	421	-	-	16	620	154	154
Indonesia	260	260	-	-	-	187	57	57	31	106	172	247	390	520	142	603
Korea, Republic of	-	-	422	422	75	475	13	374	156	778	34	830	606	3555	1946	5768
Malaysia	-	-	181	181	138	160	-	235	73	143	301	1219	1734	7017	247	1182
Philippines	-	-	-	-	-	-	11	18	43	50	-	-	-	433	-	11
Singapore	-	-	119	119	143	243	29	416	203	553	230	2117	820	1811	939	2634
Taiwan Province of China	-	-	427	427	1062	1259	-	136	233	1001	-	882	169	762	208	723
Thailand	80	80	269	269	-	-	-	14	80	1638	109	533	78	184	182	3576

/...

(Annex table 8, cont'd)

Economy	1988 Majority	1988 Total	1989 Majority	1989 Total	1990 Majority	1990 Total	1991 Majority	1991 Total	1992 Majority	1992 Total	1993 Majority	1993 Total	1994 Majority	1994 Total	1995 Majority	1995 Total
Viet Nam	-	-	-	-	-	-	-	-	-	19	-	-	-	4	-	2
Pakistan	-	-	-	-	-	-	-	-	-	106	-	-	-	-	-	-
Other Asia	-	-	-	-	-	-	-	22	-	-	-	21	-	-	-	-
Developing Europe	-	-	-	-	-	-	-	-	-	-	5	5	678	3149	621	1279
Croatia	-	-	-	-	-	-	-	-	-	-	-	-	-	-	-	-
Malta	-	-	-	-	-	-	-	-	-	-	5	5	-	-	-	-
Others	-	-	-	-	-	-	-	-	-	-	-	-	678	3149	621	1279
Central and Eastern Europe	-	-	-	-	-	-	-	106	206	206	30	295	-	917	5	426
Bulgaria	-	-	-	-	-	-	-	-	-	-	-	-	-	-	-	-
Czech Republic	-	-	-	-	-	-	-	-	-	-	-	-	-	-	-	-
Czechoslovakia (former)	-	-	-	-	-	-	-	-	-	-	-	-	-	-	-	-
Hungary	-	-	-	-	-	-	-	-	-	-	-	-	-	-	-	66
Latvia	-	-	-	-	-	-	-	-	-	-	17	17	-	-	-	-
Lithuania	-	-	-	-	-	-	-	53	-	-	-	-	-	-	-	-
Poland	-	-	-	-	-	-	-	-	-	-	-	-	-	-	-	-
Romania	-	-	-	-	-	-	-	-	-	-	-	-	-	-	-	-
Russian Federation	-	-	-	-	-	-	-	53	-	-	-	265	-	917	5	335
Slovak Republic	-	-	-	-	-	-	-	-	-	-	13	13	-	-	-	-
Ukraine	-	-	-	-	-	-	-	-	-	-	-	-	-	-	-	25
USSR (former)	-	-	-	-	-	-	-	-	206	206	-	-	-	-	-	-
Total unallocated	853	853	2494	2494	-246	-63	350	624	2010	879	2276	2802	-	-15	-4	-106

Source: UNCTAD, based on data provided by KPMG.

Note: Majority refers to business combinations of which the investor acquires at least 50 per cent voting securities of the resulting business.

Annex table 9. Cross-border mergers and acquisitions by industry, 1988-1995

(Millions of dollars)

Economy	1988 Majority	1988 Total	1989 Majority	1989 Total	1990 Majority	1990 Total	1991 Majority	1991 Total	1992 Majority	1992 Total	1993 Majority	1993 Total	1994 Majority	1994 Total	1995 Majority	1995 Total
All industries	112373	112373	121531	121531	114550	158189	53189	85569	70631	121277	68573	163140	108732	196334	134629	229368
Primary sector	7386	7386	8740	8740	6859	13753	5449	7871	2962	15959	5269	35674	7754	28514	12183	38192
Oil and gas	7216	7216	8627	8627	5367	12249	5367	7570	2406	15694	5055	35379	5849	26595	12126	37767
Agriculture, forestry and fishery	170	170	113	113	1492	1504	82	301	556	265	214	295	1905	1919	57	425
Secondary sector	52684	52684	61058	61058	49388	71872	25612	38325	36037	51219	32625	56528	58794	87181	54624	83555
Food, drink and tobacco	19786	19786	11098	11098	9873	13528	3640	5156	12339	13541	6556	9557	11373	16092	13172	15526
Textiles	1453	1453	1276	1276	867	1071	1824	2530	513	715	906	1614	1107	1916	663	1388
Paper and board	1997	1997	5970	5970	7056	7625	1681	3440	1948	3706	982	1560	4454	5019	4166	4889
Printing and publishing	9075	9075	5351	5351	756	1423	1299	2785	417	477	911	1922	3154	5840	3096	3414
Chemical and pharmaceuticals	3326	3326	12596	12596	13000	15474	5934	7440	5284	7788	11617	21036	18122	23435	17148	25074
Rubber and plastics	3179	3179	3002	3002	845	1248	1305	1403	654	888	595	813	2205	3229	2065	2757
Vehicle manufacturing	1672	1672	4749	4749	2415	12309	1786	2797	3134	4879	786	2614	2994	6986	2338	6796
Electrical and electronics	6716	6716	11817	11817	9522	11421	5803	8285	7309	10481	4223	6605	6300	10127	6257	13761
Extractive industries	1324	1324	2807	2807	3304	5818	1499	3087	2637	6828	5483	9811	5854	10611	4376	8297
Timber and furniture	228	228	945	945	335	389	12	217	454	470	9	404	709	1180	180	231
Scrap and waste	14	14	-	-	-	66	48	48	90	101	9	9	17	82	5	102
Precision engineering	2723	2723	629	629	1060	1140	733	1074	449	505	326	350	1623	1752	1123	1237
Other manufacturing	1191	1191	818	818	355	360	48	63	809	840	222	233	882	912	35	83
Tertiary sector	52303	52303	51733	51733	58303	72564	22128	39373	31632	54099	30679	70938	42184	80639	67822	107621
Construction	6818	6818	4488	4488	5730	6570	1546	2360	5888	11163	1200	3644	2829	12245	4184	8854
Distribution	1267	1267	3190	3190	3015	3593	1394	1674	1790	1895	1588	2261	4437	5340	4159	4560
Transport	1748	1748	1059	1059	2746	3868	1482	2330	971	4317	1426	4146	2194	7878	1280	4952
Retailing	9180	9180	1956	1956	4116	4706	1333	1729	2389	2665	3227	3472	3002	3614	1127	1856
Bank and finance	3782	3782	7279	7279	5784	9392	3247	6372	11471	13630	5726	10302	5906	8103	17429	19903
Insurance	8551	8551	7351	7351	8133	9909	5106	10267	1151	3932	4478	5920	8598	10400	2233	2638
Business services	1599	1599	2385	2385	1537	2099	1407	2726	809	1113	1374	2011	3010	3457	7317	8891
Real estate	1580	1580	4707	4707	2091	2832	525	1005	1908	3165	2223	8180	2352	4596	2852	5579
Engineering	10911	10911	4915	4915	2996	3769	2500	2841	2035	3372	2960	3373	4483	5355	9304	10904
Utilities	349	349	576	576	8232	10947	338	3537	211	2596	228	17905	386	8993	3282	18731
Hotels and catering	4350	4350	5607	5607	4272	4624	1407	1223	809	2909	1925	3001	2531	3826	4349	5062
Leasing	434	434	1851	1851	186	335	480	565	193	295	1612	1622	825	833	167	176
Media	670	670	3708	3708	8270	8525	733	2002	1245	2098	2008	3479	1123	4830	7978	12878
Advertising	592	592	1746	1746	535	664	39	80	39	79	127	129	12	18	21	23
Personal services	37	37	33	33	101	101	146	157	16	29	99	99	152	349	685	687
Healthcare	-	-	474	474	296	312	92	92	63	66	173	173	59	262	884	1189
Repairs	-	-	20	20	13	13	9	9	-	-	-	6	9	10	-	-
Other services	435	435	388	388	250	305	344	404	644	775	305	1215	276	530	571	738

Source: UNCTAD, based on data provided by KPMG.

Note: Majority refers to business combinations of which the investor acquires at least 50 per cent voting securities of the resulting business.

Annex table 10. Outward FDI in infrastructure-related industries, various years

(Millions of dollars and percentage)

Economy	Infrastructure-related industries				Infrastructure-related industries as share of all industries
	Construction	Communications	Transport and storage	Total	
Developed countries					
		Flows (annual average)			
Australia					
1991 - 93	34.6	...	- 120.2	- 85.6	-13.1
Denmark					
1990 - 93	4.8	...	36.7	41.5	2.5
Finland					
1993 - 95	- 2.9	...	60.2	57.4	...
France					
1992 - 94	302.7	38.6	172.3	513.6	3.7
Germany					
1994 - 95	156.0	412.3	204.8	773.1	3.1
Italy					
1992- 94	42.2	216.9	45.7	304.9	5.7
Japan					
1992 - 94	404.0	...	1 941.0	2 345.0	6.7
Netherlands					
1991 - 93	47.1	100.1	249.5	396.7	3.2
Norway					
1988 - 90	30.6	...	79.9	110.4	9.0
Portugal					
1991 - 94	2.5	5.0	7.0a	14.5	2.8
Spain					
1991 - 93	20.2	...	166.6	186.8	7.7
Sweden					
1986 - 88	77.9	...	187.0	265.0	6.9
United Kingdom					
1991 - 94	103.6	...	314.0	417.6	1.9
United States					
1992 - 94	31.3	2 038.7b	587.3	2 657.3	4.9
Total above	1 254.9	2 811.5	3 931.8	7 998.3	4.5
		Stocks			
Australia					
1980	54.3	...	116.9	171.2	7.6
1992	807.7	...	609.4	1 417.1	5.7
Austria					
1981	...	...	0.3	0.3	-
1993	376.0	...	42.7	418.8	5.5
Canada					
1984	4 473.1	2 418.2	1 653.1	8 544.4	20.4
1993	3 278.7	8 083.1	3 569.5	14 931.3	17.3
Denmark					
1982	...	...	- 1.1	- 1.1	-0.2
1990	...	...	652.7	652.7	7.5
Finland					
1980	15.1	...	2.1	17.2	2.3
1994	- 54.4	...	335.0	280.6	...

/...

(Annex table 10, cont'd)

Economy	Infrastructure-related industries				Infrastructure-related industries as share of all industries
	Construction	Communications	Transport and storage	Total	
France					
1992	2 145.3	78.3	1 812.6	4 036.1	15.1
Germany					
1985	888.7	...	776.4	1 665.1	2.2
1993	989.4	...	1 974.7	2 964.1	1.6
Iceland					
1993	...	...	6.1	6.1	5.5
Italy					
1980	...	...	26.9	26.9	0.4
1990	...	...	465.4	465.4	0.8
Japan					
1985	893.0	...	6 622.0	7 515.0	8.1
1993	3 627.0	...	23 809.0	27 436.0	6.5
Netherlands					
1985	385.3	...	574.0	959.2	2.0
1992	600.8	...	2 127.8	2 728.6	2.2
Norway					
1988	60.9	...	426.2	487.1	12.2
1993	85.4	...	1 000.5	1 085.9	8.5
Portugal					
1988	0.7	...	22.7	23.4	11.8
Spain					
1983	64.8	...	23.5	88.3	6.1
1989	176.8	...	134.1	310.9	3.4
Sweden					
1988	...	...	649.7	649.7	2.3
1991	...	...	198.9	198.9	0.4
Switzerland					
1993	...	1 322.1	968.6	2 290.6	2.6
United Kingdom					
1987	2 891.5	...	3 363.1	6 254.6	4.1
1994	2 154.7	...	4 646.9	6 801.6	2.5
United States					
1985	1 331.0	618.0	1 679.0	3 628.0	1.6
1994	767.0	9 082b	4 481.0	14 330.0	2.3
Total above					
first row	11 058.3	3 036.2	15 934.7	30 029.1	4.4
second row	14 954.5	18 565.4	46 835.0	80 354.9	4.0

Latin America and the Caribbean

	Flows (annual average)				
Brazil					
1988 - 90	75.0	...	...	75.0	27.9
Chile					
1995	13.5	...	40.7a	54.2	12.5
Colombia					
1988 - 90	0.2	7.7	...	7.9	35.0
Total above	88.7	7.7	40.7	137.1	18.9

/...

(Annex table 10, cont'd)

Economy	Infrastructure-related industries				Infrastructure-related industries as share of all industries
	Construction	Communications	Transport and storage	Total	
Stocks					
Chile					
1995	91.3	...	408.6a	499.9	16.1
Colombia					
1980	0.1	1.7	...	1.8	1.3
1990	0.7	15.3	...	16.0	4.0
Total above					
first row	0.1	1.7	...	1.8	1.3
second row	92.0	15.3	408.6	515.9	14.7

South, East and South-East Asia

Flows (annual average)					
China					
1985 - 87	3.2	...	2.2	5.4	4.1
Malaysia					
1986 - 88	0.3	...	0.3	0.1	
Philippines					
1987 - 89	-	-	15.7	15.7	42.9
Korea, Republic of					
1986 - 1988	0.1	...	0.2	0.3	0.2
Taiwan Province of China					
1992 - 94	18.2	...	52.7	70.9	0.1
Thailand					
1993 - 95	10.1	...	16.8	26.9	6.5
Total above					
1985 - 89	31.9	-	87.6	119.4	0.1
Stocks					
China					
1987	12.5	...	17.2	29.7	6.4
India					
1986	1.1	...	0.0	1.1	1.2.
Malaysia					
1988	- 24.0	...	...	- 24.0	-1.6
Korea, Republic of					
1988	36.2	...	3.2	39.4	3.5
Taiwan Province of China					
1994	117.8	...	189.8	307.6	-
Thailand					
1989	0.3	...	9.2	9.5	3.7
Total above					
1986 - 94	143.8	-	219.4	363.2	0.1

/...

(Annex table 10, cont'd)

| Economy | Infrastructure-related industries | | | | Infrastructure-related industries as share of all industries |
	Construction	Communications	Transport and storage	Total	
West Asia					
		Flows (annual average)			
Cyprus					
1993 - 95	2.6	...	0.4	3.0	22.2
Israel					
1992 - 94	49.7	...	7.3	57.0	8.7
Total above					
1992 - 95	52.3	...	7.7	60.0	9.0
		Stocks			
Israel					
1994	263.2	56.0	...	319.2	11.0
Total above	263.2	56.0	...	319.2	11.0

Source: UNCTAD, FDI database.

[a]   Including communications.
[b]   Including public utilities.

Annex table 11. Inward FDI in infrastructure-related industries, various years

(Millions of dollars and percentage)

Economy	Infrastructure-related industries				Infrastructure-related industries as share of all industries
	Construction	Communications	Transport and storage	Total	
Developed countries					
		Flows (annual average)			
Australia					
1991 - 93	30.6	146.3	178.3	355.2	7.6
Denmark					
1990 - 93	95.8	...	58.4	154.2	10.7
Finland					
1993 - 94	1.8	...	33.8	35.7	...
France					
1992 - 95	33.7	35.1	114.5	183.4	1.4
Germany					
1995	153.2	1 369.6b	565.5	2 088.2	21.3
Greece					
1987 - 89	4.4	...	3.7	8.1	1.1
Italy					
1992- 94	13.0	19.6	38.1a	70.6	2.6
Japan					
1992 - 94	0.5	37.5	31.0	69.0	1.9
Netherlands					
1991 - 93	69.0	119.7	130.7	319.4	5.4
New Zealand					
1987 - 89	- 0.6	...	1.3	0.6	0.2
Norway					
1988 - 90	- 37.2	...	41.4	4.2	0.5
Portugal					
1991 - 94	87.4	3.0	25.9a	116.3	7.3
South Africa					
1993-94	73.6	-	29.5	103.1	7.7
Spain					
1991 - 93	97.4	...	88.1	185.5	2.2
Sweden					
1986 - 88	- 0.4	...	7.2	6.8	1.0
United Kingdom					
1991 - 94	- 12.3	...	440.8	428.5	3.1
United States					
1992 - 94	- 69.0	2 330.5b	- 147.5	2 114.0	5.0
Total above	541.0	4 061.3	1 640.7	6 242.9	5.6
		Stocks			
Australia					
1980	171.2	...	159.4	330.6	2.5
1992	606.0	...	692.7	1 298.7	1.8
Austria					
1981	...	...	33.4	33.4	1.2
1993	152.2	...	151.8	304.0	2.7
Canada					
1984	3 999.3	...	990.2	4 989.5	6.9
1993	4 058.2	...	2 995.5	7 053.6	6.7

/...

(Annex table 11, cont'd)

Economy	Construction	Infrastructure-related industries Communications	Transport and storage	Total	Infrastructure-related industries as share of all industries
Denmark					
1982	...	...	36.0	36.0	7.8
1990	...	...	1 065.3	1 065.3	22.8
Finland					
1994	58.4	...	205.8	264.2	...
France					
1992	345.0	36.3	617.5	998.8	1.0
Germany					
1985	138.3	...	504.8	643.2	1.4
1993	618.1	...	1 151.6	1 769.7	1.5
Greece					
1984	...	...	630.6	630.6	12.5
Iceland					
1993	3.1	...	...	3.1	2.7
Ireland					
1986	37.9	...	39.0	77.0	1.7
Italy					
1980	...	...	127.9	127.9	1.4
1990	...	...	1 077.7	1 077.7	1.9
Japan					
1985	36.0	3.0	30.0	69.0	1.1
1993	114.0	323.0	227.0	664.0	2.2
Netherlands					
1985	248.6	...	405.1	653.7	2.6
1992	649.4	...	1 651.0	2 300.3	2.8
New Zealand					
1985	8.8	...	- 61.5	- 52.7	- 2.6
Norway					
1988	167.4	...	106.5	274.0	3.2
1993	388.3	...	382.5	770.8	5.6
Portugal					
1988	49.6	...	30.3	79.9	4.0
South Africa					
1994	158.8	-	131.9	290.7	2.9
Spain					
1983	69.8	...	59.9	129.7	2.5
1989	316.3	...	469.6	785.9	1.9
Sweden					
1988	...	...	162.4	162.4	1.6
1991	...	...	723.4	723.4	4.0
United Kingdom					
1987	280.7	...	338.7	619.5	0.6
1994	1 096.9	...	2 960.9	4 057.8	2.1
United States					
1985	4 037.0	383.0	1 459.0	5 879.0	3.2
1994	1 021.0	1 279.0b	2 405.0	4 705.0	1.1
Total above					
first row	9 244.7	386.0	5 051.9	14 682.6	2.9
second row	9 585.6	1 638.3	16 909.1	28 132.9	2.2

/...

(Annex table 11, cont'd)

| Economy | Infrastructure-related industries | | | | Infrastructure-related industries as share of all industries |
	Construction	Communications	Transport and storage	Total	
Africa					
Flows (annual average)					
Algeria					
1995	...	1.3	-	1.3	0.9
Cape Verde					
1993-95	0.1	7.1	-	7.1	56.3
Ethiopia					
1992-95	11.6	-	-	11.6	21.8
Kenya					
1992-95	0.9	0.5	-	1.4	2.3
Morocco					
1990-93	58.0	-	-	58.0	13.7
Zambia					
1993-95	5.5	-	25.9	31.4	14.1
Zimbabwe					
1993-95	0.1	-	-	0.1	-
Total above	76.2	8.9	25.9	111.0	17.1
Stocks					
Algeria					
1995	453.8	...	4.0	457.8	57.1
Botswana					
1993	30.3	-	4.7	35.0	3.7
Cape Verde					
1995	0.2	22.4	2.5	25.1	45.7
Egypt					
1995	565.2	...	-	565.2	4.2
Nigeria					
1992	71.6	...	19.9a	91.5	8.8
Total above	1 121.0	22.4	31.1	1 174.6	7.3
Latin America and the Caribbean					
Flows (annual average)					
Argentina					
1985 - 89	0.2	6.9	...	7.1	3.1
Bolivia					
1988 -89	-	-	0.1	0.1	0.2
Brazil					
1988 - 90	75.0	...	...	75.0	38.2
Chile					
1988 - 90	4.7	94.5	2.5	101.7	9.8
Colombia					
1988 - 90	8.0	0.9	...	9.0	5.3
Dominican Rep.					
1988 - 89	...	...	47.3	47.3	88.6
Ecuador					
1988 - 90	0.3	...	0.2	0.5	1.0

/...

(Annex table 11, cont'd)

	Infrastructure-related industries				Infrastructure-related industries as share of all industries
Economy	Construction	Communications	Transport and storage	Total	
Mexico					
1991 - 93	73.4	438.6	7.3	519.2	4.7
Panama					
1988 - 89	...	...	14.8	14.8	- 69.4
Paraguay					
1990	...	...	0.2	0.2	0.5
Peru					
1988 - 90	0.4	...	-	0.4	2.4
Uruguay					
1987 - 89	1.3	...	-	1.3	2.8
Venezuela					
1988 - 90	11.9	...	4.6	16.6	2.4
Total above	175.2	540.9	77.0	793.0	5.9
		Stocks			
Argentina					
1980	87.6	29.0	4.2	120.8	2.1
1992	...	...	46.0a	46.0	0.3
Bolivia					
1980	0.6	0.1	0.3	1.0	0.2
1990	0.9	0.1	0.5	1.5	0.2
Brazil					
1980	...	...	35.9	35.9	0.2
1990	...	...	60.3	60.3	0.2
Chile					
1980	21.0	0.5	5.5	27.0	3.0
1990	120.5	286.2	25.6	432.3	7.0
Colombia					
1980	3.3	32.1	...	35.4	3.3
1990	22.7	33.8	...	56.5	1.6
Dominican Rep.					
1980	...	...	16.2	16.2	6.8
1990	...	...	209.9	209.9	36.7
Ecuador					
1980	52.7	...	8.2	60.9	8.7
1990	66.7	...	19.2	85.9	6.5
El Salvador					
1980	0.6	0.1	1.3	2.0	1.3
1990	0.6	0.1	1.6	2.3	1.1
Guatemala					
1985	12.8	-	0.6	13.4	18.9
Jamaica					
1984	10.3	...	...	10.3	31.1
Panama					
1980	...	...	18.1	18.1	4.7
1989	...	...	128.5	128.5	26.1
Paraguay					
1988	0.1	-	17.2	17.3	6.9

/...

(Annex table 11, cont'd)

Economy	Infrastructure-related industries				Infrastructure-related industries as share of all industries
	Construction	Communications	Transport and storage	Total	
Peru					
1980	0.7	-	4.3	5.0	0.6
1990	2.5	-	6.6	9.1	0.7
Uruguay					
1986	2.0	...	0.4	2.4	0.8
1989	6.1	...	0.3	6.4	1.4
Venezuela					
1980	53.9	...	22.6	76.5	5.1
1990	62.4	...	14.0	76.4	2.0
Total above					
first row	245.6	61.8	134.8	442.2	1.5
second row	282.4	320.2	512.5	1 115.1	1.6

South, East and South-East Asia

Flows (annual average)

Economy	Construction	Communications	Transport and storage	Total	Share
Bangladesh					
1986 - 88	...	...	1.0a	1.0	0.5
Indonesia					
1992 - 94	71.5	...	81.6	153.1	1.1
Korea, Republic of					
1992 - 94	11.3	...	4.2	15.5	1.4
Nepal					
1994	0.8	...	2.6	3.4	3.4
Pakistan					
1991 - 93	71.2	...	- 1.0	70.1	20.5
Singapore					
1991 - 93	1 143.6	...	...	1 143.6	20.8
Taiwan Province of China					
1992 - 94	10.6	...	29.9	40.6	-
Thailand					
1993 - 95	154.0	...	...	154.0	9.3
Viet Nam					
1994	46.3	636.7	...	683.0	7.1
Total above	1 509.3	636.7	118.3	2 264.3	7.0

Stocks

Economy	Construction	Communications	Transport and storage	Total	Share
Bangladesh					
1980	2.0	...	3.1a	5.1	0.4
Hong Kong					
1986	...	...	6.0	6.0	-
1993	...	...	1 446.0	1 446.0	3.5
Indonesia					
1995	897.9	...	2 630.9	3 528.8	3.3
Korea, Republic of					
1994	90.8	...	59.1	149.9	1.2
Nepal					
1994	2.6	...	10.3	12.9	2.4

/...

(Annex table 11, cont'd)

Economy	Infrastructure-related industries				Infrastructure-related industries as share of all industries
	Construction	Communications	Transport and storage	Total	
Pakistan					
1980	6.5	...	114.6	121.1	17.6
1993	169.1	...	48.3	217.4	8.4
Papua New Guinea					
1992	...	...	6.1	6.1	0.4
Taiwan Province of China					
1994	93.1	...	322.0	415.1	-
Singapore					
1988	70.7	...	440.0	510.7	4.2
1993	3 167.8	...	904.7	4 072.5	8.4
Viet Nam					
1994	46.3	636.7	...	683.0	7.1
Total above					
first row	79.2	...	563.6	642.9	1.9
second row	4 467.7	636.7	5 421.3	10 531.8	4.8

West Asia

			Flows (annual average)		
Cyprus					
1992 - 94	...	...	0.2	0.2	0.6
Jordan					
1992 - 94	0.1	...	...	0.1	0.6
Oman					
1993 - 95	1.4	...	...	1.4	0.4
Total above					
1992 - 95	1.5	...	0.2	1.7	0.4

			Stocks		
Saudi Arabia					
1993	...	...	1.3	1.3	-

Central and Eastern Europe

			Flows (annual average)		
Czech Republic					
1992 - 94	130.1	...	...	130.1	15.7
Estonia					
1993 - 94	0.3	...	2.9	3.2	0.4
Hungary					
1993 - 94	106.5	...	283.9	390.4	19.3
Latvia					
1993 - 94	2.1	...	10.2	12.2	9.1
Romania					
1994	212.2	27.1	342.4	581.7	...
Russian Federation					
1994	95.8	...	42.6	138.4	23.8
Slovak Republic					
1993 - 94	0.3	...	0.6	1.0	0.6

/...

(Annex table 11, cont'd)

Economy	Infrastructure-related industries				Infrastructure-related industries as share of all industries
	Construction	Communications	Transport and storage	Total	
Slovenia					
1994	0.5	0.3	3.0	3.8	1.0
Total above	547.8	27.4	685.6	1 260.8	13.5
Stocks					
Belarus					
1994	-	4.9	4.0	8.9	3.1
Bulgaria					
1994	5.2	6.2	107.5	118.9	25.4
Czech Republic					
1994	480.6	...	...	480.6	12.9
Estonia					
1994	1.7	...	30.9a	32.6	10.5
Hungary					
1994	349.6	...	610.7a	960.3	12.8
Latvia					
1994	4.4	77.0	20.9	102.2	33.0
Moldova, Republic of					
1994	-	...	0.5	0.6	2.6
Poland					
1994	94.4	...	116.5a	210.9	7.4
Romania					
1994	216.2	54.2	545.5	815.9	66.5
Russian Federation					
1994	249.0	...	94.3a	343.3	10.9
Slovak Republic					
1994	7.3	...	2.6	9.8	1.9
Slovenia					
1994	3.0	1.1	12.0	16.1	1.3
Ukraine					
1994	14.9	...	18.9a	33.9	9.2
Total above	1 426.4	143.3	1 564.4	3 134.2	14.3

Source: UNCTAD, FDI database.

a   Including communications.
b   Including public utilities.

Annex table 12. Bilateral Investment Treaties
concluded from January 1994 to June 1996

Country	Date of signature	Date of entry into force
Albania		
United Kingdom	30 March 1994	30 August 1995
Czech Republic	27 June 1994	7 July 1995
Netherlands	15 April 1994	1 September 1995
Bulgaria	27 April 1994	28 January 1996
United States	10 January 1995	--
Malaysia	18 January 1995	--
Sweden	31 March 1995	1 April 1996
Russian Federation	11 April 1995	--
Romania	11 May 1995	--
France	13 June 1995	--
Denmark	5 September 1995	--
Hungary	24 January 1996	--
Algeria		
Germany	11 March 1996	--
Argentina		
Jamaica	8 February 1994	1 December 1995
Ecuador	20 February 1994	--
Bolivia	17 March 1994	--
Korea, Republic of	17 May 1994	--
Malaysia	6 September 1994	--
Portugal	6 October 1994	--
Peru	10 November 1994	--
Croatia	2 December 1994	--
Israel	23 July 1995	--
Ukraine	9 August 1995	--
Australia	23 August 1995	--
Cuba	30 November 1995	--
Armenia		
Romania	20 September 1994	24 December 1995
Cyprus	18 January 1995	--
Bulgaria	10 April 1995	--
Iran, Islamic Republic of	6 May 1995	--
France	4 November 1995	--
Germany	21 December 1995	--
Australia		
Lao People's Democratic Republic	6 April 1994	8 April 1995
Philippines	25 January 1995	8 December 1995
Argentina	23 August 1995	--
Peru	7 December 1995	--
Austria		
Estonia	16 May 1994	8 February 1995
Latvia	17 November 1994	1 May 1996

/...

(Annex table 12, cont'd)

Country	Date of signature	Date of entry into force
Azerbaijan		
Turkey	9 February 1994	--
China	8 March 1994	1 April 1995
Germany	22 December 1995	--
United Kingdom	4 January 1996	--
Bangladesh		
Netherlands	1 November 1994	--
Malaysia	12 October 1994	--
Barbados		
Venezuela	15 July 1994	31 October 1995
Germany	2 December 1994	--
Switzerland	29 March 1995	22 December 1995
Cuba	19 February 1996	--
Belarus		
United States	15 January 1994	--
United Kingdom	1 March 1994	--
Sweden	20 December 1994	--
Netherlands	11 April 1995	--
Romania	31 May 1995	--
Iran, Islamic Republic of	14 July 1995	--
Italy	25 July 1995	--
Turkey	8 August 1995	--
Ukraine	14 December 1995	--
Bulgaria	21 February 1996	--
Yugoslavia	6 March 1996	--
Belgium/Luxembourg		
Ukraine	20 May 1995	--
Estonia	24 January 1996	--
Romania	4 March 1996	--
Latvia	27 March 1996	--
Bolivia		
Argentina	17 March 1994	--
Chile	22 September 1994	--
Denmark	12 March 1995	--
Cuba	6 May 1995	--
Ecuador	25 May 1995	--
Romania	9 October 1995	--
Bosnia and Herzegovina		
Croatia	26 February 1996	--
Brazil		
Chile	22 March 1994	--
Switzerland	11 November 1994	--
Portugal	9 February 1994	--
United Kingdom	19 July 1994	--
France	21 March 1995	--
Finland	28 March 1995	--
Italy	3 April 1995	--
Denmark	4 May 1995	--
Venezuela	4 July 1995	--

/...

(Annex table 12, cont'd)

Country	Date of signature	Date of entry into force
Brazil (cont'd)		
Korea, Republic of	1 September 1995	--
Germany	21 September 1995	--
Bulgaria		
Poland	11 April 1994	9 March 1995
Sweden	19 April 1994	1 April 1995
Albania	27 April 1994	28 January 1996
Romania	1 June 1994	23 may 1995
Hungary	8 June 1994	7 September 1995
Turkey	6 July 1994	--
Slovakia	18 August 1994	9 March 1995
Ukraine	8 December 1994	10 December 1995
Georgia	19 January 1995	--
Armenia	10 April 1995	--
Spain	5 September 1995	--
United Kingdom	11 December 1995	--
Yugoslavia	13 February 1996	--
Belarus	21 February 1996	--
Cambodia		
Thailand	29 March 1995	--
Canada		
Ukraine	24 October 1994	--
Latvia	26 April 1995	27 July 1995
Philippines	10 November 1995	--
Ecuador	29 April 1996	--
Chile		
Brazil	22 March 1994	--
China	23 March 1994	--
Bolivia	22 September 1994	--
Croatia	28 November 1994	--
Czech Republic	24 April 1995	--
Romania	4 July 1995	--
Paraguay	7 August 1995	--
Ukraine	30 October 1995	--
Philippines	20 November 1995	--
United Kingdom	8 January 1996	--
Cuba	10 January 1996	--
China		
Azerbaijan	8 March 1994	1 April 1995
Ecuador	21 March 1994	--
Chile	23 March 1994	--
Iceland	31 March 1994	--
Egypt	21 April 1994	--
Peru	9 June 1994	1 February 1995
Romania	12 July 1994	1 September 1995
Jamaica	26 October 1994	--
Indonesia	18 November 1994	1 April 1995
Oman	18 March 1995	--
Morocco	27 March 1995	--
Israel	10 April 1995	--
Cuba	24 April 1995	--

/...

(Annex table 12, cont'd)

Country	Date of signature	Date of entry into force
China (cont'd)		
Yugoslavia	18 December 1995	--
Saudi Arabia	29 February 1996	--
Colombia		
United Kingdom	9 March 1994	--
Peru	26 April 1994	--
Cuba	16 July 1994	--
Spain	9 June 1995	--
Congo		
Italy	17 March 1994	--
Costa Rica		
Germany	13 September 1994	--
Côte d'Ivoire		
United Kingdom	8 June 1995	--
Croatia		
Romania	8 June 1994	--
Macedonia	6 July 1994	5 April 1995
Chile	28 November 1994	--
Argentina	2 December 1994	--
Malaysia	16 December 1994	--
Poland	21 February 1995	4 October 1995
Portugal	9 May 1995	--
Slovakia	12 February 1996	--
Turkey	12 February 1996	--
Bosnia and Herzegovina	26 February 1996	--
Czech Republic	5 March 1996	--
Cuba		
Spain	27 May 1994	9 June 1995
Colombia	16 July 1994	--
United Kingdom	30 January 1995	11 May 1995
China	24 April 1995	--
Bolivia	6 May 1995	--
Ukraine	20 May 1995	19 February 1996
Viet Nam	12 October 1995	--
Argentina	30 November 1995	--
South Africa	8 December 1995	--
Lebanon	14 December 1995	--
Chile	10 January 1996	--
Romania	26 January 1996	--
Barbados	19 February 1996	--
Cyprus		
Armenia	18 January 1995	--
Czech Republic		
Tajikistan	11 February 1994	3 December 1995
Thailand	12 February 1994	4 May 1995
Peru	16 March 1994	6 March 1995
Ukraine	17 March 1994	2 November 1995
Russian Federation	5 April 1994	--

/...

(Annex table 12, cont'd)

Country	Date of signature	Date of entry into force
Czech Republic (cont'd)		
Albania	27 June 1994	7 July 1995
Estonia	24 October 1994	18 July 1995
Latvia	25 October 1994	1 August 1995
Lithuania	27 October 1994	12 July 1995
United Arab Emirates	23 November 1994	25 December 1995
Philippines	4 April 1995	--
Singapore	6 April 1995	7 October 1995
Chile	24 April 1995	--
Venezuela	27 April 1995	--
Kuwait	8 January 1996	--
Italy	22 January 1996	--
Croatia	5 March 1996	--
Denmark		
Hong Kong	2 February 1994	4 March 1994
Romania	13 June 1994	24 August 1995
Peru	23 November 1994	17 February 1995
Venezuela	28 November 1994	--
Bolivia	12 March 1995	--
Nicaragua	12 March 1995	26 January 1996
Mongolia	13 March 1995	--
Brazil	4 May 1995	--
Albania	5 September 1995	--
India	6 September 1995	--
Dominican Republic		
Spain	16 March 1995	--
Ecuador		
Paraguay	28 January 1994	--
Argentina	20 February 1994	--
China	21 March 1994	--
United Kingdom	10 May 1994	24 August 1995
El Salvador	16 May 1994	15 January 1996
France	7 September 1994	--
Bolivia	25 May 1995	--
Germany	21 March 1996	--
Romania	21 March 1996	--
Russian Federation	1 April 1996	--
Canada	29 April 1996	--
Egypt		
Indonesia	19 January 1994	5 August 1994
China	21 April 1994	--
Romania	24 November 1994	--
Hungary	23 May 1995	--
Turkmenistan	23 May 1995	--
Uganda	4 November 1995	--
Netherlands	17 January 1996	--
Sri Lanka	11 March 1996	--
Korea, Republic of	18 March 1996	--
El Salvador		
Switzerland	8 December 1994	--
Ecuador	16 May 1994	15 January 1996
Spain	14 February 1995	20 Fenruary 1996

/...

(Annex table 12, cont'd)

Country	Date of signature	Date of entry into force
Estonia		
Israel	14 March 1994	23 May 1995
Austria	16 May 1994	8 February 1995
United States	19 April 1994	--
United Kingdom	12 May 1994	16 December 1994
Czech Republic	24 October 1994	18 July 1995
Ukraine	15 February 1995	5 May 1995
Lithuania	7 September 1995	--
Belgium/Luxembourg	24 January 1996	--
Latvia	7 February 1996	--
Ethiopia		
Italy	23 December 1994	--
Finland		
Thailand	18 March 1994	--
Brazil	28 March 1995	--
Peru	2 May 1995	--
Moldova	25 August 1995	--
Kuwait	10 March 1996	--
United Arab Emirates	12 March 1996	--
Indonesia	13 March 1996	--
France		
Turkmenistan	28 April 1994	2 May 1996
Ukraine	3 May 1994	26 January 1996
Kyrgyzstan	2 June 1994	--
Ecuador	7 September 1994	--
Philippines	13 September 1994	--
Oman	17 October 1994	--
Brazil	21 March 1995	--
Romania	21 March 1995	--
Albania	13 June 1995	--
South Africa	11 October 1995	--
Armenia	4 November 1995	--
Hong Kong	30 November 1995	--
Morocco	13 January 1996	--
Georgia		
United States	7 March 1994	--
Greece	9 November 1994	--
Bulgaria	19 January 1995	--
United Kingdom	15 February 1995	15 February 1995
Israel	19 June 1995	--
Iran, Islamic Republic of	27 September 1995	--
Germany		
Namibia	21 January 1994	Provisional application
Republic of Moldova	28 February 1994	Provisional application
Kuwait	30 March 1994	--
Costa Rica	13 September 1994	--
Barbados	2 December 1994	--
Peru	30 January 1995	--
Ghana	24 February 1995	--
Honduras	21 March 1995	--
India	10 July 1995	--

/...

(Annex table 12, cont'd)

Country	Date of signature	Date of entry into force
Germany (cont'd)		
South Africa	11 September 1995	--
Brazil	21 September 1995	--
Zimbabwe	29 September 1995	--
Armenia	21 December 1995	--
Azerbaijan	22 December 1995	--
Hong Kong	31 January 1996	--
Algeria	11 March 1996	--
Ecuador	21 March 1996	--
Ghana		
Germany	24 February 1995	--
Greece		
Morocco	16 February 1994	--
Ukraine	1 September 1994	--
Georgia	9 November 1994	--
Korea, Republic of	25 January 1995	4 November 1995
Latvia	20 July 1995	--
Honduras		
Spain	18 March 1994	--
Germany	21 March 1995	--
United States	1 July 1995	--
Hong Kong		
Denmark	2 February 1994	4 March 1994
Sweden	27 May 1994	26 June 1994
Switzerland	22 September 1994	22 October 1994
New Zealand	6 July 1995	5 August 1995
Italy	28 November 1995	--
France	30 November 1995	--
Germany	31 January 1996	--
Hungary		
Bulgaria	8 June 1994	7 September 1995
Viet Nam	26 August 1994	16 June 1995
Mongolia	13 September 1994	--
Ukraine	11 October 1994	--
Kazakhstan	7 December 1994	3 March 1996
Russian Federation	6 March 1995	--
Moldova	19 April 1995	--
Egypt	23 May 1995	--
Albania	24 January 1996	--
Iceland		
China	31 March 1994	--
India		
United Kingdom	14 March 1994	6 January 1995
Russian Federation	23 December 1994	--
Germany	10 July 1995	--
Malaysia	1 August 1995	--
Turkmenistan	1 September 1995	--
Denmark	6 September 1995	--
Italy	1 November 1995	--

/...

(Annex table 12, cont'd)

Country	Date of signature	Date of entry into force
India (cont'd)		
Netherlands	6 November 1995	--
Tajikistan	1 December 1995	--
Israel	29 January 1996	--
South Africa	1 February 1996	--
Korea, Republic of	26 February 1996	--
Indonesia		
Egypt	19 January 1994	5 August 1994
Malaysia	22 January 1994	15 June 1994
Netherlands	6 April 1994	1 July 1995
Turkmenistan	2 June 1994	--
Slovakia	12 July 1994	1 March 1995
Lao People's Democratic Republic	18 October 1994	--
China	18 November 1994	1 April 1995
Ukraine	11 April 1995	--
Spain	30 May 1995	--
Finland	13 March 1996	--
Iran, Islamic Republic of		
Armenia	6 May 1995	--
Moldova	31 May 1995	--
Belarus	14 July 1995	--
Tajikistan	18 July 1995	--
Georgia	27 September 1995	--
Philippines	8 October 1995	--
Pakistan	8 November 1995	--
Kazakhstan	16 January 1996	--
Turkmenistan	23 January 1996	--
Yemen	29 February 1996	--
Ukraine	21 May 1996	--
Israel		
Latvia	27 February 1994	9 May 1995
Estonia	14 March 1994	23 May 1995
China	10 April 1995	--
Turkmenistan	24 May 1995	--
Georgia	19 June 1995	--
Argentina	23 July 1995	--
Kazakhstan	27 December 1995	--
India	29 January 1996	--
Turkey	14 March 1996	--
Italy		
Congo	17 March 1994	--
Peru	5 May 1994	18 October 1995
Kazakhstan	22 September 1994	--
Ethiopia	23 December 1994	--
Turkey	23 March 1995	--
Brazil	3 April 1995	--
Ukraine	2 May 1995	--
Belarus	25 July 1995	--
India	1 November 1995	--
Hong Kong	28 November 1995	--
Czech Republic	22 January 1996	--

/...

(Annex table 12, cont'd)

Country	Date of signature	Date of entry into force
Jamaica		
United States	4 February 1994	--
Argentina	8 February 1994	1 December 1995
China	26 October 1994	--
Kazakhstan		
Spain	23 March 1994	--
Switzerland	12 May 1994	--
Poland	21 September 1994	25 May 1995
Italy	22 September 1994	--
Mongolia	1 December 1994	--
Hungary	7 December 1994	3 March 1996
United Kingdom	23 November 1995	23 November 1995
Israel	27 December 1995	--
Iran, Islamic Republic of	16 January 1996	--
Republic of Korea	20 March 1996	--
Korea, Republic of		
Spain	17 January 1994	19 July 1994
Philippines	7 April 1994	--
Argentina	17 May 1994	--
Greece	25 January 1995	4 November 1995
Portugal	3 May 1995	--
South Africa	7 July 1995	--
Tajikistan	14 July 1995	13 August 1995
Sweden	30 August 1995	--
Brazil	1 September 1995	--
India	26 February 1996	--
Egypt	18 March 1996	--
Kazakhstan	20 March 1996	--
Kuwait		
Germany	30 March 1994	--
Russian Federation	21 November 1994	--
Tajikistan	18 April 1995	--
Malta	19 April 1995	--
Czech Republic	8 January 1996	--
Finland	10 March 1996	--
Kyrgyzstan		
France	2 June 1994	--
United Kingdom	8 December 1994	--
Lao People's Democratic Republic		
Mongolia	3 March 1994	--
Australia	6 April 1994	8 April 1995
Indonesia	18 October 1994	--
United Kingdom	1 June 1995	1 June 1995
Latvia		
United Kingdom	24 January 1994	15 February 1995
Israel	27 February 1994	9 May 1995
Netherlands	14 March 1994	1 April 1995
Austria	17 November 1994	1 May 1996
Czech Republic	25 October 1994	1 August 1995
United States	13 January 1995	--

/...

(Annex table 12, cont'd)

Country	Date of signature	Date of entry into force
Latvia (cont'd)		
Canada	26 April 1995	27 July 1995
Greece	20 July 1995	--
Portugal	27 September 1995	--
Spain	26 October 1995	--
Viet Nam	6 November 1995	--
Estonia	7 February 1996	--
Lithuania	7 February 1996	--
Belgium/Luxembourg	27 March 1996	--
Lebanon		
Romania	18 October 1994	--
Ukraine	25 March 1995	--
Cuba	14 December 1995	--
Spain	22 February 1996	--
Lithuania		
Netherlands	26 January 1994	1 April 1995
Romania	8 March 1994	15 December 1994
Spain	6 July 1994	22 December 1995
Czech Republic	27 October 1994	12 July 1995
Venezuela	24 April 1995	--
Estonia	7 September 1995	--
Latvia	7 February 1996	--
Macedonia		
Croatia	6 July 1994	5 April 1995
Turkey	9 September 1995	--
Malaysia		
Indonesia	22 January 1994	15 June 1994
Argentina	6 September 1994	--
Bangladesh	12 October 1994	--
Croatia	16 December 1994	--
Albania	18 January 1995	--
Spain	4 April 1995	16 February 1996
India	1 August 1995	--
Peru	13 October 1995	25 December 1995
Malta		
Kuwait	19 April 1995	--
Mexico		
Spain	23 June 1995	--
Switzerland	10 July 1995	14 March 1996
Moldova, Republic of		
Turkey	14 February 1994	--
Germany	28 February 1994	Provisional application
Poland	16 November 1994	27 July 1995
Hungary	19 April 1995	--
Iran, Islamic Republic of	31 May 1995	--
Finland	25 August 1995	--
Ukraine	29 August 1995	--
Netherlands	26 September 1995	1 June 1996
Uzbekistan	21 November 1995	--
Switzerland	30 November 1995	--
United Kingdom	19 March 1996	--

/...

(Annex table 12, cont'd)

Country	Date of signature	Date of entry into force
Mongolia		
Lao People's		
Democratic Republic	3 March 1994	--
Hungary	13 September 1994	--
United States	6 October 1994	--
Kazakhstan	1 December 1994	--
Netherlands	9 March 1995	--
Denmark	13 March 1995	--
Singapore	24 July 1995	--
Russian Federation	29 November 1995	--
Romania	6 December 1995	--
Morocco		
Romania	28 January 1994	--
Tunisia	28 January 1994	--
Greece	16 February 1994	--
Poland	24 October 1994	29 May 1995
China	27 March 1995	--
France	13 January 1996	--
Namibia		
Germany	21 January 1994	Provisional application
Switzerland	1 August 1994	--
Netherlands		
Lithuania	26 January 1994	1 April 1995
Viet Nam	10 March 1994	1 February 1995
Latvia	14 March 1994	1 April 1995
Indonesia	6 April 1994	1 July 1995
Albania	15 April 1994	1 September 1995
Romania	19 April 1994	1 February 1995
Ukraine	14 July 1994	--
Bangladesh	1 November 1994	--
Peru	27 December 1994	1 February 1996
Mongolia	9 March 1995	--
Belarus	11 April 1995	--
South Africa	9 May 1995	--
Moldova, Republic of	26 September 1995	1 June 1996
India	6 November 1995	--
Egypt	17 January 1996	--
Uzbekistan	14 March 1996	--
New Zealand		
Hong Kong	6 July 1995	5 August 1995
Nicaragua		
Spain	16 March 1994	28 March 1995
Denmark	12 March 1995	26 January 1996
United States	1 July 1995	--
Norway		
Peru	10 March 1995	5 May 1995
Russian Federation	4 October 1995	--
Oman		
France	17 October 1994	--
China	18 March 1995	--

/...

(Annex table 12, cont'd)

Country	Date of signature	Date of entry into force
Oman (cont'd)		
Sweden	15 July 1995	--
United Kingdom	25 November 1995	--
Pakistan		
Tajikistan	31 March 1994	--
Spain	15 September 1994	--
Turkmenistan	26 October 1994	--
United Kingdom	30 November 1994	30 November 1994
Singapore	8 March 1995	4 May 1995
Turkey	16 March 1995	--
Romania	10 July 1995	--
Switzerland	11 July 1995	--
Iran, Islamic Republic of	8 November 1995	--
Paraguay		
Ecuador	28 January 1994	--
Peru	31 January 1994	18 December 1994
Romania	24 May 1994	--
Chile	7 August 1995	--
Peru		
Paraguay	31 January 1994	18 December 1994
Czech Republic	16 March 1994	6 March 1995
Colombia	26 April 1994	--
Sweden	3 May 1994	1 August 1994
Italy	5 May 1994	18 October 1995
Romania	16 May 1994	1 January 1995
China	9 June 1994	1 February 1995
Argentina	10 November 1994	--
Spain	17 November 1994	17 February 1996
Portugal	22 November 1994	18 October 1995
Denmark	23 November 1994	17 February 1995
Netherlands	27 December 1994	1 February 1996
Germany	30 January 1995	--
Norway	10 March 1995	5 May 1995
Finland	2 May 1995	--
Malaysia	13 October 1995	25 December 1995
Australia	7 December 1995	--
Venezuela	12 January 1996	--
Philippines		
Korea, Republic of	7 April 1994	--
Romania	18 May 1994	--
France	13 September 1994	--
Australia	25 January 1995	8 December 1995
Czech Republic	4 April 1995	--
Thailand	30 September 1995	--
Iran, Islamic Republic of	8 October 1995	--
Canada	10 November 1995	--
Chile	20 November 1995	--
Poland		
Bulgaria	11 April 1994	9 March 1995
Slovenia	12 April 1994	--
Romania	23 June 1994	30 December 1995

/...

(Annex table 12, cont'd)

Country	Date of signature	Date of entry into force
Poland (cont'd)		
Slovakia	18 August 1994	--
Viet Nam	31 August 1994	24 November 1994
Kazakhstan	21 September 1994	25 May 1995
Morocco	24 October 1994	29 May 1995
Moldova, Republic of	16 November 1994	27 July 1995
Uzbekistan	11 January 1995	29 April 1995
Croatia	21 February 1995	4 October 1995
Portugal		
Brazil	9 February 1994	--
Zimbabwe	5 May 1994	--
Venezuela	17 June 1994	7 October 1995
Russian Federation	21 July 1994	--
Argentina	6 October 1994	--
Peru	22 November 1994	18 October 1995
Chile	28 April 1995	--
Korea, Republic of	3 May 1995	--
Croatia	9 May 1995	--
Slovakia	10 July 1995	--
Latvia	27 September 1995	--
Romania		
Morocco	28 January 1994	--
Slovakia	3 March 1994	7 March 1996
Lithuania	8 March 1994	15 December 1994
Netherlands	19 April 1994	1 February 1995
Peru	16 May 1994	1 January 1995
Philippines	18 May 1994	--
Paraguay	24 May 1994	--
Bulgaria	1 June 1994	23 May 1995
Croatia	8 June 1994	--
Denmark	14 June 1994	24 August 1995
Poland	23 June 1994	30 December 1995
China	12 July 1994	1 September 1995
Viet Nam	1 September 1994	16 August 1995
Armenia	20 September 1994	24 December 1995
Lebanon	18 October 1994	--
Turkmenistan	16 November 1994	--
Egypt	24 November 1994	--
Spain	25 January 1995	7 December 1995
Ukraine	23 February 1995	--
France	21 March 1995	--
Albania	11 May 1995	--
Belarus	31 May 1995	--
Chile	4 July 1995	--
Pakistan	10 July 1995	--
United Kingdom	13 July 1995	--
Bolivia	9 October 1995	--
Tunisia	16 October 1995	--
Yugoslavia	28 November 1995	--
Mongolia	6 December 1995	--
Slovenia	24 January 1996	--
Cuba	26 January 1996	--
Belgium/Luxembourg	4 March 1996	--
Ecuador	21 March 1996	--

/...

(Annex table 12, cont'd)

Country	Date of signature	Date of entry into force
Russian Federation		
Czech Republic	5 April 1994	--
Viet Nam	16 June 1994	--
Portugal	21 July 1994	--
Kuwait	21 November 1994	--
India	23 December 1994	--
Hungary	6 March 1995	--
Albania	11 April 1995	--
Sweden	19 April 1995	--
Norway	4 October 1995	--
Yugoslavia	11 October 1995	--
Mongolia	29 November 1995	--
Ecuador	1 April 1996	--
Saudi Arabia		
China	29 February 1996	--
Singapore		
Pakistan	8 March 1995	4 May 1995
Czech Republic	6 April 1995	7 October 1995
Mongolia	24 July 1995	--
Slovakia		
Tajikistan	14 February 1994	--
Romania	3 March 1994	7 March 1996
Ukraine	22 June 1994	--
Indonesia	12 July 1994	1 March 1995
Poland	18 August 1994	--
Bulgaria	18 August 1994	9 March 1995
Uzbekistan	16 May 1995	--
Portugal	10 July 1995	--
Turkmenistan	17 November 1995	--
Yugoslavia	7 February 1996	--
Croatia	12 February 1996	--
Slovenia		
Poland	12 April 1994	--
Switzerland	9 November 1995	--
Romania	24 January 1996	--
South Africa		
United Kingdom	20 September 1994	--
Netherlands	9 May 1995	--
Switzerland	27 June 1995	--
Korea, Republic of	7 July 1995	--
Germany	11 September 1995	--
France	11 October 1995	--
Cuba	8 December 1995	--
India	1 February 1996	--
Spain		
Korea, Republic of	17 January 1994	19 July 1994
Nicaragua	16 March 1994	28 March 1995
Honduras	18 March 1994	--
Kazakhstan	23 March 1994	--
Cuba	27 May 1994	9 June 1995

/...

(Annex table 12, cont'd)

Country	Date of signature	Date of entry into force
Spain (cont'd)		
Lithuania	6 July 1994	22 December 1995
Pakistan	15 September 1994	--
Peru	17 November 1994	17 February 1996
Romania	25 January 1995	7 December 1995
El Salvador	14 February 1995	20 February 1996
Turkey	15 February 1995	--
Gabon	2 March 1995	--
Dominican Republic	16 March 1995	--
Malaysia	4 April 1995	16 February 1996
Indonesia	30 May 1995	--
Colombia	9 June 1995	--
Mexico	23 June 1995	--
Bulgaria	5 September 1995	--
Latvia	26 October 1995	--
Venezuela	2 November 1995	--
Lebanon	22 February 1996	--
Sri Lanka		
Thailand	3 January 1996	--
Egypt	11 March 1996	--
Swaziland		
United Kingdom	5 May 1995	5 May 1995
Sweden		
Bulgaria	19 April 1994	1 April 1995
Hong Kong	27 May 1994	26 June 1994
Peru	3 May 1994	1 August 1994
Belarus	20 December 1994	--
Albania	31 March 1995	1 April 1996
Russian Federation	19 April 1995	--
Oman	15 July 1995	--
Ukraine	15 August 1995	--
Korea, Republic of	30 August 1995	--
Switzerland		
Kazakhstan	12 May 1994	--
Namibia	1 August 1994	--
Zambia	3 August 1994	7 March 1995
Hong Kong	22 September 1994	22 October 1994
Brazil	11 November 1994	--
El Salvador	8 December 1994	--
Barbados	29 March 1995	22 December 1995
Ukraine	20 April 1995	--
South Africa	27 June 1995	--
Mexico	10 July 1995	14 March 1996
Pakistan	11 July 1995	--
Slovenia	9 November 1995	--
Moldova, Republic of	30 November 1995	--
Tajikistan		
Czech Republic	11 February 1994	3 December 1995
Slovakia	14 February 1994	--
Pakistan	31 March 1994	--
Kuwait	18 April 1995	--

/...

(Annex table 12, cont'd)

Country	Date of signature	Date of entry into force
Tajikistan (cont'd)		
Korea, Republic of	14 July 1995	13 August 1995
Iran, Islamic Republic of	18 July 1995	--
India	1 December 1995	--
Tanzania, United Republic of		
United Kingdom	7 January 1994	--
Thailand		
Czech Republic	12 February 1994	4 May 1995
Finland	18 March 1994	--
Cambodia	29 March 1995	--
Philippines	30 September 1995	--
Sri Lanka	3 January 1996	--
Trinidad and Tobago		
United States	26 September 1994	--
Tunisia		
Morocco	28 January 1994	--
Romania	16 October 1995	--
Turkey		
Azerbaijan	9 February 1994	--
Moldova, Republic of	14 February 1994	--
Bulgaria	6 July 1994	--
Spain	15 February 1995	--
Pakistan	16 March 1995	--
Italy	22 March 1995	--
Belarus	8 August 1995	--
Macedonia	9 September 1995	--
Croatia	12 February 1996	--
Israel	14 March 1996	--
Turkmenistan		
France	28 April 1994	2 May 1996
Indonesia	2 June 1994	--
Pakistan	26 October 1994	--
Romania	16 November 1994	--
United Kingdom	9 February 1995	9 February 1995
Egypt	23 May 1995	--
Israel	24 May 1995	--
India	1 September 1995	--
Slovakia	17 November 1995	--
Iran, Islamic Republic of	23 January 1996	--
Uganda		
Egypt	4 November 1995	--
Ukraine		
United States	4 March 1994	--
Czech Republic	17 March 1994	2 November 1995
France	3 May 1994	26 January 1996
Slovakia	22 June 1994	--
Netherlands	14 July 1994	--
Greece	1 September 1994	--

/...

(Annex table 12, cont'd)

Country	Date of signature	Date of entry into force
Ukraine (cont'd)		
Hungary	11 October 1994	--
Canada	24 October 1994	--
Bulgaria	8 December 1994	10 December 1995
Estonia	15 February 1995	5 May 1995
Romania	23 February 1995	--
Lebanon	25 March 1995	--
Indonesia	11 April 1995	--
Switzerland	20 April 1995	--
Italy	2 May 1995	--
Belgium/Luxembourg	20 May 1995	--
Cuba	20 May 1995	19 February 1996
Argentina	9 August 1995	--
Sweden	15 August 1995	--
Moldova, Republic of	29 August 1995	--
Chile	30 October 1995	--
Belarus	14 December 1995	--
Iran, Islamic Republic of	21 May 1996	--
United Arab Emirates		
Czech Republic	23 November 1994	25 December 1995
Finland	12 March 1996	--
United Kingdom		
Tanzania,United Republic of	7 January 1994	--
Latvia	24 January 1994	15 February 1995
Belarus	1 March 1994	28 December 1994
Colombia	9 March 1994	--
India	14 March 1994	6 January 1995
Albania	30 March 1994	30 August 1995
Ecuador	10 May 1994	24 August 1995
Estonia	12 May 1994	16 December 1994
Brazil	19 July 1994	--
South Africa	20 September 1994	--
Pakistan	30 November 1994	30 November 1994
Kyrgyzstan	8 December 1994	--
Cuba	30 January 1995	11 May 1995
Turkmenistan	9 February 1995	9 February 1995
Georgia	15 February 1995	15 February 1995
Zimbabwe	1 March 1995	--
Venezuela	15 March 1995	--
Swaziland	5 May 1995	5 May 1995
Lao People's Democratic Republic	1 June 1995	1 June 1995
Côte d'Ivoire	8 June 1995	--
Romania	13 July 1995	--
Kazakhstan	23 November 1995	23 November 1995
Oman	25 November 1995	--
Bulgaria	11 December 1995	--
Azerbaijan	4 January 1996	--
Chile	8 January 1996	--
Moldova, Republic of	19 March 1996	--
United States		
Belarus	15 January 1994	--
Jamaica	4 February 1994	--

/...

(Annex table 12, cont'd)

Country	Date of signature	Date of entry into force
United States (cont'd)		
Ukraine	4 March 1994	--
Georgia	7 March 1994	--
Estonia	19 April 1994	--
Trinidad and Tobago	26 September 1994	--
Mongolia	6 October 1994	--
Uzbekistan	16 December 1994	--
Albania	10 January 1995	--
Latvia	13 January 1995	--
Honduras	1 July 1995	--
Nicaragua	1 July 1995	--
Uzbekistan		
United States	16 December 1994	--
Poland	11 January 1995	29 April 1995
Slovakia	16 May 1995	--
Moldova, Republic of	21 November 1995	--
Netherlands	14 March 1996	--
Venezuela		
Portugal	17 June 1994	7 October 1995
Barbados	15 July 1994	31 October 1995
Denmark	28 November 1994	--
United Kingdom	15 March 1995	--
Lithuania	24 April 1995	--
Czech Republic	27 April 1995	--
Brazil	4 July 1995	--
Spain	2 November 1995	--
Peru	12 January 1996	--
Viet Nam		
Netherlands	10 March 1994	1 February 1995
Russian Federation	16 June 1994	--
Hungary	26 August 1994	16 June 1995
Poland	31 August 1994	24 November 1994
Romania	1 September 1994	16 August 1995
Cuba	12 October 1995	--
Latvia	6 November 1995	--
Yugoslavia		
Russian Federation	11 October 1995	--
Romania	28 November 1995	--
China	18 December 1995	--
Slovakia	7 February 1996	--
Bulgaria	13 February 1996	--
Belarus	6 March 1996	--
Zambia		
Switzerland	3 August 1994	7 March 1995

(Annex table 12, cont'd)

Country	Date of signature	Date of entry into force
Zimbabwe		
Portugal	5 May 1994	--
United Kingdom	1 March 1995	--
Germany	29 September 1995	--

Source: UNCTAD, based on national sources.

Annex table 13. Comparing main elements in key international FDI instruments

Element	Bilateral	Regional / interregional						
	Bilateral investment treaties	Investment Agreement between ASEAN countries	MERCOSUR: Protocol of Colonia on Investment (Intrazone)	APEC Non-Binding Investment Principles	Islamic Conf.: Agreement on Investment	Arab League: Unified Agreement for Investment of Arab Capital among Arab States	CoMESA: Treaty Est. the Common Market for Eastern and Southern Africa [a]	NAFTA: North American Free Trade Agreement
Legal nature	Legally binding	Legally binding	Legally binding	Voluntary	Legally binding	Legally binding	Legally binding	Legally binding
Definition of FDI: 1. Investment	Broad and open-ended; cover all types of FDI, of FDI assets and all aspects of FDI life.	Broad and open-ended; cover all types of FDI, of FDI assets and all aspects of FDI life.	Broad and open-ended; cover all types of FDI, of FDI assets and all aspects of FDI life.		Covers all investment assets and returns; investment defined as capital used in one of the permissible fields.	Covers all investment assets and returns; investment defined as capital used in one of the permissible fields.	Broad coverage of assets and activities.	Broad and open-ended; cover all types of investment (including some portfolio), investment assets and all aspects of investment life.
2. Investor	Individuals and companies having the nationality of one of the parties according to criteria set out in the instruments (in addition, often require company having a real link with the country of nationality)	Individuals and companies having the nationality of one of the parties (i.e., incorporated or constituted plus place of effective management.		Individual nationals of one of the parties and companies established in accordance with national laws.	Arab citizens who own Arab capital.		Individual nationals of one of the parties and enterprises constituted under the law of the parties and branches located in the NAFTA area, and carrying substantial business there.	Individual nationals of one of the parties and companies organized in accordance with the laws of one State Party.

Regional / interregional (cont'd)			Multilateral			
	OECD		World Trade Organization		World Bank	United Nations
Energy Charter Treaty	Codes of Liberalisation of Capital Movements and Current Invisible Transactions	Declaration on International Investment and Multinational Enterprises and related Decisions	General Agreement on Trade in Services	Agreement on Trade-related Investment Measures	Convention on the Settlement of Investment Disputes between States and Nationals of Other States; Convention Establishing the Multilateral Investment Guarantee Agency; Guidelines on the Treatment of Foreign Direct Investment	ILO Tripartite Declaration of Principles Concerning Multinational Enterprises and Social Policy; UNCTAD Multilaterally Agreed Set of Principles and Rules for the Control of Restrictive Business practices; Guidelines for Consumer Protection
Legally binding	Binding decisions of the OECD Council	Political undertaking (Declaration); binding (Decisions); voluntary (Guidelines).	Legally binding	Legally binding	Legally binding (ICSID, MIGA); voluntary (Guidelines).	Voluntary
In the energy activities only, broad and open-ended; covers all types of investment including some portfolio), investment assets and all aspects of investment life.	Covers all types of external capital transactions and of current invisible transactions other than goods, at the border.		Broad definition of commercial presence which includes FDI.			
Applicable to non-resident enterprises.	Applicable to foreign-controlled enterprises operating in the OECD area					

/...

(Annex table 13, cont'd)

Element	Bilateral	Regional / interregional						
	Bilateral investment treaties	Investment Agreement between ASEAN countries	MERCOSUR: Protocol of Colonia on Investment (Intrazone)	APEC Non-Binding Investment Principles	Islamic Conf.: Agreement on Investment	Arab League: Unified Agreement for Investment of Arab Capital among Arab States	CoMESA: Treaty Est. the Common Market for Eastern and Southern Africa [a]	NAFTA: North American Free Trade Agreement
Investment measures that affect the entry and operations of foreign investors 1. Restrictions a) Entry and establishment	Admission according to national laws but FDI is to be encouraged (in some BITs admission on the basis of national and MFN treatment).	Agreement applies only to investments specifically approved in writing and registered and upon conditions prescribed by the host country.	Entry granted on the basis of national and MFN treatment (exceptions to be included in an Annex).	Regulatory and institutional barriers will be minimized.	Transfers of capital and their utilization shall be permitted. Members shall endeavour to open various industries and economic activities.	Transfers of capital and their utilization shall be permitted and facilitated according to the economic development plans.	Dere-gulation process should be accelerated. Legal restrictions should be removed.	Establish-ment within the NAFTA area in accordance with national and MFN treatment (exceptions and various schedules including in Annexes).
b) Ownership and control	(See under entry).	(See under entry).	(See under entry).					(See under entry).
c) Operational conditions	Some BITs require that entry and residence of key foreign personnel should be permitted. A few BITs prohibit performance require-ments.	As prescribed in national laws.		The use of performance requirements should be minimized. Entry and residence of key personnel to be permitted.		Arab investor and its family are entitled to entry and residence.		Prohibits 7 types of mandatory restrictions and 4 of those also when they are linked to incentives.

Regional / interregional (cont'd)			Multilateral			
	OECD		World Trade Organization		World Bank	United Nations
Energy Charter Treaty	Codes of Liberalisation of Capital Movements and Current Invisible Transactions	Declaration on International Investment and Multinational Enterprises and related Decisions	General Agreement on Trade in Services	Agreement on Trade-related Investment Measures	Convention on the Settlement of Investment Disputes between States and Nationals of Other States; Convention Establishing the Multilateral Investment Guarantee Agency; Guidelines on the Treatment of Foreign Direct Investment	ILO Tripartite Declaration of Principles Concerning Multinational Enterprises and Social Policy; UNCTAD Multilaterally Agreed Set of Principles and Rules for the Control of Restrictive Business practices; Guidelines for Consumer Protection
Best efforts to provide national treatment and MFN treatment on entry and establishment.	Progressive liberalization of all capital movements, including all forms of FDI entry and establishment (subject to reservations).		Commercial presence is permitted in accordance with country specific schedules of commitments which form an integral part of the GATs.		States expected to admit FDI, and facilitate admission in accordance with their national laws (Guidelines).	
(See under entry).	(See under entry).		(See under entry).		Conditions on ownership and control discouraged (Guidelines).	
Prohibits some requirements (i.e., measures inconsistent with GATT Articles III and XI).		Progressive elimination of those inconsistent with national treatment. Performance requirements linked to incentives to be discouraged.		Prohibits some requirements either mandatory or linked to incentives (i.e., those inconsistent with GATT Articles III and XI).	Discriminatory operational restrictions discouraged. The employment of foreign personnel should be authorized to the extent necessary; in particular top managers regardless of their nationality; underlines importance of labour markets flexibility. Performance requirements are discouraged (Guidelines).	

/...

(Annex table 13, cont'd)

	Bilateral	Regional / interregional						
Element	Bilateral investment treaties	Investment Agreement between ASEAN countries	MERCOSUR: Protocol of Colonia on Investment (Intrazone)	APEC Non-Binding Investment Principles	Islamic Conf.: Agreement on Investment	Arab League: Unified Agreement for Investment of Arab Capital among Arab States	CoMESA: Treaty Est. the Common Market for Eastern and Southern Africa [a]	NAFTA: North American Free Trade Agreement
d) Authorization and reporting	(See under entry).	Previous approval in writing required.	(See under entry).		Permits needed shall be granted.		Administrative, fiscal and legal restrictions to intra-Common Market investment should be removed.	(See under entry).
2. Incentives				Health, safety and environmental regulations should not be relaxed as an incentive to encourage FDI.	Parties shall endeavour to offer various incentives and facilities for attracting investments.	Additional privileges to Arab investment meeting certain criteria.	Undertaking to increase awareness of the investment incentives available.	Prohibits incentives linked to certain performance requirements.
3. Standards of treatment a) National treatment	Many BITs provide no less favourable treatment than national enterprises in similar situations after establishment (exceptions include national security and vital interests of the country).	National treatment is not granted. Countries may negotiate it separately.	National treatment to foreign investors in like situations; cover entry and after entry activities).	With the exceptions in domestic laws, national treatment granted only regarding establishment, expansion, operation and protection of investments.	National treatment granted only regarding compensation for damaged caused by international civil disturbances.	National treatment granted to Arab investment.		National treatment covers establishment and all types of operations (excepted industries and activities included in negative lists and existing measures to be abolished subject to national schedules).

Regional / interregional (cont'd)			Multilateral			
	OECD		World Trade Organization		World Bank	United Nations
Energy Charter Treaty	Codes of Liberali-sation of Capital Movements and Current Invisible Transactions	Declaration on International Investment and Multinational Enterprises and related Decisions	General Agreement on Trade in Services	Agreement on Trade-related Investment Measures	Convention on the Settlement of Investment Disputes between States and Nationals of Other States; Convention Establishing the Multilateral Invest-ment Guarantee Agency; Guidelines on the Treatment of Foreign Direct Investment	ILO Tripartite Declaration of Principles Concerning Multinational Enterprises and Social Policy; UNCTAD Multilaterally Agreed Set of Principles and Rules for the Control of Restrictive Business practices; Guidelines for Consumer Protection
(See under entry).	(See under entry).	(See under entry).			States are expected to avoid making unduly cumbersome or com-plicated procedural regulations for, or imposing unnecessary conditions on, the admission of invest-ments. State will promptly issue licence and permits and grant concessions necessary for the uninterrupted operation of the admitted invest-ment (Guidelines). Approval of investment project is required to grant insurance coverage (MIGA).	
Prohibits incentives linked to TRIMs.		Provides for consultations when incentives may adversely affect the interests of mother country.		Prohibits TRIMs linked to incentives.	Incentives not recommended; if granted should be non-discriminatory; competition among States with incentives, especially tax incentives is not recommended (Guidelines).	
National treatment covers post-investment activities (exceptions to protect human life, national security etc.).		National treatment for foreign controlled enterprises, with limited exceptions subject to standstill.	National treatment to be established progressively (according to national schedules).	TRIMs prohibited in accordance with the national treatment provisions of GATT.	National treatment and non-discri-mination under the laws (exceptions to be made transparent) (Guidelines).	

/...

(Annex table 13, cont'd)

Element	Bilateral — Bilateral investment treaties	Regional / interregional — Investment Agreement between ASEAN countries	MERCOSUR: Protocol of Colonia on Investment (Intrazone)	APEC Non-Binding Investment Principles	Islamic Conf.: Agreement on Investment	Arab League: Unified Agreement for Investment of Arab Capital among Arab States	CoMESA: Treaty Est. the Common Market for Eastern and Southern Africa [a]	NAFTA: North American Free Trade Agreement
b) Most favoured nation treatment (MFN)	MFN to investments in like situations; cover post-investment activities (exceptions for members of integration schemes, protection of national security etc.). Some BITs grant MFN upon entry.	MFN to investments in like situations; cover post-investment activities (exceptions for protection of national security etc.).	MFN to investments in like situations; cover entry and after entry activities	MFN is to be extended to investors economy in relation to establishment, expansion and operations of their investments in like situations	MFN is granted in like situations in the context of the activity of the investment.	MFN is granted to Arab investment.		MFN is granted to investment in like situations; covers all aspects of investment life (exceptions to protect national security, members of free trade areas).
c) Fair and equitable treatment.	Fair and equitable treatment is granted.	Fair and equitable treatment is granted.	Fair and equitable treatment is granted.			Fair and equitable treatment granted to Arab investment.	Fair and equitable treatment shall be accorded.	Fair and equitable treatment is granted.
4. Transfer of funds	Free transfer of funds and repatriation of the investment; subject to very few exceptions in some cases (e.g., for balance of payments considerations).	Free transfer of funds and repatriation of investment.	Free transfer of funds and repatriation of investment.	Members should further liberalize towards the goal of free transfer of funds related to FDI (e.g., profits and dividends).	Free transfer of proceeds and repatriation of investment.	Right to repatriate investment and to transfer profits, etc.	Free transfer of funds and repatriation of investment.	Free transfer of funds and repatriation of investment.
5. Protection standards — a) Treatment according to international law.	Treatment according to international law is granted.	Treatment according to international law is granted.	Treatment according to international law is granted.		Treatment according to international law is granted.			Treatment according to international law is granted.

Regional / interregional (cont'd)			Multilateral			
	OECD		World Trade Organization		World Bank	United Nations
Energy Charter Treaty	Codes of Liberali-sation of Capital Movements and Current Invisible Transactions	Declaration on International Investment and Multinational Enterprises and related Decisions	General Agreement on Trade in Services	Agreement on Trade-related Investment Measures	Convention on the Settlement of Investment Disputes between States and Nationals of Other States; Convention Establishing the Multilateral Invest-ment Guarantee Agency; Guidelines on the Treatment of Foreign Direct Investment	ILO Tripartite Declaration of Principles Concerning Multinational Enterprises and Social Policy; UNCTAD Multilaterally Agreed Set of Principles and Rules for the Control of Restrictive Business practices; Guidelines for Consumer Protection
MFN covers investment activities (exceptions to protect human life, national security, members of free trade areas, etc.)			MFN granted to investment in services and services provides (limited exceptions and to be made transparent).		MFN to investments in like situations (exceptions for members of free trade areas and other limited cases to be made transparent (Guidelines).	
Fair and equitable treatment is granted.		Fair and equitable treatment is granted.	Fair and equitable treatment is granted.		Fair and equitable treatment should be granted (Guidelines).	
					Free transfer of funds and repatriation of investment (Guidelines).	
Treatment according to international law is granted.		Treatment according to international law is granted.			Treatment according to internatioal law is granted (Guidelines, MIGA).	

/...

(Annex table 13, cont'd)

Element	Bilateral	Regional / interregional						
	Bilateral investment treaties	Investment Agreement between ASEAN countries	MERCOSUR: Protocol of Colonia on Investment (Intrazone)	APEC Non-Binding Investment Principles	Islamic Conf.: Agreement on Investment	Arab League: Unified Agreement for Investment of Arab Capital among Arab States	CoMESA: Treaty Est. the Common Market for Eastern and Southern Africa [a]	NAFTA: North American Free Trade Agreement
b) Expropriation	In accordance with international law require-ments. Provide specific compen-sation standards.	In accordance with interna-tional law require-ments and upon payment of adequate compen-sation (market value, freely transferable in a convertible currency).	In accordance with interna-tional law standards and upon payment of adequate, prompt and effective (real value plus interest) compensa-tion.	FDI should not be expropriated except for a public purpose and on a non-discrimina-tory basis, according to law, and against prompt payment of adequate and effective compensa-tion.	FDI should not be expropriated except for a public purpose and on a non-discrimina-tory basis, according to law, and against prompt payment of adequate and effective compensa-tion.	FDI should not be expropriated except for a public purpose and on a non-discrimina-tory basis, according to law, and payment within on year from dispossession date.	Parties should refrain from nationali-zation, or, in the the event of expropria-tion pay adequate compensa-tion.	Expropriation should be in accordance with interna-tional law require-ments. Provides specific compen-sation standards.
c) Recourse to international means for settlement of disputes between investors and states.	Recourse to international means for investor-state dispute settlement accepted (e.g., ICSID, UNCITRAL).	Recourse to international means for investor-state dispute settlement accepted (e.g., ICSID, UNCITRAL).	Recourse to international means for investor-state dispute settlement accepted (e.g., ICSID, UNCITRAL).	Members accept that investor-state disputes will be settled promptly through arbitration procedures acceptable to both parties.	Investor-state disputes should be submitted to the arbitration tribunal established under the Agreement.	Investor-state disputes should be submitted to the Arab Investment Court established under the Agreement.	Recourse to international means for investor-state dispute settlement accepted.	Recourse to international means for investor-state dispute settlement accepted (mechanisms include ICSID, UNCITRAL, etc.).
6. Transparency				All invest-ment laws, regulations, adminis-trative guidelines and policies are to be made publicly available in a readily accessible manner.				Reporting of relevant measures to monitor negative lists.

Regional / interregional (cont'd)	OECD		Multilateral			
			World Trade Organization		World Bank	United Nations
Energy Charter Treaty	Codes of Liberalisation of Capital Movements and Current Invisible Transactions	Declaration on International Investment and Multinational Enterprises and related Decisions	General Agreement on Trade in Services	Agreement on Trade-related Investment Measures	Convention on the Settlement of Investment Disputes between States and Nationals of Other States; Convention Establishing the Multilateral Investment Guarantee Agency; Guidelines on the Treatment of Foreign Direct Investment	ILO Tripartite Declaration of Principles Concerning Multinational Enterprises and Social Policy; UNCTAD Multilaterally Agreed Set of Principles and Rules for the Control of Restrictive Business practices; Guidelines for Consumer Protection
Expropriation should be in accordance with international law requirements. Provides specific compensation standards.					Expropriation should be in accordance with international law requirements. Provides for detailed definitions of compensation standards (Guidelines).	
Recourse to international means for investor-state dispute settlement accepted (mechanisms include ICSID, UNCITRAL, etc.).					Recourse to international means for investor-state settlement of disputes accepted (Guidelines). Provides mechanisms for conciliation and arbitration in disputes between a State and private foreign investors (ICSID).	
Relevant laws subject to GATT transparency requirements.	Reporting on relevant measures. OECD to monitor compliance with Codes.	Reporting on relevant measures to monitor compliance with national treatment commitments.	Duty to make available relevant laws.	Duty to make available relevant laws.	Publication of adequate information about legislation is encouraged (Guidelines, MIGA).	

/...

(Annex table 13, cont'd)

Element	Bilateral	Regional / interregional						
	Bilateral investment treaties	Investment Agreement between ASEAN countries	MERCOSUR: Protocol of Colonia on Investment (Intrazone)	APEC Non-Binding Investment Principles	Islamic Conf.: Agreement on Investment	Arab League: Unified Agreement for Investment of Arab Capital among Arab States	CoMESA: Treaty Est. the Common Market for Eastern and Southern Africa [a]	NAFTA: North American Free Trade Agreement
7. <u>Measures dealing with broader concerns</u> a) Restrictive business practices					Requires investments to avoid anti-competitive behaviour.			Has competition rules but fails to define un-competitive behaviour and use trade remedy laws.
b) Consumer protection and health safety standard								
c) Labour standards								
d) Corporate behaviour				Acceptance of FDI is facilitated when FDI abide by the laws of the host country.				

Regional / interregional (cont'd)			Multilateral			
	OECD		World Trade Organization		World Bank	United Nations
Energy Charter Treaty	Codes of Liberali- sation of Capital Movements and Current Invisible Transactions	Declaration on International Investment and Multinational Enterprises and related Decisions	General Agreement on Trade in Services	Agreement on Trade- related Investment Measures	Convention on the Settlement of Investment Disputes between States and Nationals of Other States; Convention Establishing the Multilateral Invest- ment Guarantee Agency; Guidelines on the Treatment of Foreign Direct Investment	ILO Tripartite Declaration of Principles Concerning Multinational Enterprises and Social Policy; UNCTAD Multilaterally Agreed Set of Principles and Rules for the Control of Restrictive Business practices; Guidelines for Consumer Protection
Encourages governments to introduce and apply competition rules.		Multinational corporations should not use practices that abuse market position.			The guidelines are based on the general premise that equal treat- ment of investors in similar circumstances and free competition among them are prerequisites of a positive investment environment.	Defines anti-competi- tive behaviour of enter- prises; prescribes subs- tantive national norms and international cooperation mecha- nisms to avoid such behaviour (RBP). Introduces standards to protect consumers from abuse of market position by transna- tional corporations (GCP).
		Establish standards on consumer protection for TNCs.				Establish comprehen- sive standards on consumer protection (GCP).
		Establish standards on employment and labour relations for TNCs.				Prescribe detailed standards on employ ment and labour conditions for TNCs (ILO Declaration).
		Establish comprehensive standards for the behaviour of TNCs.			Guidelines apply to bona fide private investments (Guidelines).	

Source: UNCTAD, based on UNCTAD-DTCI, 1996a.

a   Most of CoMESA provisions reflected in this table relate to investment into CoMESA.

Select list of UNCTAD publications on
Transnational Corporations and Foreign Direct Investment

A. Individual studies

International Investment Instruments: A Compendium. Sales No. E.96.IIA.12 (the set).

Foreign Direct Investment, Trade, Aid and Migration. 100 p. Sales No. E.96.II.A.8.

Incentives and Foreign Direct Investment. 98 p. Sales No. E.96.II.A.6.

World Investment Report 1995: Transnational Corporations and Competitiveness. 491 p. Sales No. E.95.II.A.9. $45.

World Investment Report 1995: Transnational Corporations and Competitiveness. An Overview. 51 p. Free-of-charge.

Small and Medium-sized Transnational Corporations: Executive Summary and Report on the Osaka Conference. p. 60. UNCTAD/DTCI/6. Free-of-charge.

World Investment Report 1994: Transnational Corporations, Employment and the Workplace. 482 p. Sales No. E.94.II.A.14. $45.

World Investment Report 1994: Transnational Corporations, Employment and the Workplace. An Executive Summary. 34 p. Free-of-charge.

World Investment Directory. Volume IV: Latin America and the Caribbean. 478 p. Sales No. E.94.II.A.10. $65.

Liberalizing International Transactions in Services: A Handbook. 182 p. Sales No. E.94.II.A.11. $45. (Joint publication with the World Bank.)

Accounting, Valuation and Privatization. 190 p. Sales No. E.94.II.A.3. $25.

Environmental Management in Transnational Corporations: Report on the Benchmark Corporate Environment Suvey. 278 p. Sales No. E.94.II.A.2. $29.95.

Management Consulting: A Survey of the Industry and Its Largest Firms. 100 p. Sales No. E.93.II.A.17. $25.

Transnational Corporations: A Selective Bibliography, 1991-1992. 736 p. Sales No. E.93.II.A.16. $75. (English/French.)

Small and Medium-sized Transnational Corporations: Role, Impact and Policy Implications. 242 p. Sales No. E.93.II.A.15. $35.

World Investment Report 1993: Transnational Corporations and Integrated International Production. 290 p. Sales No. E.93.II.A.14. $45.

World Investment Report 1993: Transnational Corporations and Integrated International Production. An Executive Summary. 31 p. ST/CTC/159. Free-of-charge.

Foreign Investment and Trade Linkages in Developing Countries. 108 p. Sales No. E.93.II.A.12. $18.

World Investment Directory 1992. Volume III: Developed Countries. 532 p. Sales No. E.93.II.A.9. $75.

Transnational Corporations from Developing Countries: Impact on Their Home Countries. 116 p. Sales No. E.93.II.A.8. $15.

Debt-Equity Swaps and Development. 150 p. Sales No. E.93.II.A.7. $35.

From the Common Market to EC 92: Regional Economic Integration in the European Community and Transnational Corporations. 134 p. Sales No. E.93.II.A.2. $25.

World Investment Directory 1992. Volume II: Central and Eastern Europe. 432 p. Sales No. E.93.II.A.1. $65. (Joint publication with ECE.)

World Investment Report 1992: Transnational Corporations as Engines of Growth: An Executive Summary. 30 p. Sales No. E.92.II.A.24.

World Investment Report 1992: Transnational Corporations as Engines of Growth. 356 p. Sales No. E.92.II.A.19. $45.

World Investment Directory 1992. Volume I: Asia and the Pacific. 356 p. Sales No. E.92.II.A.11. $65.

B. Serial publications

Current Studies, Series A

No. 28. *Foreign Direct Investment in Africa*. 119 p. Sales No. E.95.II.A.6. $25

No. 27. *The Tradability of Banking Services: Impact and Implications*. 195 p. Sales No. E.94.II.A.12. $50.

No. 26. *Explaining and Forecasting Regional Flows of Foreign Direct Investment*. 58 p. Sales No. E.94.II.A.5. $25.

No. 25. *International Tradability in Insurance Services*. 54 p. Sales No. E.93.II.A.11. $20.

No. 24. *Intellectual Property Rights and Foreign Direct Investment*. 108 p. Sales No. E.93.II.A.10. $20.

No. 23. *The Transnationalization of Service Industries: An Empirical Analysis of the Determinants of Foreign Direct Investment by Transnational Service Corporations*. 62 p. Sales No. E.93.II.A.3. $15.00.

No. 22. *Transnational Banks and the External Indebtedness of Developing Countries: Impact of Regulatory Changes*. 48 p. Sales No. E.92.II.A.10. $12.

No. 20. *Foreign Direct Investment, Debt and Home Country Policies*. 50 p. Sales No. E.90.II.A.16. $12.

No. 19. *New Issues in the Uruguay Round of Multilateral Trade Negotiations*. 52 p. Sales No. E.90.II.A.15. $12.50.

No. 18. *Foreign Direct Investment and Industrial Restructuring in Mexico*. 114 p. Sales No. E.92.II.A.9. $12.

The United Nations Library on Transnational Corporations. (Published by Routledge on behalf of the United Nations.)

Set A (Boxed set of 4 volumes. ISBN 0-415-08554-3. £350):

Volume One: *The Theory of Transnational Corporations*. 464 p.

Volume Two: *Transnational Corporations: A Historical Perspective*. 464 p.

Volume Three: *Transnational Corporations and Economic Development*. 448 p.

Volume Four: *Transnational Corporations and Business Strategy*. 416 p.

Set B (Boxed set of 4 volumes. ISBN 0-415-08555-1. £350):

Volume Five: *International Financial Management*. 400 p.

Volume Six: *Organization of Transnational Corporations*. 400 p.

Volume Seven: *Governments and Transnational Corporations*. 352 p.

Volume Eight: *Transnational Corporations and International Trade and Payments*. 320 p.

Set C (Boxed set of 4 volumes. ISBN 0-415-08556-X. £350):

Volume Nine: *Transnational Corporations and Regional Economic Integration*. 331 p.

Volume Ten: *Transnational Corporations and the Exploitation of Natural Resources*. 397 p.

Volume Eleven: *Transnational Corporations and Industrialization*. 425 p.

Volume Twelve: *Transnational Corporations in Services*. 437 p.

Set D (Boxed set of 4 volumes. ISBN 0-415-08557-8. £350):

Volume Thirteen: *Cooperative Forms of Transnational Corporation Activity*. 419 p.

Volume Fourteen: *Transnational Corporations: Transfer Pricing and Taxation*. 330 p.

Volume Fifteen: *Transnational Corporations: Market Structure and Industrial Performance*. 383 p.

Volume Sixteen: *Transnational Corporations and Human Resources*. 429 p.

Set E (Boxed set of 4 volumes. ISBN 0-415-08558-6. £350):

Volume Seventeen: *Transnational Corporations and Innovatory Activities*. 447 p.

Volume Eighteen: *Transnational Corporations and Technology Transfer to Developing Countries*. 486 p.

Volume Nineteen: *Transnational Corporations and National Law*. 322 p.

Volume Twenty: *Transnational Corporations: The International Legal Framework*. 545 p.

Transnational Corporations (formerly *The CTC Reporter*).

Published three times a year. Annual subscription price: $35; individual issues $15.

Transnationals, a quarterly newsletter, is available free of charge.

United Nations publications may be obtained from bookstores and distributors throughout the world. Please consult your bookstore or write to:

United Nations Publications

Sales Section
Room DC2-0853
United Nations Secretariat
New York, N.Y. 10017
U.S.A.
Tel: (1-212) 963-8302 or (800) 253-9646
Fax: (1-212) 963-3489

OR

Sales Section
United Nations Office at Geneva
Palais des Nations
CH-1211 Geneva 10
Switzerland
Tel: (41-22) 917-1234
Fax: (41-22) 917-0123

All prices are quoted in United States dollars.

For further information on the work of UNCTAD Division on Investment, Enterprise Development and Technology, please address inquiries to:

United Nations Conference on Trade and Development
Division on Investment, Enterprise Development and Technology
Palais des Nations, Room E-8006
CH-1211 Geneva 10
Switzerland

Telephone: (41-22) 907-5707
Telefax: (41-22) 907-0194

QUESTIONNAIRE

World Investment Report 1996:
Investment, Trade and International Policy Arrangements
Sales No. E.95.II.A..

In order to improve the quality and relevance of the work of the UNCTAD Division on Transnational Corporations and Investment, it would be useful to receive the views of readers on this and other similar publications. It would therefore be greatly appreciated if you could complete the following questionnaire and return to:

Readership Survey
UNCTAD Division on Investment, Enterprise Development and Technology
United Nations Office in Geneva
Palais des Nations
Room E-8006
CH-1211 Geneva 10
Switzerland

1. Name and address of respondent (optional):

   _____

   _____

   _____

   _____

2. Which of the following best describes your area of work?

Government	☐	Public enterprise	☐
Private enterprise institution	☐	Academic or research	☐
International organization	☐	Media	☐
Not-profit organization	☐	Other (specify)	_____

3. In which country do you work?   _____

4. What is your assessment of the contents of this publication?

Excellent	☐	Adequate	☐
Good	☐	Poor	☐

5. How useful is this publication to your work?

Very useful ☐　　　Of some use ☐　　　Irrelevant ☐

6. Please indicate the three things you liked best about this publication:

_____

_____

_____

7. Please indicate the three things you liked least about this publication:

_____

_____

_____

8. If you have read more than the present publication of the UNCTAD Division on Investment, Enterprise Development and Technology, what is your overall assessment of them?

Consistently good ☐　　　Usually good, but with some exceptions ☐

Generally mediocre ☐　　　Poor ☐

9. On the average, how useful are these publications to you in your work?

Very useful ☐　　　Of some use ☐　　　Irrelevant ☐

10. Are you a regular recipient of *Transnational Corporations* (formerly *The CTC Reporter*), the Division's tri-annual refereed journal?

Yes ☐　　　No ☐

If not, please check here if you would like to receive a sample
copy sent to the name and address you have given above ☐